THE EUROPEAN COMMISSION
OF THE TWENTY-FIRST CENTURY

The European Commission of the Twenty-First Century

HUSSEIN KASSIM, JOHN PETERSON, MICHAEL
W. BAUER, SARA CONNOLLY, RENAUD DEHOUSSE,
LIESBET HOOGHE, AND ANDREW THOMPSON

OXFORD
UNIVERSITY PRESS

OXFORD
UNIVERSITY PRESS

Great Clarendon Street, Oxford, OX2 6DP,
United Kingdom

Oxford University Press is a department of the University of Oxford.
It furthers the University's objective of excellence in research, scholarship,
and education by publishing worldwide. Oxford is a registered trade mark of
Oxford University Press in the UK and in certain other countries

First Edition published in 2013

Impression: 1

British Library Cataloguing in Publication Data
Data available

Library of Congress Cataloging in Publication Data
Data available

ISBN 978-0-19-959952-3

Printed and bound by CPI Group (UK) Ltd, Croydom, CR0 4YY

We dedicate this book to our partners and families, who have lived through the project with us. In appreciation of your forbearance, and with our love.

Preface

The idea for this project was born in a workshop, convened by John Peterson, at the University of Edinburgh on 8–9 February 2006. John was the leader of a team working on 'The Commission and the European Civil Service' in the EU-Consent Network of Excellence, which was funded under the European Union's (EU) Sixth Research Framework. Although the discussion was relatively well informed, the academics in the room—some of us who have spent many years studying the European Commission—felt that despite the scholarly attention directed at the organization, important questions remained unanswered.

Our usual approach to conducting research on the Commission was at least partly responsible. Subject on our side to constraints of time and money, we generally try to interview as many officials as are willing to meet us and to put questions to them about whatever topic we are currently investigating. In this way over the years many of us have clocked up hundreds of interviews. Although this approach has its rewards, getting to know the Commission and its staff by traipsing through the streets of Brussels has its limitations. I suggested to John that a large-scale survey would enable us to capture the views of far more officials than we could possibly ever hope to meet face-to-face and to elicit a far more representative sample of opinion and perspectives from within the organization. In this way, we could better understand the Commission and the people who work for it. The appointment of a new Secretary-General made the moment opportune.

John and I tested the idea with friends and colleagues, sounded out potential collaborators, and floated the idea with senior officeholders in the Commission. To our delight—and our surprise, in the case of the latter—all were encouraging. To cut a long story short, the breakthrough came when John found himself with an opportunity to explain the project to Commission President José Manuel Barroso at the University of Edinburgh, where Barroso was being awarded an honorary degree. As a former academic, President Barroso could see the value of the project and offered his endorsement. Catherine Day, the Secretary-General of the Commission and its highest-ranking permanent official, was equally supportive.

We were extremely grateful, not only for the green light to proceed with what has been a truly privileged experience, but also because we recognized the significance of the decision. Allowing an outside team of researchers to investigate the background, beliefs, and attitudes of staff is courageous for any organization. For a body such as the Commission that is continually in the spotlight and whose status is a source of almost daily controversy, it was especially courageous. We would be bound to uncover opinions that would be unwelcome, if not unsurprising, to senior officeholders, and stumble into the malcontents who oppose official policy, sometimes vehemently. Our admiration was only the greater as so few organizations, public or private, have been prepared to open themselves up in this way.

We have accumulated many other debts since that workshop in Edinburgh. Our first and foremost debt is to the European Commission; notably the 1901 Commission staff members who completed the online survey and in particular the more than 200 who consented to face-to-face interviews. If these respondents had not been prepared to spare their time or share their experience, the project would not have been possible. There are a number of particular individuals within the Commission, or formerly of it, to whom we are especially grateful. They include: Catherine Day, Olivier Bailly, Luc Tholoniat, Jonathan Faull, Sabine Weyand, Matthew Baldwin, Stefaan de Rynk, Daniele Dotto, Emiel Weizenbach, Emer Daly, Cesare Onestini, and Jim Cloos. Their help and support has been invaluable.

We have benefited greatly from the expertise and insight of several scholars. Charlie Jeffery offered advice at the very beginning that proved invaluable. Carolyn Ban, Morten Egeberg, Ed Page, and Jarle Trondal have been critical friends, who have encouraged us, but also forced us to reflect and rethink at key points along the way. We are grateful to the participants in countless conference panels and workshops for helpful comments and suggestions.[1] In addition, Christina Boswell, Charlotte Burns, Laura Cram, Francesca Gains, Didier Georgakakis, Miriam Hartlapp, Klaus Goetz, Gary Marks, Anand Menon, Julia Metz, B. Guy Peters, Christian Rauh, Susanne K. Schmidt and Anchrit Wille read and helped us improve early drafts of what become the chapters of this book.

The EU Consent Network and the UK Economic and Social Research Council (ESRC Grant no. RES-062-23-1188) provided the funding of the research on which this book is based. We are grateful to both. We also express our gratitude to Françoise Girard and David Knott—old friends of Hussein and Sara's—whose generous donation, following the dip of the Pound Sterling

[1] They include: Council of European Studies conference, Barcelona, 24–26 June 2011 and Montreal, 15–17 April 2010; *Public Administration in the Multilevel System* session, Humboldt-Universität, Berlin, 23–24 June 2011, ECPR Pan-European Conference; European Union Studies Association, Boston, 2–3 March 2011; Europa Institute Annual Mitchell lecture, Edinburgh, 24 February 2011; EXACT Marie Curie International Training Network workshop, Edinburgh, 9 December 2010; European Group of Public Administration, Toulouse, 8 September 2010; European Consortium for Political Research Fifth Pan-European Conference, Porto, 23–26 June 2010; ARENA Research Seminar, University of Oslo, 8 June 2010 and 10 May 2010; Political Studies Association, University of Edinburgh, 1 April 2010; and EU-Consent meetings, Edinburgh, 4–6 March 2009, 20 July 2006, and 15 May 2006 and, Paris, 21–22 June 2006.

against the Euro, enabled us to make the most of a unique research opportunity. Tanja Börzel and Thomas Risse very kindly funded an authors' workshop co-hosted by the Wissenschaftzentrum Berlin für–Sozialforschung at the Freie Universitat Berlin/Kolleg-Forschergruppe, 7–8 February 2011, which gave us an important opportunity to present and discuss chapter drafts.

A number of people have worked with us or for us, or have otherwise offered their assistance. We are very grateful to Marina Shapiro for her statistical work in weighting the samples at the beginning of the project, to Elizabeth Bomberg, Rosalind Cavahagn, Pascal Duchauchoy-Creuzin, Madeleine Dobie, Anna-Lena Hogenauer, Hagen Streb, Nicholas Veron, and Sabine Weyand for helping with queries relating to the translation of the questionnaires into French and German, and to Mark Dittmer-Odell and Ines Mosgalik for stalwart assistance in the field. We have been extremely fortunate to employ an excellent research assistant in Louise Maythorne in Edinburgh and an outstanding research administrator in Vanessa Buth in Norwich. Both also participated with us in multiple interviews in Brussels; their efforts have been truly indispensable.

Members of the research team have, moreover, incurred individual debts. Michael Bauer would like to thank Philipp Studinger for his assistance with data analysis. Sara Connolly expresses her gratitude to UEA for granting her the period of study leave that enabled her to work on the project and the ongoing commitment of the University to interdisciplinary research. Liesbet Hooghe is grateful to Ben Crum, Simon Hug, Julia Langbein, Gary Marks, Jerome Schafer, Pascal Sciarini, and Jarle Trondal for comments on drafts, as well as to the Dutch National Science Foundation, the Center for European Studies at Chapel Hill, and the KFG 'The Transformative Power of Europe' for supporting her research. Hussein Kassim has learned much about the Commission from conversations with Dionyssis G. Dimitrakopoulos, Fernando Garcia Ferreiro, Anne Stevens, Handley Stevens, Martin Westlake, and, especially, Anand Menon, as well as (at the very beginning) Martin Mauthner. Colleagues at UEA, including John Street, Lawrence Hardy, Liki Koutrakou, and David Milne have offered support and encouragement at various stages of the project. Andrew Thompson would like to thank Debbie Menezes for work with data analysis.

Finally, as Principal Investigator (or 'leader') of the research team, I should like to record my gratitude to Dominic Byatt at OUP, who has been an enthusiast for the project since when we first mentioned it to him, and to Lizzy Suffling, Carla Hodge, and Howard Emmens for their work on the book's production. Above all, wholehearted thanks are owed to my six collaborators and co-authors in this epic enterprise. Both the project and this book are the product of the combined endeavour, talents, and knowledge of all the research team. It has taken its time, but here it is at last!

Hussein Kassim, Norwich, 5 December 2011

Contents

List of Tables

List of Figures

Abbreviations

AD	Administrator
AST	Assistant
BEPA	Bureau of European Policy Advisers
DG	Directorate-General
DG ADMIN	Directorate-General for Personnel and Administration
DG AGRI	Directorate-General for Agriculture and Rural Development
DG BUDG	Directorate-General for Budget
DG CLIMA	Directorate-General for Climate Action
DG COMM	Directorate-General for Communication
DG COMP	Directorate-General for Competition
DGT	Directorate-General for Translation
DG DIGIT	Directorate-General for Informatics
DG EAC	Directorate-General for Education and Culture
DG ECFIN	Directorate-General for Economic and Financial Affairs
DG ELARG	Directorate-General for Enlargement
DG EMPL	Directorate-General for Employment, Social Affairs and Inclusion
DG ENER	Directorate-General for Energy
DG ENTR	Directorate-General for Enterprise and Industry
DG ENV	Directorate-General for the Environment
DG HOME	Directorate-General for Home Affairs
DG HR	Directorate-General for Human Resources and Security
DG INFSO	Directorate-General for Information Society and Media
DG JLS	Directorate-General for Justice, Freedom and Security
DG JUST	Directorate-General for Justice
DG MARE	Directorate-General for Maritime Affairs and Fisheries
DG MARKT	Directorate-General for Internal Market and Services
DG MOVE	Directorate-General for Mobility and Transport
DG REGIO	Directorate-General for Regional Policy
DG RELEX	Directorate-General for External Relations
DG RTD	Directorate-General for Research and Innovation
DG SANCO	Directorate-General for Health and Consumers
DG TAXUD	Directorate-General for Taxation and Customs Union

DG TRADE	Directorate-General for Trade
DG TREN	Directorate-General for Transport and Energy
ECHO	Humanitarian Aid
EEAS	European External Action Service
EP	European Parliament
ESTAT	Eurostat
EUCIQ	The European Commission in Question (research project)
IAS	Internal Audit Service
IGC	Inter-Governmental Conference
JRC	Joint Research Centre
OIB	Infrastructures and Logistics—Brussels
OIL	Infrastructures and Logistics—Luxembourg
OLAF	European Anti-Fraud Office
SCIC	Interpretation
SG	Secretariat-General
SJ	Legal Service
TEC	Treaty establishing the European Community
TEU	Treaty on European Union
TFEU	Treaty on the functioning of the European Union

1

Introduction: The European Commission in Question[1]

The European Commission is one of the world's most powerful international administrations. With major executive and enforcement responsibilities, a key role in the management of the European Union's (EU) finances and expenditure, and a monopoly over the right to bring forward proposals in most areas of EU legislation, the Commission occupies a central position in the European Union.[2] Located at the heart of the EU's administrative system, its influence extends far beyond Brussels. As well as affecting the domestic politics and policy of the EU member states, the Commission's action has consequences for international regulation, bilateral and multilateral international negotiations, and relations between Europe and other regions of the globe. Considered historically to have been the 'engine' of European integration, it is the subject of perennial debate[3] and the object of strong, often extreme, opinion.[4]

Unsurprisingly, the Commission has attracted considerable scholarly attention,[5] but much about the organization and its staff is not well known or understood. Who, for example, are the officials who work for the Commission? What are their professional and educational backgrounds? Is the

---

[1] 'The European Commission in Question' (EUCIQ) is the title of the research project on which this book is based. See <http://www.uea.ac.uk/psi/research/EUCIQ>.

[2] For perspectives on changes in the Commission's influence over time, see Kassim and Menon (2004, 2010). For an alternative view of the Commission's influence, see Moravcsik (1999).

[3] For discussions of the role of the Commission, see, e.g., Lindberg (1963), Hallstein (1965), Spinelli (1967); Coombes (1970); Monnet (1978); Christiansen (1997); Lequesne (1997); Moravcsik (1999); Schmidt (2000); Shore (2000); Pollack (2003); Trondal (2008).

[4] The British conservative philosopher, Roger Scruton, charges, for example, that European Commissioners 'have the death of Europe in their hearts' (2009: 33).

[5] There are a handful of historical studies that analyse the European Commission and its predecessor bodies, beginning with Haas's seminal study of the European Coal and Steel Community (1958), and continuing with Coombes (1970) and Michelmann (1978) through to Abélès et al. (1993). Among recent studies, see Page (1997); Peterson (1999); Shore (2000); Hooghe (2001); Stevens and Stevens (2001); Dimitrakopoulos (2004); Dumoulin (2007); Franchino (2007); Suvarierol (2007); and Georgakakis (2012).

Commission an administration of lawyers? What motivates officials to pursue a career in the European Commission? What are their beliefs about the role that the Commission should play in Europe, where decision-making authority should reside, and where the European Union is heading? What have been the enduring consequences of the reform programme undertaken by the Commission under the Presidency of Romano Prodi (1999–2004) or the effects of measures implemented under José Manuel Barroso's Presidency (2004–14)? How effective is leadership and coordination within the organization? How do officials view the 2004 and 2007 enlargements and how has the experience affected the Commission? And how does the European Commission compare with other bureaucracies—both in domestic political systems and among international organizations? These questions are the starting points for the present enquiry.[6]

Their limited exploration hitherto has not prevented the spread of myths about the people or the organization. In the public mind, the Commission is populated by zealous 'Eurocrats' who want always and everywhere to extend the Union's influence and, thereby, their own power—a view also voiced routinely by some mainstream politicians and others.[7] In an era of general anti-bureaucratic sentiment (see du Gay 2000, 2005; Peters 2001), the Commission is viewed as the arch bureaucracy—remote, non-responsive, over-mighty, interfering, interventionist. It is depicted as antiquated and resistant to change, combining the worst characteristics of continental European bureaucracies (Stevens and Stevens 2001; Balint et al. 2008).

There are echoes of these views in academic analyses, but a constant refrain in scholarly work is that the Commission escapes easy categorization. Studies informed by a public choice or new public management approach Commission bureaucrats as budget-maximizers or competence-expanders.[8] According to such scholarship, Commission officials are driven by a desire 'to build Europe' and thereby to increase their powers.[9] Studies from a public

---

[6] Hooghe (2001, 2005); Georgakakis and de Lassalle (2007); Suvarierol (2007); Bauer (2008); Ellinas and Suleiman (2011); Landfried et al. (forthcoming) study subsets of Commission officials. Carolyn Ban's (2013) forthcoming study, like the current volume, is anchored in a large-scale survey of the entire Commission.

[7] For example, Douglas (now Lord) Hurd, UK Foreign Secretary (1989–95), remarked famously in November 1991 on 'the apparent wish of the European Commission to insist on inserting itself in the nooks and crannies of everyday life' (cited in Stuart 2004: 226).

[8] The theoretical proposition that bureaucrats are motivated by budget or competence maximization was developed in American public administration (Niskanen 1971; Calvert et al. 1989), but the idea has also taken hold as an analytical category in studying relations between national bureaucracies and political principals in Europe (see, for instance, Dunleavy 1990). More recently, it has been applied to the study of the European Commission (see Pollack 2003; Franchino 2007).

[9] In her study of officials in the early 1980s, Willis (1982: 4) noted that 'a key additional requirement in the early days was that staff should be devoted Europeans, who by the zeal and commitment to the goal of integration would maintain the momentum of the Commission's

administration perspective examine how the Commission compares with other bureaucracies in terms of leadership,[10] political or administrative centralization, coordination, and the capacity to adapt (Metcalfe 2000; Stevens and Stevens 2001; Kassim 2004a, 2004b, 2008). There is, of course, a tension between these approaches. While the studies predicated on a 'maximization' premise cast the Commission as a monolithic organization, those working from a public administration perspective highlight its internal fragmentation (Balint et al. 2008).

This volume takes a new look at the Commission. It investigates the origins and backgrounds of Commission officials, their career trajectories and beliefs, and the inner workings of the organization that they serve. Drawing on unique primary source material collected by the authors,[11] the chapters that follow offer a detailed examination of the European Commission at the beginning of the twenty-first century.

RESEARCHING THE EUROPEAN COMMISSION

For much of the organization's history, the literature on the Commission was sparse. Well into the 1980s, writings on the Commission opened with a ritual expression of surprise at the paucity of scholarship on the subject beyond the classic studies produced by Coombes (1970) and Michelmann (1978). Since the 1986 Single European Act, however, the literature has become so voluminous that this ritual refrain is no longer warranted.[12] Moreover, scholarship on the Commission has not only broadened, but has become more sophisticated. Analysis of the organization has moved beyond the terms of the traditional, if narrow, self-marginalizing debate between neofunctionalism and intergovernmentalism (Schmidt 1996; Hooghe 2001: 1–5). Scholars writing on the Commission increasingly draw on mainstream approaches in political science (see Page 1997, 2012; Hooghe 2005a; Smith 2004), public administration (see Egeberg 2006; Trondal 2007) and other sub-disciplinary perspectives. Authors have contributed to understanding the organization's early history (Heyen and Wright 1992; Loth et al. 1998; Dumoulin 2007), key

---

process towards it'. Shore (2000: 140) attests to the continued importance of commitment to the European idea nearly two decades later.

[10] For studies of leadership in international organizations, see Claude (1959); Cox and Jacobsen (1973); Young (1991); Barnett and Finnemore (1999); Janning (2005); Tallberg (2006); Deese (2008).

[11] The project on which this book is based collected data from two main sources: an online survey, and a structured programme of interviews (see below).

[12] The bibliography assembled by Szarek and Peterson (2007) testifies to the extent to which the literature on the Commission has grown.

structures and actors (Endo 1999; Joana and Smith 2002; Smith 2004; Spence and Edwards 2006; Kassim 2012), officials (Page 1997; Hooghe 2001), its internal operation (Ross 1995; Stevens and Stevens 2001; Spence and Edwards 2006; Kassim 2006), interaction with other bodies (Egeberg 2006), and the role that it plays in decision making (Pollack 1996, 1997a), policy development (Schmidt 2000; Pollack 2003) and treaty negotiations (Christiansen 2002; Falkner 2002; Beach and Christiansen 2007; Kassim and Dimitrakopoulos 2007).

Yet, despite the invaluable insights that it affords, the existing literature is limited in terms of the questions it poses and the approaches it adopts. One reason is that much of the literature has been principally concerned with estimating the Commission's relative influence in EU decision making (see Sasse et al. 1977; Schmidt 2000; Pollack 1996, 1997a, 2003; Jupille 2004). This preoccupation with the Commission as a political actor has inevitably led to a focus on the organization's interaction with other bodies rather than investigation of its inner workings. Moreover, analyses typically proceed from the assumption that the Commission is a unitary player rather than an internally differentiated organization (Cram 1993; Hooghe 2001; Kassim and Dimitrakopoulos 2007). Such tendencies overlook the possibility that exploration of the Commission's internal processes may in fact hold the key to understanding preference formation within the organization (Hooghe 2005a; Hartlapp 2011) and thereby its external behaviour (see, for example, Kassim and Dimitrakopoulos 2007).

Some scholars have sought to open the 'black box' and have offered important insights into how the organization functions as an administration. However, these analyses have often been confined to particular groups or actors. Attention has been focused on Commission Presidents (Ross 1995; Peterson 1999, 2004), the Commission Presidency (Endo 1999; Kassim 2012), the College (Peterson 2012) or members of the Commission (Joana and Smith 2002, 2004; Smith 2003), the *cabinets* (of personal advisers to Commissioners; see Ritchie 1992; Egeberg and Heskestad 2010), middle managers (Bauer 2008), the Directorates-General (DGs) (or permanent 'services'; see Hooghe 2001), the Secretariat-General (Kassim 2006), and individual Directorates-General (Wilks 1992; Cram 1994; Cini 1996). Attempts to provide systematic overviews of the Commission, however, are somewhat sparse, and coverage of the organization's various parts somewhat uneven.

A further limitation concerns the tendency to treat the Commission as a *sui generis* or singular administration. In the older literature, this inclination reflected a preoccupation with the capacity of the Commission to fulfil its treaty-given mission to drive integration forward (see Coombes 1970)—a particular concern in the 1960s and 1970s. However, even where the emphasis has not been on the Commission's developmental role, scholars have been distinctly wary of comparing the Commission with other bureaucracies. Works such as Balint et al. (2008) are rare exceptions. Such restraint is surprising, since public bureaucracies have much in common. They perform generic functions and confront similar challenges. Even if they operate in distinct institutional environments, modern bureaucracies offer policy advice, and implement and enforce policy. Similarly, as organizations, there is much that they share. They must, for example, motivate staff and manage interdepartmental coordination. No organization if it is to survive, moreover, can avoid adapting to changing pressures and demands from outside and from within. These common tasks and challenges would appear to provide obvious grounds for comparison, and though data on other administrations is often difficult to find,[13] the failure of scholars working on the Commission to draw on taxonomies, concepts, models, or theories from the comparative study of bureaucracies or of organizations is hard to explain (Metcalfe 2000 is one of few exceptions).

The paucity of studies comparing the Commission and other international administrations is especially surprising. Despite some early attempts in this direction (see, especially, Siotis 1964), it is only in the recent past that scholars, for example, Bauer and Knill (2007), Balint et al. (2008) and Trondal et al. (2010), have sought to undertake more systematic comparisons. Still rarer are comparisons between the Commission and national administrations,[14] or theoretically-inspired case studies focused on the Commission (see Bauer 2002). Although some recent comparative work on administrative reform does include the Commission as a case study (Pollitt and Bouckaert 2000; 2004, 2011; Bauer and Knill 2007), such research is sparse.

An additional limitation relates to source material. Many studies are based on secondary sources, which can be constraining. Those drawn on primary materials often base their extrapolations on small-sample surveys or informal interviews.[15] This approach may make it possible to generate hypotheses, but is not usually sufficient to test them confidently. For this purpose larger, representative, datasets are necessary, as they increase the chances that findings will be robust.

---

[13] The scarcity of data has led some scholars of public administration to resort to ingenious efforts to draw comparisons between national administrations (see, e.g., Peters 2003: Chapter 3, especially Tables 3.1, 3.2, and 3.3). However, the OECD now regularly publishes systematic cross-national data on aspects of public management, such as public governance, public employment and management, and budgeting and public expenditures, which makes informed comparison considerably easier.

[14] There is a literature on how national administrative models have influenced the shape and practices of the Commission (see, e.g., Stevens and Stevens 2001; Ritchie 1992; and Page 1997).

[15] Coombes (1970) quotes from interview material, but does not state how many interviews were conducted within the organization, or with whom, while Michelmann (1978) conducted 172 formal interviews with Commission officials. His study draws on responses to two questionnaires: one, to which 604 responded, was administered to 1200 officials in grades A4 to A7; the other, to which 320 responded, was administered to 334 Heads of Unit and other A3s. Page (1997), by contrast, is based on analysis of the biographical data of 2,300 officials of grade A4 or above extracted from *The European Companion* and *Who's Who*. Hooghe (2001) conducted 137 semi-structured interviews from a population of 200 senior officials. Stevens and Stevens (2001) draw on over forty. Ban (2013), who conducted a survey administered to several thousand officials, offers the one study that can, like this book, draw on a large-scale survey.

Responding in large part to the limitations of the existing literature, this book departs in four respects from previous work. First, it approaches the Commission primarily as an organization or administration. Instead of focusing on its role and influence in decision making, this volume is concerned with the Commission's staff and with the organization's internal operation. Second, instead of directing attention to individual parts of the Commission, this book examines the organization as a whole in an attempt to understand both its vertical and horizontal dynamics. Third, the study draws upon an established conceptual repertoire in comparative public administration to pose questions about the Commission familiar to students of bureaucracies—for example, about how and why officials use personal networks, the availability and circulation of information within the organization, and the attitudes of bureaucrats to politics, internal administrative reform, and external political reform.[16] Where data permits, the book attempts to compare the Commission with other administrations. Finally, rather than relying on secondary sources, this study is based on primary material generated by the research team. At the empirical core of the book is a 'once-in-a-generation' survey of Commission staff, complemented by more than two hundred interviews conducted by the project team.

THE AIMS OF THE BOOK

The book's central ambition is to develop an understanding of the Commission that builds on the experience, testimony, and insight of the people who work for the organization. It aims not only to examine the internal functioning of the Commission and its personnel, but also to explore the beliefs and behaviour of officials. In particular, it investigates how the Commission has responded to two major challenges: administrative reform and enlargement. The volume is not structured around a single dependent variable, but attempts to develop a multi-perspective understanding of the organization. It proceeds from the premise that, in order to gain a full picture of an organization, it is insufficient merely to examine structures and procedures. Attention needs also to be paid to the origins, experience, and attitudes of its staff.

The eight chapters that follow address five themes.[17] Chapter 2 examines the background and career experience of Commission personnel. It asks: Who

---

[16] See, e.g., Armstrong (1973); Dogan (1975); Aberbach et al. (1981); Page and Wright (2000); Pollitt and Bouckaert (2004, 2011); Bauer and Knill (2007); Gains and John (2010).

[17] This volume is co-authored. Each chapter has a primary author who is the first named as follows: Chapter 1 is co-authored by Hussein Kassim (general introduction), Andrew Thompson (survey and mixed methods), Liesbet Hooghe (beliefs: a conceptual framework), and Sara Connolly (independent variables); Chapter 2 Sara Connolly and Hussein Kassim; Chapter 3 John Peterson, Sara Connolly, and Andrew Thompson; Chapter 4 Liesbet Hooghe; Chapter 5

are the people who work for the organization? At what stage in their professional life do they join the Commission, and why? Where do they come from and what expertise do they bring? What is their career trajectory thereafter? Such concerns have been of long-standing interest in the literature on public administration, where scholars have investigated the social origins of the servants of the state[18] and the extent to which public bureaucracies are representative of the communities that they serve (see, for example, Kingsley 1944; Van Riper 1958). They have also reflected on the skills that public service requires, and whether these should be developed before or after entry (Boussaert et al. 2001: 87–96).

In the case of the Commission, however, there have been relatively few attempts to investigate the backgrounds of officials. The exception is nationality, where since the early days of the European Communities member governments have been concerned to ensure that a fair share of their nationals are recruited by the organization. The limited interest in other characteristics of Commission staff, such as their educational backgrounds or professional experience, however, has allowed accepted wisdoms about officials to go unchallenged and untested, among them the belief that the Commission is populated by law graduates or that its officials are likely to have spent their entire career in the public sector. Such perceptions are, of course, not neutral. They imply that the Commission is an inward looking and defensive organization, short on creativity, and lacking the diversity of experience or expertise needed to meet the challenges of a changing world.

Examinations of the career paths of Commission officials are also surprisingly scarce. Discussions of career development feature routinely in the study of administration, but detailed analyses of career-building and of horizontal and vertical mobility in the European Commission are rare.[19] Little is known, for example, about the number of Directorates-General in which an official is likely to serve in the course of a career, how long it takes for an entry-level recruit to advance to a middle or senior management post, whether the nationals of some member states progress more rapidly than others, or whether men achieve promotion more quickly than women. These issues and their implications for the Commission and for officials are investigated in Chapter 2. As well as examining the educational and professional

Renaud Dehousse and Andrew Thompson; Chapter 6 Hussein Kassim, John Peterson and Sara Connolly; Chapter 7 Hussein Kassim, John Peterson and Sara Connolly; Chapter 8 Michael Bauer, Sara Connolly, and Hussein Kassim; Chapter 9 John Peterson, Sara Connolly, and Andrew Thompson; Conclusion: Hussein Kassim, Liesbet Hooghe, John Peterson, Michael Bauer, Sara Connolly, and Andrew Thompson.

[18] See, e.g., Halsey and Crewe (1968); Armstrong (1973); Aberbach et al. (1981); Kessler (1986); Derlien and Mayntz (1988); Quermonne (1991).
[19] Exceptions are Michelmann (1978); Page (1997); on the College of Commissioners, see Döring (2007).

backgrounds of staff, it looks at their motivations for joining the Commission and investigates career mobility within the organization. It considers the extent to which the Commission has genuinely become a career civil service, where staff members join at entry level and make their way up through the ranks to middle and senior management positions.

Chapter 3 addresses how officials navigate the Commission. The way in which individuals negotiate the workplace has been a long-standing interest of students of public administration and scholars of organizations.[20] The formal and informal contacts that they form and how they use these connections are an important aspect of employee behaviour, whether in the public or the private sector. In the literature on the Commission, the general importance of informal networks has often been explained as a reaction to the insistence on formal hierarchy (see, for example, Spence 1994; Shore 2000: 196–200). Existing studies have examined networks as an instrument of leadership (Ross 1995) or coordination, or have emphasized the tendency of officials to construct informal networks with fellow nationals (Suvarierol 2007). There has, however, been little systematic investigation of how Commission officials view personal networks, on what basis—for example, nationality, language, or party affiliation—contacts are established, and what functions they perform. Drawing on responses to a series of questions posed in the online survey and in follow-up interviews, Chapter 3 addresses these issues.

The two chapters that follow examine the beliefs of Commission officials. While there are a significant number of empirically-informed analyses of beliefs held by national bureaucrats that follow seminal works by Aberbach et al. (1981), Mayntz (1984), Suleiman (1984), Derlien and Mayntz (1988), Mayntz and Derlien (1989), Derlien (2003), and Schwanke and Ebinger (2006),[21] comparable studies of Commission officials are scarce. Chapter 4 charts Commission officials' views on the governance, ideological direction, and policy responsibilities of the European Union. Influenced by the bureaucratic politics approach, the tendency in the EU literature has been to assume that officials are inclined towards federalism, want to centralize power in Brussels, and instinctively support the 'Community method', a conception of the Union that places the Commission at the heart of European integration.[22] Chapter 4 tests and challenges these assumptions. Chapter 5, by contrast, focuses on the constituency of Commission officials who support the 'Community method'. With the status, role, and powers of the Commission challenged by other EU

[20] On networks within organizations, see Brass (1984); Morgan (1986); Burt (1992); Degenne and Forsé (1999); Cross et al. (2001); McPherson et al. (2001); Kilduff and Tsai (2003), Cross and Parker (2004); Wasserman and Faust (2007).
[21] In addition to Hooghe (2001, 2005) and Ban (2013), mentioned above, Ellinas and Suleiman (2011) is also based on a survey; for analysis from an anthropological angle, see Abélès et al. (1993) and Shore (2000).
[22] Preston (1995); Devuyst (1999); Wallace (2010); Dehousse (2011).

institutions, most notably the European Council and the European Parliament, this chapter examines how adherents of this conception have responded and investigates their views on a series of other issues.

Chapters 6 and 7 examine respectively leadership and coordination. Chapter 6 investigates leadership under the Barroso Commission. Although the period during which Jacques Delors held the Commission Presidency (1985–95) was covered by a number of important studies (Grant 1994; Ross 1995; Endo 1999; Drake 2000), Commission leadership since 1995 has attracted considerably less attention, despite the contrasting styles of Delors's successors on the one hand and the successive treaty reforms that have strengthened the office since the Treaty of Amsterdam on the other. Chapter 6 examines the extent to which José Manuel Barroso has been able to realize his vision of presidential leadership, looks at how his Presidency is perceived at different levels of the organization, and considers how officials rate Commission Presidents from Delors to Barroso along four dimensions: setting a policy agenda, effectively managing the house, delivering on policy priorities, and defending the Commission in the EU system.

Chapter 7 looks at coordination in the organization. This theme has featured in many studies of the Commission, but few scholars have sought systematically to investigate the effectiveness of vertical and horizontal coordination at political and administrative levels (though see Kassim and Peters 2008). This chapter compares the views of *cabinet* members and staff in the services. It examines relations between the *cabinets*, between Directorates-General, and between *cabinet* members and services as seen from both sides. It also considers the changing role of the Secretariat-General and the attitudes of Commission personnel to its rising profile.

The chapters that follow examine how two major challenges—administrative reform and enlargement—have affected attitudes and work practices. Chapter 8 investigates the views of officials on administrative reform. Although the Kinnock–Prodi reforms implemented between 2000 and 2005 have attracted considerable scholarly attention (Levy 2003, 2004, 2006; Kassim 2004a, 2004b, 2008; Levy and Stevens 2004; Bauer 2006; Ellinas and Suleiman 2007, 2008),[23] neither the attitudes of officials towards the reforms nor their impact on the organization has been charted in detail. This chapter examines both.

Chapter 9 addresses the 'big bang' enlargement of 2004 and 2007. Existing research has focused mainly on how it affects the working of the EU institutions and the Commission's legislative role (see for example Dehousse et al.

---

[23] The programme of administrative reform implemented during this period is referred to as the 'Kinnock–Prodi reforms' throughout. As Reform Vice-President, Neil (now Lord) Kinnock led the process, but Commission President Romano Prodi also introduced a number of important measures.

2006; Best et al. 2008; Odell 2010). There has been much less analysis of perceptions from within the organization on how the Commission handled the recruitment of officials from the new member states or the institutional consequences of enlargement, or how enlargement has affected the Commission's internal functioning. Moving beyond early assessments (Peterson 2008; Peterson and Birdsall 2008), this chapter investigates whether officials from the new member states are distinct in terms of their beliefs and attitudes, and gauges the effect on the organization.

SOURCES, MIXED METHODS, AND TESTIMONY AS RESOURCE AND OBJECT

The book draws on original primary material created by the project team. The findings it reports are based on three main sources of data (see Figure 1.1):

- a once-in-a-generation online survey administered in the autumn of 2008,
- a series of interviews with a sub-set of self-selected respondents to the online survey conducted between January and March 2009, and
- a structured programme of follow-up interviews with senior officials carried out between May and November 2009.

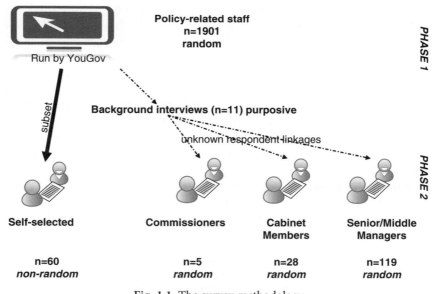

Fig. 1.1 The survey methodology

The study was conducted entirely independently of the Commission. However, the project team benefited from cooperation with members of the *cabinets* of Commission President José Manuel Barroso and Commissioner for Administration (and Vice-President) Siim Kallas, as well as officials in the Commission's Secretariat-General and the evaluation unit in the Directorate-General of Personnel and Administration. Together they provided access to the personnel data needed to generate a representative online survey and representative follow-up interviews. Importantly, the team sought and secured full academic independence in the design and conduct of the survey and subsequent interviews.[24]

The Surveys

The online survey is at the project's heart.[25] The questionnaire, which is reproduced in the appendices asked respondents for information about their background, motivation for joining the Commission, career experience, economic and cultural values, preferred conception of the EU as a political system, and their views on the internal operation of the Commission, administrative reform, and enlargement. Where appropriate, questions were informed by those used in earlier surveys of national civil servants to allow comparability, and of Commission officials in order to permit longitudinal analysis. Thirty-five Commission officials assisted with the piloting and pre-testing of successive versions of the questionnaire, and YouGov, the market research agency, which created the link to the online version, offered advice on the structure and presentation of the survey.

The project was concerned mainly with staff involved in policy. The online survey targeted *cabinet* members and administrators (AD)—one of two categories of permanent officials in the Commission[26]—in services with policy or policy-related responsibilities.[27] A stratified random sample of 4,621

---

[24] As a condition for carrying out the project, the research team undertook to comply with the data protection rules governing officials of the European administration. Members of the research team also agreed to guarantee the anonymity of respondents and to treat the responses of interviewees as confidential. As well as signing a confidentiality agreement concerning use of the data, members of the research team committed themselves to ensuring that it would not be possible to identify a particular individual from the comments or remarks cited or the description of the respondent or interviewee given in any published output.

[25] In line with recent practice, an internet survey was chosen in order to maximize response rates and provide greater protection of anonymity. Internet surveys are more versatile in format, easier to administer, and more error-proof than other instruments. In addition, they are particularly well-suited for elite actors, who value their efficiency and flexibility.

[26] For a description of the status of a permanent official and these two roles, see <http://ec.europa.eu/civil_service/job/official/index_en.htm>.

[27] Assistant-grade officials and officials working in translation, interpretation and support services were excluded. As the result of a technical error, however, the survey was inadvertently sent to a number of translators. As the project was concerned with officials working in policy-related Directorates-General, responses from translators do not feature in the analyses reported

Table 1.1 Targeted and achieved sample relative to the total population of the Commission in 2008 and in 2011

Sample Group	Population Size (2011)	Population Size (2008)	Target Sample Size	Achieved Sample Size	
	N	N	n	n	%*
Cabinet members*	199	203	203	54	27
Senior Managers (DG/DDG/ Directors) and Advisers/ Assistants to Directors-General	339	482	482	195***	40
Middle Managers (HoU)	1,163	1,081	1,081	429	40
Principal Administrators, Administrators	10,530	12,964	2,855	1,149	40
Other/preferred not to say				74	
TOTAL	12,032 + Cabinet	14,730	4,621	1,901	41

* Approximate percentages.
** Cabinet members may be classed as permanent or temporary officials.
*** Senior Managers (114) and Advisers (81).

officials—or approximately a quarter of 14,730 administrators employed in Brussels and Luxembourg in September 2008—as well as all *cabinet* members,[28] were included.[29] The targeted sample included all members of cabinets, all senior and middle managers (n = 1,563), and a random sample of other AD staff (i.e. administrators not holding management positions) in 31 policy-related DGs (n = 2,855). It was proportionate to gender, age together with length of service and nationality of officials, but it oversampled officials from the twelve newest member states (by 25 per cent) to make possible meaningful comparisons between them and officials from member states that joined before 2004). Table 1.1 shows the population at the time of the survey in autumn 2008 (and 2012 for an updated comparison), target sample, and achieved sample for the on-line survey of all policy-related AD staff in the Directorates-General, plus members of cabinets.

The achieved sample was 1,901, representing a 41 per cent response rate. It is interesting to note that approximately 40 per cent of each category of seniority responded, apart from *cabinet* members, for whom the response

below. Neither proportional iterative fitting (see below) nor, therefore, the representativeness of the results was affected.

[28] *Cabinet* members may be permanent officials or employed as temporary agents (see <http://ec.europa.eu/civil_service/job/temp/index_en.htm>, accessed 8 May 2012).

[29] 'Seconded national experts', also called 'detached national experts' <http://ec.europa.eu/ civil_service/job/sne/index_en.htm>, were not included in the sample. It is not known how many 'temporary staff in research', who can work in permanent posts under the research budget in six DGs (Research, Information Society, the Joint Research Centre, Energy and Transport, Enterprise and Fisheries) were included in the sample.

rate was just over a quarter. As some sub-populations—for example, nationals from the smallest member states—were marginal, a process of iterative proportional fitting was implemented to weight the data to reflect the true population proportions of each category within the stratification as closely as possible. This ensured that the achieved sample, on which the analysis presented in the chapters that follow is based, is representative of seniority, gender, age and length of service, nationality, and officials from the 'old' (that is, the EU-15) and 'new' (the EU-12) member states.

One hundred and twenty-four respondents to the online survey volunteered for further participation in the study. Interviews were conducted with sixty of this self-selecting sample, for two purposes. The first was to test interpretations of the responses to the online survey. The second was to inform the design of the interview templates for the follow-up interview programme. A mix of open and closed questions was used.

Prior to carrying out the elite group interviews, a purposive sample of eleven expert advisers in diverse roles within the Commission was chosen to illuminate or clarify certain aspects of how the organization worked. The intent was to ensure that questions would be meaningful to respondents and would produce greater insights into the functioning of the Commission. The sample comprised Heads of Unit (4), advisers (3), members of *cabinet* (2), a Director, and a policy officer.

Follow-up face-to-face interviews were conducted with officials drawn from a stratified sample. The sample included the following: all Commissioners, all Directors-General, a random sample of middle managers, and two members of each *cabinet*. In terms of the achieved sample, interviews were conducted with 5 Commissioners, 28 *cabinet* members, 42 senior managers, and 77 middle managers.[30] A template set of questions was constructed for each, customized as appropriate for each target constituency (the templates used for Commissioners, *cabinet* members, and middle and senior managers are included as appendices).[31] These interviews helped to provide an insight into the possible causal mechanisms that underlie the statistical associations revealed by the online survey. The aim was also to ensure comparability with classic attitudinal research in comparative public administration, which has mainly relied on semi-structured qualitative interviewing and used *ex post* coding.

The surveys were conducted against the background of important developments inside and outside the Commission (see Figure 1.2). The Lisbon Treaty's protracted ratification ran for more or less the whole period of the online survey and into the period of face-to-face interviews. The financial

---

[30] Five expert advisers were consulted.
[31] All involved a mix of open and closed questions, except for the Commissioner template featuring exclusively open questions. The data from the closed questions was aggregated and is cited throughout the text.

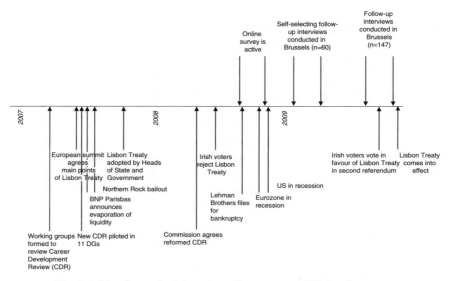

Fig. 1.2 Timeline: administration of surveys and EU developments

crisis broke out some months before the online survey was activated. Internally, the Career Development Review (CDR), the system of appraisal introduced as part of the Kinnock–Prodi reforms, was re-examined in late 2007 and a major amendment was introduced in 2008. The new system was rolled out and became operational throughout the fieldwork period.

A mixed methods design

The use of data from two different sources was a distinctive part of the project's design. The large-scale survey made it possible to collect the views of nearly two thousand respondents, providing rich data for statistical analysis. The semi-structured interviews, meanwhile, generated more modest quantitative data, but also source material for qualitative analysis. This use of mixed methods performs three functions. The first is expansion beyond the quantitative data, since interviews make it possible to consider issues that are more usefully explored discursively. Second, the interviews offer complementarity. They help interpret results, resolve puzzling findings, and understand why officials respond as they do. Triangulation—the third—is used occasionally to corroborate the findings using both sources of evidence.

Mostly, in the chapters that follow, interview material performs the function of complementarity. It serves to offer insights into the reasoning behind the quantitative data. For this reason, quotations from the interviews are cited to give a sense of the range of views within the organization rather than their frequency or distribution. However, the interviews were also used to examine the views of officials on issues that are more usefully explored face to face. For whichever purpose it is cited, the interview material quoted in the chapters that follow has been anonymized.

The combination of data sources and the mixed methods approach deliver a richer product than is possible by exclusive reliance on a single method. Although all the chapters report descriptive statistics and most use multivariate analysis in examining the quantitative data, the particular analysis that is undertaken, the sources used, and the combination of methods varies from chapter to chapter. The examination of personal networks in Chapter 3, beliefs in Chapter 4, and the 'Community method' in Chapter 5 draw almost exclusively on data from the online survey. By contrast, the discussions of nationality (Chapter 2), leadership (Chapter 6), coordination (Chapter 7), reform (Chapter 8), and enlargement (Chapter 9) use responses to the online survey, data from the interviews, and interview testimonies. The mixed methods approach is arguably best exemplified in these five chapters. The specific usage, however, also varied. Expansion featured in discussion of personal contacts and networking (Chapters 3 and 5), *cabinets*, their role and functioning (Chapter 7), leadership (Chapter 6), and reform (Chapter 8). Complementarity was employed to explore nationality (Chapter 2), beliefs and partisanship (Chapter 4), coordination (Chapter 7), and leadership (Chapter 6). Triangulation, meanwhile, was used most extensively in examination of leadership (Chapter 6).

Variation in the extent to which mixed methods were employed and in the specific usage can be explained mainly by the differences in scope between the online survey and the interview questionnaires (see Appendices 1–5). Some topics featured only in one or the other. For example, questions about professional and educational background, career progression, views about the scope of EU competencies, and the detail of administrative reform were asked only in the online survey. By contrast, questions on the operation and role of the *cabinets* featured prominently in the face-to-face interviews.

One final point is important. For the purposes of analysis, the text that follows frequently distinguishes between middle and senior managers, on the one hand, and administrators on the other. In formal terms, however, all are administrators. No easier shorthand is in common currency.

Testimonies as resource and object

The coverage of a multiplicity of themes of varying ontological type is a feature that distinguishes the book. In the existing literature, studies tend either to investigate the beliefs of officials (see, for example, Hooghe 2001) or to examine factors and procedures relating to Commission personnel and the organization and its structures (see Page 1997; Stevens and Stevens 2001; Spence with Edwards 2006). This volume aims to do both. It proceeds on the premise that the testimony of officials offers insight into the functioning of the Commission and that the views and experience of the people who work for the organization offer a key to understanding its functioning. It rejects as excessively rigid the epistemological claim that soliciting the preferences of interview-subjects offers a glimpse only into an assumptive world.

The chapters that follow report the responses from the online survey and (in most chapters) the interviews. They examine the distribution of opinion among respondents on the various issues on which they have answered questions and use the data as evidence to test hypotheses drawn from the existing literature. They then seek to explain the distribution of attitudes among respondents. With respect to the former, the claims are theme-specific. There is no single overarching thesis that links the themes addressed. This is not so in regard to the beliefs expressed by respondents, where there are general theories transcending particular subjects about why officials adopt the positions that they do. Hypotheses derived from these theories, detailed below, are tested in the chapters that follow.

BELIEFS: A CONCEPTUAL FRAMEWORK

This study examines the rich palette of attitudes and beliefs held by Commission officials on several subjects, and aims to shed light on the variation in the positions they take. The approach is guided by two basic principles.[32] The first is that men and women are rational beings who are in general motivated by values and beliefs as well as rational interest.[33] Values or beliefs are mostly acquired through socialization and learning, and interests are acquired in a process of more or less bounded calculation. Sometimes beliefs and interests combine to reinforce particular attitudes; sometimes they pull in different directions.[34] Second, men and women almost always live and work in a

[32] For general discussions, see Searing (1994); Chong (2000). For applications to the Commission, see Hooghe (2001, 2005a); Bauer (2008).

[33] An alternative approach is to elide the distinction between values and interests (see Chong 2000), by conceptualizing people as bounded rationals (Simon 1985). This kind of approach usually defines rationality thinly as responding to apparent cost–benefit considerations. While appealing in principle, such an approach is impractical to implement. What are the boundaries of thin rationality? What cannot be reduced to cost–benefit? What is, in other words, *not* rational? The approach here differs in that it sets out posts in the sand by defining *a priori* what is meant by rational interest. This makes it possible to formulate falsifiable expectations.

[34] This study follows standard definitions in political psychology on values, beliefs and attitudes (Feldman 2003; Taber 2003). *Values* refer to 'enduring beliefs that a specific mode of

multiplicity of institutional contexts. For Commission officials, the institutional contexts are territorial (especially, but not only, national) and functional. The push-and-pull of territorial and non-territorial loyalties and interests can change attitudes.

Socialization and utility maximization

Socialization theory states that individuals acquire attitudes by internalizing the values of the groups or institutions in which they live or work. This view emphasizes affective group ties—identities—and longstanding personal dispositions. What motivates individuals is, in March and Olsen's (1989) well-known phrase, 'a logic of appropriateness' or in Börzel and Risse's terms (2009) 'normative rationality'. Utility maximization theory, in contrast, maintains that attitudes reflect the desire to maximize utility. Individuals hold particular views because they are rational in the light of costs and benefits. March and Olsen describe this as a 'logic of consequentiality'; others call it 'instrumental rationality'.

The operationalization of these theories requires definition. Thus, for the purposes of this study, utility is defined in terms of career benefits and national benefits: Commission officials can be expected to consider how reforms may affect their career chances or the material situation of their country. How to understand utility is intensely debated. Proponents of thick rationality conceive of utility in terms of individual wealth maximization, while proponents of thin rationality take the view that any object or value can be maximized, so long as individuals act consciously and consistently (Kato 1996; Levi 1997; Yee 1997). This study takes a less demanding position. Utility refers to material interests, such as career interests, rather than to wealth maximization. Commission officials have more generous remuneration packages than some public officials (though

---

conduct or end-state of existence is personally or socially preferable to an opposite or converse mode'; examples are the values of liberty, social justice, ambition, responsibility, success. It is common to look for how people prioritize values, and political ideologies are one way in which individuals can summarize how they rank-order values. *Beliefs* refer to statements about how the world is. A belief can be equated with knowledge if the belief is true, and if the believer has a justification (plausible assertions or evidence) for believing it is true. *Attitudes* are statements about how the world should be (or not be); attitudes reflect how much an individual likes (or dislikes) a person, place, thing, or event. Beliefs are statements about what is believed to be; attitudes are judgments. In this study, the dependent variables are mostly attitudes towards particular objects: on reform, enlargement, coordination, leadership, EU policy-making, etc. Sometimes they are beliefs—statements about what officials think is true—as for example on actual EU policy scope, on the role of the Secretary-General, or on the decline or increase in power among the institutions. Most of the time, values and beliefs (or belief systems, such as political ideology or governance views) are among several plausible sets of independent variables that could shape attitudes.

not to their counterparts in the private sector), which may reduce the appeal of salary rises and increase that of promotions or prestige assignments.

In practice, individuals are often motivated by a combination of norms and utility. Utility maximization prevails when attitudes are perceived to have material consequences that can be estimated with some accuracy, are large enough to matter, are transparent, and when an individual's choice is likely to affect the outcome (Sears and Funk 1991; Young et al. 1991). Socialization is most likely when the opposite holds. Hence utility maximization can be expected to shape attitudes on matters that affect career chances, such as administrative reform, coordination in the Commission, career development, or work practices. Attitudes on diffuse beliefs, such as EU governance, EU ideology, the Community method, or the policy scope of the European Union, can be expected to be subject to socialization.

Territorial and functional contexts

It is unlikely that the Commission determines officials' attitudes. Unity of purpose is fictional in any public administration, but there is good evidence that this maxim is particularly true regarding the Commission (Spierenburg 1979; Cini 1996; Page 1997; Kassim and Dimitrakopoulos 2007). As discussed in later chapters, fragmentation in services and agencies, geographical dispersion in Brussels and across the European Union, relatively weak horizontal coordination and stronger vertical coordination are not conducive to forging a homogeneous, single-purposive service. Directorates-General (DGs) or groups of DGs develop distinctive institutional environments. Rather than a single-purpose service, the Commission is a conglomerate of DG coalitions.[35]

Moreover, the wider political context is salient in Commission officials' daily work. Commission officials are players in a political system in which authority is shared across territorial levels (Peterson and Bomberg 1999; Hooghe and Marks 2001; Bartolini 2005). They are attuned to national environments—governments, administrations, interest groups, public opinion, parties—as well as to European-wide contexts, which are to some extent ideological. Contestation between market liberals and social democrats, social liberals and conservatives, and materialists and post materialists permeates EU policy-making (Marks and Steenbergen 2004; Hix 2005; Kriesi et al. 2008; Manow et al. 2008; van Apeldoorn et al. 2009).

Commission officials work in an institutional context where functional loyalties and interests related to the Commission, the Directorate-General

---

[35] Hypotheses about how Directorates-General coalesce into functional groups with coherent attitudes are discussed below.

		Institutional context	
		FUNCTIONAL	TERRITORIAL
Logic of influence	SOCIALIZATION	**Commission socialization** *(length of service)* **DG socialization** *(e.g. years in a DG core activity;* *market-correcting DG;* *market-enhancing DG)* **Positional socialization** *(e.g. years in an administrative primary* *function; years in a cabinet)* **Political ideology** *(left/right; liberal/conservative)* **Governance beliefs** *(supranationalismvs. other; Community* *method supporters)*	**Enlargement socialization** *(EU–12 vs. EU–15; accession* *wave)* **National political system** *(e.g. national experience with* *multi-level governance)* **Career in national admini -stration** *(length of career)*
	UTILITY MAXIMIZATION	**Bureau-maximization** *(e.g. works in: a spending DG;* *management DG; power DG)* **Positional maximization** *(e.g. works currently as senior official;* *works in a cabinet; works in an* *implementation job)*	**Enlargement utility** *(EU–12 vs. EU–15)* **National utility** *(e.g. net beneficiary vs. net* *contributor; country size;* *governance efficacy)*
CONTROLS		*Selective recruitment (pre-Delors, Delors, interregnum,* ***Barroso recruits)*** *Self-selection (motivation)* *Age, Gender, Education,* *International education, prior career, multiple nationality*	

Fig. 1.3 Possible sources of influence on officials' attitudes

(DG), the *cabinet*, or their position in the hierarchy compete with territorial loyalties and interests related to national administrations, national political systems, and national publics. Philosophical belief systems pertaining to the role of government in the economy and people's lives also play a role. These represent the building blocks for attitude formation in the Commission. By combining type of institutional context (territorial or functional) with logic of influence (socialization or utility maximization), a series of possible influences on Commission officials' attitudes can be highlighted.

Overview

Figure 1.3 summarizes these possible sources of influence on officials' attitudes. Table 1.2 operationalizes these as independent variables. How officials are influenced, and with what results, are questions taken up in subsequent chapters. Here the rationale for each variable is set out.

Table 1.2 Operationalization of independent variables

Commission socialization	Years in the Commission for each respondent. *Source*: self-reporting (Q4).
Age	At the time of the survey (2008-year of birth). *Source*: self-reporting (Q123).
DG core activity	Classification of services and DGs on the basis of whether the core function is spending (management), legislation (producing new legislation), regulation and enforcement (upkeep and enforcement of acquis/comitology), internal support services, or external relations. *Source*: coding on the basis of the Commission's Annual Management Reports, in which each DG explains its functions and activities and sets out its budget, and self-reporting (Q116). This information is summarized in seven responses: Spending DG; Regulatory DG; Legislative DG; Internal DG; External DG; Spending and regulation DG; Spending and legislative DG.
DG spending levels	Classification of DGs based on the levels of spending reported in the Commission's Annual Management Reports. Levels of spending are classified as high if they are above €10,000 million, large if they are between €1,000 million and €10,000 million, medium if they are between €300 million and €1,000 million and small if they are below €300 million. *Source*: coding on the basis of the Commission's Annual Management Reports, in which each DG explains its functions and activities and sets out its budget, and self-reporting (Q116).
Management DG	Dichotomous variable taking on the value of 1 if a respondent works in a management DG, defined as being DG Budget, DG Admin, Internal Audit, Anti-Fraud Office, and the Secretariat-General. *Source*: self-reporting (Q116).
Market-enhancing DG	Dichotomous variable taking on the value of 1 if a respondent works in a DG with responsibility in market-enhancing area of policy, i.e. competition, economic and financial affairs, enterprise and industry, internal market services, taxation and customs union, trade. *Source*: self-reporting (Q116).
Market-correcting DG	Dichotomous variable taking on the value of 1 if a respondent works in a DG with responsibility in market-correcting area of policy, i.e. development, education and culture, employment and social affairs, environment, EuropeAid, health and consumer protection, humanitarian aid, regional policy, research. *Source*: self-reporting (Q116).
Power DG	Dichotomous variable taking on the value of 1 if a respondent works in a policy area with strong Commission initiative—a policy area meets certain criteria on level and scope of EU authority. Using a five-point scale developed on the basis of formal Treaty rules by Börzel, policies score 3 or higher on level of authority (3 = shared EU and national competencies) and 3.75 or higher on scope (3.75 = exclusive right of Commission initiative + full judicial review + codecision). Policy scores are averaged across the Amsterdam, Nice and Constitutional Treaties and then allocated to the most closely associated DG. Non-policy DGs (e.g. legal service, Secretary-General) are scored 0. *Source*: Börzel (2005) and self-reporting (Q116).

Current position	Summarized in four responses: Member of cabinet; Senior manager = Director-General, Deputy Director-General, Director, Adviser; Middle-manager = Head of unit; Administrator. *Source*: self-reporting (Q20).
Primary function	Administrative primary functions: steering jobs, relational jobs, implementation jobs, support jobs. *Source*: self-reporting (Q23).
Cabinet experience	Dichotomous variable taking on the value of 1 if a respondent is currently working in a cabinet *or* has previously worked in a cabinet. *Source*: self-reporting (Q20 and Q24_1).
Left/Right ideology	Individual responses on an 11-point scale (0 to 10, 5 is the mid-point) reporting personal philosophy; standardized around the mean. 'People often think of themselves in terms of their personal philosophical stance on economic issues. Some favour an active role for government on economic policy questions. Others look primarily to markets. Where would you place yourself in terms of economic philosophy?' *Source*: self-reporting (Q125).
Liberal/Conservative ideology	Individual responses on an 11-point scale (0 to 10, 5 is the mid-point) reporting personal philosophy; standardized around the mean. 'People often think of themselves in terms of their personal philosophical stance on social and cultural issues. Many people who consider themselves liberal tend to favour expanded personal freedoms on (for example) abortion, same-sex marriage and so on People on the conservative side tend to favour more traditional notions of family, morality, and order. Where would you place yourself in terms of social-cultural philosophy?' *Source*: self-reporting (Q126).
EU governance beliefs: • *supranationalists* • *state-centrists* • *institutional pragmatists* • *other*	Four dichotomous variables that categorize officials according to their views on the appropriate balance of power among Commission, member states, and European Parliament. Four types are constructed from responses on two survey questions. *Source*: self-reporting (Q127 and Q128); see Chapter 4 and Hooghe (2012) for details.
EU-15 or EU-12	Variable that takes on a value of 1 if a respondent is a citizen of one of the fifteen older member states and a value of 2 if a respondent is a citizen of one of the twelve newest member states. *Source*: self-reporting (Q120).
Accession wave	Five-way classification based on accession waves, whereby 1 = 1952 (founding six, EU 6); 2 = 1973 (Denmark, Ireland, UK: first enlargement), 3 = 1981 and 1986 (Greece, Spain, Portugal: Mediterranean enlargement), 4 = 1995 (Austria, Finland, Sweden: Northern enlargement), 5 = 2004 and 2007 (ten former communist countries + Cyprus, Malta: CEE +). *Source*: self-reporting (Q120).
Country size	Country's population in 2008 (in '000s). *Source*: Eurostat.
Governance efficacy	Country average for 1996–2006. Government effectiveness is one of six measures developed by the Worldwide Governance Indicators project by the World Bank. These aggregate indicators are based on hundreds of variables measuring various dimensions of governance, taken from 35 data sources provided by 33 different organizations. The data reflect the views on governance of public sector, private sector and NGO experts, public opinion and firm surveys. *Source*: Kaufmann, Kraay, Mastruzzi (2009) (<http://info.worldbank.org/governance/wgi/index.asp>).

(continued)

Table 1.2 Continued

Multilevel governance	Regional authority index for each member state (average for ten years, 1996–2006), a measure of the extent of self-rule and shared rule for each intermediate tier of regional government. Standardized around the mean. *Source*: RAI dataset by Hooghe et al. (2010).
Community method supporters:	Dichotomous variable that categorizes officials according to their views on the Community method, based on their responses to two survey questions. *Source*: self-reporting (Q128 and Q130); see Chapter 9 for details.
Career in national administration	Years of prior service in national/regional/local administration. *Source*: calculated from self-reported career history (Q10_2 and Q12 (banded), whereby 1 = up to 1 year, 1.5 = 1 to 2 years, 4 = 2 to 5 years, 8 = 5 to 10 years, 13 = 10 to 15 years, 18 = more than 15 years).
Pre Delors recruits	Dichotomous variable taking on a value of 1 entered the Commission before the Delors presidency (i.e. before 1985). *Source*: calculated on the basis of self-reported entry to the Commission (Q4).
Delors recruits	Dichotomous variable taking on a value of 1 entered the Commission under the Delors presidency (i.e. between 1985 and 1995). *Source*: calculated on the basis of self-reported entry in the Commission (Q4).
Interregnum recruits	Dichotomous variable taking on a value of 1 if entered the Commission under the Santer or Prodi presidency (i.e. between 1996 and. 2004). *Source*: calculated on the basis of self-reported entry in the Commission (Q4).
Barroso recruits	Dichotomous variable taking on a value of 1 if entered the Commission under the Barroso presidency (i.e. from 2005). *Source*: calculated on the basis of self-reported entry in the Commission (Q4).
Motivation	Series of 12 dichotomous variables extracted from the question: 'Why did you choose to follow a career in the European Commission? (Please choose as many as are relevant). Options: Job stability; Promising career prospects; Competitive remuneration; Commitment to Europe; Commitment to a particular policy area; Quality of the work; I was asked to apply.' On the basis of spontaneous answers on 'other' we created the following additional categories: I liked the international aspects of the job; My professional development/training made this a logical choice; Family/personal reasons; Because public service is important to me; I want to influence policy. *Source*: self-reporting (Q2).
Gender	Dichotomous variable whereby 0 = male and 1 = female. *Source*: self-reporting (Q124).
Education	The responses to the question of main subject of degree are grouped into six responses: 1 = Law, 2 = Economics and business, 3 = Politics, International relations or another social science; 4 = Arts and the humanities; 5 = Mathematics, computing, engineering, physical or life science; 0 = no response or prefer not to say. *Source*: self-reporting (Q7 and Q8).
International education	Dichotomous variable that takes a value of 1 if the respondent studied outside his country of citizenship. *Source*: self-reporting (Q9).

Prior experience	Series of 12 dichotomous variables extracted from the question: 'What career did you follow before joining the European Commission? (Please choose as many as are relevant) Options: International organization, Non-EU; National civil service; Party politics; Trade union or social movement; private enterprise, liberal professions; education and research; journalism and PR; Other EU organization; None; Other, prefer not to say'. *Source*: self-reporting (Q10_1 to Q10_12).
Multiple nationality	Dichotomous variable where 0 = if respondent has one nationality and 1 = if respondent has dual or multiple nationality. *Source*: self-reporting (Q122).

The Commission as Context

The most immediate environment for officials is the Commission as an organization. Two basic processes guide how and why experiences within the organization shape attitudes of Commission officials. These processes are particularly salient for younger officials:

Commission socialization. The assumption in neofunctionalist and intergovernmental theories of European integration is that the Commission is pro-integrationist. This supposition harks back to Jean Monnet (1978), one of the EU's 'founding fathers', who instilled pro-European values and objectives in creating the institution. The socialization logic expects officials to internalize these norms as they work longer in the Commission.

Bureau-maximization. Utilitarian reasoning builds on public choice theory to argue that bureaucrats support bureau-maximizing strategies—budget expansion, bureaucratic discretion, better status and work conditions—in order to maximize career benefits (Niskanen 1971; Calvert et al. 1989; Dunleavy 1991; Moe 1997; Pollack 2003).[36]

It is possible that socialization or bureau-maximization lead Commission officials to want *in general* more EU competences, greater Commission autonomy, or larger Commission budgets. However, socialization and bureau-maximization can also work at a disaggregated level: the policy area, the DG, the position. Furthermore, officials do not join the Commission as blank slates. They have particular philosophical views and they are shaped by experiences or laden with interests related to their national or regional background.

---

[36] The power of socialization or utility maximization varies inversely with age and experience. New experiences are more formative when a person has few relevant prior experiences (Searing et al. 1976; Levy 2003). Utility calculations lose salience as officials grow older because anticipated career benefits decrease as retirement approaches.

Policy field and DG

The problems that confront officials, and the legal frameworks in which they are addressed, diverge sharply across services. At the time the survey was conducted, the Commission was composed of 26 Directorates-General, 19 services and six executive agencies. How does a DG shape an official's attitudes?

> *DG core activity.* DGs tend to have a core activity (see Table 1.3), which can be expected to influence an official's views on, for example, administrative reform or the EU's policy scope. Regulation and enforcement is the primary activity of health and consumer protection, internal market, or competition. Preparing legal rules is central in the DGs for employment, environment, justice and home affairs, transport, and energy. The EU's budget of €141.5 billion (2010 figures) is spent mainly in regional policy, agriculture, research, development, and aid. The field of external relations is sometimes described as its own universe with four big planets: trade, external relations (DG RELEX, since 2010 partitioned), development, and enlargement. A relatively diverse group of DGs and services are concerned with institutional and internal affairs, including personnel management, inter-service coordination, budget, statistics, legal support, and financial control. Some DGs are strongly present in more than one activity, and they are coded accordingly.

> *Management.* DGs vary in the extent to which management is central to their task description. Historically, the European Commission has been less a manager and more 'the engine of European integration' on account of its constitutionally guaranteed monopoly of legislative initiative and its competence to bring infringement proceedings (Tallberg 2000, 2002; Pollack 2003; Dehousse 2011). These powers set it apart from national administrations and all but a handful of international administrations.[37] However, over the past decade the Commission has become more attentive to administrative performance (Kassim 2004a, 2004b, 2008; Bauer 2007; Cini 2007). Services with a primary role in monitoring managerial performance can be expected to frame distinctive attitudes.

> *Legal competence.* Commission policy-making is regulated by a strict legal framework. Some services, such as competition or trade, handle supranational competencies, while others deal with intergovernmental issues. Sometimes the differences run within DGs, but most services have a dominant trait. DG Employment mostly operates through soft law, even though the gender equality unit, which was part of this DG until moved to Justice, Fundamental Rights and

---

[37] Exceptions include the Commission de la Communauté Économique et Monétaire de l'Afrique Centrale (CEMAC), the European Economic Area (EEA), the International Monetary Fund (IMF), and the Southern African Development Community (SADC), where the organ that is the functional equivalent of the European Commission has the monopoly of legislative initiative. In the European Economic Area (EEA), the European Commission itself exercises a near-monopoly (Hooghe et al. forthcoming).

Table 1.3 Classification of Directorates-General by function (2009)

Directorates-General	Staff	Primary or first task	Secondary or second task	Total budget (€millions)	Total spending (€ millions)
Administration (ADMIN)[1]	604	Internal Services (100%)		€932.4	€932.4
Agriculture and Rural Development (AGRI)	943	Regulatory (75%)	Enforcement (25%)	€54893.2	€49160.2
Budget (BUDG)	397	Internal Support (100%)		€276.7	€276.7
Communication (COMM)	489	Internal Support (100%)		€212.8	€210.1
Competition (COMP)	669	Enforcement (75%)	Regulatory (25%)	€87.7	€87.7
Development (DEV)	269	External (100%)		€3974.0	€3974.0
Economic and Financial Affairs (ECFIN)[3]	471	Regulatory (100%)		€430.2	€414.8
Education and Culture (EAC)	494	Spending (100%)		€1403.1	€1366.1
Employment, Social Affairs, Equal Opportunities (EMPL)[3]	618	Legislative (50%)	Spending (50%)	€11184.5	€11199.3
Enlargement (ELARG)	216	External (75%)	Spending (25%)	€1078.6	€1414.7
Enterprise and Industry (ENTR)[2]	741	Spending (50%)	Regulatory (50%)	€660.8	€570.6
Environment (ENV)[2]	561	Legislative (100%)		€460.0	€367.8
EuropeAid (AIDCO)[4]	568	Spending (100%)		€5476.9	€4459.3*
European Anti-Fraud Office (OLAF)[3]	340	Internal Support (100%)		€78.4	€74.2
External Relations (RELEX)[2]	645	External (100%)		€3112.1	€3112.1
Fisheries and Maritime Affairs (MARE)	266	Regulatory (75%)	Spending (25%)	€976.9	€695.3
Health and Consumer Protection (SANCO)	675	Regulatory (100%)		€664.7	€573.1
Humanitarian Aid (ECHO)	160	Spending (100%)		€796.3	€796.3
Informatics (DIGIT)	396	Internal Support (100%)		€141	€141
Information Society and Media (INFSO)	803	Spending (50%)	Regulatory (50%)	€1510.4	€1353.7
Internal Audit Service (IAS)	84	Internal Support (100%)		€1.7	€1.7
Internal Market and Services (MARKT)	417	Regulatory (75%)	Enforcement (25%)	€64.4	€64.4
Joint Research Centre (JRC)	1763	Research (100%)		€370.8	€365.7**
Justice, Freedom and Security (JLS)[5]	433	Legislative (75%)	Spending (25%)	€924.6	€675.8
Legal Service (SJ)	545	Internal (100%)		€182.2	€182.2
Regional Policy (REGIO)	355	Spending (100%)		€38514.3	€38514.3***
Research (RTD)	1210	Spending (100%)		€4659.7	€4514.6

(continued)

Table 1.3 Continued

Directorates-General	Staff	Primary or first task	Secondary or second task	Total budget (€millions)	Total spending (€ millions)
Secretariat-General (SG)[3]	465	Internal Support (100%)		€182.2	€182.2****
Taxation and Customs Union (TAXUD)	366	Regulatory (100%)		€129.8	€104.9
Trade (TRADE)	445	External (75%)	Regulatory (25%)	€78.5	€77.0
Transport and Energy (TREN)[3,6]	913	Legislative (50%)	Spending (50%)	€2735.4	€2284.2
SCIC and DGT	701 + 2,220	Internal Support (100%)		€374.5	€374.5

Notes: Classification is based on DG's own categorization of strategic objective. Secondary categories are included only where such activities are prominent or repeatedly noted. Where first and secondary typologies are given as both 50%, neither is considered primary. Budgetary figures provided by DG BUDG and refer to the year 2009 (<http://eur-lex.europa.eu/budget/data/D2010_VOL4/EN/index.html>).

1 From 2010, DG Human Resources (HR)

2 From 2010, new DG Climate Action (CLIMA) formed from parts of DGs ENTR, ENV, and RELEX

3 Data from 2010 Annual Management Plan (AMP). AMPs for 2008 and 2009 not available

4 Activities funded by budgets of other DGs.

5 Split into DG Home Affairs (HOME) and DG Justice (JUST) 2010

6 Split into DG Transport (MOVE) and DG Energy (ENER) 2010

* = General EU budget for external assistance managed by EuropeAid

** = direct research

*** = combined figure, including Secretariat General

**** = combined figure, including Legal Service

Source: Annual Management Plans, European Commission Directorates-General (various), 2008, 2009

Citizenship in January 2011, can rely on well-developed Court jurisprudence. DG Competition is the Commission's supranational power house with the authority to conduct dawn raids, break up monopolies, forbid mergers, and fine countries or multinationals, although the DG's small directorate on state aid works closely with member states. DGs with strong legal competence—power DGs—might plausibly induce officials to hold distinctive attitudes (Hooghe 1999).

Policy principles. Policy-making concerns the allocation of values. DG Market's mission is to deepen market competitiveness by, for example, reducing red tape, while DG Employment's objective is to watch over equity and fairness in the market through regulation. The former may not inevitably be incompatible with the latter, but different sets of values—competitiveness and equity—are privileged in certain policy contexts.

Position

A second source of variation relates to the positions that officials occupy in the Commission's hierarchy. Each position comes laden with distinct expectations, experiences, and interests. Three sources of positional difference are important:

Current position. Senior officials engage routinely in tasks that rarely concern junior officials: they lead and motivate a team, set strategic priorities, take responsibility for the DG's finances and budget, negotiate with member states, stakeholders, or the European Parliament, represent the Commission to the outside world, defend their DG in inter-service battles, and interact with their Commissioner and the College. Conversely, senior officials do not tend to accumulate expertise on a problem, manage a dossier from cradle to maturity, author green or white papers, write executive summaries, participate in technical working groups on a regular basis, or immerse themselves in a policy area for a lifetime.

Administrative function. The Directorate-General for Administration classifies all positions in four task categories: steering jobs, relational jobs, implementation jobs, and support jobs. This classification has been adopted in this study in the expectation that type of activity may shape attitudes.

Cabinet experience. Cabinets are the heart and soul of Commission politics; here European objectives, member state priorities, and policy-making meet. Officials may become *cabinet* members because they possess the values and attitudes that make a *cabinet* member successful, or they may acquire these values on the job. The bottom line is that officials who have had *cabinet* experience are likely to hold different attitudes from those who have not.

Values and beliefs

A third source is the 'set[s] of beliefs about the proper order of society and how it can be achieved' (Erikson and Tedin 2003). Human beings care about consistency between their core beliefs and their attitudes about specific objects. The role of three sets of core beliefs is considered:

Economic left/right. The European Commission has been alternately attributed a bias in favour of market integration (van Apeldoorn et al. 2009; Scharpf 2010) and market-correcting policies (Majone 1996). To what extent do Commission officials' personal beliefs about the role of government in markets predispose their attitudes?

Liberal vs conservative. With the expansion of Europeanization to asylum and immigration, citizenship, culture, education, and foreign policy, EU policy-making is affecting European societies' identities. It is difficult to conceive of Commission officials as neutral arbiters, all the more so because European integration has been understood as a project that emphasizes cosmopolitanism and progressive social values (Inglehart 1977; Vachudova and Hooghe 2009; Risse 2010).

EU governance. How the EU should be governed, and by whom, is contested. This book pursues two lines of enquiry to categorize divergent opinions. One asks how Commission officials conceive of the appropriate balance of power among Commission, member states, and European Parliament: supranationalism, state-centrism, or institutional pragmatism (Hooghe 2012). A second considers the Community method, which has formed the constitutional foundation for the Commission's special role in the European construct (Dehousse 2011).

Territoriality and nationality

Previous research has found that territoriality, and in particular nationality, profoundly shapes the way a person thinks about European issues (Hooghe 2001, 2005; Beyers 2005). The challenge is to theorize what it is about being British, Bulgarian or Belgian that makes this so.

EU-12. For the purposes of this study, EU-12 refers to the twelve member states that joined the European Union in 2004 or 2007. These recent members can be expected to have distinctive interests and values stemming from the collective break with communism and authoritarianism (Kitschelt 1992; Kitschelt et al. 1999; Vachudova 2005; Rohrschneider and Whitefield 2009).[38] Socialization and utility combine to suggest that EU-12 officials have distinctive attitudes on a range of EU issues.

Accession wave. Each enlargement writes its own history in anticipated benefits, hopes, and contestation (Dehousse et al. 2006; Peterson and Birdsall 2008). Hence the discourse that accompanies each accession is distinctive, and these discourses may frame perceptions in the aftermath.

[38] The island-states of Cyprus and Malta experienced non-communist authoritarian rule for a period of their post-colonial past.

Country size. By virtue of its size, EU government can produce public goods with transnational economies of scale (Alesina and Spolaore 2003). Small countries can expect to benefit more in trade, security, insurance against asymmetrical shocks, bargaining power, scale in research, or tackling transnational problems. Small countries can also use the European Union to tie down bigger powers.

Governance efficacy. European government may be perceived as a substitute for national government if the latter is ineffective (Sanchez-Cuenca 2000). Member states differ widely in their governing capacity, and officials from countries with less effective public authorities may have reason to desire a stronger Europe or a stronger Commission.

Multilevel governance. Individuals from federal or regionalized countries are familiar with sharing authority, and extending shared rule to the European level encounters fewer habitual barriers (Hooghe 2001; Risse 2005). It is also less costly to implement since it builds upon, rather than challenges, the status quo. A stronger Europe, European Commission, or more EU competencies should come easier to individuals from multilevel polities.

Career in national administration. National bureaucrats often develop a sense of national public service, adopt particular national administrative styles, and are linked into national networks (Suleiman 1984; Page 1997). Commission officials who worked in a national administration or as diplomat prior to joining the Commission could be primed towards less Europe, less Commission initiative, and a more modest Commission (Egeberg 1999; Hooghe 2001).

Additional influences

Selective recruitment. In the past, senior officials were not infrequently para-chuted by fiat of the Commissioner, often after consulting the member state with an interest in the position (Page 1997). The so-called 'Delors mafia', as top officials hired under Jacques Delors were sometimes labelled, was formed this way, and a sizeable number became stalwarts of the Delors agenda (Ross 1995). Commissioners and national governments no longer have discretion to tailor recruitment to their political agenda, but while strict rules minimize, they cannot entirely eliminate, selective recruitment. We examine whether the Barroso Commission has geared recruitment to officials sympathetic to managerial reform (Georgakakis and de Lassalle 2008).

Self-selection. Prior research has demonstrated that top officials are much more likely to have an attachment to Europe than either national elites or public opinion (Hooghe 2005). It is plausible that candidates for Commission jobs are more favourable to the goals of European integration than non-candidates. To take account of self-selection, officials were asked why they joined the Commission (Searing 1994).

Controls: Controls for the purposes of this study are age, gender, type of education, international education, prior professional experience, and multiple nationality. Controls gain theoretical meaning in relation to particular objects. For example, in Chapter 8, it is hypothesized that economics graduates and officials with a private sector background are favourably disposed to an administrative reform that strengthens managerial principles.

The chapters that follow test hypotheses informed by the conceptual schema set out in Figure 1.3 in order to explain variation in the views held by Commission officials on particular issues. A subset of the above variables is used in both descriptive and multivariate analyses throughout.

CONCLUSION

The extensive literature on the European Commission that has emerged in recent years provides a starting point for this study. However, as the above discussion has contended, existing scholarship has significant limitations. First, it has mostly focused on the Commission as a political actor rather than as an administration or organization. It may well be that the Commission's ability to be an effective political actor is determined—perhaps quite directly—by how well its administration works. Second, past research has overwhelmingly focused on part of the organization—its President, a particular DG, or how it has handled a particular policy or piece of legislation—rather than the Commission as a whole. One frequent effect is that existing work falls victim to the familiar 'blind men and elephants' problem (see Puchala 1971): it is assumed that the whole resembles one of a number of differing parts. Third, the Commission is often portrayed as unique or *sui generis*, which in key respects it is, but this characterization tends to preclude comparison with other administrations, national and international. The Commission may have exceptional powers for an international administration, but it performs many of the same tasks and functions undertaken by all bureaucracies and confronts similar challenges.

Finally, and most importantly, existing research on the European Commission draws on 'small n' samples. Most studies are based on small numbers of interviews or rely on secondary literature or official EU publications. To conduct a 'large n' study of the sort that is presented in this volume requires exceptional access to the Commission itself, as well as the committed efforts of a 'large n' of its officials. It also needs significant funding and calls for a large research team, with diverse, but complementary, skills.[39]

---

[39] Kassim, Peterson, and Dehousse have conducted research of a mainly qualitative character, while Bauer and Hooghe have used both qualitative and quantitative methods in their work. Connolly is an economist, experienced in applied econometric techniques, while Thompson is a specialist in quantitative methods.

2

The Commission and its Personnel

Public bureaucracies in the modern world must endeavour to meet three demands.[1] They need to command a high level of specialist expertise so that they can carry out the tasks entrusted to them. They should be representative of the political community that they serve if they are to have the knowledge and command the legitimacy necessary to carry out their responsibilities. They should also, if they are to be genuinely independent of the constituencies that they serve, be able to offer their employees the prospect of career progression and advancement over a working lifetime. These requirements apply no less to the European Commission. Indeed, for an international administration, and one, moreover, with far-reaching powers, they are at least as important as for national administrations and, perhaps, even more so.[2]

This chapter assesses the extent to which the Commission of the twenty-first century meets these criteria. It looks first at expertise. According to the existing literature, Commission officials are highly educated (Michelmann 1978: 24; Page 1997: 69). A high percentage, moreover, are lawyers (Michelmann 1978: 24; Page 1997: 75; Shore 2000: 135). A widespread view is that 'Eurocrats', as Commission officials are often styled, are typically career bureaucrats, who have spent their entire working lives in the public sector, if not in Brussels. This perception, together with the view that the Commission is an administration of lawyers, suggests an organization that is likely to be formalistic in outlook, limited in imagination, and lacking the experience and expertise necessary to confront the challenges of the twenty-first century. Second, studies of the Commission administration suggest that the larger member countries are under-represented among its staff, especially in the upper echelons of the organization (Page 1997: 42–9). Such an imbalance, should it persist, is likely to be problematic for the

---

[1] See Weber (1964) on *inter alia* expertise and hierarchy. Kingsley (1944) is the *locus classicus* on representation and bureaucracy. See also Meier (1975) and Dolan and Rosenbloom (2003).

[2] A different standard of democracy is thought to apply to international organizations (Scharpf 1999: ch. 1). National administrations are integrated into the domestic political system, but since international organizations have no clear chain of input legitimacy, their claim rests principally on output delivery.

Commission, the member states concerned, and the European project more broadly. Third, previous studies report that in the Commission horizontal mobility is low (Michelmann 1978: 28; Page 1997: 34–5; Williamson 1998; Stevens and Stevens 2001: 103–4), women are seriously under-represented, especially at management levels (Stevens and Stevens 2001: 108–14; Spence and Stevens 2006: 103–4), and career progression is slow, unpredictable, and subject to interruption or blockage when high politics intervenes (Coombes 1970: 141–65; Page 1997: 26, 41–2, 49, 51–2; Stevens and Stevens 2001: ch. 5).

Drawing on data from the online survey and face-to-face interviews, this chapter examines each of these accepted wisdoms about the Commission. It looks at the educational qualifications and professional backgrounds that officials bring to the organization. It addresses the issue of nationality and the extent to which nationals are present in the Commission in proportion to their share of the EU population.[3] It investigates the career trajectories of officials after they enter the Commission, as well as the motivation that leads officials to pursue a career in the organization. Focusing on career development, it looks at staff mobility between Directorates-General, promotion—especially whether certain nationals are promoted more rapidly than others and whether there are gender differentials—and career-building on the part of managers and members of *cabinets*.

The chapter presents four main findings. The first is that the Commission as an organization possesses a far wider range and diversity of expertise than is often thought. It shows that the Commission is not populated overwhelmingly by lawyers, and repudiates the view that its officials have only limited experience of the world beyond the EU quarter in Brussels. Second, it confirms that the larger member states remain under-represented within the organization, especially within its upper echelons. An analysis of career position and career progression by gender shows that there are relatively few women in middle and senior management positions, but those who are in those posts reached them more rapidly than their male counterparts—a third finding. The fourth is that, although there is strong evidence of career-building by officials, a significant proportion of managers and of *cabinet* members have not made their way through the ranks of the organization, but have been recruited from outside. As a result the career progression of officials who joined the organization at entry level has been interrupted or blocked.

The chapter begins with a general introduction to recruitment and promotion processes in the Commission, providing a reference point for the discussion that follows. A second section looks at the people who work for the Commission. It investigates the educational and professional backgrounds of Commission staff, and it examines the extent to which nationals of EU

---

[3] See also chapters 3, 4, and 8 below.

member states are present in the organization relative to their share of the Union's population. Career development is explored in a third section. This part of the chapter considers why officials choose to pursue a career in Brussels, mobility between departments, promotion, and career-building.

RECRUITMENT AND PROMOTION IN THE EUROPEAN COMMISSION

Although, when the Communities were created, some had argued that the Commission administration should be staffed by civil servants seconded from the administrations of the member states for fixed periods,[4] an alternative model, supported by Walter Hallstein, the first Commission President, appeared to win the day. The Commission put in place a 'career-based' system (OECD 2009: 78) that matched Hallstein's ambition for the Commission to be a permanent, career civil service. In systems of this type, officials are recruited by competitive selection to the entry ranks and progress up the career ladder on merit. Top performers can in time expect to move into senior management positions, which are open only to public servants.[5] Only by adopting such a system, Hallstein believed, could the Commission command the expertise and exercise the independence necessary to perform the responsibilities foreseen for it under the treaties (Noël 1998; von der Groeben 1998).

The Staff Regulations, adopted in 1961,[6] laid the foundations for a career-based system. As in the French national administration, officials are recruited to the Commission on merit according to their performance in a competitive entry examination, the *concours*.[7] In the Commission, these competitions can take a variety of forms. They can be open and general, or limited to candidates either from particular countries or with particular professional expertise. Once they have entered the Commission, officials are obliged by Article 11 of the

---

[4] See especially Siotis (1964); Scheinman (1966: 761, fn 21); and Peterson (1971). Shore (2000: 132) argues more generally that: 'the major tensions and cleavages in the integration process, particularly those arising from the encounter between intergovernmental and supranational visions of Europe, [were] played out in the Commission's staffing and management practices'.

[5] By contrast, in 'position-based' systems, 'candidates apply directly to a specific post and most posts are open to both internal and external applicants' (OECD 2009: 78).

[6] The Staff Regulations (Commission 1962) have been updated several times since. See <http://ec.europa.eu/civil_service/docs/toc100_en.pdf>. These rules apply not only to the staff of the Commission, but to employees of all EU institutions.

[7] Candidates have their applications screened to ensure that they comply with specific requirements made in the call, such as age, qualification, and professional experience. They take a pre-selection test, which may involve multiple-choice test, a specialist expertise test, and a language test. A written examination follows, before a final oral examination. Successful candidates are placed on a reserve list, circulated to the Directorates-General, who use it to identify suitable candidates for vacant posts. See Stevens and Stevens (2001: 76–80, 87–9, 90–2).

Staff Regulations to act independently of any national or sectoral interest, and on behalf of the Commission and the Commission alone.

The career structure in the Commission was designed to allow progression. Under the original system, which persisted until the Kinnock–Prodi reforms of 1999 to 2004 (see Chapter 8), the staff of all EU institutions were divided into four categories that corresponded to varying levels of educational attainment. For example, A grade, or administrative, staff were responsible for policy work and required a university degree or equivalent, while B grade officials performed executive tasks and needed a school-leaving certificate.[8] Each category was divided into grades—there were eight for A officials—and each grade was further graduated into either six (A1, A2, and A8) or eight steps (A3 to A7). One idiosyncrasy of the system was that these grades were not necessarily aligned with function or level of responsibility although Directors-General and deputy Directors-General tended typically to hold the grade of A1, Directors A2, and Heads of Unit A3, A4 or A5 (see Table 2.1).

Most officials joined the Commission at the entry level of their respective grade. In the old system, for administrators this was A7 or A8 (though A7 required two years professional experience).[9] All officials were entitled under

Table 2.1 Grades and posts: old and new

Old System		New System		
Category A Personnel				
Director-General	A1	Director-General	AD 16	
Director	A2		AD 15	
Head of Unit	A3–A5	Director	AD 14	
Administrator	A5	Head of Unit	AD 14	
	A6		AD 13	
	A7		AD 12	
Assistant Administrator	A8		AD 11	AST 11
			AD 10	AST 10
			AD 9	AST 9
		Administrator	AD 8	AST 8
				AST 7
				AST 6
				AST 5

Source: <http://ec.europa.eu/civil_service/docs/toc100_en.pdf>

[8] Secretarial and clerical responsibilities were performed by category C officials, while D officials were usually drivers or performed manual duties.

[9] In line with the idea that the European administration should be permanent, independent, and a career civil service, the staff unions have sought to limit general, open competitions to the entry grades. Competitions were held for entry to the higher grades but, for the same reason, were limited. In 2011, the ceiling was set at 20 per cent of entrants each year. Moreover, until it was abolished in 2002 on the grounds of age discrimination, an upper age limit of 45 was applied for administrators. This was a controversial change among Commission officials (Stevens and Stevens 2001: 182).

the Staff Regulations to advance by one step within their grade every two years (Article 44), but promotion to the next grade was selective and depended on merit. According to the Staff Regulations, the performance of all members of staff would be assessed on the basis of a report to be completed at least once every two years.[10] Based on this procedure, Stevens and Stevens (2001: 98) estimated that it would take on average from fifteen to twenty years for an official to progress from A7 to A4. Although the most talented officials might make it to the most senior positions, 'the pyramid narrow[ed] sharply towards the top'.

The Kinnock–Prodi reforms enacted a comprehensive overhaul of both the career structure and promotion procedures (see Chapter 8).[11] The new career structure, which came into force on 1 May 2004 to coincide with the Eastern enlargement, replaced the original four staff categories with two status functions on a single spine.[12] The career span for Assistants (AST) runs from grades 1 to 11, with AST1 to AST4 as entry grades, and for Administrators (AD) from 5 to 16, where the entry levels are AD5 to AD8. As with the old system, grade and functions are not automatically correlated, but in practice there are associations at certain points (see Table 2.1). Similarly each grade under the new structure has a number of 'seniority steps' (now five in number, except for AD16, where there are three) and officials automatically advance one step every two years. The new promotion procedures were intended to create a system that would motivate staff by offering advancement on the basis of proven merit and to reward performance rather than seniority. A new system of annual appraisal, the Career Development Review (CDR),[13] replaced the discredited reporting system (discussed in Chapter 8) and was intended to serve as the basis for promotion.

---

[10] The report, completed by a line manager, comprised three sections, inviting comments on ability, efficiency and conduct in the service (Stevens and Stevens 2001: 100). However, the system did not work very effectively. Reporting was patchy, assessments tended to be inflationary due to a concern on the part of managers to avoid litigation, and owing to problems with the formal system, parallel systems of confidential reporting developed (Stevens and Stevens 2001: 101).

[11] Promotion, according to the Spierenburg Report (1979: 32) was 'irregular and haphazard'.

[12] For the scales, see Annex 1 of the *Staff Regulations of Officials the European Communities* (Commission 2004: 43–4, available at <http://ec.europa.eu/civil_service/docs/toc100_en.pdf>). The new structure was intended to remove the bottlenecks that had limited movement between staff categories under the traditional system (see Chapter 8). The initial plan had been to introduce a single scale, but this was abandoned. Although the system eventually introduced succeeded in removing many of the rigidities that had previously impeded mobility, AST officials need to pass an examination to move to AD status and there is a quota on the number of officials who can move from AST to AD in any period.

[13] See <http://ec.europa.eu/reform/2002/chapter02_en.htm#3>. The CDR is discussed in Chapter 8.

Nationality and the distortion of the career-based system

Though the mechanisms for a career-based system were put in place in the early 1960s, the operation of the model was soon compromised by the demands of nationality.[14] The Commission needs to employ officials from all the states that are members of the Union. Without the knowledge, expertise and connections brought by member state nationals familiar with policies and political systems at home, the Commission would not be able to carry out its responsibilities. Nor in the absence of officials from all EU member states would its claim to embody the common interest be credible. On the grounds of effectiveness and legitimacy, the Commission therefore inscribed in the Staff Regulations a commitment to maintain a 'geographical balance' within the administration.[15]

This vague formulation was not sufficient to satisfy member governments. The insistence of capitals on 'fair shares' for their nationals (Page 1997: 41) led to the introduction of practices and mechanisms that established nationality as a key criterion in personnel decisions, although such consideration was against the spirit of the Commission's independence, the strictures of the Staff Regulations, and the jurisprudence of the Court of First Instance (Stevens and Stevens 2001: 46–7). The determination of member governments to ensure the presence of their nationals in appropriate numbers at all levels of the organization, together with the transformation of the *cabinets* into the agents of national governments (see Coombes 1970; Ritchie 1992), seriously distorted the possibility of career progression on the basis of merit alone.

Governments were successful both in carving out a permanent presence in the Commission administration for their nationals and in establishing permanent channels of influence. Informal quotas were an important device. Governments agreed a formula for the allocation of top administrative posts (Coombes 1970: 141),[16] and, unlike recruitment to junior positions, these

---

[14] For career progression to work effectively, a bureaucracy needs to be relatively stable and personnel decisions free of external interference. These conditions do not obtain in the case of the Commission, however, where the size and structure of the administration are determined by the budgetary authority (the Council of Ministers and the European Parliament), where member governments exerted pressure on personnel decisions, and where enlargement has necessitated large scale recruitment of nationals from incoming member states.

[15] Despite the apparent incompatibility of the two goals, the commitment to 'geographical balance' and appointment on the basis of merit featured in the same provision of the Staff Regulations: 'Recruitment shall be directed to securing for the institution the services of the officials of the highest standard of ability, efficiency and integrity, recruited on the broadest possible geographical basis from among nationals of Member states of the communities' (Article 27). Article 29, meanwhile, explicitly excludes nationality as a criterion for appointment or promotion. As Cris Shore (2000: 141) observes, a formal commitment to strict national quotas would have been both illegal and taboo. At the same time, organizational charts from the Commission's earliest operation show that detailed consideration was paid to maintaining a national balance.

[16] Informal quotas had existed for the top three grades of the European Coal and Steel Community (Conrad 1992: 68).

appointments were made by the College.[17] Governments also sought to plant their flags in departments in policy areas of key national interest, and often succeeded.[18] Thus, for example, the Director-General of DG Agriculture was often French, the Director-General of DG Competition German and the Director-General of DG Economic and Financial Affairs Italian (Page 1997: 54; see also Michelmann 1978: 484).[19] More generally, the governments of the Six decided that as a whole the administration should be staffed in rough proportion to the relative size of national contributions to the Community budget (Lindberg 1963: 72).[20] The precise balance was reviewed and revised at every round of enlargement until 2004.[21] With each accession, a proportion of posts at all levels of the organization were reserved for officials from the incoming states (Ziller 2000: 361).

Furthermore, the personal offices of the Commissioners became agents through which member governments asserted their claims to 'fair shares'.[22] *Cabinets* actively monitored appointments to ensure that the quota for their nationals among top managers was respected (Coombes 1970: 256) and played a key role in selecting compatriots for positions reserved for their nationals (Coombes 1970: 256; see also Joana and Smith 2002: 119 fn 1). These 'machinations' were compared by an unnamed *cabinet* member quoted by Spence and Stevens (2006: 199–200) to 'a game of chess': The *chefs de cabinet* 'know the people and the vacant posts and keep it all pretty much in their heads'. Where

[17] If suitable candidates of the appropriate nationality could not be found inside the Commission, the Staff Regulations permitted use of 'a procedure other than the competition procedure' for appointments to the most senior grades.

[18] Quoting from a Commission document published in 2002, Spence and Stevens (2006: 200) comment on the organization's somewhat disingenuous discussion. Observing that the procedure for making appointments to senior posts 'mirrored the established, rather complex European decision-making process', the document continues: 'It ultimately led Member States to share out management posts at the Commission among themselves under a sort of quota system, even reaching the stage where Member States were almost claiming certain posts as being theirs by right'.

[19] The case of Frenchman Guy Legras, who was Director-General of DG Agriculture for fifteen years, provides an extreme example of the national flag system.

[20] This translated into a share of one quarter each respectively for France, Germany, Italy, and the Benelux countries.

[21] For 1973, the target for the four large states and Benelux was set at 18.4 per cent each, and for Ireland and Denmark 4 per cent each (see Michelmann 1978: 478; Christoph 1993: 531). For the southern enlargement, see Viñas (2001: 120) and for the northern enlargement, see Stevens and Stevens (2001: 120). However, there were no strict national quotas for lower or middle grades in 2004 (Michelmann 1978: 27–8). Significantly, Michelmann (1978: 111) found that in the five DGs (Economic and Financial Affairs, Competition, Social Affairs, Agriculture, and Transport) that were at the heart of his study 'staffing so nearly corresponds to the theoretical allocation'.

[22] Hallstein had 'wanted to keep them small' (Ritchie 1992: 99), 'since it was accepted that as cabinet members would be of the same nationality as the Commissioner, they would work against his aim of strengthening *l'ésprit communautaire*' (Lemaignen 1964: 49–50). However, 'several Commissioners, including the French and Italians, argued that substantial *cabinets* were necessary because of the heavy workload' (Ritchie 1992: 99).

there were no appropriately qualified nationals in the services, a *cabinet* would bring in outsiders. Senior appointments, moreover, were thrashed out at so-called 'non-meetings' of the *cabinets*.[23]

As their influence and importance grew, *cabinets* themselves became a stepping stone to high office, including for members of *cabinets* who had been recruited from outside the Commission (Noël 1992: 152; Egeberg 2003: 140). Towards the end of a College's mandate, it was common practice for a management position in the services to be found for such individuals without their having to submit to the usual requirements for entry into the organization. This practice, known as *parachutage*, was bitterly resented by career officials not least because it blocked their own prospects for promotion (Bellier 1994: 256; Page 1997: 81; Joana and Smith 2002: 51–84).[24]

Although nationality became a major consideration in personnel policy, a number of safeguards existed to prevent national interests from compromising the Commission's independence. In order, for example, to prevent the colonization of parts of the administration by particular member states, it was not permitted for compatriots to occupy adjacent senior management positions (Page 1997: 59). Nor could a Director-General head a service for which a Commissioner of the same nationality was responsible.[25] At a cultural level, powerful norms largely inhibited officials from acting as representatives for their country of origin in carrying out their responsibilities within the Commission. Despite the importance of nationality in recruitment and promotion, Michelmann (1978: 29) concluded in the late 1970s that 'civil servants themselves do not perceive nationality to be a problem in everyday working relations with their fellow civil servants from other member states'.

In the recent past, the Commission has taken steps to reduce the influence of nationality as a consideration in personnel decisions. The Kinnock–Prodi reforms introduced new appointment procedures for senior officials that aimed to insulate the process from outside interference.[26] They also abolished

[23] Spence and Stevens (2006: 186) note that at least one former Secretary-General refused to attend these meetings.

[24] The individual concerned would not have to sit the *concours* for senior positions, but for middle management posts a special competition would have to be arranged. On *parachutage*, see Spierenburg (1979: 104); Page (1997: 49–51); Stevens and Stevens (2001: 72, 81–4); Spence and Stevens (2006: 201). Joana and Smith (2002: 77) found that a significant number of officials gained promotion in this way.

[25] In this sense, national representation was *passive* rather than *active* (for the distinction, see Mosher 1968: 12).

[26] The new Code of Procedure (European Commission 2000) required a vacancy notice with detailed job profile to be published in the case of all appointments at grade AD16. A rapporteur of equivalent grade to the post to be filled draws up a shortlist, taking geographical balance and the need to recruit women into account. The candidates are interviewed by an advisory committee, chaired by the Secretary-General. Once the interviews have been conducted, the Commissioner responsible for the Directorate-General is presented with a list from which an appointee is selected in agreement with the President of the Commission and the Commissioner

the system of informal national quotas, and ended the practice of national flags. Other reforms were directed at the *cabinets* (see Chapter 7). In order to loosen the ties between *cabinets* and the capital of the Commissioner's home state—and to make *cabinets* more European—first Prodi and later Barroso imposed a multinationality requirement. Since 2005 at least three nationalities must be represented in a *cabinet*, while the *chef* and deputy *chef* should not come from the same member state.[27]

THE PEOPLE WHO WORK FOR THE COMMISSION

The public administration literature suggests that the origins and backgrounds of bureaucrats are important for at least three reasons: the tasks entrusted to public bureaucracies in the modern world assume that they command a high level of specialist expertise (Page 1992: 9); the socialization of bureaucrats creates biases which are likely to influence their work (Kingsley 1944; Sheriff 1976); and knowledge of where bureaucrats come from is a democratic entitlement.[28] Who, then, are the people who work for the Commission?

The EUCIQ online survey asked respondents to provide information about their main educational qualifications, professional background and experience, and nationality.[29] The dataset thereby generated made it possible to test accepted wisdoms and to examine whether findings from earlier studies still held true. The results concerning nationality show a similar picture to that found by Page (1997); namely, that the larger member states are under-represented. However, the view that the Commission is overwhelmingly populated by lawyers or that officials tend to have spent their entire working lives in the organization are exposed as myths.

Educational background: an administration of lawyers?

A first finding comes as no surprise: the staff of the Commission are well-educated and cosmopolitan. No fewer than 70 per cent of officials hold a postgraduate degree, and 58 per cent have studied in more than one country.

responsible for personnel and administration. A similar process has been introduced for Directors. A key role is played by a Consultative Committee for Nominations, composed of a group of Directors-General, and chaired by the Secretary-General.

[27] See Chapter 6.

[28] The Commission publishes key data concerning its personnel at <http://ec.europa.eu/ civil_service/about/figures/index_en.htm>.

[29] The questionnaire asked respondents for their present nationality and, since some officials may have dual citizenship, to indicate whether they hold more than one nationality.

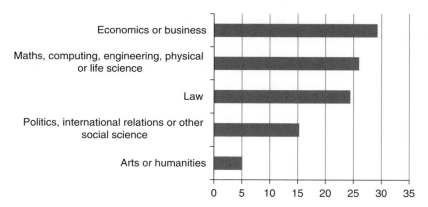

Fig. 2.1 Subject of main degree (% reporting each subject area)

Note: n = 1,793. % of those who answered question.

An overwhelming majority—69 per cent—have completed degrees in either the social sciences or law (see Figure 2.1). Just over a quarter (26 per cent) have science training, but only 5 per cent graduated with a degree in the arts or humanities. Examination of recruitment over time shows little change in these proportions.[30]

A second finding, however, challenges conventional wisdom about the Commission. While just under a quarter of respondents reported that their main educational qualification was in law, no fewer than 29 per cent had studied economics or business, and 26 per cent were maths, computing, engineering or science graduates. Twelve per cent completed studies in political science, international relations, or public administration. There are also gender differences relating to degree subject. Men are more likely to have a background in economics, but women outnumber men in law and politics. Men are much more likely to have a science training, whereas women are more likely to be among (the small number of) arts or humanities graduates.

More generally, the educational background of officials in the organization is impressively diverse. The Commission commands a wider range of expertise than is often thought. Some specialists, unsurprisingly, are concentrated in particular services. The Legal Service has the highest concentration of lawyers, and DG Economic and Financial Affairs has the highest percentage of economists. While lawyers are concentrated in a relatively small number of medium-size Directorates-General, mostly concerned with compliance, enforcement and regulation, economists are found in significant numbers

---

[30] Drawing on data drawn from sources published 1991–3, Page (1997: 78) reported that 52.5 per cent of officials in EU organizations came from a social sciences background, 36.6 per cent from law, 25.3 per cent from science, and 15 per cent from the arts.

Table 2.2. Distribution of officials by educational qualification across DGs

Directorate-General	Law	EUCIQ sample	Number of officials
Legal Service (SJ)	92.3%	52	352
Justice Freedom and Security (JLS)	45.5%	55	360
Competition (COMP)	44.4%	63	599
Internal Market and Services (MARKT)	43.5%	62	403
Taxation and Customs Union (TAXUD)	43.2%	44	356
Trade (TRADE)	42.9%	49	422
Office for Infrastructure and Logistics in Brussels (OIB)	33.3%	12	402
Secretariat-General (SG)	31.4%	51	462

Directorate-General	Economics or business	EUCIQ sample	Number of officials
Economic and Financial Affairs (ECFIN)	86.8%	53	467
Eurostat (ESTAT)	62.5%	24	593
Budget (BUDG)	58.5%	41	390
Development (DEV)	50.0%	22	263
Internal Audit Service (IAS)	50.0%	20	73
Regional Policy (REGIO)	47.7%	65	538
Employment Social Affairs Equal Opportunities (EMPL)	44.4%	72	577
Enlargement (ELARG)	43.8%	32	224
Humanitarian Aid (ECHO)	38.5%	13	163
Education and Culture (EAC)	36.7%	49	486
Trade (TRADE)	36.7%	49	422
Competition (COMP)	36.5%	63	599
Agriculture and Rural Development (AGRI)	35.8%	106	918
Internal Market and Services (MARKT)	33.9%	62	403
Taxation and Customs Union (TAXUD)	31.8%	44	356

Directorate-General	Mathematics, computing, engineering, physical or life sciences	EUCIQ sample	Number of officials
Informatics (DIGIT)	74.4%	39	367
Research (RTD)	70.3%	128	1,188
Joint Research Centre (JRC)	57.1%	14	1663
Information Society and Media (INFSO)	55.6%	54	818
Fisheries and Maritime Affairs (MARE)	45.2%	31	247
Health and Consumer Protection (SANCO)	45.2%	62	604
Environment (ENV)	41.6%	89	522
Energy and Transport (TREN)	33.8%	74	867
Enterprise and Industry (ENTR)	33.7%	104	731

Note: n = 1,793.

across several Directorates-General that perform a variety of functions (see Table 2.2). Scientists are also distributed widely across the Commission. The highest concentrations are in DGs Informatics, DG Research and Information, and the Joint Research Centre, but significant numbers work in, for example, DGs Information Society and Media, Maritime Affairs and Fisheries, Health and Consumers, and Environment.

Professional experience and background: career bureaucrats?

A third finding, which challenges the view that officials have had limited professional experience and which also shows similarities with earlier studies (see Michelmann 1978; Page 1997), is that Commission officials command a diverse range of professional experience. Contrary to the popular image, the Commission is not staffed by employees who have spent their entire working life in the organization. No fewer than 96 per cent of EUCIQ respondents worked somewhere else before they joined the Commission.

Even more significant, perhaps, the Commission is not overwhelmingly staffed by career bureaucrats (see Figure 2.2). The data from the online questionnaire shows consistently that, over the past four decades, at least a third of respondents worked in business before they joined the Commission–a figure that does not include, moreover, the 11.9 per cent who were recruited to the Commission from the liberal professions. Although currently a plurality of officials (40 per cent) have worked in national administrations, this proportion represents a forty-year high and appears to be associated with the northern and eastern enlargements. Until the mid-1990s, that is for the greater part of the organization's history, more officials came into the Commission from the private sector than from any other background.[31] Education and research lie third in the list (24 per cent). More generally, the figures covering the last forty years do not show any overall trend as to whether officials are more likely to come from the public or the private sector.

As with educational qualifications, an analysis was undertaken to see if officials with certain professional backgrounds were concentrated in particular Directorates-General. The distribution by professional background is shown in Table 2.3. The departments with the highest proportion of officials who had worked in public administration were DGs Environment, Taxation and Customs Union, and Trade. DGs Administration and Personnel, Budget, Communication, Transport and Energy, Enlargement, Enterprise, Informatics, Information Society and Media, Market, Joint Research Centre, Legal Service, and Research and Innovation, by contrast, were those with the highest

[31] It is interesting to compare these figures with those reported by Page (1997:76): civil service 43 per cent; private sector 35 per cent; education 34 per cent; free (liberal) professions 10 per cent.

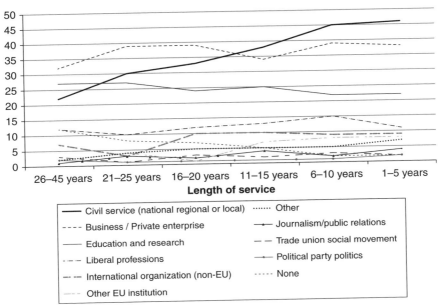

Fig. 2.2 Previous career by year joined Commission (% within length of service)

Note: n = 1,848.

proportion of officials with private sector experience. DG Communication had a 50:50 split.

Nationality and representation

In spite of the member states' insistence on 'fair shares', previous studies (with the exception of Michelmann (1978)) have found considerable variation in the presence of nationals relative to their country's share of the EU' population. Drawing on data from 1993, Page (1997: 44) reported that some larger countries were under-represented, while several small states had more officials than the size of their population would suggest (Spence 1997: 82–89; Stevens and Stevens 2001: 118; House of Lords 1998: 111). Using a measure of fair shares 'based upon the difference between numbers of officials from each member state compared with the number of officials one would expect if employment were strictly proportionate to member state population' and where a value of zero signifies that the representation of nationals is exactly proportionate to population, Page (1997: 44) found significant disproportion-ality at all levels of the organization.[32] Germany, Italy, Spain, and to a lesser

---

[32] The mismatch tends to be lowest in the A category, suggesting that nationality consider-ations may have come into play in the pre-selection phase of the *concours* (Page 1997: 46).

Table 2.3 Distribution of officials between DGs by professional background (% within DGs)

Directorate-General	Civil service	Private sector or liberal professions	Education or research	International organization (includes other EU institutions)
Administration (ADMIN)	49	54	22	15
Agriculture and Rural Development (AGRI)	44	39	39	8
Budget (BUDG)	25	60	22	15
Communication (COMM)	50	50	20	13
Competition (COMP)	37	46	42	13
Development (DEV)	35	35	27	30
Economic and Financial Affairs (ECFIN)	47	38	49	8
Education and Culture (EAC)	39	37	29	14
Employment Social Affairs Equal Opportunities (EMPL)	33	44	30	16
Energy and Transport (TREN)	28	66	26	11
Enlargement (ELARG)	31	50	11	28
Enterprise and Industry (ENTR)	32	52	37	16
Environment (ENV)	52	49	45	10
EuropeAid (AIDCO)	42	48	22	24
External Relations (RELEX)	38	46	12	17
Fisheries and Maritime Affairs (MARE)	48	48	36	10
Health and Consumer Protection (SANCO)	47	27	37	11
Humanitarian Aid (ECHO)	36	36	3	14
Informatics (DIGIT)	28	70	29	3
Information Society and Media (INFSO)	13	74	35	13
Internal Market and Services (MARKT)	44	56	41	11
Interpretation (SCIC)	21	38	26	10
Joint Research Centre (JRC)	29	64	15	14
Justice Freedom and Security (JLS)	29	47	52	9
Legal Service (SJ)	39	55	36	35
Regional Policy (REGIO)	47	39	2	11
Research (RTD)	30	52	16	17
Secretariat-General (SG)	46	28	70	12
Taxation and Customs Union (TAXUD)	57	45	50	9
Trade (TRADE)	52	38	30	12
Total	40%	33%	24%	12%

Note: n = 1,848.

extent the UK were under-represented in A1, A2, and A3 posts. The Netherlands and Denmark, and, to a lesser extent, Greece had a greater proportion of their nationals at these senior grades than their relative share of the EU population would suggest. For Ireland, Belgium, and (especially) Luxembourg, the proportion was even higher.

The picture in 2008, drawn from Commission data, shows that large member states continue to be under-represented among junior officials (see Table 2.4). That Britain scores badly (504 fewer than its share of the total EU population would suggest) is perhaps predictable in view of that country's

Table 2.4 Disproportionality index, 2008 and 2012

	2008				2012			
Nationality	All AD staff	AD 5–10	AD 11–13	AD 14–16	All AD staff	AD 5–10	AD 11–13	AD 14–16
Austria	59	9	45	5	59	−1	51	9
Belgium	978	489	420	69	992	507	418	68
Bulgaria	102	187	−77	−9	150	213	−58	−5
Cyprus	51	49	−2	5	44	40	1	4
Czech Republic	48	165	−105	−12	44	142	−88	−10
Germany	−732	−323	−352	−57	−741	−490	−215	−36
Denmark	116	20	90	7	104	11	85	8
Spain	−169	−113	−43	−14	−192	−206	15	−1
Estonia	91	99	−10	2	99	104	−7	2
Finland	190	61	128	2	188	52	134	2
France	−265	−183	−81	−1	−345	−331	−21	7
United Kingdom	−791	−504	−255	−32	−885	−679	−181	−24
Greece	242	10	209	23	234	0	207	26
Hungary	121	226	−99	−6	115	203	−84	−4
Ireland	118	26	75	17	114	19	81	14
Italy	−334	−172	−122	−40	−373	−307	−35	−31
Lithuania	107	139	−32	0	104	128	−24	1
Luxembourg	31	2	21	7	30	1	22	6
Latvia	83	102	−19	1	92	104	−14	1
Malta	97	94	0	2	103	99	2	2
Netherlands	12	−38	44	5	−6	−73	58	9
Poland	−264	197	−416	−45	−263	124	−350	−36
Portugal	125	−24	143	6	117	−46	155	8
Romania	−121	144	−239	−26	−52	160	−190	−21
Slovakia	63	121	−54	−4	58	105	−44	−3
Slovenia	108	127	−20	1	105	117	−13	1
Sweden	97	25	70	3	89	5	84	1

Source: European Commission, DG Human Resources and Security, Statistical Bulletin.

enduring Euroscepticism, but the extent of Italian (−172), French (−183), and especially German under-representation (−323) is surprising.[33] Under-representation is also a problem at management levels (AD11 to AD16) for these states: the figure for Germany is −409, for the UK −287, for Italy −162, and for France −82. Among the smaller member states, nationals from Ireland, Greece, and especially Belgium score more highly among administrators and managers than their share of the total EU population would suggest.

---

[33] Concern at this shortfall has led the UK government to restore the European Fast Stream for British civil servants.

One further observation is important. The online questionnaire was carried out in 2008 when the programme to recruit officials from the 'new' member states in central and Eastern Europe had not been completed. The larger countries, Poland and Romania, were under-represented. Poland had a 'deficit' of 264 and Romania 121, which drew unfavourable comment.[34] By contrast, Hungary, Slovenia, Lithuania and Bulgaria each had more than a hundred officials more than suggested by their respective shares of the total EU population. The Commission's recruitment initiative from the EU-12 had been completed by 2010. As the data for 2012 in Table 2.4 shows, however, disproportionality among the EU-12 remained an issue. Poland's shortfall had been reduced by one, while Romania's fell by 69.

As the informal quota system was historically policed most vigorously at Director-General level, it is worth focusing on the nationality of the incumbents of these top posts. As Table 2.5 shows, there is little evidence of the operation of a quota system under either Barroso I or Barroso II. Whether this result is an unalloyed benefit is a matter for debate. On the one hand, the stranglehold of governments may have been relinquished, enabling the Commission to enjoy genuine organizational independence and allowing officials promotion to these top positions on merit. On the other hand, the effectiveness and legitimacy of the organization may be problematic in respect of those countries, big or small, that have few nationals in senior positions.[35]

The planting of national flags is also less in evidence in the Commission of the twenty-first century. The top posts in certain Directorates-General tend no longer to be occupied by officials from the same member states. In the second year of Barroso II, for example, the Director-General of DG COMP was Dutch, and his predecessor British. DG AGRI was headed by a Spaniard, who had succeeded a Frenchman. The Director General of DG ECFIN, meanwhile, was Italian, and his predecessor German.

Both developments can be attributed largely to reforms adopted by the Prodi Commission. The new appointment procedures have given the Commission greater organizational independence, and considerably limit the opportunities for outside interference (Egeberg 2003; Wille 2007; Balint et al. 2008; Fusacchia 2009). In addition, a rule enforcing compulsory mobility for senior officials limits the length of time that a Director-General can normally remain in the same position to five years.[36]

---

[34] See, for example, <http://reuniting-europe.blogactiv.eu/2009/09/25/mr-barroso-be-fair-to-the-east>.

[35] In 2009, the most senior Maltese official in the Commission, for example, was a head of unit.

[36] During his first term, Barroso shuffled senior offficeholders in November 2005, November 2006, and January 2009.

Table 2.5 Change in the nationality of Directors-General, 1995–2012

Directorate-General	Director-General	Nationality	Tenure	
			From	To
Secretariat-General	David Williamson	British	1978	1997
	Carlo Trojan	Dutch	1997	2000
	David O'Sullivan	Irish	2000	2005
	Catherine Day	Irish	2005	
DG I/External Economic Relations/Trade	Horst Krenzler	German	1987	1996
	Hans-Friedrich Beseler	German	1996	1999
	Mogens Peter Carl	Danish	2000	2005
	David O'Sullivan	Irish	2005	2010
	Jean-Luc Demarty	French	2011	
DG RELEX	Guy Legras	French	1999	2003
	Eneko Landaburu	Spanish	2003	2009
	Joao Vale de Almedida	Portuguese	2009	2010
	David O'Sullivan (first chief operating officer of the EEAS, 2011)	Irish	2010	2011
DG II/ECFIN/FC	Giovanni Ravasio	Italian	1997	2001
	Klaus Regling	German	2001	2008
	Marco Buti	Italian	2008	
DG IV/COMP	Manfred Caspari	Italian	1980	1990
	Alexander Schaub	German	1995	2002
	Philip Lowe	British	2002	2010
	Alexander Italianer	Italian	2010	
DG V/EMPL/Social Affairs, Employment, Social Affairs and Equal Opportunities	Allan Larsson	Swedish	1995	2000
	Odile Quintin	French	2000	2006
	Nikolaus van der Pas	German	2006	2009
	Robert Verrue	French	2009	2011
	Koos Richelle	Dutch	2011	
DG VI/AGRI	Guy Legras	French	1984	1999
	Jose Manuel Silva Rodriguez	Spanish	1999	2002
	Fabrizio Barbaso	Italian	2002	2003
	Jose Manuel Silva Rodriguez	Spanish	2003	2006
	Jean-Luc Demarty	French	2006	2010
	Jose Manuel Silva Rodriguez	Spanish	2010	
DG XV/MARKT	John Mogg	British	1993	2002
	Alexander Schaub	German	2002	2006
	Jörgen Holmquist	Swedish	2007	2010
	Jonathan Faull	British	2010	
DG XVI/REGIO	Eneko Landaburu	Spanish	1986	1999
	Guy Crauser	Luxembourgeois	2000	2003
	Graham Meadows	British	2004	2007
	Dirk Ahner	German	2007	2012
	Walter Deffaa	German	2012	

(continued)

Table 2.5 Continued

Directorate-General	Director-General	Nationality	Tenure	
			From	To
JAI	Adrian Fortescue	British	1999	2003
	Jonathan Faull	British	2003	2010
	Francoise Le Bail (Justice)	French	2010	
	Stefano Manservisi (Home)	Italian	2010	

Attitudes to nationality: results from the survey

The online survey posed two questions about nationality.[37] The first sought to elicit the views of officials on the following proposition: 'Some argue that posts in the Commission should be distributed on the basis of geographical balance.' Respondents were invited to record the intensity of their views on a five-point scale, from 'strongly agree' to 'strongly disagree'. The second question was intended to examine the importance of nationality in the working life of Commission officials.[38] The aim was to gain an understanding of whether officials believe that nationality influences how colleagues approach their job and whether, in particular, there is a view in the organization that an official should not deal with an issue that is salient to their home state. It was also intended to test the claim made by Michelmann (1978: 28) that an emphasis in recruitment and promotion 'results in nationality becoming over-emphasised as an attribute of each civil servant'. Thus, in the online survey respondents were asked to express their views on the proposition that: 'Some think that it is problematic for Commission officials to manage dossiers of special interest to their own member state'.

[37] These questions are, of course, not exhaustive. Other aspects of nationality were investigated elsewhere in the online survey and in follow-up interviews. For example, Chapter 3 considers nationality as a factor in personal networks. However, the project did not investigate stereotyping or the impact of language differences. See Michelmann (1978: 27–31) and Abélès et al. (1993) for discussion of nationality in its broader operation.

[38] An earlier study quoted the following reflection on the subject offered by an official: 'I don't think that the nationality difference is very strong at all in terms of how people act ... [I]n the reality of the day-to-day work, does it make a lot of difference? Quite frankly, it does not' (Hooghe 2001: 190).

On 'geographical balance',[39] respondents were split: 48 per cent declared that they were opposed, 35 per cent that they were in favour. There was a similar division on the second question: 51 per cent of respondents did not consider it problematic for officials to handle issues of special interest to their country of origin. Thirty-four per cent, however, disagreed. Taken together, the responses suggest that roughly half of the Commission's staff do not believe either that nationality should play a decisive role in recruitment or that in their work officials are likely to show bias in favour of their home state. More than a third, however, hold the opposite view.

Further analysis showed that there was an overlap between the respondents who oppose 'geographical balance' and those who do not think it problematic for officials to manage special dossiers involving their home country. The two groups are not, however, coterminous. Of those who disagree that posts should be distributed on the basis of geographical balance, 60 per cent disagree that it is problematic for officials to manage special interest dossiers which relate to their own member state. Just under 30 per cent agree and 12 per cent are neutral.

Geographical balance and diversity in the Commission

In an attempt to explore the reasoning that underlay these responses, middle and senior managers were asked in follow-up interviews for their reflections on the responses to the online survey. Specifically, they were asked whether they were surprised that 48 per cent of respondents opposed the idea of geographical balance while 35 per cent supported it, and that 34 per cent of respondents thought that it was problematic for officials to manage dossiers of special interest to their own member state but 51 per cent did not consider it to be a problem. The aim was to examine whether the interviewees detected a tension between acceptance of officials handling their own national dossiers and rejection of a geographical balance in recruitment and promotion. The question elicited some interesting responses:

'One of the best things about . . . the Commission is working in this intercultural environment. It's fantastic, and you forget nationality a lot of the time, and that is brilliant' (interview 45);

'I always forget that I am working with people who have another nationality than me' (interview 92);

'[I]f European citizens exist all, they exist here' (interview 44);

---

[39] The term 'geographical balance' is taken directly out of the Staff Regulations (see footnote 15).

'[W]ith waves of enlargement it's become less obvious what people's nationality is, and one doesn't really care . . . [I]t's certainly not something that you can ever throw at people. It's never a weapon or a tool' (interview 78).

Only a very small number dissented from this view. For example, one middle manager who joined the Commission in 1989 contended that 'the European spirit . . . was higher, bigger than it is now [in 2009] . . . People take a more nationalistic approach' (interview 94).

Support for national diversity was universal among interviewees. The view expressed by a deputy Director-General was typical: 'You need mixed teams, you need mixed skills, you need mixed cultural bases to come to the best outcomes' (interview 139). However, support for diversity rarely translated into an advocacy of quotas, still less for the reservation of particular posts for nationals from particular member states.[40] In the words of one middle manager: 'I'm against such an application of geographical balance if it means that posts have a national flag and if it's too rigorously applied . . . [though] I see the need for us to have some kind of representation at the highest level' (interview 126). According to another: 'We are a unique institution and we represent twenty-seven member states, and member states want to see themselves reflected in the composition of the major institution, so I would understand if there's some support for geographical balance, although not rigidly' (interview 9). Having commented that 'the UK is systematically under-represented. I think this is detrimental for the UK and it's detrimental for the Commission', a Director in a large spending DG continued, 'having said that, I think the idea of a quota would not be line with the principles of the institution' (interview 122).

The importance of having nationals from all member states was asserted on a number of grounds. Legitimacy was key among them. A Head of Unit in a service with outward-facing operational responsibilities noted, for example, that 'the real thing we need to do is to show the outside world that we are neutral. And for that, we need perhaps to take account of the geographical thing' (interview 45).

Often pragmatic considerations were mentioned in the same breath as legitimacy. Without the presence of officials from all the member states, the Commission would not only lack the expertise necessary to carry out its responsibilities effectively, but its actions would not be seen as acceptable. One Director-General observed on this point: 'It is good that not just the Commission as a whole, but that every service has a certain representation of all [cultural viewpoints] that make it also more likely that the results from

---

[40] Although some officials voiced concern that without a mechanism for ensuring fair representation, smaller member states would be under-represented. One official from such a state observed: 'For me, some form of geographical balance is necessary. Otherwise, we are penalized as being a microstate' (interview 48).

policy-making will respond to expectations of all parts of Europe and it makes the acceptability of the proposals better' (interview 133). The under-representation of the UK within the Commission administration was identified as a particular problem:

'If one country isn't represented at all, or is significantly under-represented, I think that it poses a problem of perception and maybe some problems in reality.... [W]hy a certain policy or formulation of it won't play in the United Kingdom ... won't come to the attention of the Commission if there isn't sufficient UK voice at the very top tables. And that's important because there's no point in the Commission proposing a policy or a line or a technical solution if in fact that isn't going to work' (interview 69).

Without native speakers, the Commission would not be able to carry out its responsibilities. For one senior manager in a large DG, it was simple: '[Y]ou can't manage programmes if you don't have people who speak the language' (interview 122). A similar view was expressed by a middle manager in another large DG: 'I am dealing with implementation ... and the best for me is to hire the people who speak the language' (interview 98). A head of unit opined: '[L]anguage is a cultural vehicle among other things, along with a communication vehicle, and therefore it is very important that in the discussions with the member states officials hav[e] a nationality or know the language of that member state' (interview 32). For one Director in an internal service: 'With 27 member states and 11 languages you clearly need to be able to have native speakers on file ... You can never ask someone not originating from Latvia to deal with Latvian cases because nobody else masters the language' (interview 72). This was imperative, given the technical areas in which the Commission is engaged: 'In some cases people who're very fluent in English can be used for cases against the UK, but even then if you're not a native speaker and you're fighting against lawyers from the City, it's a tall order. So we tend to use nationalities because that's their strength. In DG Competition, for instance, it's quite commonly accepted that people who master the language deal with the case' (interview 72).

Understanding how the political and legal systems of the member states work was also an important reason for recruiting as broadly as possible:

'[W]e have to rely on the fact that people understand their member state, and we have to have an enormous resource of people from different member states to understand how to operate, and to develop policy in the member state concerned' (interview 17);

'[I]t's important to have officials who know the legal situation in the member states' (interview 8);

'[I]f you ask a young brilliant Polish student who has just joined the Commission to find ways to attack the Polish government on some state aid dossier, you will find them eager to do so, and they're very good at it' (interview 72).

At the same time, few thought that nationality should be the most important, still less the only, consideration in recruitment or promotion. According to one head of unit: '[T]here should be some geographical balance, especially for the higher jobs in the Commission, but it should by no means be the only criteria' (interview 52). Another thought that '[Any geographical balance] should not be too strict, because then you will get less competent people at the top' (interview 45). Indeed, most went out of their way to emphasize the importance of merit, competence and talent. Only a small minority believed that nationality should be entirely disregarded. A middle manager in a small operational service declared: 'For me, nationality should not play a role' (interview 5).

Interviewees recognized that support for diversity did not come without a price. Some individuals would lose out either in recruitment or promotion, on account of the measures necessary to ensure the presence of nationals from all member states within the administration. One Director observed: '[W]e've seen how difficult it is ... [I]f you have ten new countries and some of them very big, it means that all of a sudden you cannot employ any more people from the old member states' (interview 3). According to one middle manager, it was unavoidable: '[S]ometimes you see [young] people ... taking very senior positions, [when] the only advantage they have is they come from a new member state ... [but it's] part of the game ... [I]f we want Estonia, Malta, Cyprus, Lithuania to have the feeling that they're accepted, they're recognized, then sometimes you have to pay the price; they have some junior people taking senior positions, but that's the fact of life. I don't really see a problem. Sometimes it creates an individual frustration ... It's the price you pay as an individual' (interview 9). Another took a similar view: 'ideally, in an organization like ours, you would recruit people in relation to their merit, ... their competences, and their abilities to do the job, not on the basis of where they came from. That's the way the World Health Organization operates. The political reality is, and ... this affects all of us ... that we do have to try to recruit to get some kind of balance, and the Sec[retariat]-Gen[eral] operates these kinds of policies. ... Yes, they are distorting, but on the other hand ... for the long-term ..., you have to work on trying to find some balance ... [W]hen you're trying to fill posts, you have to try to seek some kind of spread of talent ... across the member states' (interview 17).

In summary, the interviews with managers suggest that the disagreement with geographical balance expressed by 48 per cent of respondents to the online survey should not be interpreted as opposition to diversity. Rather it represents repudiation of a form of that policy that operates through quotas. In fact, interviewees believe that the Commission administration needs nationals from all member states if it is to perform its functions effectively and if its actions are to be regarded as legitimate.

Nationality and neutrality

Interviewees were also prompted for their reflections on the survey response to the question of whether officials should manage issues that were of special interest to their state of origin. Though they recognized the potential dangers and took the view that not only impartiality, but the appearance of impartiality was important, an overwhelming majority sided with the 51 per cent of survey respondents who did not consider such a situation to be problematic. Indeed, in line with the support for diversity on the grounds of the need for the Commission to command language skills and national expertise to which the quotations in the preceding section testify, many thought that it was inevitable that nationals would be handling dossiers that were salient to their home state, since in many cases—for example, dealing with national or subnational authorities that are beneficiaries of EU spending programmes, or investigating state aid in small member states—only nationals would have the necessary linguistic skills or the legal and political expertise.[41]

Interviewees offered a number of explanations. Some appealed to the administrative culture of the Commission, with its emphasis on independence. Thus, the deputy Director-General of one powerful DG stated: 'I don't think it's a problem, because I fundamentally trust the neutrality of Commission officials, so I don't see an ethical issue ... [W]e have high standards in recruitments ... and we are an independent civil service' (interview 139). Most thought that neutrality had been thoroughly inculcated as a norm: '[A] lot of people will actually be more tough with their own member state, more exigent because they want to show that they're neutral' (interview 45).

Others pointed to a series of controls, constraints and checks-and-balances within the Commission. Some, such as the hierarchical structure of DGs and collective decision-making by the College, where a dossier is handed up a line of superiors and discussed by other departments, as well as the *cabinets*, are long-standing. Rules, such as those that preclude the appointment or continuation in post of a Director-General coming from the same home country as the Commission to whom he or she is responsible, or occupation of adjacent senior positions by compatriots, are also historic and were intended to prevent any particular member state from potentially gaining undue leverage or influence over policy.

Working in multinational teams is a further example. One middle manager in a DG with major responsibilities in the member states recognized the importance of both allocating the task to the expert within the team and

---

[41] However, one interviewee suggested that officials did not like to be put in this position: '[I]t is true that you do feel uncomfortable when you deal with a dossier that is of great interest in your own member state because it makes your life more difficult ... and mostly because you feel that you are being supervised even more intensely ... I think many ... colleagues will try to avoid dealing with these files' (interview 60).

ensuring oversight to prevent potential abuses: 'We are nineteen in all and we are . . . thirteen nationalities . . . We need a balance, because we need to get the nationals who may understand better than non-nationals the workings of the member state; at the same time, we want to avoid situations of potential conflict of interest' (interview 16). Other mechanisms—oversight and monitoring by managers, 'the four eyes' principle, and working in teams—are standard management techniques.

Several officials mentioned the changes introduced by the Kinnock–Prodi reforms in wake of the resignation of the Santer Commission as key factors. Reference was made to detailed financial management control procedures, internal auditing, and compulsory rotation, as well as a greater emphasis on 'ethics and improved management' (interview 107). One veteran official thought that there had been a change over time and attributed this to the introduction of greater controls after 1999: '[When I first joined the Commission] there was a school of thought here that you didn't deal with files from your own country. And that was the wisdom of the time . . . But that has changed now' (interview 79).

Overall, although they were sensitive to how it might be perceived as a problem, the middle and senior managers interviewed did not consider that it was problematic for officials to handle dossiers that were of particular interest to their home country. They believed that the culture within the Commission administration, as well as controls inside and outside the unit, reduced the risk that any official might be tempted to treat their home state more favourably.

CAREER DEVELOPMENT: MOTIVATION, MOBILITY, AND PROMOTION

The responses to the EUCIQ online survey provided rich data on the career experience of Commission officials. It asked respondents why they had chosen to follow a career in the European Commission. It asked when they had joined the organization, in which DGs they had worked, when, and in which order, and what positions they had held. The responses made it possible to report not only on the motivation that led officials to pursue a career in the organization, but how horizontally mobile they have been, and how their career has developed. It also makes it possible to assess the proportion of officials who have risen through the ranks as against those who have been directly recruited from the outside to positions in management or the *cabinets*.

The reasons that lead individuals to decide to work in a particular organization are likely to reflect, but also to influence, that body's identity and culture, which in turn affects how the organization is perceived from the outside. In the Commission's case, there is an assumption that the organization is an expansionist body, populated by federalist-inclined officials who want always to extend the competencies of the Union and therefore their own power (see also Chapters 4 and 5).[42] According to this view, officials move to Brussels because they are motivated by idealism: they want to 'build Europe'.

A second view emphasizes material motivations.[43] From this perspective, the decision to work for an organization is based largely on the expected financial return. Hood and Peters (1994: 27), for example, argue that better rates of pay and working conditions explain the attraction of Brussels. They observed that in the early 1990s the salaries of top EU officials were around 37 per cent higher than those of their counterparts in national civil services (Hood and Peters 1994: 27). Page (1997: 23) also holds that the appeal of a career in the Commission is influenced by the relative earning opportunities available. He suggests that salary levels in an individual's home state are especially important and notes that the attractiveness of Brussels as a career option is therefore likely to vary between member countries.[44]

The online survey presented officials with a list of possible reasons as to why they had chosen to pursue a career in the European Commission:

- Job stability
- Promising career prospects
- Competitive remuneration
- Commitment to Europe
- Commitment to a particular policy area
- Quality of the work
- I was asked to apply
- Other
- Prefer not to say

Respondents were invited to select as many as were relevant. Four main findings can be reported. First, a majority of officials cited European idealism as a motivation for choosing to follow a career in the European Commission (Figure 2.3). No fewer than 71 per cent of respondents indicated that they had made the decision based on a 'commitment to Europe'.

An analysis of data was then undertaken to see whether longer-serving officials were more likely to invoke 'building Europe' as a motivation. Although the percentage of officials who cited this reason did vary over

---

[42] Hooghe (2001) is, of course, an exception.
[43] In his examination of the development of DG Competition, for example, Wilks (1992) contends that, though earlier generations of officials may have joined out of idealism, they have long been supplanted by more career-minded cohorts.
[44] Page (1997: 43) cited the conclusion of an internal Commission study from the early 1990s that noted a 'shortage of candidates from well-off member states' (Personnel and Administration 1992: 23).

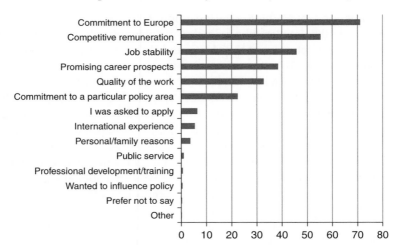

Fig. 2.3 Motivation for joining the Commission

Note: n=1,789.

Table 2.6 Reasons stated for choosing a career in the Commission by length of service

	Length of service						
	1–5 years	6–10 years	11–15 years	16–20 years	21–25 years	26–45 years	All
Commitment to Europe	66	71	74	76	75	71	71
Competitive remuneration	57	60	55	52	50	54	55
Job stability	52	51	42	38	40	35	46
Promising career prospects	43	38	32	32	39	41	39
Quality of the work	36	36	35	29	26	27	33
Commitment to a particular policy area	24	26	22	23	17	16	22

Note: n=1,789.

time, there was little evidence of a socialization effect.[45] However, officials who joined the Commission in 2003 or after were slightly less likely (66 per cent) to cite 'to build Europe' as a motivation (see Chapter 9).

Second, commitment to a particular policy area has become more significant as a motivation over time (Table 2.6). This may reflect the extent to

---

[45] Between 74 and 76 per cent of officials who joined between eleven and twenty-five years ago cited commitment to Europe as a motivation.

which, since the Maastricht treaty, the European Union has become a major actor or decision-making arena in a range of policy areas in which a job in the Commission has therefore become sought after. The third finding is that job stability has grown in importance. While cited as a reason for moving to Brussels by a quarter of respondents who were recruited between 1963 and 1982, it was mentioned by a third or more of officials who joined between 1983 and 2002, and by more than 40 per cent of more recent recruits.

Finally, competitive remuneration is an important motivation. It was cited as a reason by at least half of the respondents to the online survey, no matter at which point over the past forty years they had moved to Brussels. Material considerations were more important, however, for officials who joined the Commission during or since the late 1990s. However, a test of the hypothesis, derived from the work of Hood and Peters (1994) and Page (1997), that material considerations matter more for nationals from member states where the average salary level at home is relatively low compared with pay in the European Commission, was negative. Officials from countries where rates of pay were relatively high were not less likely to cite competitive remuneration as a reason for choosing to follow a career in Brussels, nor were officials from member states where rates of pay are low more likely so to do.[46]

In summary, the motivations of Commission officials for choosing to pursue a career in the organization are more complex than the image of staff as federalist idealists suggests. Although a significant majority of officials chose to join the Commission in order 'to build Europe',[47] material considerations figure strongly as a factor and commitment to a policy specialism has become increasingly important.

National administrations vary considerably in the extent to which they actively promote horizontal mobility.[48] In the UK, movement between ministries is considered a positive asset for both individual employees and the civil service as a whole. By contrast, in Germany, the Netherlands, or Sweden it is common for public servants to spend their entire career within a single department.

In the Commission's case, commentators—albeit with access to differing data sources—have arrived at different estimations concerning the rate of mobility. Bourtembourg (1987: 505–9) found that, of the 74 A grade officials who had passed the concours in the 1970s, 44 remained in the same DG ten years later and 27 had changed, of whom 10 had switched DGs twice. The

---

[46] Countries were classified as high, medium or low income based on the average earnings in the year of the survey. There were no statistically significant differences between nationals from each of the three groups in the responses to this question.

[47] Although as Chapter 4 shows, they do not all share the same vision of Europe.

[48] See Bossaert et al. (2001: 97–104) for an overview and comparison.

Williamson Report, by contrast, found that between 1990 and 1997 'an average of only 800 staff (about 4 per cent) moved from one DG to another each year' (cited in Stevens and Stevens 2001: 103).

Scholars have also arrived at different verdicts about whether mobility in the Commission is such a problem. Page (1997: 35), for example, questioned whether the 40 per cent rate reported by Bourtembourg in 1987 was really so low. Those who have considered it problematic identify a number of sources for what they take to be a low rate of mobility. Spierenburg (1979: 4–6) listed 'excessive specialization', 'over-elaborate hierarchies', and 'inflexible responses to changing priorities', while Coombes (1970) pointed to the autonomy of individual DGs and the absence of a strong human resources department at the centre of the organization. Stevens and Stevens (2001: 104), meanwhile, suggested on the one hand that managers in the Commission did not want to lose their best staff members, especially when it was so difficult to appoint replacements, and on the other that stubborn resistance on the part of officials to move often led to challenges in Court (Stevens and Stevens 2001: 47).

The data from the online survey shows that 47 per cent of officials have served in a single department. More than half of the workforce have worked in more than one Directorate-General (Figure 2.4; see Page 1997: 35). However, analysis of the data shows there is considerable variation at departmental level (see Table 2.7). DG External Relations is at the upper end of the scale. Officials in this DG had on average served in 2.5 departments. DGs Research and Innovation, Agriculture, Competition, Environment, and Health and Consumer Protection, meanwhile, are at the lower end. Officials in these services have on average worked in just under two (between 1.74 and 1.81) Directorates-General. This variation can be explained by the different skills that are required by the departments in question. DG External Relations was a generalist department, but the five where the mobility is low have technical responsibilities, which require their staff to have specialist training and expertise The possibilities for career progression in other Commission departments is likely to be low for these officials.

A count regression model was used in order to identify the variables that determine levels of horizontal mobility.[49] The results revealed that neither gender nor previous career were significant. Education, however, was important in two main instances. Officials with a degree in science tend to be relatively immobile. Economists, by contrast, have worked in a relatively high number of Directorates-General. Unsurprisingly, seniority and length of service

---

[49] The dependent variable in this model was the number of DGs that each individual in the sample reports having worked in.

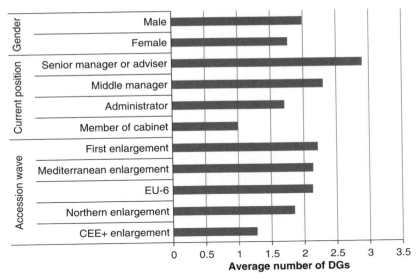

Fig. 2.4 Horizontal mobility: average number of DGs by gender, position, and accession wave

Note: n=1,759.

were also linked with higher levels of mobility. Similarly, officials who joined the Commission on account of their commitment to a particular policy area tended not to have moved frequently between DGs.[50]

Promotion in the Commission has been problematic, as the discussion above has outlined (see also Chapter 8). Three findings emerged from the online survey. The first is that the average age at which officials entered the Commission is 32 for female and 34 for male officials. This is consistent with the finding that all but a handful of officials had prior work experience before they joined the Commission. It also shows that there has been little change since the mid-1990s (Page 1997: 75). Unsurprisingly, officials recruited directly from outside the administration to a *cabinet* position or a senior or middle management post tend to be slightly older—36—when they join the Commission.

The second concerns the extent to which Hallstein's ambition of a career-based administration has been realised. An analysis of career-building was conducted with the aim of discovering whether managers and *cabinet* members had made their way up through the ranks of the Commission, or been

---

[50] The survey was conducted too soon after the reforms introduced by the Prodi Commission to assess the effects of measures that were intended to improve horizontal mobility at junior and middle management levels.

Table 2.7 Number of DGs by current DG

Directorate-General	Mean	N	Std. Deviation
Communication (COMM)	3.1	24	2.0
Humanitarian Aid (ECHO)	2.8	14	1.6
Enlargement (ELARG)	2.6	32	1.0
Administration (ADMIN)	2.6	39	1.6
Joint Research Centre (JRC)	2.5	14	0.9
External Relations (RELEX)	2.4	69	1.4
EuropeAid (AIDCO)	2.4	50	1.3
Education and Culture (EAC)	2.2	51	1.4
Office for Official Publications of the European Communities	2.2	31	0.9
Fisheries and Maritime Affairs (MARE)	2.2	31	1.2
Secretariat-General (SG)	2.1	50	1.3
Budget (BUDG)	2.1	40	1.0
Justice Freedom and Security (JLS)	2.1	55	1.4
Employment Social Affairs Equal Opportunities (EMPL)	2.1	73	1.3
Informatics (DIGIT)	2.1	40	1.0
Enterprise and Industry (ENTR)	2.0	104	1.1
Energy and Transport (TREN)	1.9	74	1.3
Regional Policy (REGIO)	1.9	66	1.0
Taxation and Customs Union (TAXUD)	1.9	44	1.8
Health and Consumer Protection (SANCO)	1.8	62	1.0
Development (DEV)	1.8	23	0.7
Environment (ENV)	1.8	88	0.9
Trade (TRADE)	1.8	50	0.8
Competition (COMP)	1.7	63	1.0
Agriculture and Rural Development (AGRI)	1.7	106	1.1
Internal Market and Services (MARKT)	1.7	61	1.0
Legal Service (SJ)	1.7	51	0.9
Research (RTD)	1.7	128	1.1
Information Society and Media (INFSO)	1.6	54	0.8
Economic and Financial Affairs (ECFIN)	1.5	53	0.9
Interpretation (SCIC)	1.5	39	1.0
Eurostat (ESTAT)	1.4	26	0.8
European Anti-Fraud Office (OLAF)	1.4	13	0.5
All DGs	2.0	1759	1.2

Note: n = 1,759.

recruited to those positions from the outside. An investigation of the careers of individuals who had been recruited directly to management or *cabinet* posts was also undertaken.

The main finding is that, although there is evidence of significant career-building among senior managers, middle managers and *cabinet* members, a substantial proportion of officials within each category had been recruited directly into those positions from outside the service (see Table 2.8). Either respondents reported that this was the first position that they had held in the Commission or they had not worked previously as an administrator. Of

Table 2.8 Percentage of *cabinet* members, middle managers, and senior managers who have previously held positions within the Commission

Current role	Previous roles					
	Cabinet	Senior management	Middle management	Administrator	Other	None
Member of *cabinet*	19	2	26	52	9	26
Senior manager or adviser	27	41	55	43	3	15
Middle manager	9	3	38	63	10	9
All non-adminstrative grades	11	8	31	46	7	12

Note: n = 680 (*cabinet* officials, senior managers, middle managers only).

senior managers or advisers, more than 40 per cent had previously served as administrators and more than half had been middle managers.[51] An even larger proportion of middle managers—60 per cent—had served in more junior roles. However, 68 per cent of middle managers were career officials (314 of 463), while 32 per cent (149) had been recruited directly from outside the Commission. The picture for senior managers was different and surprising, since external recruits (74) outnumbered career officials (56).

These findings are significant for two main reasons. First, they show that the degree to which the Commission can be considered to be a career-based service, where officials enter the lower levels of the administration and can expect to be promoted to management level, is limited. The career paths of such officials are likely to be blocked by outsiders who have been recruited to management positions, which is likely to have a negative effect on morale. Second, the figures in both cases are far higher than for earlier periods. The 32 per cent of middle managers recruited from outside the Commission is considerably higher than the 12 per cent reported by Page (1997: 51). Similarly, at 57 per cent, the proportion of senior managers recruited from outside the Commission is far higher than the 30 per cent reported by Willis (1982) and Page (1997: 51) in the 1980s and 1990s.

At the same time, analysis of the data suggests that the high proportion of external recruits is associated to some degree at least with the recruitment exercise linked to the 2004 and 2007 enlargements. Twenty-seven per cent of outside recruits had joined the Commission in the preceding five years. More generally, a significant proportion of respondents whose current position was their first in the organization had given lengthy service to the Commission.

[51] Just over 40 per cent had previously held a position in senior management and over a quarter had worked in *cabinets*.

The same was true of those reporting that they had only held one job previously in the Commission and that that had been at management level Sixteen per cent of external recruits had served in the Commission for twenty-six years or more. Eighteen per cent of managers with only one previous job in management had turned in ten or more years of service, 20 cent more than sixteen years, 24 per cent more than twenty-one, and 19 per cent twenty-six or more. In other words, though they had not made their way up from the lower levels of the organization, they had become long-standing servants. Furthermore, the number of external recruits to management positions needs to be put into context. Within the EUCIQ sample, no fewer than 86 per cent of officials reported that their first job in the Commission had been as an administrator. Thus, the vast majority had entered the organization at a junior grade.

In the case of *cabinets*, there were apparently competing expectations. *Cabinets* had historically been a route for outsiders to enter the Commission, typically from the Commissioner's home civil service, before embarking on a high-flying career in the services. However, recent reforms have denationalized *cabinets* (Egeberg and Heskestad 2010), lowered the grades at which *cabinet* members are employed, and have made *parachutage* considerably less attractive.[52] As a result, serving in a *cabinet* may no longer have the appeal, either for outsiders or for insiders, that it once commanded.

The findings from the EUCIQ data show that direct recruits are present in *cabinets* in high numbers and in higher proportions than previously. No fewer than 37 of the 87 *cabinet* members who answered the question in the online survey—or 42 per cent—reported that their current position was their first in the Commission. Page (1997: 51) estimated in the mid 1990s that about 12 per cent of *cabinet* members were in this category. That the proportion is now 30 percentage points higher is a significant finding.

Perhaps, as with managers, the high percentage of outsiders in cabinets in 2008 is to be explained by eastern enlargement. In other words, there has been no upward trend over time. The large numbers are to be explained by a one-off event that brought twelve new member states into the Union. Further support for viewing this period as exceptional comes from evidence of career-building among the 58 per cent of non-outsiders–those who worked their way up through the organization. Of the fifty *cabinet* members who had worked previously in the Commission, 26 per cent had been middle managers, and 52 per cent administrators.

---

[52] The highest management position to which officials exiting *cabinets* are likely to be ap-pointed is Head of Unit, which is a more junior role than past parachutees would have targeted.

Promotion: Party, Cabinet Experience, Nationality, and Gender

The responses to the online survey provided information making it possible to examine the career trajectories of Commission officials. A first step was to calculate the average length of time that it took officials to become middle and senior managers from the time that they joined the Commission. This made it possible to assess whether nationality by wave of accession, *cabinet* experience or gender had an impact on the speed of career progression. The effects of partisan affiliation, using testimony from interviews with managers and members of *cabinet*, were also assessed.

Analysis of the data showed that middle managers in the Commission had on average taken fourteen-and-a-half years of their eighteen years' service to attain their current positions. Senior managers, meanwhile, had served on average for twenty-one years and had waited nineteen years before their promotion to Director or Director-General. A first finding concerned nationality. The online survey data showed that nationals from countries that had joined the Commission in the northern and the eastern enlargements had reached middle management positions significantly more rapidly than the average. The same was true in regard to the speed with which officials reached senior management positions.

The second finding concerned the impact of *cabinet* experience. As *cabinets* have been considered glamorous and prestigious places to work, it is widely believed that the experience of working in a cabinet enhances the career opportunities within the organization (Page 1997: 81). However, in the analysis of the data collected for the current project no significant difference was found, in terms of the time taken to reach middle or senior management positions, between those who had and those who had not worked in a *cabinet*.[53]

The third finding related to gender. Existing scholarship has shown the Commission to be an organization where historically women have been under-represented, concentrated in lower grades, and largely absent from senior posts. The Commission initiated action to address the gender imbalance as long ago as 1978. Until the northern enlargement, however, progress was slow (Penaud 1989; Page 1997: 70–4; Spence 1997: 89–91; Stevens and Stevens 2001: 108–14). Ten years after the creation of a standing Joint Committee on Equal Opportunities for Men and Women in 1984, women

---

[53] These findings contrast with the figures released by Siim Kallas, Commissioner for Administrative Affairs, in 2005. He indicated that in the Prodi Commission 15 per cent of A1 (now AD 15–16) and 14 per cent of A2 (AD 14–15) posts had gone to *cabinet* members. Under the Santer Commission (1995–9), the figures had been 20 per cent and 16 per cent and under Delors (1989–94) 19 per cent and 24 per cent (Cronin 2005).

still accounted for only 13.5 per cent of A grade officials and 5.4 per cent in the top grades.

Measures implemented since the mid-1990s, including a series of Action Programmes, changes implemented as part of the Kinnock–Prodi reforms, and recruitment associated with the eastern enlargement (European Commission 2011, Ban 2010), have achieved a degree of success. When it launched its new Equal Opportunities Strategy in December 2010, the Commission noted that the proportion of senior management posts held by women had risen from 4 per cent in 1995 to 21.4 per cent in 2009 and in middle management from 10.7 per cent to 23.3 per cent (European Commission 2010: 3). In comparative terms, in 2010 the Commission had a higher percentage of women in senior positions than Belgium, Ireland, the Netherlands, France, and Germany, as many as Norway and Finland, and fewer than Italy, Austria, the UK, Spain, Sweden, Portugal, and Greece (OECD 2009: 71).[54]

The EUCIQ online survey asked officials whether: 'It is now as easy for women to advance their careers as men'. Forty-six per cent of respondents agreed or strongly agreed; 25 per cent were neutral.[55] This perception was tested against official Commission census data from 2008 (Commission 2008) and against data from the survey sample. Although Commission headlines in official documentation report gender parity. The in overall staff numbers, a breakdown by grade shows that the percentage of women diminishes with each upward step of the career hierarchy (see Figure 2.5). Although Catherine Day has been Secretary-General since 2006, female managers are still a rarity. Analysis of the EUCIQ data showed, though, that the small number of women who have reached middle and senior management positions have done so more rapidly than their male counterparts (see Table 2.9). The same is not true of *cabinets*, where women typically have had to accumulate more years of service than men before being selected to be a member of a Commissioner's personal office.

A fourth, and final, finding concerns partisan affiliation (see also Chapters 3 and 4). A first aim was to investigate whether partisanship was an important influence as it had been in the Delors Commission, where socialist networks played a key role in mobilizing support across the organization (Grant 1994; Ross 1995). A second was to determine whether the relevance of partisanship to recruitment, promotion or role distinguished the *cabinets* from the administration. Managers and cabinet members were asked: 'How important is party affiliation or party sympathy of officials in the Commission?' The interviewees were invited to offer one of five possible responses:

---

[54] The data for these other administrations was collected in 2005.

[55] The gender breakdown of responses to this question is instructive: 79 per cent of the respondents who agreed or strongly agreed were men; 71 per cent of those who disagreed or strongly disagreed were women.

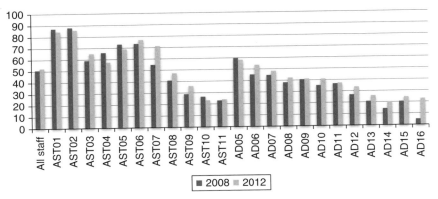

Fig. 2.5 Percentage of female officials at each grade in 2008 and 2012

Source: 2008 data from European Commission, DG Human Resources and Security.

Table 2.9 Average length of service before current position (years)

Current position	All	Male	Female	Career officials	Direct entry	*Cabinet experience*
Senior manager or adviser	19.02	19.45	17.50	20.87	17.18	21.40
Middle manager	14.56	14.86	13.44	13.43	17.72	13.48
Member of *cabinet*	9.68	8.68	11.13	8.93	12.00	9.68

Note: n = 680 (*cabinet* officials, senior managers, middle managers only).

- Party affiliation is very important
- It is important
- Sometimes it plays a role, sometimes not
- It is not very important
- It does not play any role at all

Their responses suggest not only that political partisanship does not play a major role in the life of the Commission, but that it is also far less important in the *cabinets* than is often assumed.

In regard to the Commission administration, no fewer than 70 per cent of managers thought that that party affiliation was not very important or not important at all for top officials. Their views were often emphatically expressed:

- '[I]n the services, it has no importance' (interview 52)
- 'Zero' (interview 133)
- 'I don't know the affiliations of any of my colleagues' (interview 162).[56]

Cabinet members were somewhat more evenly divided, although a majority took the same view: 54 per cent (fifteen of the twenty-eight interviewed) thought that political partisanship was not very important or plays no role for top managers, 36 per cent that is sometimes plays a role, and only 7 per cent (two of the twenty-eight interviewed) that it is important.[57]

Findings concerning party affiliation in the life of *cabinets* were no less dramatic. Only 5 per cent of managers thought that the party affiliation of *cabinet* members was important or very important.[58] Thirty-eight per cent believed that it sometimes played a role, and 29 per cent that it was not very important or did not play any role. The split of opinion among *cabinet* members was very similar. Only 7 per cent (two of the twenty-eight interviewed) considered party affiliation to be important or very important, while 36 per cent believed that it sometimes plays a role. Forty per cent, however, considered that partisanship is either not very important or plays no role. Since *cabinets* have historically served as the private offices of their Commissioners, been staffed predominantly by the Commissioner's fellow nationals and political intimates, and thought to balance the party card, these findings are highly significant.[59]

---

[56] Some respondents speculated that it might play a role somewhere in the Commission, even if they had no direct experience themselves. One Director, for example, replied: 'Not at all, except that now and then you hear rumours about one or other' (interview 82). In similar vein, a middle manager offered the view: 'I think it matters for senior management' (interview 20). Similarly, one *chef de cabinet* reflected that 'there are at least suspicions that party affiliation can play a role in which top officials, and I mean, really top officials get which jobs, or whether they get jobs at all.... But is it party affiliation? Is it nationality?... [I]f you're a particular nationality, and you're being pushed for a top job, and you've got the wrong party card, I have a suspicion that sometimes that it can impact; it certainly did in the past, and maybe less so now. It's hard to tell' (interview 84).

[57] In the view of one cabinet member, however: 'It is not unimportant at all. I have seen people hired in this Commission who wouldn't have been hired if they hadn't had the right party, so that happens to be true' (interview 74).

[58] One Director, who had served in three *cabinets*, remarked: 'I don't think it has been an issue in any of these *cabinets*' (interview 60). According to another: 'I've been in *cabinets* for a long time. It's irrelevant there as well' (interview 72).

[59] Combined with the denationalization of the cabinets (see Chapter 6), the limited relevance of political partisanship points to nothing short of a transformation of their composition and role. As one *chef de cabinet* observed: '[A]lthough *cabinets* are still political, it is less party political and more policy political, and—and that has also become much more pronounced with...the denationalization...of *cabinets*....[W]e're not involved in—in, if you like, in [domestic] politics or anything like that. It's...pure Commission politics that we tend to be involved in....[I]t is much better not to have a Commissioner surrounded by certain people of the same nationality with one token foreigner, you know, so that you—you become more conditioned by one particular national approach. I think it is much healthier the way things have evolved' (interview 96).

The interview testimonies of *chefs de cabinets* and other *cabinet* members offer illustrations of the range of views and some of the reasoning behind the opinions expressed. For two *chefs de cabinet*, party was simply not relevant:

> [I]t's not something I know about people. I don't know if somebody is from which party.... I was never asked or it's just not an issue (interview 134).

> [W]e don't ask. I mean we have now in our cabinet okay, roughly ten people who deal with substance. I can easily say that there are three or four we don't know, either me or Commissioner their political affiliation. We never ask (interview 105).

Two others averred that party affiliation would not be a consideration in recruitment to a *cabinet*:

> In cabinets my boss would deliberately not have asked a number of the members what their party affiliation was ... [W]hen we are recruiting, we would never ask somebody (interview 86).

> Recruitment of cabinet members is ... done not on the basis of which party or which ideological system do you belong to. It's mainly based on what is your CV, what are your experiences, and where have you worked (interview 7).

The irrelevance of party was stressed by the *cabinet* members of Commissioners who were technocrats rather than politicians:

> My present Commissioner and even the previous one were not really party members, so that's good (interview 152).

> Helping the Commissioner manage his or her links to a political party? Not at all important, because he's not a member of a political party (interview 34).

Other interviewees considered it normal that *cabinet* members had party affiliations, but thought that for the most part it would not problematic even if they had different political leanings:

> [T]he Commissioner is in one political family; I am on the other political family. We have two members in the third political family ... [I]t shows that it doesn't matter really ... if you don't disagree on substance (interview 58).

Those *cabinet* members who did think partisanship matters offered quite different rationales. Interviewees believed Commissioners are likely to be more successful if they have a range and variety of networks than if they draw only on their own party. To have multiple party links was therefore an asset for a *cabinet*. Thus:

> '[A] Commissioner would really miss out on the collegial work if she or he would surround himself with people from their own party' (interview 72).

> '[A] good and clever cabinet ... will have more than one political-party political affiliation' (interview 53).

As the functions of a *cabinet* are inherently political and a key role of the *cabinet* is to support the work of the Commissioner in a political environment, the channels afforded by party links are invaluable. For one Head of Unit:

> '[Party]'s not important, but party interest, or political interest or sensitivity to party issues, yes' (interview 9).

Maintaining good relations with the political groups in the European Parliament, for example, is important to ease the passage of legislation. For this reason:

> [A]ll Commissioners feel that links to the European Parliament are very important, and that takes two forms really, two key dimensions. One is your portfolio responsibilities, guiding those through the channels in Parliament, something that we obviously spend a lot of time on [as part of] our direct portfolio responsibilities because we have Parliament there. But the other one is links to the political group in Parliament . . . And there the cabinet has given, because that is not something where you can ask the DG to gather support. That comes from the cabinet (interview 104).

> [The] Commissioner is going to see that it is important that we have a link open to liberals, socialists, and EPP. That is enough (interview 105).

> [M]y Commissioner meets her political group and Parliament for dinner every month. I'm not a liberal, but I have to go to liberal dinners and all the rest . . . to at least understand people's particular view of the world is (interview 62).

For some *cabinets*, maintaining a link between the Commissioner and the party at home is important, but interviewees were at pains to emphasize that rather than a general function of the *cabinet* this was a responsibility delegated to one or two of its members:

> [T]he link to the home state and the link to the political party is not [the responsibility of] the whole of the cabinet, but . . . people within the cabinet, those who came with him (interview 7).

> [L]ink to the home state? . . . [T]here is one person in the cabinet, in particular, who has that, but we had the same in the Patten cabinet that was our sort of backyard boy who took care of the links back to London, and—well, in this case [a Scandinavian member state], and maybe more importantly . . . help manage the link to the political party (interview 104).

A general view was simply that the importance of partisanship differs between *cabinets*. The variation may reflect differences in national practice, political culture or Commissioner preferences:

> [I]t varies from country to country. I think in some countries it's still quite important because it can help you advance your career (interview 96).[60]

> It depends on the cabinet. For this cabinet, completely irrelevant. The Commissioner wanted people on the basis of competence, in fact, she was quite keen

---

[60] Denmark, Ireland and the UK were cited as examples where party had little or no role, Austria, Belgium and Germany where it might.

to have people of different backgrounds, which might include party affiliation, simply because she was keen to have a broad church. In some cabinets, . . . if you're not a party member, then you'd better not . . . [be] there . . . [H]ere it was completely irrelevant (interview 84).

You would know in certain countries that it's very unlikely that the cabinet, head of cabinet comes from a party opposite to the party of the commissioner, in some countries. I mean, the corporatist countries, you know (interview 62).

I think the Commission is a strange mixture. I have come from a background where I would like to think that . . . any Minister I have worked with has no idea about what my political affiliations are—that I would do the same job for anybody. It is part of the way I am just built [but] [t]hat is not the system in all administrations here. [In the case of officials from] France and German[y] . . . those affiliations are known and you know people are promoted because of political affiliations when a certain party is in power. . . . Once I got used to it, it was all right. . . . My experience with politicians is they do and they can because they look at who can deliver results for them. And if you can't deliver results it doesn't matter what side you are on you know (interview 68).

CONCLUSION

This chapter has examined expertise, representativeness, and career progression—key features of concern to scholars of public administration—in the case of the European Commission. The findings, based on a detailed dataset, offer important insights into the organization and its personnel. Four sets of findings are important. The first is that the Commission is able to draw on a broader and more diverse range of expertise than accepted wisdoms about the organization suggest. Data from the EUCIQ online survey shows that the Commission is not populated overwhelmingly by lawyers. Also, contrary to the assumption that officials have typically spent their entire working life in the Commission, the vast majority of officials had in fact had a prior career before they joined the Commission. Importantly, a large segment of officials moved to the Commission from the private sector.

Second, the Commission administration is representative in the sense that all twenty-seven member states are present in the services. A concerted effort has led to improved recruitment from the countries of the EU-12 that joined the Union as a result of the 2004 and 2007 enlargements. At the same time, some of the large member states are under-represented, though to varying degrees. The shortfall in the number of officials from France, Germany, Italy, and the UK is a source of anxiety for the Commission, as well as in the member states concerned. It raises concerns not only about the organization's effectiveness, but also about perceptions of its legitimacy.

Third, despite Hallstein's intentions, the realisation of a career-based civil service has only been partially achieved. For much of the Commission's history, the main obstacle has been the claims of the member states to 'fair shares'. Nationality, including the recruitment exercise undertaken with the 2004 and 2007 enlargements, routinely distorted promotion and career prospects within the organization. Although the changing role of the *cabinets* (see Chapter 7) and the Kinnock–Prodi reforms have largely downgraded nationality as a consideration in appointments, enlargement has continued to act as an impediment. Thus, a significant proportion of middle managers and especially senior managers did not rise up through Commission ranks, but had been recruited directly to those posts from the outside. For the Commission as for any international organization, a trade-off between the claims of representativeness on the grounds of effectiveness and legitimacy, and of career progression based on merit, is apparently inescapable. Only the terms of that trade-off change over time.

Finally, albeit somewhat marginally, both the presence and the promotion prospects for women within the organization have improved. To that extent, various action programmes and especially the reforms enacted under the Prodi Commission appear to have borne fruit. However, there are still relatively few women in middle and especially senior management positions. Further action will be necessary if women are to be better represented at all levels of the organization.

3

Navigating the Commission

All modern administrations—including the Commission—operate on the basis of rules and procedures that specify how officials interact to perform tasks for which their institution has responsibility. Such rules are usually codified: that is, they are collected together into a system or 'code'. An administrative code conventionalizes formal rules. It draws from them principles and expectations about, for example, how information is communicated, which officials must be consulted on or approve specific pieces of work, and how tasks are divided between different categories of official.[1]

Yet, no administration works purely on the basis of formal rules. In fact, the most common frustration associated with bureaucracies arises when they become rigidly rules-bound, inflexible, and cannot adapt to specific contingencies (see Crozier 2009). Just as laws can never be written to cover every imaginable exigency in social life, it is impossible for any administrative code to specify a 'best' procedure—as opposed to a *correct* procedure—for dealing with every imaginable situation.

It is only a slight exaggeration that all important scholars of public administration have sought to specify how officials have to improvise to perform their work. Niklas Luhmann (1964) developed the notion of *brauchbare Illegalität*: literally, 'useful illegality'. Renate Mayntz (1966) argued that 'bad' or rigid rules are almost inevitably 'flexibilized' by officials, who engage in 'spontaneous adaptation'. On the specific question of how officials communicate with one another, Herbert Simon (1997: 213–4) insists that:

> No matter how elaborate a system of formal communication is set up in the organization this system will always be supplemented by informal channels . . . it may be conjectured that weakness of the formal system of communications and failure to secure an adequate measure of coordination through that system probably encourage the development of cliques. The coordination function that cliques perform under such circumstances is closely analogous to the

---

[1] Some students of public administration, such as Wilson (1991), would also subsume informal rules and practices under the term 'code'.

coordination function performed by political machines in a highly decentralized governmental structure like the American system.

By this account, public administrations end up working more like urban American political machines, with their much-deserved reputation for cronyism and improvisation, as opposed to Weberian, rule-bound automatons.

The European Commission is a multi-national administration, relatively young, and engaged in knowledge-intensive work. It wields powers that are far more formidable than those of any other international administration. At the same time, the Commission is resource-poor and procedure-rich—the latter less as a consequence of its formal code than because the EU's member states are principals who frequently are reluctant to delegate to the Commission as their agent; they thus often 'load' the tasks that they assign to the Commission with strict controls, which results in complicated and extensive procedures that must be followed.

This chapter is concerned with how, in such circumstances, Commission officials 'navigate', or plan, direct, or plot a path to the successful completion of their work. It seeks to answer the question: how do officials find the resources, expertise and knowledge needed to perform knowledge-intensive work *despite* onerous and complicated rules of procedure?

Part of the answer, at least, is through networks: groups of interconnected officials. The Commission operates within an institutional system in which it, along with the other main EU institutions, mostly succeed or fail together (see Peterson and Shackleton 2012). The Commission is also dependent for resources and expertise on a diverse range of experts, officials, and other policy stakeholders who do not work for its administration. As such, it nearly always succeeds or fails as a member of networks that extend beyond the Commission to its counterparts from other EU institutions, European national capitals, and members of (for lack of a better term) 'European civil society'. Networks that are concerned with specific EU policies—that is, *policy networks*, are horizontally-composed 'cluster(s) of actors, each of which has an interest, or "stake", in a given . . . policy sector and the capacity to help determine policy success or failure' (Peterson and Bomberg 1999: 8). Most work on network governance in Brussels finds distinct networks that correspond to discrete policy sectors or (much less often) connect them. The Commission often has considerable influence on their composition and ways of working.

Our data shed light on one particular type: personal networks *within* the Commission, or the people to whom Commission officials turn for information or advice on professional matters. We thus have only a partial picture of how Commission officials navigate the Brussels machine. But we find that many officials agree that the use of informal networks is necessary to get their work done. We are able to add considerably to knowledge about how networks within the Commission are composed and used, and thus how the administration *really* works, as opposed to how the Commission's formal rules and procedures prescribe that it should work.

We begin by putting the Commission in context: we identify the key factors that condition how its officials navigate. Second, we review several different research literatures—with increasing degrees of specificity for the case at hand—on organizational networks, network governance, networks in the EU, and networks within the Commission for evidence about what determines how they are composed and work. Our third section presents EUCIQ survey data on networks within the Commission and 'mines' it for clues about how officials navigate. Fourth, we complement the survey's findings by drawing on our interviews with managers. Our central arguments, drawn together in the conclusion, may be summarized as:

- networks are valued by most officials who must navigate the administration;
- officials rely on networks most of all for procedural advice;
- most officials rely more on their personal networks the longer they serve; and
- nationality is a secondary but certainly not unimportant determinant of network membership.

THE COMMISSION IN CONTEXT

Understanding how the Commission works begins by understanding the nature of its work. It is focused on complex policy problems—such as counter-terrorism, people and drug trafficking, regional development, and environmental protection. Many of these qualify as what public policy specialists call 'wicked problems' (Rittel and Webber 1973): persistent, relentless, unstructured, contested, highly technical, and having to be dealt with in a context of uncertainty. Climate change, energy security, and migration control all qualify: they are issues on which there is often little consensus about the definition of the problem, let alone about solutions.

By nature, wicked problems are *horizontal* problems: they arise because of multiple, interdependent policy failures spread across multiple policy sectors. They can only be solved (if they can be solved at all) via coordinated action by officials with different policy responsibilities. Wicked problems resist resolution by traditional, 'established "stovepiped"'—that is, rigidly segmented—'systems of problem definition, administration and resolution' (Weber and Khademian 2008: 336).

To its considerable cost, the Commission is a highly segmented adminis-tration. Its internal fragmentation is an historical legacy of European integra-tion, as the Commission (2001: 28) itself has admitted: 'step by step integration, which has characterized the [EU's] development, has tended to slice policies into sectoral strands, with different objectives and different tools; over time the capacity to ensure... coherence has diminished'. As such, the Commission has both a uniquely challenging policy agenda and appears to be structured in a way that makes it singularly ill-equipped to perform its work. Of course, the problems of sectoral fragmentation alongside a powerful need for coordination are by no means exclusive to the Commis-sion. Still, Peters and Wright (2001: 158) argue that while 'managing the problems of fragmentation, sectoralization and policy interdependence is not peculiar to Brussels... the extent and nature of those problems in Brussels is of a different order from that prevailing in the member states' (see also Metcalfe 1992).

These challenges magnify the importance of the Commission's detailed and onerous administrative code. It was not always thus, as during the early years of the European Economic Community the Commission operated on the basis of few besides informal rules and procedures. Yet, one heirloom of the intensive round of administrative reform following the mass resignation of the Santer Commission in 1999 is strict rules that govern how it spends money, utilizes staff, and exchanges information. It is set out in the *statut*—or *Staff Regulations of the Officials of the European Communities* (see Chap-ter 2)—running in its English version to 167 pages with nine Titles, over one hundred articles, and thirteen annexes.[2] Although it is shorter than terms and conditions specified for (say) British or German civil servants, it is by many accounts considerably less flexible (Spence and Stevens 2006: 175). Reveal-ingly, a new and reformed *statut* was formally implemented on 1 May 2004, thus showing both the profound impact on the Commission of that year's enlargement (see Chapter 9) as well as the laboriousness of the process of agreeing the *statut*: it took five years from the time of the Santer Commission's downfall.

Moreover, the Commission has far more powers than it has resources. Given the major policy responsibilities it bears, it is a remarkably small administration of around thirty thousand officials.[3] The Commission relies

---

[2] The *statut* applies to all EU institutions except the European Investment Bank and European Central Bank.

[3] In the mid-1990s there existed 0.8 of a European civil servant (taking into account *all* European civil servants, including the Commission) compared to 322 national civil servants for each 10,000 EU citizens. Spence (2006: 178) offers the caveat that 'such comparisons are of doubtful relevance. The Commission is directly responsible for the implementation of very few policies... and that is what generally requires large numbers of staff'. However, the Commis-sion's relative dearth of officials concerned with implementation, combined with its need to

heavily on actors with the expertise and resources that it, as an administration, lacks. Such actors include private firms and associations, non-governmental organizations, and (especially) national administrations. As such, many Commission officials must navigate even beyond the EU's institutional system to succeed in their work.

But the institutional system of which the Commission is a part demands extensive exchange and coordination between institutions. The EU system is one of shared more than separated powers (see Peterson and Shackleton 2012). Almost nothing important can be agreed without the consent of all three main players in its legislative triangle: the Council (of Ministers), European Parliament, and the Commission itself. Commission officials can therefore become almost as familiar with the other EU institutions as with their own.

Thus, the Commission is highly 'stove-piped', its administrative code is burdensome, it is resource-poor, and it is heavily dependent for its success on its relationship with other EU institutions. And still it is tasked with trying to solve 'wicked problems', whose very nature makes it unlikely that they can be solved by administrations that strictly observe their own administrative code, especially one as cumbersome as that under which the Commission operates. For the Commission more than most public administrations, '[t]he challenge . . . is that they can do their jobs by the book and still not get the job done' (Kettl 2002: 22).

Against this backdrop, five key features characterize the Commission as an administration. First, in formal terms, the Commission is rigidly *hierarchical*, reflecting its French-style origins. One official contrasts life in the administration with his involvement in the European Parliament:

> Commuting as I did between the Commission and the European Parliament, I quickly noted a difference in the atmosphere between the two institutions. The Commission had a strict hierarchy and a business-like approach . . . The Commission used formal methods of address (for example, the *vous* form in French), whereas everyone in the Parliament was quickly on first name terms, even the assistants and translators. The Commission was a political machine. The Parliament was a political club. (Eppink 2007: 62)

The Commission's Directorates-General (DGs)—its equivalent of ministries—work under the political direction of the College of Commissioners. Each DG, on paper at least, 'has many of the characteristics of a classic Weberian pyramid' (Spence and Stevens 2006: 187). They are headed by a Director-General, with Directors heading functional divisions, and 'units' within each division consisting of a Head and several desk officers. Hierarchy in the

design policies that can be implemented in 27 different member states, makes it even more important that its officials have strong and extensive personal networks in national civil services.

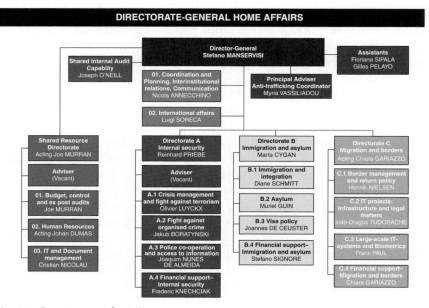

Fig. 3.1 Organigram of a DG

Source: < http://ec.europa.eu/dgs/home-affairs/chart/docs/organigramme_en.pdf >, accessed 5 December 2011.

Commission is reflected in its (in Brussels-speak) 'organigrams' that set out the chain of command for all DGs (see Figure 3.1).

These structures determine the pathway for dossiers, a second defining feature of the Commission (see Cini 1996: 152; Nugent 2001: 242). Dossiers are specific pieces of work or proposals whether legislative (such as regulations) or not (consultative 'Green Papers'). They are central to the work of the administration above all because the Commission holds a monopoly on the right of initiative in EU legislation. One unit—and, in fact, one official—almost always takes the lead on each dossier and prepares it for its journey to the Director-General's desk. The Commission may be the only administration in the world that organizes its work almost exclusively on such a basis. One effect is to atomize the administration: officials must and do consult widely, but responsibility for the progress of most dossiers lies squarely on the shoulders of individuals. Another effect is to enhance the importance of personal networks. The dossier system means that the Commission—more than most administrations—relies on the strength of ties between officials with different types of expertise, knowledge, and skills.

The strength of such ties is particularly important because few dossiers are the exclusive preserve of one DG. Inter-service consultation on them is often long, laborious, and antagonistic. As Stevens and Stevens (2001: 79) note:

an official who wishes to take the views of colleagues in six or seven other Directorates-General is expected to pass a draft upwards to the Director-General, who will pass it to the other Directors-General, who will pass it downwards to the appropriate members of their staff. Responses will take the same route in reverse.

All dossiers also must be checked by the Secretariat-General, to ensure they have been prepared following the Commission's rules of procedure, before they go to the College. It became accepted wisdom, especially under the Barroso Presidency, that almost nothing could be done against the wishes of the Secretariat-General (Kassim 2006: 79). This point was reinforced institutionally under Barroso's 'Better Regulation Agenda', which required all legislative proposals to include an impact assessment that specified what precise effects any proposed policy would have, and faced being scrutinized by an Impact Assessment Board within the Secretariat-General. One Director in DG Market described the Board as 'all Barroso's people. They can stop anything'.[4]

But *coordination* between DGs—a third key feature of how the Commission works—is even more complicated than that. The Budget and Financial Control Directorates-General have to be consulted on all proposals that spend money. DG Personnel and Administration must be formally involved on anything that affects personnel. The Legal Service must scrutinize any proposal before it reaches the College. That coordination is taken seriously is reflected in the growth of standing inter-service groups, which offer a permanent structure for coordination between specific DGs, from 63 groups in 1993 to 224 by 2006.

Still, it is frequently claimed that the Commission has 'inadequate capacities for effective coordination', which contributes significantly to its 'management deficit' (Spence and Edwards 2006: 148). As a consequence, officials piloting a dossier frequently resort to informal contact with other desk officers so that agreement between DGs can precede formal inter-service consultation and thus avoid long delays before decisions are reached (Stevens and Stevens 2001: 176). More generally, the process by which dossiers finally reach the College— long and tortured if done 'by the book'—is an important reason why learning to circumvent formal procedures is essential for officials who wish to thrive, or even survive, in the Commission (Hooghe 2005: 878).

A fourth feature of life in the Commission is *impermanence*. One source of flux is frequent changes in Commissioners and portfolios, with the latter often created or adapted in response to the ambitions of new Commissioners, the Commission President, or pressure from Member States. The need to create more portfolios to assign to an enlarged college post-2004 illustrates the point. Responsibility for DG SANCO—Health and Consumer Protection—had to be split between two Commissioners and a barely plausible portfolio for

---

[4] Non-EUCIQ interview conducted by one of the authors, 21 November 2006.

'multilingualism' created when new Bulgarian and Romanian Commissioners arrived in 2007. Numerous Directors-General have faced the management headache of having parts of their service pulled in varying directions or split off to a new DG. One such shake-up took place in 2010 (with delays into 2011) when the DG for Justice, Freedom and Security (which itself had started as a unit in the Secretariat-General in the early 1990s) was split into two DGs: DG Home Affairs concerned with immigration and asylum, and DG Justice to focus on citizenship and judicial cooperation. One consequence of so much chopping and changing is highly centralized management systems to cope with frequent transformations.

Increases in staff mobility, despite its acknowledged virtues, have been another source of impermanence. Directors-General now must change posts every five years. They are obliged to identify staff in 'sensitive posts' with personnel or financial responsibilities who are subject to compulsory re-deployment every seven years. The Commission also makes extensive use of irregular posts—Temporary Agents and Detached National Experts (who remain on the payroll of their government, firm, or NGO)—to cope with shortages in human resources. To illustrate, in 1992 when the need for expertise on Eastern Europe became urgent, it was estimated that nearly one-third of staff working for the Commission did so on a non-statutory basis (Spence and Stevens 2006: 193).

Without doubt, the single most powerful source of impermanence—as well as a final fundamental feature of the Commission's work—has been *task expansion*: the tendency for the EU, and thus the Commission, to take on new and more diverse policy responsibilities. Over time, the Commission has become more 'polycentric', with increasingly more and more dissimilar centres of power and control. Police and judicial cooperation, monetary union, and crisis management are all very distinctive policies in which the Commission is involved despite having no role in these areas twenty years ago.

Thus, the Commission faces numerous obstacles to the effective perform-ance of its work. It, like many administrations, must surmount rigid hierarch-ies to design solutions to complex policy problems. More than most, it deals with 'wicked problems' that demand extensive coordination across services. Its strict hierarchy, the dossier system, its problems of coordination, state of impermanence, and the frequency with which it is given new tasks make it something between difficult and impossible to do its work by the book. As such, it is perhaps not surprising that the Commission has been characterized as *distinctive* in that it is not a:

> conventional machine bureaucrac[y] with [a] large staff . . . engaged in continuing routine administrative work. Instead [its DGs] are strategic nodes in politico-administrative networks working with and through national administrations as

well as with other institutions and organisations at the European level (Spence and Edwards 2006: 129).

There is evidence in the EUCIQ project data to suggest that many Commission officials agree. In response to the online survey a clear plurality of officials who responded[5]—around 44 per cent—agreed that the Commission had to rely 'more on informal networks than formal hierarchies' to get its work done. Only around 30 per cent disagreed (see Figure 3.2). Personal networks thus seem to be an important asset as officials seek to navigate the administration.

Just as we have put the Commission in perspective, informal networks linking its officials must be put into perspective by considering the nature of networks in organizations generally and those involved in EU governance more specifically. These tasks are the focus of the next section.

THE COMMISSION AND THE NATURE OF NETWORKS

Students of organizational behaviour—many in the field of business studies—have increasingly focused on social networks as critical to innovation and success in modern organizations that are 'flatter' and less hierarchical than their predecessors. Much of this work seeks to help managers identify, evaluate, and support networks that naturally arise between employees who rely on them to do their work (see Nohria and Eccles 1992; Borgatti and Cross 2003). For example, Cross and Parker (2004) stress the importance of bridging strategically important disconnects, eliminating information bottlenecks, and locating the key 'connectors' in social networks within organizations. Very recent work focuses on issues such as employee or customer retention and marketing to increasingly ubiquitous online social networks (see Ballinger et al. 2011; Nitzan and Libai 2011; Porter et al. 2011).

Social science research on network structures has expanded significantly in recent years (see Powell 1991; Thompson et al. 1991; Thompson 2003). Social networks are of obvious interest to sociologists (see Marsden 2005; McPherson et al. 2009; Porter et al. 2011), but they have become increasingly a focus of research on public administrations (Brass 1984; Gibbons 2004) or public policy. Increasingly, work on how policies are made or implemented[6] within networks is comparative, with policy outcomes linked to network structures (see Marsh and Rhodes 1992; Marsh 1998; Kriesi et al. 2006), especially in policy areas that

---

[5] Around 12 per cent did not answer or responded 'don't know'.
[6] On policy-making, see Heclo 1978; Dunn and Perl 1994; Grande and Peschke 1999; De Jong and Edelenbos 2007. On implementation, see Hall and O'Toole 2000; Kamarck 2007; Yesilkagit and Blom-Hansen 2007.

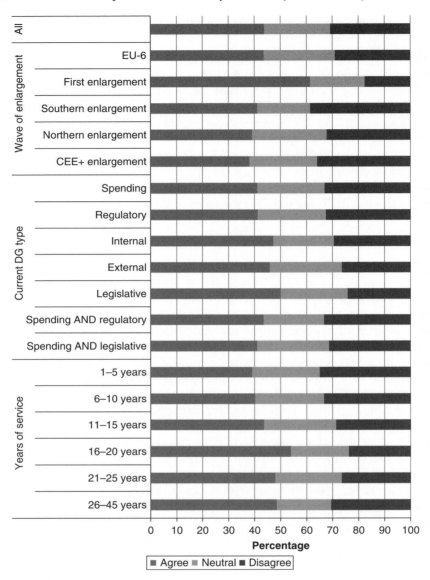

Fig. 3.2 Are networks important?

Note: Valid %. n = 1,617; full sample = 1,846. 3.9% not sure, and 8.5% missing responses.

demand extensive international cooperation (Slaughter 2004; Slaughter and Zaring 2006).

Nevertheless, it is plausible to conclude that our knowledge of networks as social constructs remains primitive (see König 1998; Peterson and O'Toole 2001). Debates about whether policy network analysis is an 'approach, a theory or loose construct' (Kettl 2002: 111) can seem insular, personal, and even petty (see Dowding 2001; Marsh and Smith 2001). Yet, research that seeks to put 'theoretical meat on metaphorical bones' (Peters 1998a: 26) at least raises interesting and pertinent questions about modern governance.[7] What makes network analysis distinctive is its 'focus on the relationships between the players' (Kettl 2002: 111), its concern for the horizontal over the hierarchical, and its search for explanations at the point of interstitial links between actors (see Rhodes 1997). Network analysis is a 'framework for defining a central problem' (Kettl 2002: 112): specifically, how are outcomes negotiated between stakeholders that have the capacity to determine policy success or failure but also are unable to impose outcomes?

Research that deploys network analysis to explain EU governance has proliferated since the mid-1990s.[8] There is no shortage of sceptics who cast doubt on the utility of the approach. For some, governance in Brussels is too fluid for actors to develop enduring exchange relationships. By this view, the network that forms to negotiate on one dossier is rarely identical to the network that forms around the next (see Kassim 1994).[9] For others, what matters in EU governance is the formal, legal framework for policy-making. There obviously exists no legal mandate to sustain policy networks (see Börzel 1998; 2010).

Nevertheless, there are at least three reasons to believe that '[t]he EU is replete with policy networks' (Jordan and Schout 2006: 256; see also Peterson 2009: 105–7). First, EU governance is concerned with the externalities of globalization and deep economic interdependence of EU member states. It is thus by necessity multinational. Technological progress makes it increasingly easier for goods, people, services, and information to cross borders. But it also makes regulation of such movement highly complex and technical. It is well-established in the research literature that network governance is most likely to arise in sectors where experts are empowered by their technical expertise and policies are shaped or set at the international level.

Second, as we have noted, the EU is a highly differentiated polity (see Rhodes 1997). It is intensely polycentric, with decision rules and dominant actors—political and technocratic, public and private—that vary enormously between policy sectors. Turf battles are frequent, especially where dossiers

---

[7] They include the role of ideas in linking policy specialists (Kisby 2007), whether networks may become institutionalized in a 'new institutionalist' sense of established norms (Blom-Hansen 1997), and whether the existence of identifiable policy networks necessarily leads to 'network governance' (Damgaard 2006).

[8] See Peterson 1995; Ansell et al. 1997; Dehousse 1997; Ward and Williams 1997; Bomberg 1998; Daugbjerg 1999; Grande and Peschke 1999; Nunan 1999; Peterson and Bomberg 1999; Jordan and Schout 2006; Suvarierol 2007, 2009; Kern and Bulkeley 2009; Peterson 2009.

[9] This view might be one that was more plausible in the early 1990s when the EU's policy agenda was far less extensive *or* intensive than it is today.

provoke rivalries between actors with policy concerns that clash, such as agricultural productivity versus environmental protection. 'Firewalls' between policy sectors are high: EU policy networks are commonly viewed as discrete and disconnected from one another. Every EU policy sector has its own 'dedicated' Commissioner and DG, Council and (usually) European Parliament (EP) committee, as well expert and advisory committees. Yet, despite the EU's polycentricity, what most policy sectors have in common is that power is shared (more than divided) between the Union's main institutions: the Commission, Council and Parliament. In short, the EU usually can act only after extensive exchange between the administrations of its institutions, which naturally gives rise to informal networks that facilitate such exchange.

Third, again, the EU is centrally concerned with wicked policy problems that transcend divisions between policy-specialized administrations. The 'central problem' addressed by network analysis, formulated above, can be put a more specific way in the case of the EU: how do multiple public administrations—usually, together with civil society—build the capacity to solve complex problems? Doing so is mostly a matter of effective knowledge exchange—to the point where a 'useable *new* knowledge base for effective problem-solving' is created (Weber and Khademian 2008: 335). This task is 'particularly acute for networks built around wicked problems, where the differences between participants are deep and the barriers to knowledge transfer, receipt and integration are distinct' (Weber and Khademian 2008: 335). As seen in inter-service consultation within the Commission, the EU has witnessed a considerable increase over time in formalized and permanent links between different policy-specialized officials.

Against this backdrop, the Commission itself can be easily handicapped or even hamstrung by its own internal, fragmented structure. The ability of the Commission to engage effectively and defend its own position in EU policy networks depends on the capacity of its own officials to navigate 'the house' and produce unified, well-informed and fully prepared positions that have the backing of the administration as a whole. Unless Commission officials network effectively with each other, the Commission cannot expect to be a force for effective European public policies.

Previous research on networks in the Commission, according to Suvarierol (2009: 10) has 'so far has not opened this black box. Networks have remained mainly as subjects of anecdotes or circumstantial references'. Her survey of existing research leads her to claim that it is 'frequently argued that nationality forms an important basis for forming networks in and about the European Union (EU) institutions' (Suvarierol 2009: 1).[10] Accordingly, Shore (2000: 199) cites an official in DG Administration who claims:

---

[10] This claim is made in relation to (*inter alia*) Peterson (1995) and Hooghe (1999, 2001). The latter simply notes that the one characteristic that all EU actors share is a nationality and that

Yes, there is a French Mafia in the Commission. But there is also an English Mafia. You have Mafiosi everywhere, but there are different kinds of Mafiosi: there is a gay Mafia, a freemasons' Mafia, an *Opus Dei* Mafia, a Socialist and a Communist Mafia.

Shore (2000: 200) goes further to argue that '[n]etworks are ... central to understanding the way the Commission works in practice ... the "Brits", Danes and Swedes—with their anti-patronage cultures—fail to grasp the networking dynamics of the Commission's internal culture'. Others stress the importance of different kinds of network. For example, Grant (1994) and Ross (1995) both contend that Jacques Delors's hand-picked operatives— who shared the Commission President's own ideological agenda—formed a sort of 'parallel administration' in the Commission. Both academics (see Schnabel 2002) and journalists (Stares 2005) have claimed the existence of a 'Bruges mafia' within the Commission: graduates of the College of Europe that have developed relationships while studying become a privileged caste with Bruges playing the same role as the *grandes écoles* whose graduates dominate the French civil service (see Suleiman 1974).

Regardless of what are the bases for social networks within the Commission, a necessary but far from sufficient condition for the Commission to succeed is that its officials must navigate within their *own* administration to find the resources and expertise needed to do their work effectively. Logically, officials must create and maintain personal networks that link them to other officials who can offer support, guidance, and know-how to perform knowledge-intensive work. So what determines how personal networks within the Commission are constructed?

NETWORKS IN THE COMMISSION

As EUCIQ survey data presented in Figure 3.2 suggests, many Commission officials believe that networks linking officials across 'the house' are important. Similarly, much existing research concludes that the Commission operates in large part through informal networks, since hierarchies are—in practice— weak or blurred.[11] One of us, in a previous monograph on the Commission,

---

national Permanent Representations (the Brussels equivalent of embassies) may act as the 'ringleaders' of national networks in the EU (75). But it makes no claim that nationality is the most important basis for networks in the Commission.

[11] Indicative are the frequent references to '*Système D*' in Spence with Edwards (2006), which refers to the French slang term for a system that relies on 'débrouillard' (muddling through). A variant is '*Système démerder*'.

found herself resorting to use of the term 'network' no fewer than 76 times (Hooghe 2001).

The most centrally-focused study of networks in the Commission to date is that of Suvarierol (2007). Her core argument is that her findings expose the 'myth of nationality' as a determinant of networks in the Commission. The study finds, for example, that 53.7 per cent of respondents stated that 'nationality is not a shaping factor for their work' and 60.5 per cent of officials surveyed have 'a purely multinational network which does not include any official of their own nationality' (Suvarierol 2007: 82–3).[12]

The study's findings should be considered in the context of three caveats. First, the data set is generated from 82 respondents drawn from four DGs.[13] The number of cases is quite large for a study carried out by a lone researcher. But it is obviously far smaller than the data set—both from the survey and interviews—on which the present study relies.[14] Second, the subject of nationality is sublimated in Suvarierol's (2007: 65) questionnaire and not mentioned until its very end on the grounds that the Commission's 'organisational discourse . . . embraces supranationality as the norm' and '[w]ith its link to nationalism, nationality is unacceptable in the formal discourse' (Suvarierol 2007: 81). Third, the study was carried out in 2005–6: that is, in the wake of organizational reforms that made the Commission considerably more 'European'. These reforms, for example, eliminated 'national flags' on key posts (see Chapter 2) and required *cabinets* to have at least three nationalities. Studies of networks pre-reform (such as they are) might well have been undertaken in an era when nationality was more important in the Commission.

Despite these caveats, Suvarierol's study could be viewed as the state of the art in terms of our knowledge about networks in the Commission. As such, we replicated its key questions in our own survey. But the EUCIQ survey also posed the direct question (not included in Suvarierol's survey): 'In your experience, what are the most important bases for informal networks in the Commission?' Respondents were asked to choose the most important two bases[15] for networks in the Commission and rank them in importance.

---

[12] At the same time, Suvarierol (2007: 79) found that 57.3 per cent of her respondents 'said nationality mattered' as a factor in determining the membership of networks in the Commission.

[13] Because one official responded to only half of the survey questions, most calculations rely on 81 responses (Suvarierol 2007:71).

[14] To illustrate the point, the timing of Suvarierol's fieldwork—2005, when the recruitment of EU-12 officials had barely begun—meant that only two EU-12 officials (both Czech) were represented in her data set. The far larger survey carried out for the present study (see Chapter 1 for details) received valid responses from 349 EU-12 officials (including 33 Czech officials) to the question that was, for example, the basis for Figure 3.2.

[15] In fact, respondents were asked to choose the *three* most important and to rank them. However, a technical fault in the online survey meant that officials could only choose two ranked choices.

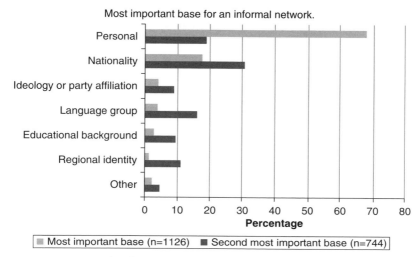

Fig. 3.3 What factors determine the composition of networks?
Note: n = 1,846.

While we should be cautious about generalization,[16] the data strongly suggest that informal networks are based significantly less on nationality, language, or party affiliation or ideology than on simple personal contact between officials in the course of their work (see Figure 3.3).[17] Party connections are relatively insignificant and the overwhelming majority of officials who chose this option—no fewer than 92 per cent who did—were officials from EU-15 member states. There is no clear evidence of, for example, the 'College of Europe/Bruges mafia' mentioned above.[18]

A separate survey question posed to administrators only (data from which we examine below) asked how officials first met other officials who now formed part of their personal network. By far the largest group reported that they met in a professional context (see Figure 3.4).

Here we might note Suvarierol's (2007: 144) finding that, by far, most Commission officials made first point of contact with the most important

---

[16] Questions that asked respondents to choose the 'most' and 'second most important' basis for personal networks yielded a considerable amount of missing data. To illustrate, the percentage of respondents who were 'unsure' (4.2) or simply did not reply (34.8) when asked to choose the most important basis for their own network adds to no less than 39 per cent (n = 720). The total for the 'second most important' basis question was 59.7 per cent (n = 1101). No other questions in the survey yielded anything close to as much missing data, so the conclusions presented in this section are more contestable than nearly all others offered in this volume.

[17] The choice 'personal contact' included the clarifying phrase '(e.g. worked in same unit or team)'.

[18] Not all those who stated 'other' specified what it comprised, but Bruges or the College of Europe were never mentioned by any respondent. Those who did indicate what it comprised cited such a broad range of bases that any additional categories based on 'other' would be underspecified.

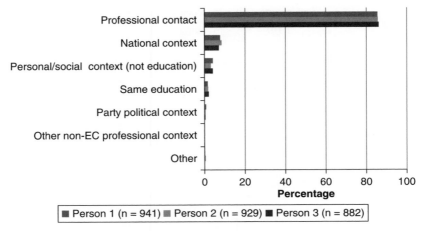

Fig. 3.4 How did officials meet members of their network?

Note: n=1,846.

members of their personal network in a 'professional/Commission-related' context. More than 90 per cent of first contacts were made in this way. Over half resulted from officials working in the same DG or unit. As such, there is strong evidence from multiple sources that what determines the membership of informal networks in the Commission is simply the experience of officials' working lives.

However, our data contain grounds for qualifying the 'myth of nationality' thesis. Nationality seems to be the second most important determinant of the membership of personal networks, and by a considerable margin over the next most important (ideology/party affiliation and language; see Figure 3.3). It is a stronger basis of network membership for some nationalities and types of official than others. The data shown in Figure 3.5 suggest that nationality is important for newer officials and generally decreases in importance as early-career officials gain experience.[19] Curiously, though, the importance of nationality is more pronounced among those who have been in the Commission for a very long time—that is more than 20 years—while language features more among the more recent arrivals.[20]

In sum, there is powerful evidence to suggest that contact with other officials in the day-to-day work of the Commission is the most powerful

---

[19] The importance of personal contact, rather than nationality or language, increases with the seniority of the respondent, albeit a weak association as shown by Cramer's V statistic (Cramer's V), which is a measure of the strength of the association (0: min; 1: max). We also resort in this chapter to the probability measure of 'p', which reflects the margin of error. As a rule of thumb, a 'p' below 0.05 is statistically significant. In the case of this question, the values are $p = 0.028$; Cramer's $V = 0.084$.

[20] For example, language was chosen as the most important determinant of network membership by 7 per cent of officials with 1–4 years of experience, as opposed to only 1 per cent with 11–19 years experience ($p = 0.001$; Cramer's $V = 0.103$).

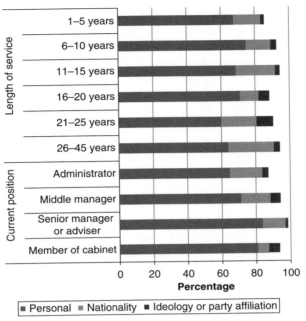

Fig. 3.5 Most important bases for informal networks by length of service and current position

Note: Valid %. n = 1,126; full sample = 1,846. 4.2% not sure, and 34.8% missing responses.

determinant of network membership. The importance of personal contact, rather than nationality or language, increases with the seniority of the respondent, although the association is somewhat weak (see Figure 3.5).[21] Our data are ambiguous about length of service and seniority since (again) very long-serving officials are more likely to report that nationality determines network membership. What is unambiguous is that while nationality is not unimportant, it is clearly less important than personal contact.

Having examined 'headline' findings from the survey's data on networks, we now shift to an examination of some of its fine grain. We confront the questions: what types of official are more likely to rely on informal networks to do their work? How fluid or static are networks? How are they used?

Who Relies on Networks?

Our findings about which officials rely most on their networks are more tentative than virtually all other findings from our study because a relatively

[21] p = 0.028; Cramer's V = 0.084.

large share of administrators (the only category of official asked) did not respond to the survey's questions that inquired about their own personal network. It is also conceivable—if unlikely—that officials may have reported that they believe networks in the Commission are important but that they themselves do not rely on their own network to navigate the house. Despite these caveats, however, we uncovered statistically significant findings about who relies on networks.

For example, EU-15 officials are far more likely to agree that the Commission must rely on informal networks than EU-12 officials (shown as 'CEE + enlargement' in Figure 3.2).[22] There are also significant differences between different accession waves. Networks are considered important especially by officials whose countries joined in 1973 (shown as 'First enlargement' in Figure 3.2).[23]

The data reveal no discernible differences between types of DGs with respect to their views on the importance of informal networks.[24] Figure 3.2 suggests (faintly) that officials in legislative DGs are more likely to think networks are important. But DGs in which at least 50 per cent of survey respondents think networks are important are a very mixed bag: they include Agriculture (AGRI), Education and Culture (EAC), Eurostat (ESTAT), Interpretation (SCIC) and the Legal Service (SJ).[25]

We also find some evidence that informal networks are viewed as more important by officials who have been in the Commission for longer periods (but are not necessarily more senior).[26] When length of service is broken down by five-year periods, a parabolic effect appears. Informal networks are considered most important by those who have been in the Commission for 16–20 years, but decreasingly so either side of this range (as shown in Figure 3.2).[27]

Who Networks with Whom?

Our study sought to generate original knowledge but also to build on existing research. As such, EUCIQ survey respondents were offered one of the same core questions offered to officials in Suvarierol's study. The intent was to allow for comparison—2005 versus 2008—by extending the 'longitude' of the prior study.

---

[22] $p = 0.043$; Cramer's V = 0.083.   [23] $p < 0.001$; Cramer's V = 0.101.

[24] $p = 0.357$.

[25] Even if we assume that the scale is a ratio scale, there is an insignificant statistical relationship with the perceived importance of informal networks between the different DG types ($p = 0.114$).

[26] $p = 0.027$; gamma = 0.126. (The gamma statistic is a measure of strength of association between two ordinal variables: 0 = minimum; 1 = maximum.)

[27] $p = 0.036$; gamma = 0.126.

Table 3.1 The 'myth of nationality' in 2005

'I would now like to focus on the persons within the European Commission you regularly turn to for information or advice for your (policy-making) work. With this, I do not necessarily mean the officials whom you have to contact due to your task description and obligations, like your boss or direct colleagues. Please take into consideration all types of contact (in person, phone, email, etc.)'.
- Only 18% of same nationality
- Only 33% speak native language
- Only 50% chance that contact person is from same region (north/south)

Note: n = 241 network contacts.
Source: Suvarierol 2007.

Table 3.1 summarises Suvarierol's data underlying her claim that it is a 'myth' that Commission officials primarily network with officials of their own nationality. Language is also, it is claimed, a non-issue for most officials. There is some evidence to sustain the view that cultural affinities between officials from the same regions of Europe—such as the Nordic or Mediterranean countries—makes them more likely to network with one another. Generally, however, Suvarierol (2007: 83) paints a portrait of a post-national, truly *European* Commission based on findings such as (for example) that more than 60 per cent of her respondents had an entirely multinational network with no other official of their own nationality.

The EUCIQ survey posed a nearly identical question to that posed by Suvarierol (see Table 3.1). The precise wording we used was: 'We would like to ask you about the people to whom you regularly turn for information or advice on *professional matters* (in person, phone, e-mail, and so on). We do *not* necessarily mean the Commission officials whom you have to contact due to your responsibilities or the regulations of the house, such as your manager or direct colleagues. *We do not wish to know who may be part of your own professional network. We wish to know about the nature of networks in the Commission generally'.*[28] Respondents were asked to think of three personal contacts, and then to answer the following set of questions about the relationship with each contact:

- 'How long have you known this person? (years);
- On which issues do you usually consult this person? [indicate more than one if you'd like]. The options given were: career issues; policy advice; procedural advice; other;
- How did you *first* meet? The options given were: professional contact; national context; party political context; other;

[28] The question was asked of administrators only, and not managers, since the survey posed a range of questions to the latter on recent administrative reforms and new management codes and tools.

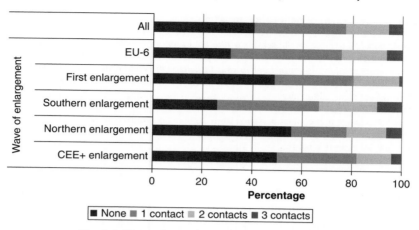

Fig. 3.6 Network members of the same nationality
Note: n = 828; 2,484 contacts.

- Gender: M or F;
- Age of this person: your age group, at least 10 years younger, at least 10 years older;
- What is this person's country of nationality?
- Do you share the same mother tongue?
- Usual language of communication? The options given were: your's, their's, third language, it varies;
- Ideological affinities? The options given were: similar to yours, quite different, don't know.'

Our results cast considerable doubt on the 'myth of nationality' thesis. They reveal a high probability that officials network with colleagues of their own nationality, with a majority—nearly 59 per cent—of those who cited three contacts and answered for all three[29] having at least one contact of the same nationality (see Figure 3.6). This figure is more than three times higher than that reported by Suvarierol and is based on a sample that is more than ten times larger.

The likelihood that officials had network contacts of their own nationality varied considerably by wave of accession. Figure 3.6 shows that same nationality contacts were considerably more likely amongst officials whose member state was part of the initial EU-6 or the Mediterranean (or 'southern') enlargements of the 1980s. More than two-thirds (around 68 per cent) of officials

---

[29] The share of cases left blank by officials asked to report on three members of their own network was 43 per cent.

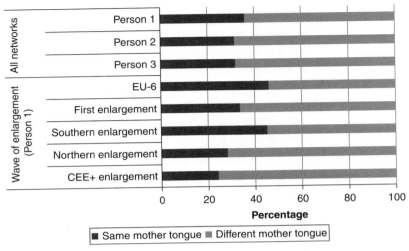

Fig. 3.7 Use of mother tongue within network

Note: Person 1, n = 941; Person 2, n = 929; and Person 3, n = 882.

from the original six reported a contact of their own nationality, while the figure for Iberian officials was more than 75 per cent. A much higher share of Spanish or Portuguese officials, along with their Bulgarian and Romanian counterparts (around 12 per cent in all cases), reported that their network consisted *exclusively* of contacts that shared their nationality.

However, the survey appeared broadly to confirm Suvarierol's findings about language (see also McDonald 1997). About one-third of officials reported that members of their network had the same mother tongue as themselves (see Figure 3.7). Sharing one's mother tongue with the first network contact shows a distinct pattern in relation to the waves of accession (and hence nationality), being more likely for officials from the EU6 and Spain and Portugal.[30]

Although the differences are not great, the first named contact is most likely to speak the same language as the respondent and the third contact least likely. However, it appears unusual for officials to communicate with their contacts in the latter's mother tongue. Instead, most use a third language. The norm is for officials to use the same language all the time with individual network contacts (even if different languages are used with different contacts; see Figure 3.8).

There are distinct differences between nationalities as to which language they speak with their network contacts, as shown for 'Person 1' (see Figure 3.8).[31] Leaving aside a sample of two Luxembourgers, the officials most likely to speak their own language are, in descending order, the French,

[30] p = 0.001; Cramer's V = 0.132.   [31] p < 0.001; Cramer's V = 0.350.

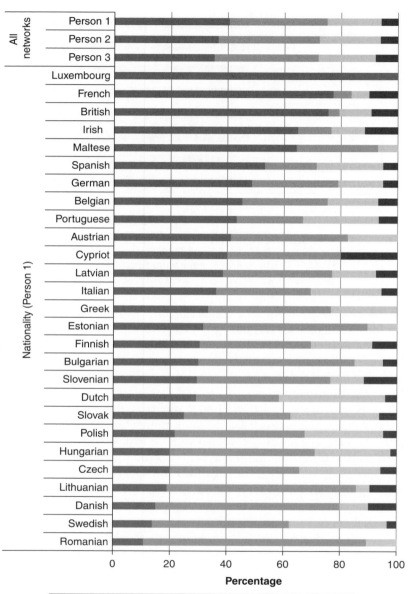

Fig. 3.8 Use of language within network

Note: Person 1, n = 941; Person 2, n = 929; and Person 3, n = 882.

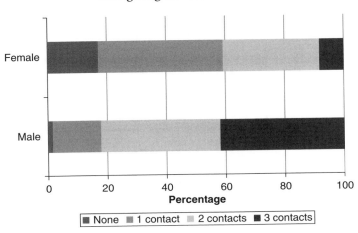

Fig. 3.9 Network members of the same gender

Note: n = 828; 2,484 contacts.

British, Irish, Maltese and Spanish. It is interesting to note that French officials, who tend to bemoan the declining use of their language, appear able to work on the basis of the longstanding injunction that 'the language of the Commission is French' (quoted in McDonald 1997: 58). Meanwhile, those more likely to speak in a third language are from the smaller EU-12 countries, which have quite distinctive languages, or from the Nordic states.

The question of whether officials shared a similar ideology to their network contacts appeared to encounter some considerable degree of reticence among EUCIQ survey respondents. More than one-third were not sure or did not wish to say whether they held similar ideological views to their network contacts. For those who did respond, around three-quarters believed they had similar ideological viewpoints.

The survey data suggest a strong tendency for network contacts to be male, both for male and female respondents (see Figure 3.9).[32] Across all three contacts, around two-thirds of network contacts were male, with men significantly more likely to be an official's first contact. When shown these results, a very senior Commission official summed up by saying, 'so men talk to men and women talk to anyone'.[33]

Yet, there is evidence of an increasing feminization of networks (see Figure 3.10). This pattern advanced with the northern enlargements of 1973 and 1994, but not with the southern or eastern enlargements.[34] A similar

[32] p < 0.001; CV = 0.490.
[33] Non-EUCIQ interview conducted by one of the authors, 8 July 2009.
[34] p = 0.012; Cramer's V = 0.148.

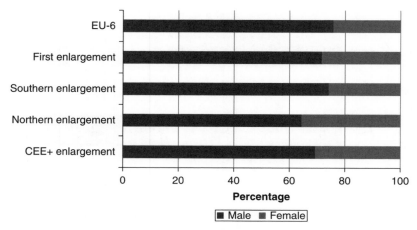

Fig. 3.10 Gender of first network contact by accession wave

Note: n = 941.

relationship is found in relation to shorter length of service: relatively newer recruits were more likely to network with female officials. The survey found little variation between network contacts in terms of relative age, with clear majorities of all contacts in the same age group, and most of the others at least 10 years older (see Figure 3.11).

The data also suggest that personal networks link younger officials with older and more senior ones who may act as mentors. As might be expected, younger officials were more likely to consult older contacts, but also—surprisingly and (to a somewhat lesser extent)—vice versa: that is, older officials were more likely to have younger officials in their network[35] (see Figure 3.11). Most officials' network contacts were senior to the officials themselves (see Figure 3.12).

Whether an official's network contacts tended to be more senior or junior in grade was very much determined by age. Figure 3.12 shows that younger officials were more likely to have network contacts who were senior to themselves, and, conversely, the contacts of older officials were more likely to be in lower grades.[36] Here, it bears recalling that all respondents were administrators, and only one-third were aged 46 or older. However, this result is predictable: until 2002 the Commission generally only recruited new officials aged under 45 (the age limit was nullified by the European Ombudsman). Moreover, not all older administrators can be considered 'time-servers' who have failed to be promoted to a management post: nearly one-third of

[35] p < 0.001; Cramer's V = 0.371.   [36] p < 0.001; Cramer's V = 0.178.

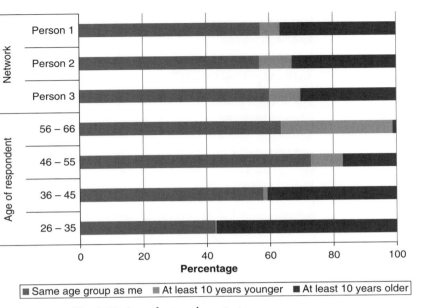

Fig. 3.11 Age of network contacts

Note: Person 1, n = 941; Person 2, n = 929; and Person 3, n = 882.

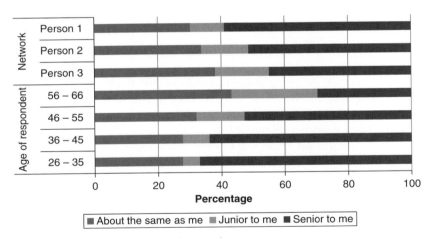

Fig. 3.12 Grade of network contacts

Note: Person 1, n = 941; Person 2, n = 929; and Person 3, n = 882.

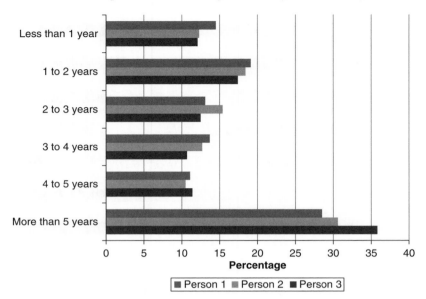

Fig. 3.13 Length of time in network

Note: Person 1, n = 941; Person 2, n = 929; and Person 3, n = 882.

respondents to this question aged 46 plus were from EU-12 states who, by definition, had served in the Commission for five years or fewer in 2008.

How Fluid are Networks and How are They Used?

The EUCIQ survey yielded ambiguous results on the fluidity of networks. On one hand, over one quarter of contacts had been in officials' networks for more than five years. On the other, between 15 and 20 per cent had been contacts for only one to two years (see Figure 3.13).

Network contacts are most commonly consulted for procedural advice, followed by policy advice, and finally career issues. The last of these tends to be discussed with (only) one network contact. Very few officials consult their network contacts about personal issues (see Figure 3.14). Using officials' first network contacts as an exemplar (see Figure 3.15), younger officials are more likely to consult their network contacts for careers advice,[37] which is also reflected in length of service.[38] There is little variation between DGs, besides some (weak) evidence that officials working in external DGs are more likely and those in internal DGs less likely to seek policy advice from members of their networks.[39]

---

[37] p = 0.013; Cramer's V = 0.101.   [38] p = 0.014; Cramer's V = 0.100.

[39] Around 60 per cent of officials in external DGs consulted their first network contact for policy advice, compared with around 38 per cent of officials in internal DGs; p = 0.015; Cramer's V = 0.105.

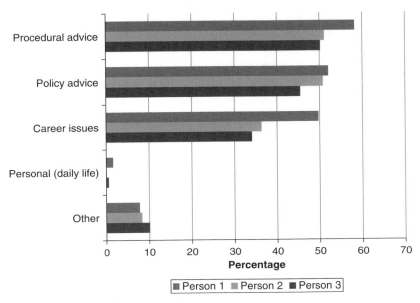

Fig. 3.14 Consultation issues

Note: Person 1, n = 941; Person 2, n = 929; and Person 3, n = 882.

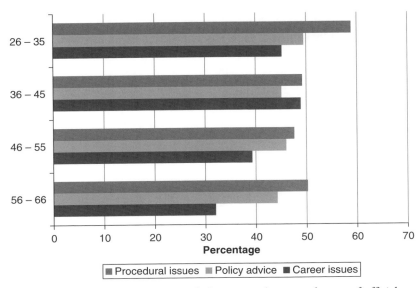

Fig. 3.15 Consultation issues with first network contact by age of official

Note: Person 1, n = 941.

In sum, most officials appear to have longstanding network contacts, but there is also evidence of considerable fluidity. Procedural advice is what respondents seek most often from their network contacts, although policy advice runs a close second. Many Commission officials have one 'go to' network contact for career advice. Younger officials tend to network with older and more senior officials. Generally, the survey uncovers genuinely new findings, and ones that are more substantiated than those of previous studies, about informal networks in the Commission. But how do we *explain* them?

EXPLAINING NETWORKS IN THE COMMISSION

The post-survey interviews with managers[40] offered us the chance to try to explain why the survey found what it did about internal networks in the Commission. In this case, we used mixed methods in the pursuit of complementarity: that is, to try to explain what the survey found and enhance our understanding of the results. Our sample for the interviews was limited in size—119 managers—and relatively large shares of interviewees did not offer clear answers to our questions about networks.

Managers were asked whether they were surprised that political party affiliation was rarely chosen by survey respondents as the most important basis for determining network membership. An impressive majority of interviewees—around two-thirds—were *not* surprised. Only a few were.[41]

Interviewees were then asked whether the importance of party political affiliation had increased or diminished over time. A large share—more than half—of managers gave no clear answer. But a majority that did indicated that party affiliation had either decreased (17 per cent) in importance or remained the same (25 per cent). Almost none thought it had increased in importance.[42]

---

[40] Questions about informal networks in the Commission were not put to *cabinet* members because it was felt that the (very limited) time available for interviews was better spent on issues directly related to the work and role of *cabinets*.

[41] The totals were 36 yes ('I am surprised'), 80 no, and 3 don't know/no response/difficult to interpret. In fact, 'ideology or party affiliation' was chosen more often as a basis for networks than 'education' or 'regional identity'. But the gap between these three options was very marginal and much larger shares of respondents chose 'personal', 'nationality', or 'language group' (see Figure 3.3). The very small share of survey respondents who reported first meeting their network contacts in a 'political party' context is also worth noting (see Figure 3.4).

[42] Next, managers were asked whether the finding that party political affiliation was chosen as an important basis for informal networks almost exclusively by long-serving EU-15 officials matched their own experience. Again, a majority of managers (56 per cent) did not give an unambiguous answer. Those who did were split, with a slightly larger share (24 per cent) saying it did *not* correspond with their own experience.

The interviews with managers also offered a test of the 'myth of nationality' thesis. Managers were told (erroneously[43]) that around half of all survey respondents indicated that nationality was an important determinant of network membership, and were asked if this result was surprising. A large share—more than half—replied that it was unsurprising.[44] When asked whether nationality as a determinant of network membership had changed over time, a large share (again) of managers offered no clear answer. But of those that did (about a third of all interviewees), far more indicated that nationality had decreased in importance or stayed the same over time.[45]

Interviewees were also presented with the finding that nationality was a less important determinant of the membership of networks for more senior officials. Asked whether they found this finding 'odd', a (slim) majority of interviewees responded unambiguously. Of those that did, far more (44 per cent) found this result to be 'about right' than found it 'odd' (only 15 per cent).

Finally, managers were asked whether the very high share of officials who indicated that personal contact, such as working in the same unit, was the most important basis for informal networks was higher or lower than might be expected. This time, a majority of interviewees gave a clear answer. And a clear majority who did expected this result.[46]

Thus, the interview data suggest that most managers believe that party affiliation is relatively unimportant as a bond between officials in the Commission. More seem to believe that it has decreased than increased in importance over time. One Head of Unit offered the following comment:

> Am I here to pursue the agenda of one political party? That's clearly not relevant. Am I here to focus on . . . the president's agenda? Yes, then that is very high on my priorities list. And does the president have political convictions? Does he belong to a political party? Yes, he does. But this is not my agenda. This is my political master's agenda (interview 36).

Traditionally, party affiliation has played an important role in determining selection and job prospects in some national administrations, especially in continental Europe.[47] The Commission seems to be an outlier in this respect.

---

[43] As may be seen from Figure 3.3, far fewer than half—in fact, only around a quarter—of survey respondents chose 'nationality' as an important basis for personal networks. The error arose from a failure to notice that, more accurately, around half as many respondents chose 'nationality' as 'personal'. The result is that our test of the 'myth of nationality' thesis in this case is less robust than it should be.

[44] The totals were 19 yes, 60 no, and 40 don't know/no response/difficult to interpret.

[45] Asked if the importance of nationality as a basis for network membership had changed over time, around 20 per cent thought it had decreased in importance, 13 per cent thought it had stayed the same, and only 3 per cent thought it had increased in importance.

[46] A total of 13 expected a higher figure, 19 lower, 42 about the same, and 45 gave no clear response.

[47] The Commission also may be contrasted with the (highly partisan) European Parliament administration. See, for example, Brand (2007).

Our test of the 'myth of nationality' thesis via interviews with managers yields the interesting result that a majority would have been unsurprised if the survey had yielded a much higher rate of choice of 'nationality' as a basis for informal networks than it actually did. There is some evidence that managers believe that nationality has declined in importance over time. And many find it natural that nationality is a less important basis for the membership of the networks of more senior officials. Finally, we find more evidence that contact in day-to-day work life determines the membership of most officials' networks.

CONCLUSION

Much of our evidence about informal networks in the Commission is tentative. A good 'chunk' of it is limited to administrators: the way that networks are used and composed may well be different for managers or *cabinet* members. Our knowledge of networks as social structures remains primitive more generally. The same is the case when it comes to networks in EU governance. Suvarierol (2007: 10) is not wrong to claim that much existing work on Brussels policy networks has been based on 'anecdotes or circumstantial references'.

Nevertheless, our findings are derived from a data set that is much larger than those of past studies. EUCIQ thus offers genuinely new knowledge about informal networks in the Commission. To be clear, we have focused on only one kind of network in one EU institution. There is far more research to be done, particularly on the relationship between the strength or effectiveness of informal networks in the Commission and its ability to participate effectively in policy networks that link it to other EU institutions and civil society.

The hypothesis that many Commission officials rely on informal networks to do its work seems validated by our evidence. One official with twenty-five years of service in the Commission put it simply: 'networks in the Commission are very important. You are handicapped without one'.[48] It also appears that informal networks are used by officials to seek procedural advice more often than any other kind of advice. These findings may be viewed as unsurprising given the Commission's onerous rules of procedure and administrative code. Putting the Commission in comparative perspective, a senior policy adviser in the Clinton administration expresses a mainstream view:

As the economy has become global, the need for global governance measures has increased. But international bureaucracies have proved even less attractive to states than their internal, domestic bureaucracies. The bureaucracies of the UN

---

[48] Non-EUCIQ interview conducted by one of the authors, 28 August 2009.

and the *emerging EU bureaucracy in Brussels* are rife with 'bugs' in their operating systems and burdened with suspicion about their degree of accountability' (Kamarck 2007: 100; emphasis added).

In short, informal networks may be important because they allow officials to do their jobs despite the 'bugs' in the Commission's 'operating systems', or the EU's more generally.

Here, it is worth mentioning an issue that increasingly preoccupies the study of networks, and on which our data set is effectively silent: that is, how networks are managed. In his treatment of the 'transformation' of governance in the twenty-first century, Kettl (2002: 168) insists that public managers increasingly 'need to harness their hierarchies to manage . . . networks, often side by side with traditional programs that continue to be managed through authority-driven structures . . . *Public managers need to rely more on interpersonal and interorganizational processes as complements to—and sometimes substitutes for—authority*' (emphasis in original).

This point applies both to the Commission and to the EU more generally. If the EU really is 'replete with policy networks', then someone has to manage them. Concern for the management of EU policy networks is reflected in Pollitt and Bouckaert's (2004: 235) claim that while the Commission is the prime candidate to act as their manager, it is also internally very fragmented and in a weak position to manage cross-sectoral networks. They lament that its officials are not trained in techniques such as network audits or management (Pollitt and Bouckaert 2004: 270). One of the prime weaknesses of EU governance may well be that its institutional system generally, and the Commission specifically, lacks capacity for network management (see Metcalfe 2000, 2004; Jordan and Schout 2006). Future research needs to focus on the Commission's status in wider, inter-institutional networks and how it might step up to the plate to manage them, perhaps drawing on some of the business studies research that we have mentioned.

Where EUCIQ *has* shed new light is on which types of officials think networks are important and thus, we may infer, most often rely on them. Most officials rely more on their networks the longer they serve (at least until they near retirement). The finding that officials who have been in the Commission for 16–20 years consider informal networks important, but that officials on either side of this range find them less important, is intriguing. One possible explanation, which merits further investigation, is that officials rely on their own personal networks at the peak of their working life in the Commission. After that, they gradually become less 'plugged in', including to their own personal contacts.

Among our most interesting findings are that EU-15 officials are more likely to believe that the Commission must rely on informal networks, and that considerably more think ideology or party political affiliation is an

102 *The European Commission of the Twenty-First Century*

important basis for their membership. One hypothesis—which we explore in Chapter 9—is that the 2004 and 2007 enlargements have, on balance, both made informal networks less important and party or ideology less a determinant of their memberships. The most common assumption about networks in the existing literature is that *trust* is the main determinant of the cohesiveness of networks. Has enlargement brought a decline in trust within the Commission? The present study cannot answer this question. Future studies might well seek to do so.

The present study *can*, however, confront the 'myth of nationality' thesis. Our evidence suggests that nationality is by no means an unimportant basis for network membership, and that it is more important for some nationalities than for others. Only slightly more than one-third of survey respondents reported having no network contacts who shared their nationality. Whether that is a lot or a little depends on one's expectations, but it is clearly not consistent with nationality being a myth. The older officials are, the more is nationality reported as a determinant of the membership of personal networks. One plausible explanation for this finding is that nationality determined membership of networks more in the past than it does now in the Commission. And it *is* striking that only about 5 per cent of officials have networks composed exclusively of their fellow nationals.

We find more evidence that the Commission is not fragmented along linguistic lines than that it is 'post-national', although even here there is evidence that certain nationals—the French and British amongst them—mostly use their mother tongue in their work. Generally, our evidence suggests that the Commission is becoming more post-national over time. There is, for example, support for the hypothesis that nationality is a more important determinant of personal networks for officials at the beginning and end of their careers. But we would struggle to agree that nationality does not matter as a basis for informal Commission networks, or that it is a 'myth'.

At the same time, our data strongly suggest that the constitution of Commission officials' networks is determined mostly by their experience of working in the administration, as opposed to other sources of affinity. In line with previous studies, respondents first met their network contacts almost exclusively in a professional context. Very few officials use their networks for exchanges on personal matters. The portrait that emerges is a Commission that is business-like and focused on its work. Evidence to suggest that beliefs or ideology are an important basis for network membership is thin. But ideology and what Commission officials believe matter in other ways. We seek to show how in Chapter 4.

4

What Officials Believe

Over the past few decades the European Union has been transformed from a system for interstate collaboration to a polity (Hix 1994; Caporaso 1996; Marks et al. 1996; Hooghe and Marks 2009) in which Commission officials are active players. They initiate and implement EU decisions across a broad swathe of policies, frame the European interest, and represent the European Union in international forums. Their attitudes and beliefs help shape Europe's future. This chapter describes their views on the governance, ideological direction, and policy scope of the European Union.

There is considerable variation among Commission officials about how the balance of power between the Commission, member states, and European Parliament should look. Differences range from supranationalism and state-centrism to institutional pragmatism. We begin by outlining these conceptions, show their relative strength in the Commission, and then examine to what extent territorial and functional factors help us understand variations in EU governance beliefs. In the next sections, we document ideological diversity among Commission officials and explore whether DGs have indeed recognizable partisan make-ups. In the final section, we examine which policies, Commission officials desire to centralize or decentralize, and how intensely, and we take up the question whether bureaucratic politics motivates Commission officials' beliefs on Europe's policy agenda.

COMMISSION OFFICIALS AND EU GOVERNANCE

What form of EU governance is favoured by Commission officials? What, in their view, is the appropriate balance of power among the Commission, member states, and European Parliament? There are several viable options:

- an intergovernmental or state-centric Union which conceives the Commission as an agent under close member state supervision; that is, member states steer the course of European integration (Moravcsik 1998);

- a proto-federal or supranational European Union in which the Commission is the primary authority. This vision was theorized by early neo-functionalists (Lindberg and Scheingold 1970). Later work refined the argument by highlighting the role of the European Court of Justice as the engine of integration and downplayed the teleology associated with the original formulations (Sandholtz and Stone Sweet 1998);

- a multilevel polity in which the Commission and the member states are interlocking and complementary institutions (Marks et al. 1996). This option echoes Ernst Haas, who observed in *The Uniting of Europe* that the European Coal and Steel Community constituted 'a hybrid in which neither the federal nor the intergovernmental tendency has clearly triumphed' (Haas 1958: 526–7). He described it as a fundamental departure from traditional conceptions of government.

State-centrism has broad support amongst Europe's publics and national elites; and since national loyalties and interests may influence Commission officials' beliefs, some of these views are likely to carry over into the Commission. The supranational and multilevel options are in line with the general expectation that Commission officials favour strong European Union institutions. This is consistent with utility maximization, according to which bureaucrats are bureau-maximizing (Pollack 2003). It also chimes well with an organizational understanding that expects the views of Commission officials to be shaped by organizational location (Egeberg 2001). And it corresponds with the observation that, given a choice, few individuals pursue careers in an organization with antithetical values.

Supporters of a federal Union or a multilevel polity find common ground in their defence of the Treaty rules that invest the Commission with the monopoly of legislative initiative and the member states (or the Council of Ministers) with the power to pass legislation. Haas drew attention to this institutional innovation in the ECSC Treaty, which became later known as the Community method (Weiler 1991; Wallace 2000; Dehousse 2011).

The Community method has ambiguous constitutional implications. Commission President Walter Hallstein believed that it required federalism (Hallstein 1963: 168). But Haas thought that the Community method was a stable equilibrium, and apparently so does the Commission: 'The Community method . . . provides a means to arbitrate between different interests by passing them through two successive filters: the general interest at the level of the Commission; and democratic representation, European and national, at the level of the Council and European Parliament, together the Union's legislature' (Commission 2001: 8). When stripped of its federal ambition, the Community method side-steps institutional power struggles by regulating

Table 4.1 EU governance views

	Some people want the College of Commissioners to become the government of Europe.	Some argue that member states—not the Commission or European Parliament—should be the central players in the European Union.
Strongly agree	7.4	1.1
Agree	29.9	7.1
Neither agree nor disagree	16.1	11.8
Disagree	26.2	40.7
Strongly disagree	13.5	34.3
Not sure/missing	6.9	4.9

Note: Percentages; n = 1,846.

the separate roles of Commission and member states in policy-making, and that is an attractive strategy for defenders of the Commission in a time of resurgent nationalism (Hooghe 2012). So the method has been linked with federalism and with multilevel governance. The Community method party is diverse indeed—a theme we explore in Chapter 5.

Where do officials stand on these three options? Table 4.1 provides the distribution of responses on two statements concerning power relations between the Commission and member states. There is considerable ambivalence. The first statement expresses the supranational view that 'the College of Commissioners should become the government of Europe'. As many Commission officials disagree as agree with the statement, and 16 per cent sit on the fence. The state-centric statement that 'member states—not the Commission or European Parliament—should be the central players in the European Union' produces a more uniform picture: 75 per cent oppose, though 20 per cent would not object.

Figure 4.1 typologizes Commission officials on EU governance based on their responses to these statements. Supranationalists agree that the College of Commissioners should be the government of Europe and disagree that member states should remain the central pillars, while state-centrists disagree with the former and agree with the latter. But some officials—institutional pragmatists—believe that *neither* the College of Commissioners *nor* the member states should be the kernel of European government. From the survey, 13.3 per cent of Commission officials can be classified as state-centrists, 36.6 per cent as supranationalists, and 29.1 per cent as institutional pragmatists. One out of five officials cannot be placed into any of these categories.

Table 4.2 breaks these percentages down by rank, gender, and EU-12 vs EU-15. The strongest difference runs along gender lines. Women are much less likely to be supranationalists. Interestingly, this echoes the finding from

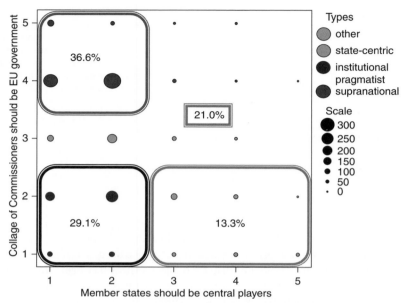

Fig. 4.1 EU governance options and types of Commission officials

Note: n = 1,698. Five-point scales ranging from 1=strongly disagree; 2=disagree; 3=neither disagree nor agree; 4=agree; 5= strongly agree.

Table 4.2 EU governance options by seniority, gender, and enlargement

	Commission (all)	Top officials	Rank and file	Men	Women	EU-15 officials	EU-12 officials
Supranationalists	36.6	39.5*	36.1*	40.4**	29.8**	38.8**	30.4**
State-centrists	13.3	9.2*	13.5*	12.0*	15.8*	12.8	14.7
Institutional pragmatists	29.1	29.4	28.7	27.2*	32.6*	28.9	29.7
Other	21.0	21.8	21.7	20.4	21.8	19.5*	25.2*
N	1,692	119	1,498	1,068	614	1,278	401

Note: Percentages. * indicates that differences of means is significant at 0.05 level and ** at 0.01 level between subgroups, e.g. men are significantly more likely to be supranationalists than women, and EU-15 officials are more likely to be supranationalists than EU-12.

public opinion studies that women are slightly more reluctant than men to embrace European integration (Gelleny and Anderson 2000; Nelsen and Guth 2000). Some have explained this in terms of economic interest: women are more vulnerable to economic competition and might be wary of the single market. Others emphasize cultural or even biological differences: women are compassionate and less competitive and are more circumspect about power battles. This might explain why women are predisposed to institutional pragmatism.

EU-12 officials are less likely to be supranationalist and more likely not to fall in any of these categories, although these differences wash out once we exert controls (see below). An official's nationality, DG location, self-selection, and gender tell a more convincing story.

There is much that unites supranationalists, state-centrists, and institutional pragmatists. They tend to agree that a) the Commission should not focus on managing existing policies; b) posts in the Commission should not be distributed to achieve geographical balance; c) officials should put loyalty to the Commission over DG loyalty. Table 4.3 shows that for each of the six statements, absolute majorities in three categories endorse the same direction. But three differences stand out.

First, state-centrists are least opposed to the Commission focusing more on management (statement 1). This fits the expectation that state-centrists are more willing to 'normalize' the Commission in the mould of a standard bureaucracy. Second, state-centrists are most sceptical and supranationalists least sceptical (statement 3). This is surprising. The Commission's monopoly of initiative is essential to its special role in the European Union's system of

Table 4.3 Attitudes by EU governance type

	Percentage who agree strongly or tend to agree		
	Supranationalists	Institutional pragmatists	State centrists
Commission as Manager vs Commission as Initiator			
1. The Commission should primarily focus on managing existing policies rather than developing new ones.	10.0	12.0	24.8
2. The more member states the EU has, the more important is the Commission's role as policy initiator.	65.6	69.0	63.1
3. The Commission should share its sole right of initiative with the European Parliament.	37.6	32.1	29.8
Accommodate national interests vs Independent of national interest			
4. Some argue that posts in the Commission should be distributed on the basis of geographical balance.	34.2	37.1	41.3
5. It is more important to have one Commissioner per member state than to have a smaller and more efficient College.	20.2	32.0	36.8
Loyalty to DG vs Loyalty to Commission			
6. Commission officials work for their DG first, then for the Commission.	29.2	29.8	42.0

Note: Percentage of respondents agreeing strongly or tending to agree with the statement (as opposed to disagreeing strongly or tending to disagree or neither agreeing nor disagreeing).

multilevel governance, and one would expect supranationalists to be keen to defend it. Perhaps the reason is that supranationalists desire the Commission to be the sole government, accountable to a democratic parliament, while state-centrists (and institutional pragmatists) are content with the Commission's status as a bureaucracy—albeit with special powers. Third, state-centrists and institutional pragmatists are much less concerned about accommodating national interests, be this through 'geographical balancing' or by tolerating one Commissioner per member state, than supranationalists, who are strongly opposed (statements 4 and 5).

Explaining beliefs on EU governance

What makes someone a supranationalist, state-centrist, or institutional pragmatist? Past research suggests that territorial and functional (or professional) loyalties and interests shape EU governance views among European elites (Egeberg 2001; Hooghe 2001, 2005; Beyers 2005; Bauer 2008; Hooghe 2012). Our analysis provides strong support for these conjectures, but we also find that other factors, in particular the reason for joining the Commission (motivation) and gender, help explain EU governance views.

Figure 4.2 suggests there are considerable differences among nationalities in the distribution of supranationalists, institutional pragmatists and state-centrists. Belgians and Italians are heavily over-represented among supranationalists; state-centrists come disproportionately from Britain, Slovakia and Sweden; and institutional pragmatists from Portugal, Slovenia and the Netherlands. Four national characteristics in particular predispose nationalities to state-centrism, supranationalism, or institutional pragmatism:

- *Multilevel governance.* Supranationalists and institutional pragmatists come disproportionately from countries with extensive decentralization, and state-centrists come disproportionately from unitary countries.[1]

- *Religion and state building.* State-centrists come disproportionately from protestant countries; supranationalists and institutional pragmatists from Catholic countries.[2] There is congruence here with the finding in

---

[1] Operationalized as the average score on the regional authority index for each member state over ten years (1995–2006), a measure of the extent of self rule and shared rule for each intermediate tier of regional government. *Source*: RAI dataset by Hooghe et al. (2010), accessible at <http://www.unc.edu/~hooghe>. The difference is significant at the 0.001 level between state-centrists and supranationalists; institutional pragmatists rank in between.

[2] Operationalized as the percentage of Protestant population for each member state in 2008, standardized around the mean. *Source*: US State Department's *International Religious Freedom Report 2008* (accessible at <http://www.state.gov/g/drl/rls/irf>). Difference of means between state-centrists on the one hand and institutional pragmatists and supranationalists on the other is significant at the 0.001 level.

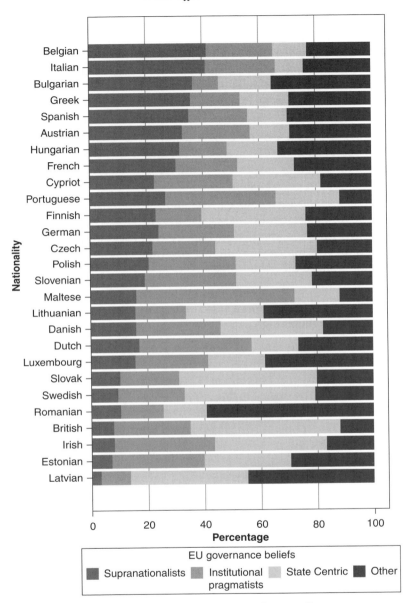

Fig. 4.2 EU governance types and nationality

European public opinion research that support for supranationalism tends to be strongest in Catholic societies (Nelsen et al. 2001; Madeley 2008; Boomgaarden and Freire 2009). Stein Rokkan emphasized how religious strife split Europe into territories that rejected Rome and those that embraced it. Protestant state churches became central instruments for nation builders in Northern and Central Europe, whereas the Catholic Church remained supranational (Rokkan and Urwin 1983).

- *Country size.* State-centrists come disproportionately from large countries; supranationalists from smaller countries. This is consistent with the expectation that the smaller the country, the greater the benefits of large-scale European government.

- *Governance efficacy.* State-centrists and institutional pragmatists come disproportionately from countries with effective governance; supranationalists from less effective governance countries. Substituting a federal European government for national government is attractive if the latter cannot produce the public goods.[3]

Attitudes differ also systematically across Directorates-General (DGs), but the differences are not as pronounced as for nationality. One finding and one non-finding deserve highlighting:

- *Technical expertise DGs.* Institutional pragmatists work disproportionately in DGs with technical content; state-centrists and supranationalists in DGs with political content. Where shared technical know-how is a basis for effective policy-making, institutional power battles are irrelevant. Institutional pragmatists are over-represented in DGs such as Fisheries, Environment, Development, or Information Society. Our data do not enable us to tease out whether this is because institutional pragmatists self-select (or are recruited) for technical DGs, or because the policy environment socializes and incentivizes people who work there.

- *DGs with strong legal competence.* DGs that exercise the Commission's monopoly on initiating legislation are *not* home to a disproportionately large number of supranationalists, and DGs with extensive routinized member state involvement do *not* harbour more state-centrists. We tested these propositions in terms of socialization as well as utility. To the extent

[3] Government effectiveness is a measure developed by the Worldwide Governance Indicators project of the World Bank. These aggregate indicators are based on hundreds of variables measuring various dimensions of governance, taken from 35 data sources provided by 33 different organizations. The data reflect the views on governance of public sector, private sector and NGO experts, public opinion and firm surveys. *Source*: <http://info.worldbank.org/governance/wgi/index.asp>. Differences between state-centrists and institutional pragmatists on the one hand and supranationalists on the other are significant at the 0.001 level.

that DG experience shapes attitudes, one would have expected otherwise. However, the data do not bear this out.

Territorial loyalty and DG experience explain the bulk of the variance in EU governance views, but three additional factors merit mention.

- *National administration.* Commission officials who worked in a national administration or as a diplomat prior to joining the Commission are significantly more likely to be state-centrist and less likely to be supranationalist. This is consistent with earlier work (Hooghe 2001), and it conforms to the expectation that former national bureaucrats export state-centred views acquired at home to their new job.

- *Motivation for joining the Commission.* Respondents who joined because of a commitment to Europe are more likely to be supranationalists or institutional pragmatists, and less likely to be state-centrists. Commitment to Europe is the most common motivation—72 per cent mention it, but only 57 per cent of state-centrists do so against 80 per cent of supranationalists and 69 per cent of institutional pragmatists. Twenty-three per cent mention commitment to a policy supranationalists are under-represented, while and institutional pragmatists over-represented among them. Interestingly, institutional pragmatists are also over-represented among those who were asked to apply, and among those who say they joined because they like to work in an international environment, or because of personal or family reasons—reasons noticeable for being non-committal on the institutional power balance between Commission and member states.[4]

- *Gender.* As indicated above, women are significantly more likely to be institutional pragmatists or state-centrists, and less likely to be supranationalists. The EU governance gender gap is most pronounced in the EU-15.

These patterns are robust in multivariate analysis.[5] National background is powerful in distinguishing state-centrists from supranationalists, while DG location helps explain who are the institutional pragmatists. State-centrists are most likely to come from countries with limited multilevel governance, countries with larger populations, and from Protestant countries. Supranationalists come from countries with multilevel governance, smaller countries, countries with less governance effectiveness, and non-Protestant countries. State-centrists and supranationalists are thus mirror images. Institutional pragmatists stand apart from both groups—not so much in terms of where they come from, but on account of their professional profile: they tend to work in policy

---

[4] These last three differences are not statistically significant because of the small number of officials involved.

[5] See Hooghe (2012) for a detailed analysis.

DGs with high technical content where shared technical knowledge reduces institutional power struggles.[6] Their motivational core is consistent. They came to Brussels for primarily apolitical reasons: to work on a policy problem they care about, to be in an international environment, or because family or circumstance brought them there.

Beliefs about the future

In separate interviews with senior managers and heads of unit, we presented respondents with three conceptions of the European Commission's role in EU governance:

- the Commission as policy initiator and guardian of the treaties;
- the Commission as an administration serving the Council and the Parliament;
- the Commission as the government of Europe.

These conceptions are not directly comparable to the governance types outlined above, but there are affinities. The first option describes the Community method, the second option is consistent with state-centrism or intergovernmentalism, and the third comes closest to Hallstein's federal conception.

We asked which of these three conceptions of the Commission do respondents prefer, and which of these will the Commission be closest to ten years from now. Figure 4.3 reveals a sharp distinction between desires and expectations. Eighty-one per cent prefer the Community method, but only 43 per cent believe it will survive beyond ten years. Eight per cent support the federal conception, but only 2.5 per cent see it as the Commission's future. The sharpest contrast is on the Commission as administration: just 1 per cent support this, but 21 per cent expect it to be the Commission's future.[7] There is a grim realization among senior officials that the role of the Commission is changing in an undesirable direction and one over which they have little control.

---

[6] Dichotomous variable taking on the value of 1 if a respondent works in a policy DG that demands above average technical expertise, i.e. Agriculture, Development, Environment, EuropeAid, Fisheries, Information Society and Media, Internal Market, Joint Research Centre, Taxation and Customs Union. Differences between institutional pragmatists and state-centrists are significant at the 0.05 level and at the 0.10 level with supranationalists.

[7] A large number of interviewees did not respond to the second question. When these missing values are excluded the numbers change to 56 per cent (Community method), 27.5 per cent (administration), and 3.3 per cent (government).

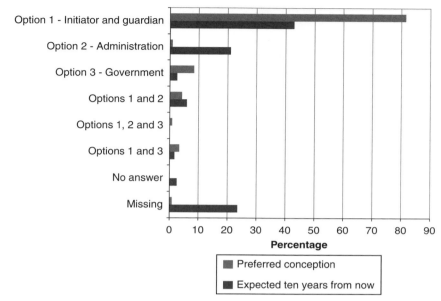

Fig. 4.3 Preferences and expectations about the Commission's role
Source: Face-to-face interviews with heads of unit and senior managers (n = 119).

COMMISSION OFFICIALS AND POLITICS

Scholars, politicians, and media commentators attribute ideological bias to Commission bureaucrats, although there is little agreement on the direction of this bias. A strand of the political economy literature understands the European Union as an agent of big capital (van Apeldoorn et al. 2009). This is consistent with the purported bias of the Rome Treaty in favour of market integration. Ironically, many politicians and political pundits blame the European Commission for exactly the reverse. In 1988, British Prime Minister Margaret Thatcher famously accused the Delors Commission of plotting socialism through the back door. Vaclav Klaus, the Czech president, contemptuously describes the Commission as socialist. We therefore venture into highly charged political terrain when we poll Commission officials on their economic and social-cultural philosophy:

- 'People often think of themselves in terms of their personal philosophical stance on economic issues. Some favour an active role for government on economic policy questions. Others look primarily to markets. Where would you place yourself in terms of economic philosophy?' ranging from 0 (a greater role for government) over 5 (centrist) to 10 (greater role for markets).

Table 4.4 Ideology by seniority, gender, and enlargement

	Commission (all)	Top officials	Rank and file	Men	Women	EU-15	EU-12	Political Parties EU-15	Political Parties EU-12
Economic left/right dimension									
Mean	5.47	5.45	5.47	5.48	5.44	5.19**	6.27**	5.10	4.99
Median	5.00	6.00	5.00	5.00	5.00	5.00	7.00	5.00	4.70
St.Dev.	1.98	2.13	1.97	2.02	1.92	1.93	1.91	2.07	2.10
N	1,676	122	1,555	1,060	616	1,248	428	114	73
Social-cultural dimension									
Mean	3.68	3.51	3.69	3.72	3.61	3.53**	4.13**	5.66	5.08
Median	3.00	3.00	3.00	3.00	3.00	3.00	3.00	5.75	5.00
St.Dev.	2.49	2.45	2.50	2.45	2.57	2.37	2.77	2.00	2.15
N	1,676	122	1,555	1,060	610	1,248	428	114	73

Note: ** indicates that differences of means are significant between subgroups at p < .01. EU-12 political parties are to the economic left of EU-12 Commission officials and the difference is statistically significant; officials of either part of Europe are significantly more socially liberal than are political parties.
Top officials = senior managers.
Rank and file includes administrators other than senior managers.

- 'People often think of themselves in terms of their personal philosophical stance on social and cultural issues. Many people who consider themselves to be liberal tend to favour expanded personal freedoms on (for example) abortion, same-sex marriage, and so on. People on the conservative side tend to favour more traditional notions of family, morality, and order. Where would you place yourself in terms of social-cultural philosophy?' ranging from 0 (more liberal) to 10 (more conservative).

Table 4.4 presents these dimensions on 0 (left) to 10 (right) scales. On the economic spectrum, European Commission officials are centrist, leaning slightly to the right (mean = 5.47). On the social liberal/conservative dimension, Commission officials are left of centre (mean = 3.68). Variation on social values is greater than on economic values.

One of the most striking findings in the survey is evident from the last four columns in Table 4.4. EU-12 officials are considerably more right wing in economic terms and less social-liberal than their EU-15 colleagues.[8] Both differences are highly significant. Moreover, EU-12 officials are quite a bit more pro-market than political parties in their home countries. They are also more socially liberal. EU-12 officials are *not* representative of their societies. They are mobile,

[8] It is well documented that the ideological profile of parties in the older member states of Western Europe differs considerably from most recent member states (Marks et al. 2006). That is why we compare officials from the EU-15 with EU-15 political parties and officials from the EU-12 with EU-12 political parties. The political party positioning for a country is the average of political parties weighted for party vote in the national election in or prior to 2006. *Source*: 2006 Chapel Hill Expert survey on political parties (Hooghe et al. 2010).

Western-educated, have tenuous ties to communist networks, tend to be outspoken critics of the former regimes, and are usually successfully integrated in the 'Western' world. As a result, they are motivated to embrace market values and cosmopolitanism, often with the zeal of recent converts. One might have expected differently. A compelling line of argument, developed by Kitschelt et al. (1999) and Vachudova (2005), is that the revolutions left a communist legacy—radical economic egalitarianism and anti-democratic authoritarianism—that continues to shape values and political preferences. EU-12 officials might have been to the economic left and more socially conservative than their EU-15 counterparts. We find signs of somewhat greater conservativism, but quite a bit more market liberalism than among their Western colleagues.

Understanding ideological variation in the Commission

Ideology is prior to Commission employment. Whether a person is a market liberal rather than a social democrat or liberal rather than conservative is determined earlier in life.[9] Explaining the origins of Commission officials' ideological beliefs is therefore beyond the scope of this study, but perhaps the data can shed light on ideological variation in the Commission. Let us examine three sources of variation: territory, DG location, and EU governance views.

National political economy and economic ideology. Figure 4.4 illustrates average positioning on the economic spectrum by nationality. There is a left-oriented southern cluster and an economically liberal Central and Eastern European cluster. However, there is no Scandinavian cluster and, interestingly, officials from 'market-liberal' Britain stand shoulder to shoulder with 'Rhine-capitalist' Germans and Dutch. Hence our findings only partly confirm the expectation that nationalities upload their country's political-economic model: that the British make the case for market liberalism, Germans and French for Rhine capitalism, Scandinavians for social democracy, and Southerners for a Mediterranean model oriented around the family (Brinegar and Jolly 2005; Callaghan 2010). As noted above, the difference between EU-12 officials and EU-15 officials trumps that between any smaller country groupings, but that difference cannot be attributed to divergent national socialization. The reasons why EU-12 officials are more market-liberal than their EU-15 colleagues appear to be personal rather than national, as we elaborate in Chapter 9.

Policy families and economic ideology. Officials in market-correcting DGs, such as Regional Policy, Social Policy, or Environment, are less pro-market than those in market-enhancing DGs, such as Trade or Competition (Table 4.5).

---

[9] Though it is possible that ideological priors could be affected by experiences in the Commission. About potential genetic bases for ideological proclivities, see Alford et al. (2005).

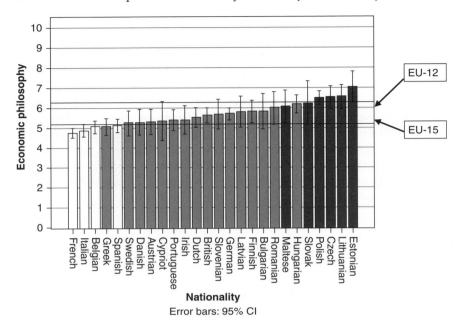

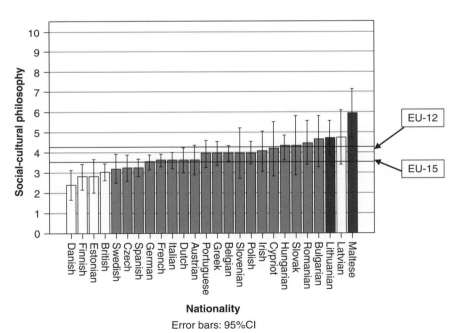

Fig. 4.4 Ideology by nationality

Note: n = 1,676, with n ≥ 18 or higher for each nationality (Luxembourg excluded). The bars represent the mean value by nationality, and the whiskers the 95 per cent confidence intervals. Darker- and lighter-coloured bars at either end highlight which nationalities have ideologies that differ significantly from the overall average (one-tailed t-tests at p < 0.05).

Table 4.5 DG location and ideology

	Economic left/right		Social liberal/conservative	
All DGs	Mean = 5.47		Mean = 3.68	
Market-enhancing DGs	Strongly more to the right	6.02 (.000)	—	3.76 (.411)
Market-correcting DGs	Strongly more to the left	5.02 (.000)	—	3.55 (.215)
Spending DGs	Strongly more to the left	5.08 (.000)	—	3.62 (.789)
Regulatory DGs	Strongly more to the right	5.83 (.000)	Strongly more conservative	3.96 (.005)
Legislative DGs	—	5.35 (.404)	—	3.55 (.586)
Internal DGs	—	5.35 (.221)	More liberal	3.40 (.049)
External DGs	—	5.44 (.786)	More liberal	3.28 (.041)

Note: Figures in brackets report p-values of t-tests on whether the mean for officials in a DG group is significantly different from the mean for officials outside the DG group.

This corresponds with scholarly accounts that highlight how key Commission services are dominated by particular ideological factions. Wilks (1996, 2005) has argued that neoliberalism among DG Competition officials provided a major impetus for enhanced EU authority in competition policy. Ross (1995), Hooghe (1996), and Falkner (1998) have documented how particular Commission services have been motivated by social-democratic ideas regarding EU cohesion and social policy. Students of EU gender and anti-discrimination policy describe how the Commission services have pushed a progressive agenda (Chicowski 2007; Caporaso and Tarrow 2009).

DG core activity and ideology. A more general pattern of ideological sorting emerges when one coalesces DGs according to their core activity.[10] Economically left officials are over-represented in spending DGs, while economically right-wing officials are found disproportionately in regulatory DGs. Regulatory DGs are also distinctly more conservative, while officials in external relations—and surprisingly, also internal DGs such as the Secretariat-General, Administration or the Legal Services—are more socially liberal.

EU governance views. State-centrists are to the economic right of supranationalists and institutional pragmatists.[11] This is consistent with the notion that the right favours intergovernmentalism to create regime competition, while the left favours supranationalism to increase the EU's capacity to regulate

---

[10] This operationalization simplifies the 7-category variable 'DG core activity' described in Chapter 1 into five categories. A DG is allocated to one of five categories (regulatory, legislative, spending, internal, external) if it is primarily or secondarily involved in this activity. DG activity is assessed on the basis of the Commission's Annual Management Reports, in which each DG explains its functions and activities and sets out its budget.

[11] Difference of means tests for economic philosophy between state-centrists on the one hand and institutional pragmatists and supranationalists on the other hand are significant at the 0.001 level; on socio-cultural philosophy means are different at the 0.05 level. Institutional pragmatists and supranationalists are not significantly different in their ideology.

markets (Hooghe and Marks 1999). One might also expect officials with socially liberal views to be more supportive of European authority and conservative individuals to be less supportive (Inglehart 1970; Marks et al. 2006; Risse 2010). But tests show that the difference is not statistically significant (see footnote 11).

Policy-making concerns the allocation of values. The values that the Commission allocates vary from policy to policy, and—strikingly—the values that the employees in those policy fields hold vary in tandem. Market-correcting DGs attract officials sympathetic to an active, equilibrating role for government on economic questions, and market-enhancing DGs appeal to market liberals. Services that disburse money appeal more to social-democrats, and regulatory services are more economically conservative. On economic ideology, DG location is a surer predictor than nationality. There is only one exception: the ideological difference between EU-12 and EU-15 officials.

Interpersonal variation on the socio-cultural dimension—though greater—is less easily understood. This study confirms that officials are considerably more socially liberal than citizens, but that is to be expected given their advanced education, public sector profession, person-oriented work with a high degree of control over pace and content, international lifestyle, and high income (Kitschelt 1994; Oesch 2006). Social-cultural values cluster only in a very minor way by DG group: external DGs draw more social liberals, and regulatory DGs attract more conservatives. Nor do they differ significantly between top and rank, between individuals with a lot of or a little multinational experience, or by EU governance type. Variation in socio-cultural values appears to be explained by the same set of factors at work in the general population: social conservatives are over-represented among EU-12 officials, older officials, officials from non-Protestant countries, and among right-of-centre officials. There are very few indications that the European Commission or the EU political context influence ideological positioning on socio-cultural values.

The meaning of 'political'

Commission officials did not feel constrained in conveying their ideological beliefs. Thirty-four officials preferred not to answer the questions on their ideological leanings. This was not more than the number that withheld their year of birth (n = 34) or gender (n = 17). It is possible that we helped respondents along by describing the ideological dimensions as 'philosophical views or stances'. A more plausible explanation is that Commission officials are quite capable of distinguishing between philosophical core values and party politics. The former are accepted and valued as input in the job; the latter's influence is much rarer and much more contested.

We received a taste of the former in face-to-face interviews with senior managers. We asked forty Directors and Directors-General how much they enjoy the political side of their work. Twenty-eight (70 per cent) say they like it very much, six 'like it but have some reservations', and one person accepts it as 'part of the job', against just two people who do 'not like it that much' and three people for whom 'there is no political side'. Moreover, despite being reluctant to share the monopoly of legislative initiative with the European Parliament (68 per cent disagree, 24 per cent agree),[12] middle and senior managers are generally respectful of the role played by Council and European Parliament. Of 116 individuals in face-to-face interviews, 86 per cent disagree with the statement that the 'European Parliament and/or the Council of Ministers too often interfere with the work of the European Commission' while 11 per cent agree. As Bauer and Ege (2011: 25) observe, 'Commission officials perfectly fall into the conceptual category of "image II" bureaucrats, i.e. demonstrating a clear ability to distinguish between a power-based and a policy-based understanding of political work' (see also Aberbach et al. 1981).

Engagement in party politics is a different matter. While we did not ask officials which party they voted for in the last elections or whether they are members of a party, we asked them whether party affiliation was an important basis of informal networking in the Commission. Party affiliation was flagged in fourth place among six options (see Chapter 3). Eighteen per cent ticked it as first or second most important base; it was preceded by personal connections in the workplace (83 per cent), same nationality (49 per cent), and same language group (20 per cent), but beat shared educational background (13 per cent) and shared regional identity such as Nordic or Mediterranean (10 per cent).[13]

The minor role of partisanship was corroborated in face-to-face interviews with 116 senior and middle managers (see also Chapters 2 and 10). When asked directly about party membership, 85 per cent said they were never a member of a party and only 9 per cent claimed to be active or passive members.[14] This appears to be much lower than in many national administrations (Bauer and Ege 2011).[15] Table 4.6 reports on two questions about the relative role of party affiliation in Commission work. Party politics is

---

[12] Middle management and senior officials from the online survey. Among junior officials, there is a somewhat greater willingness to share initiative power with the European Parliament (52 per cent disagree, and 37 per cent agree).

[13] Middle and senior managers in the online survey (n = 228).

[14] The question reads: 'If you don't mind us asking, do you belong to a political party?' with the following response options: No, never; In the past, not anymore; Yes, but I am not active; Yes, and I am still active. Our team argued long about the wisdom of including a question that was perceived to be very sensitive, but of randomly selected interviewees only two people (1.7 per cent) chose not to respond. Perhaps the perceived sensitivity of partisanship for bureaucrats is more in the minds of political scientists than of the bureaucrats.

[15] Hard comparative evidence is sketchy. Bauer and Ege refer to a 2005 study of German top officials, where 48.5 per cent of interviewed German top officials reported that they were a member of a political party.

Table 4.6 The role of partisanship

	How important is the party affiliation or party sympathy of officials in the Commission?	How important is party affiliation for cabinet members?
Party affiliation is very important	0.9	4.3
It is important	3.4	15.5
Sometimes it plays a role, sometimes not	20.7	38.8
It is not very important	46.6	20.7
It does not play any role at all	25.0	8.6
Don't know/prefer not to say	3.5	20.2

Note: Percentages from face-to-face interviews. Respondents are middle and senior managers (n = 119; 92 per cent are from EU-15).

presumed to be more important for *cabinet* members than for other officials, but the overall perception is that party affiliation does not matter a great deal.

Since responses to the two questions are quite highly associated,[16] they can be combined in a factor 'perception of party politicization'. Four factors are significant predictors of perceived party politicization (Appendix 6). First, heads of unit are more likely than directors or directors-general to believe party affiliation is important. Second, people on the economic right are more likely to report politicization. This is consistent with the view that the pro-market bias in the treaties requires centre-left partisan mobilization to push through a market-correcting agenda; market liberals enjoy the structural advantage of having their preferences built into the rules (Scharpf 2010). Third, officials from countries with a tradition of politicized administrations are more likely to find politicization in the Commission.[17] Our evidence does not enable us to settle whether they simply project experience from their home country on the Commission, or whether officials from countries with

---

[16] The Pearson correlation is 0.34 (n = 100).

[17] Politicization scores developed by Balint et al. (2008) for fifteen EU countries. The additive index uses existing formal organizational rules, adding up to seven dichotomous items. Each item is coded as '1' (i.e. politicized) if the condition in the brackets is satisfied. 1. Senior staff is usually recruited from the administration itself (no); 2. Senior staff is recruited through formal procedures prior to the appointment (no); 3. Senior staff can be dismissed by the minister without cause (yes); 4. Senior staff can be replaced when the government changes (yes); 5. The incumbent minister can appoint senior staff (yes); 6. A formalized *cabinet* system exists (yes); 7. The appointment of *cabinet* staff is formalized (no). Greece is most politicized and Britain least (Bauer and Ege 2011).

politicized civil services are more exposed to politicization in the Commission. The first would suggest that perceptions rule experience, and the second that experience in the Commission could be nationally specific.

Fourth, the longer ago officials joined the Commission the more likely they perceive party politicization. Disaggregating our sample into three groups— officials recruited during or before the Delors presidency (before 1995); officials recruited in the period between Delors and Barroso (1995–2004); and officials who entered during the Barroso presidency (2005 onwards)—sheds sharp light on this: the first group is three times more likely to perceive politicization than the third group, with the second group in the middle. This may reflect a tension between rapidly declining politicization in the Commission and people's capacity to update their views. Delors recruits entered a highly politicized institution, but this context was altered by subsequent reforms. The current Commission bureaucracy is not free of party (and national) politics, but its daily operation and personnel policy are much less affected by it than before (Bauer and Ege 2011). However, updating political beliefs with new experiences happens slowly.

COMMISSION OFFICIALS AND POLICY SCOPE

The theory of bureaucratic politics predicts that bureaucrats prefer to expand policy competences or budgets to enhance their status and power, and support expansion of their particular policy field more than others (Calvert et al. 1989; Niskanen 1994; Pollack 2003; Franchino 2007). We examine this argument in two steps: first by asking whether there is a general tendency to shift policy authority to the European Union; and second by investigating whether there is a specific tendency for officials to fight for their policy corner. The evidence supporting these two bureaucratic arguments is weak. Commission officials' attitudes on policy scope in general, and on the kind of policies that should be centralized, are guided by ideology and EU governance views rather than by career interests.

Commission officials were asked to evaluate both the actual and desirable distribution of authority between member states and the EU on eleven policies:

We are interested in your views on the distribution of authority between member states and the EU on a range of policies.
- Please start by giving us your assessment of the *actual* distribution in 2008. Where is each policy decided?
- Where *should* this policy be decided?

Respondents were prompted to select a position on an eleven-point scale from 0 (exclusively national/subnational) to 10 (exclusively EU). By subtracting actual from desirable policy we get a read on Commission officials' attitudes towards the *status quo*. Positive values indicate a desire for decentralization, and negative values for centralization. Foreign and security policy and asylum and immigration policies lead the list. The smallest shifts are desired for competition, trade, and regional policy. Interestingly, officials want to roll back centralization in agriculture.

Centralization across the board?

European Commission officials want more EU authority by an average of 1.58 on an eleven-point scale, which is a shift of 14 per cent. That is consistent with the most basic prediction of bureaucratic politics.

However, there is no universal desire for more Europe. Desired change appears highest for policies that are least centralized, though this is not a consistent trend. Social policy—perceived to be the most decentralized—is not on the Commission officials' top centralization list, and the three most centralized policies (competition, trade, agriculture) are assessed very differently. At the individual level, there is even greater variation. Individual correlations between actual and desired scope range between –0.36 and –0.51 (depending on the subcategory). These are negative, suggesting that officials generally want more centralization for the most decentralized policies, but they are also moderate, suggesting that officials have divergent views and use more discriminating criteria than an across-board 'power-maximization' frame.

Men are not more inclined to shift authority to the EU than women, and junior not more than senior officials. However, junior officials are keener on centralizing environment, foreign and security, or social policy, and men are more inclined to roll back EU agricultural policy and are more enthusiastic about centralizing foreign and security policy. In bivariate analysis, EU-12 officials appear no more nor less inclined to shift EU authority than their EU-15 colleagues. However, they are less likely to want to centralize asylum and immigration policy or foreign and security policy, the top two policies in demand for centralization. This is balanced by the fact that they are more in favour of EU regional policy than their EU-15 colleagues. What emerges is a qualified picture that suggests that the utilitarian argument—that bureaucrats support bureau-maximizing strategies—needs more scrutiny.

In a multivariate analysis of variation in overall desired policy scope, beliefs and ideology are more powerful than nationality and DG location (see Appendix 7).

Table 4.7 Desired shifts in EU authority in eleven policy fields

	Actual policy scope	Desired policy scope	Desired shift in centralization	Desired ranking of policies	Desired policy scope by subgroup					
					Senior officials	Other	Men	Women	EU-15	EU-12
EU Authority Mean	5.42	7.00			6.8	7.0	7.01	7.00	7.0	6.9
St.Dev.	(1.22)	(1.30)			(1.37)	(1.30)	(1.27)	(1.38)	(1.30)	(1.34)
1. Competition	8.0	8.3	+ 0.3	2						
2. Trade	8.0	8.4	+ 0.4	1						
3. Agriculture	7.7	6.9	−0.8	7	7.4*	7.8*	6.8*	7.1*		
4. Environment	6.2	7.7	+ 1.5	3					5.6**	6.0**
5. Regional development	5.2	5.7	+ 0.5	10						
6. Development	5.1	6.7	+ 1.6	8						
7. Energy	4.9	7.6	+ 2.7	4					7.1*	6.8*
8. Asylum and immigration	4.1	7.1	+ 3.0	5						
9. Police and judicial cooperation	4.0	6.5	+ 2.5	9						
10. Foreign and security	3.4	7.0	+ 3.6	6	6.4**	7.1**	7.1*	6.8*	7.1**	6.7**
11. Social policy	3.2	5.0	+ 1.8	11	4.6*	5.1*				

Note: Means are reported where differences are significant whereby *significant at 0.05 level; ** significant at 0.01 level.

- *EU governance views.* By far the most powerful predictor of how much centralization officials want is whether they are state-centrist or supranationalist. All other things being equal, a state-centrist's optimal level of centralization is 0.69 points lower than that of an institutional pragmatist and 1.24 points lower than a supranationalist's ideal point on a scale of 11.

- *Ideology.* Socially liberal officials are more in favour of centralization than conservatives, and left-wing officials also tend to be more in favour than those on the economic right. These effects are robust even when we control for EU governance type. In other words, the fact that state-centrists tend to be market-liberal and supranationalists tend to be on the left does not swallow the *independent* effect of economic philosophy on desired policy centralization.[18]

- *Religion and state building.* Officials from Protestant countries are less likely to support centralization. This echoes a deeply engrained suspicion against supranational authority, anchored in the intertwined history of Protestantism and state building in Northern and Central Europe (Rokkan and Urwin 1983).

- *Country size.* Officials from smaller countries are more in favour of centralizing authority, which is consistent with a public good argument. More targeted national utility factors are weak: officials are not more in favour of centralization if they are from trading nations, from member states that are net beneficiaries of the EU budget or its structural funds, or from countries with lower governance efficacy.

- *East vs West.* EU-12 officials are less likely to support centralization—an effect that cannot be reduced to ideology, EU governance, gender, or country characteristics.

- *Core activity.* Officials from external DGs (Trade, RELEX, Development, Enlargement) are more likely to support centralization than the average official. They are the only functional group standing out.

In explaining variation on the general desire for EU policy scope, DG location is weak. However, disaggregating policy scope into meaningful policy families reveals a more differentiated picture. Table 4.8 compares average desired

---

[18] The differences between men and women and between senior and junior officials wash out once we take into account EU governance beliefs and ideology. Indeed, as observed earlier, men are more likely to be supranationalist and women state-centrist; senior officials are more market-liberal than junior officials. However, the EU12/EU15 difference strengthens under controls.

Table 4.8 Desired policy scope disaggregated by policy family

		All policies		Market-enhancing policies		Market-correcting policies	Security policies
Commission		7.00		8.39		6.30	6.83
[ST.Dev]		[1.30]		[1.48]		[1.53]	[1.94]
Market-enhancing DGs	↔	6.9	↑	8.5	↓↓	6.0	↔ 6.8
Market-correcting DGs	↔	7.0	↔	8.3	↔	6.3	↔ 6.8
Spending DGs	↔	7.0	↓	8.3	↔	6.3	↔ 6.9
Regulatory DGs	↔	6.9	↔	8.4	↓↓↓	6.1	↔ 6.8
Legislative DGs	↔	7.0	↔	8.3	↔	6.3	↓↓ 6.6
Internal DGs	↔	7.1	↔	8.4	↔	6.4	↔ 6.9
External DGs	↑↑↑	7.4	↑↑↑	8.9	↑↑	6.6	↑↑↑ 7.3
State-centrists	↓↓↓	6.2	↓↓↓	7.9	↓↓↓	5.5	↓↓↓ 5.8
Institutional pragmatists	↓↓	6.9	↔	8.3	↓	6.2	↓↓ 6.6
Supranationalists	↑↑↑	7.4	↑↑↑	8.7	↑↑↑	6.7	↑↑↑ 7.4

Note: Averages for each subgroup. ↑↑↑ or ↓↓↓ indicate significance levels of t-tests on whether the mean for officials in a group is significantly different from the average for officials outside that group. ↑↑↑ or ↓↓↓ = < .001; ↑↑ or ↓↓ = < .01; ↑ or ↓ = < .05; and ↔ = no significant difference. All policies = all eleven policies (scope); Market-Enhancing policies = competition, trade; Market-correcting policies = environment, regional development, development, social policy; Security policies = asylum and immigration, police and justice cooperation, foreign and security policy.

scope for market-enhancing policies (competition, trade), market-correcting policies (environment, development, regional development, social policy) and security policies (asylum and immigration, police and justice, foreign and security) across types of DGs.

Commission officials' wish for EU authority is selective and explicable in terms of DG location. Grouping DGs by their policy principles produces intelligible differences: officials in market-enhancing DGs want to bolster EU authority in competition and trade much more than their colleagues in other DGs, and are less keen on EU authority in market-correcting policies. Officials in market-correcting DGs lean in the other direction, though they are less distinctive as a group than their colleagues in market-enhancing DGs. Selective centralization (or decentralization) is also apparent when DGs are grouped by core activity, with regulatory DGs harbouring the most reluctant supporters of EU authority in market-correcting policies and spending DGs the most reluctant supporters of market-enhancing EU policies. As expected, officials in internal and legislative DGs do not have distinctive preferences.

There is one exception to the measured and selective preferences of Commission officials: those from external DGs favour EU centralization across the board and, as we have seen above, this preference cannot be explained away in terms of their EU governance views, ideology, or nationality.

Bureau-maximization?

The evidence above casts doubt on the assumption that Commission officials have a general desire for greater EU authority. Their preferences are measured and explicable. However, is it not possible that officials promote their policy corner rather than Commission authority in general? Do they? The short answer is: partly. Table 4.9 reports independent means t-tests comparing desired EU authority between the DG 'owning' the policy and all others. One-tailed tests are reported here because the expectation is that officials from the DG that owns the policy should be more enthusiastic about EU authority than officials from other DGs.

We test nine policies that are commonly identified with one DG and for which we have statistically meaningful samples: competition, trade, agriculture, social policy, regional policy, environment, justice and police cooperation, asylum policy, and foreign and security policy.[19] Three of the nine policies conform to the expectation (trade, agriculture, foreign and security). No other reaches significance at the 0.05 level.[20] One policy goes in the

Table 4.9 Does 'bureaucratic politics' work?

Policy		Desired EU authority in policy field		
	EUCIQ sample size	Owner-DG	Others	Significance (one-tailed)
Trade	47	9.5	8.4	**0.000**
Competition*	53	8.1	8.3	0.279
Agriculture	93	7.7	6.9	**0.000**
Social policy	70	5.3	5.0	0.158
Regional development	59	6.0	5.7	0.064
Environment	81	7.8	7.7	0.414
Foreign and security policy	65	7.6	6.9	**0.000**
Asylum and immigration	50	7.5	7.0	0.057
Police and judicial cooperation	50	6.5	6.5	0.426

Note: Desired EU authority on a 0–10 scale with 0 (exclusively national/subnational) to 10 (exclusively EU). Differences of means significant at 0.001 level are in bold.

* With respect to competition policy, officials in the owner-DG tend to be less in favour of centralization than officials outside the DG. The reported t-test parameter is one-tailed.

[19] Testing is constrained by the limited sample size of DGs, by the fact that policies may be fragmented across several DGs (or parts of DGs), or because policies are diverse with respect to the appropriate balance of national/EU authority.

[20] On 1 July 2010, the former DG for Justice, Freedom and Security was partitioned into two DGs, one for home affairs (DG Home), which deals with immigration and asylum, and one for justice and fundamental rights (DG Justice), which deals with citizenship and judicial

opposite direction: officials in DG Competition lean towards *less* EU authority for their policy field than officials outside their DG. The difference is not significant, but it lends added credence to the conclusion that our evidence provides hardly a ringing endorsement of bureaucratic politics!

CONCLUSION

This chapter surveys core beliefs of Commission officials: their basic conceptions of EU governance, and their political ideology. It then examines how these shape their views on politics and EU policy-making. We find considerable variation and substantial structure, and we relate these to controversies regarding the institution.

The European Commission has sometimes been portrayed as hungry for a supranational Europe with the Commission in the driver's seat. We do not find much evidence for this view. The 'party of the willing' is a minority of 36 per cent. They want the College of Commissioners to be the government of Europe and do not want member states to be the central pillars. They cohabit with 13.3 per cent state-centrists, who want the opposite, and with nearly 30 per cent institutional pragmatists who believe that *neither* the College of Commissioners *nor* the member states should be the kernel of EU government. Some 20 per cent avoid taking a position.

National background is powerful in distinguishing state-centrists from supranationalists, while DG location helps explain who are the institutional pragmatists. State-centrists are most likely to hail from countries with limited multilevel governance, larger populations, and Protestant state churches, and they are more likely to be former national civil servants. Supranationalists come from countries with multilevel governance, smaller countries, countries with less governance effectiveness, and non-Protestant countries. The types are not distinctive in age, seniority, length of service, or transnational experience, but they are different in gender (supranationalism is disproportionately male) and ideology (supranationalists are more left-wing and more socially liberal than state-centrists). State-centrists and supranationalists are in many ways each other's alter egos. Institutional pragmatists stand apart from both groups—not so much in terms of national background, but on account of their professional profile: they work in policy DGs where shared technical knowledge reduces institutional power struggles. Their motivational core is consistent with this. They came to Brussels for primarily apolitical reasons: to work

---

cooperation. Our survey was conducted before the split and so we use the same DG for asylum and immigration policy and for police and judicial cooperation.

on a policy problem, to be in an international environment, or for family reasons.

While these three types have their differences on the future balance among Commission, member states and Parliament, their disagreement is bounded. Europe is desirable and a source of motivation for all. They tend to agree that a) the Commission should have power of initiative; b) Commission officials should be watchful of national influence; and c) officials should be loyal to the political positions of the College. However, state-centrists are pro-management and others are much less so; institutional pragmatists do not want to choose between Commission and member states as sources of authority; supranationalists are much more worried about geographical balancing. Supranationalists may be followers of Monnet, Hallstein, or Delors, and institutional pragmatists may appreciate Haas's hybrid form of governance, but state-centrists in the Commission are not disciples of de Gaulle, Thatcher, or Klaus.

The European Commission has been accused of being neoliberal, and it has been charged with plotting socialism. Neither is true. European Commission officials are distinctly centrist on the economic left–right spectrum, albeit leaning slightly to the right. They are a fair echo of European societies, at least in the EU-15. Officials from the EU-12 are more market-liberal than their societies, but that does not make them *neo*-liberal. The Commission is more distinctive on the social liberal/conservative dimension, where officials display the liberal bent to be expected of highly educated, internationally inclined, mobile, and prosperous public sector professionals.

The distribution of ideology is far from random across services. Policy-making is about the allocation of values, and the values that the Commission allocates vary from policy to policy. It is striking that the values of the employees vary in tandem. Market-correcting DGs attract officials sympathetic to an active role for government, and market-enhancing DGs appeal to market liberals. Services that disburse money appeal more to social-democrats, and regulatory services are economically conservative. On economic ideology, DG location is a surer predictor than nationality. There is only one exception: EU-12 officials are more market-liberal than EU-15 officials. On social ideology, the differences are more a matter of personal demographics and less of institutional context. There is again one exception: EU-12 officials are more conservative than EU-15 officials.

The European Commission is a test case for bureaucratic politics theory, which predicts that bureaucrats seek to maximize power. The evidence supporting the thesis is mixed. European Commission officials do want, in the aggregate, more EU authority in the eleven policy areas that we asked them to evaluate. The desired shift is significant but hardly radical: an average of 1.6 on an 11-point scale (from 5.4 to 7). There is significant variation both across officials and across policies. EU governance views and ideology provide strong cues for Commission officials in steering their *general* preference on whether policy authority should be centralized at EU level or decentralized to national and subnational governments. National interest (small countries want more EU authority) and national socialization (Protestant countries want less) help too, but only secondarily. DG location explains *which* policies Commission officials would like to centralize, and which ones not. The desire to centralize is selective and measured; it seems to be driven by reason and values rather than some instinctive reaction to maximize Commission power. But if DG location explains variation on particular policies, does this conceal a tendency for officials to defend their policy corner—over and above that of their colleagues? The answer is: only partially. On the basis of our data, we conclude that the pertinence of the bureaucratic politics argument has been overrated.

5

The Commission in the EU Institutional System: A Citadel under Siege

A common view of administrations is that they are eager to expand their influence by resorting to a wide range of tools, ranging from technical expertise to the budget (Niskanen 1971). The Commission is no exception to the rule: its officials are often described in the press and by politicians as power-hungry—'*technocrates européistes*' in the words of former French foreign minister Hubert Védrine[1]—and the organization itself as a 'self-serving bureaucracy', to quote German centre-right MEP Ingebord Grässle.[2] Similarly, there is no shortage of scholarship that describes it as a 'utility maximizer' eager to expand its influence (Pollack 2003), casts it as a 'purposeful opportunist' trying to draw maximum benefit from its often limited powers (Cram 1993; Héritier 1999), or criticizes the continuous erosion of national powers it is conducting as a form of 'integration by stealth', that neither its political principals (the member states) or its citizens desire (Majone 2005).

It is fair to say that the Commission has at its disposal a wider range of resources than the secretariats of most international organizations. The treaty invites it to act independently from external pressures; so does its official institutional ideology, the 'Community Method' (CM), developed by the founders of the EU (Dehousse 2011). The Commission's broad formal powers include a near-monopoly of legislative initiative and the discretionary power to bring about infringement proceedings against member states that fail to comply with EU law—two important prerogatives in their own right that, when skilfully combined, enable it to play a leading role in legislative procedures (Schmidt 2011). Unlike the Council, its members (in the College and in the services) work full-time on European issues, and it is better equipped than either the Council or the Parliament to have a cross-cutting view on the wide range of policies conducted or affected by the Union. Last but not least, given the limited development of party politics at the European level, it is also less

---

[1] Quotation taken from *Le Monde*, 29 June 2010.
[2] As reported in *European Voice*, 29 July 2010.

bothered than its domestic counterparts by purely political considerations. This explains why the CM has always been defended by the Commission leadership. Even President Barroso, who is often suspected of revisionist leanings, systematically pays lip service to it. Reacting to the multiplication of French and German unilateral initiatives during the financial crisis, he notably stressed that the best guarantee for 'preserving the coherence' of EU action was the CM, involving the European Commission as the guardian of the EU Treaties to prevent possible divisions (Barroso 2011).

In this chapter, we assess what is left of the CM (on the beliefs of Commission officials, see Dimitrakopoulos 2008), after nearly two decades of powerful challenges to the Commission's authority. In contrast with Chapter 4, the purpose here is not to provide the reader with an overall map of officials' beliefs, but merely analyse whether officials are still inspired by the classical view of their institution's role, and how they envisage its relationships with other institutions and actors. We begin by recalling the main changes that have taken place in the governance of the EU in the period following the Maastricht treaty (1992), as this forms the background against which we must assess officials' current views. We then analyse how large is support for the CM in today's Commission, and discuss a number of factors that might affect it. Finally, we examine CM supporters' views on the evolution of the EU institutional system.

THE POST-MAASTRICHT ENVIRONMENT

Since Maastricht, the European Commission, which was long regarded as the main engine of integration, has lost substantial ground. Even though its formal powers have not been curtailed, its authority has been challenged in various ways. From the beginning of the 1990s on wards, the level of support has collapsed; opinion polls have unanimously confirmed the fact that the 'permissive consensus' that enabled the European venture to be launched is now nothing but a memory (Hooghe and Marks 2009). Around the same time, the national governments began to show signs of growing impatience with what they saw as an unlimited increase in the powers of the EU, and therefore of the Commission. Counterweights have proliferated. The 'pillar structure' of the Maastricht treaty was undoubtedly the first expression of this new tendency: the member states agreed to undertake common actions in areas such as foreign policy, security, and justice, traditionally the preserve of the state, but only on condition that the role of the supranational institutions was reduced. Even in traditional areas of Community intervention such as the internal market, member governments appeared reluctant to strengthen the Community structure, which led to the setting up of multiple autonomous bodies. Today, over thirty administrative agencies operate alongside the

Commission and the national governments in areas including the fight against drug addiction, food security, and health and safety in the workplace. In other areas, the gap between the administrative tasks and the resources allocated to the Commission has resulted in the systematic use of subcontractors, some of which were implicated in the fraud and mismanagement that brought about the downfall of the Santer Commission (Committee of Independent Experts 1999). Typically, when functional needs for a stronger European impetus start to be felt, national governments systematically insist on responding through ad hoc structures, rather than entrusting the Commission with new tasks. Over the last two decades, we have been witnessing, *inter alia,* the creation of offices such as the High Representative for the Common Foreign and Security Policy, the presidency for the Eurogroup and the President of the European Council. The Commission has been relegated to a secondary role while the heads of state and government assume an overall role of guidance and control.

In the meantime, the Commission has also faced growing pressure on the side of the European Parliament. To remedy the notorious 'democratic deficit' from which the European political system is said to suffer, a strong dose of parliamentarianism has been injected at the European level; the European Parliament's financial, legislative, and supervisory powers have been strengthened. The Treaty of Lisbon describes it as a co-legislator, on the same footing with the Council, in most policy areas. Equally importantly, the Parliament has acquired considerable influence over the appointment of the Commission. To strengthen the links between the Parliament and the 'executive', it has been given the power to elect the Commission President and, although its 'vote of approval' concerns the College as a whole rather than individual commissioners, it has secured the creation of a hearing procedure inspired by the US experience, which has enabled it to influence the distribution of portfolios within the Commission and even its composition.

In general terms, the European Parliament's rise in power has been achieved largely to the detriment of the Commission. The generalization of legislative co-decision and the parallel development of 'early agreements' (Shackleton 2000; Héritier and Farrell 2003) have constrained the Commission's ability to shape EU legislation resulting from its right of initiative, giving rise to concerns in some quarters of the administration (Costa et al. 2011). The Parliament enjoyed decisive influence over some of the most controversial proposals of recent years, such as the services (or Bolkestein) directive or the REACH regulation (Crespy 2010). In a wide range of areas, ranging from the supervision of the Commission's exercise of its executive powers by committees composed of national officials (comitology) to the negotiation of external agreements, the Commission has had to come to terms with a vocal partner, eager to secure a seat at the table. Its spending power is now subject to close scrutiny by the EP's budget control committee.

In addition to the transformation of its institutional environment, the Commission's services have gone through major changes. The forced resignation of the Santer Commission in 1999, following allegations of mismanagement, has had a lasting impact on the institution. It has encouraged the development of a new role model, where the emphasis is no longer on the missionary role to be played by an administrative elite in charge of 'making Europe', but rather on its managerial role, in tune with the world fashion of 'new public management'. Successive reforms of administrative management (the Kinnock–Prodi reforms) and of recruitment procedures, largely inspired by this new model, have been resented by insiders as externally imposed (Bauer 2008; Georgakakis 2010; see also Chapter 8).

Put together, all these factors easily explain why the Commission is widely viewed as a power in decline (Kassim and Menon 2004). This view finds a strong echo in our survey: 61.7 per cent of our respondents think that the EU has lost ground to national capitals, 58.7 per cent believe that power has been usurped by the European Parliament; and a majority of them regards the Delors years as a 'golden era' in which the Commission clearly was Europe's agenda-setter (see Chapter 6). But how do they respond to these developments? There are two main possibilities: officials from the reformed Commission could try to adjust to the new setting and attempt to define a new role for themselves; or they could display a besieged citadel's attitude, through attachment to the official dogma, nostalgia for a glorious past, and reluctance to accept a more modest role. As will be seen, both can be discerned, albeit to different degrees, among our respondents.

WHAT ROLE FOR THE COMMISSION?

No one will be surprised that there is still wide support within the Commission for a vision of the EU in which it plays a key role, without being hindered excessively by national governments or the EP. The survey shows that amongst our respondents there is strong (79 per cent) opposition to the idea that the member states' grip over decision-making should be tolerated and, notwithstanding the widespread supremacy of the parliamentary democracy model in Europe, a majority (57.8 per cent) is of the opinion that the European Parliament should not be given a right of legislative initiative. When it comes to the Commission's own place in the EU system, the classical view of the Commission's policy-making role still holds firm. While just over half accept that the Commission's role in policy management and coordination has expanded, an overwhelming majority (79.8 per cent, with over 40 per cent holding the view strongly) declare themselves opposed to the idea that it should primarily focus on managerial duties. Nearly two-thirds are convinced that the Commission's role as policy initiator is gaining more importance as a result of enlargement.

The combination of all these elements might be read as confirmation of a wide support for the CM, where the Commission pulls the strings by bridging the gap between the rival interests of national governments and the opposed viewpoints of the Council and the Parliament. At the same time, the dominant view seems to be that the Commission should act as honest broker rather than as a hegemon. There is a clear recognition that the Commission should not aspire to unrivalled supremacy in the Union, since a relative majority of the respondents who express an opinion (42.6 per cent) declare themselves opposed to the idea that the Commission might aspire to become the government of the EU. If one were to stop here, one could easily believe that the average Commission official's conception of their own role has not been dramatically affected by the post-Maastricht developments. Yet thinking on the part of officials is much more complex than this rapid overview of the data suggests. First, as Chapter 4 has shown, there is a significant diversity in officials' images of Europe and of their own role. Even though support for a classical view of the Commission's role remains strong, it coexists with alternative perspectives, be they state-centric or supranationalist (Hooghe 2012). Second, one may wonder how cohesive the group of supporters of the CM actually is, and to what extent it may differ from officials who do not adhere to the classical vision of the Commission.

To answer these questions, we defined on the basis of the above data an 'ideal type' derived from the main tenets of the CM doctrine: the faithful disciple is expected to believe that the Commission is something more than the secretariat of an international institution, traditionally confined to narrowly defined tasks; in the EU context it, rather than the member states or the Parliament, is expected to be the main agenda-setter. One could have opted for a more elaborate definition of the CM, but we decided to stick to a minimalist derivation for two reasons. First, despite the Commission's efforts to 'codify' the basic tenets of the doctrine, for example in its White Paper on governance (Commission 2001), there is no commonly received understanding of the concept. Second, adopting a broad definition allowed us to examine how much support some ideas, such as the view of the Commission as a would-be 'government of Europe', enjoy in the CM camp. Adherence to the CM was therefore defined using responses to a question on officials' views of EU governance, and singling out two criteria: disagreement with the idea that 'member states—not the Commission or European Parliament—should be the central players in the European Union' and with the view according to which 'the Commission should primarily focus on managing existing policies, rather than developing new ones'. As a result, our CM supporters are less prone to centralization than the 'supranationalist' camp described in Chapter 4. Interestingly, the data reveal a strong endorsement of the CM, so defined, among Commission officials: a large number of our respondents (61.7 per cent, 1139 persons) adhere to the criteria we set.

WHO (STILL) BELIEVES IN
THE COMMUNITY METHOD?

Beyond the size of the pro-CM party, it is interesting to know who its members are and the factors that shape their view of the Commission's role. The scholarly literature suggests two paths in particular that are worth exploring. First, it has been shown that officials' views on EU governance are generally influenced by their national background (Hooghe 2001). One could, for instance, imagine officials from the founding countries, immersed in EU policy-making for over half a century, to be more favourable to the CM than newcomers from the countries that joined in 2004 or later. Similarly, with the CM having been largely conceived to protect the rights of smaller countries from undue pressure from their larger partners, one would expect this cleavage to affect officials' beliefs. Past professional experience could also be relevant in at least two ways. Given the official adherence of the Commission hierarchy to the CM, acculturation effects might imply that the longer an official's career in the Commission, the more he or she would be inclined to be supportive. By contrast, it might be expected that those who have worked in a national administration prior to joining the EU bureaucracy would find it more difficult to support a system characterized by a clear transfer of authority to the supranational level.

Ideological factors are more difficult. From the standpoint of economic philosophy, European integration can be looked at in radically opposed ways. On the one hand, one might expect support for a free market to positively influence support for the CM, which has played a key role in the establishment of the single market; on the other, left of centre parties tend today to vest greater hopes in supranational regulation to compensate for the erosion of states' regulatory powers. On the whole, therefore, we did not expect this variable to have a major influence on our findings. In contrast, it would seem natural for more socially libertarian officials to be 'more comfortable with European identity' (Hooghe 2012). Further insight on the ideological motivation behind officials' support for the CM can be expected to exist among those who joined the Commission due to their commitment to building Europe.

In looking at the evidence from the 62 per cent of our survey respondents who adhered to our definition of the CM, we can test the above hypotheses. Thus, the importance of nationality is partially borne out in our data

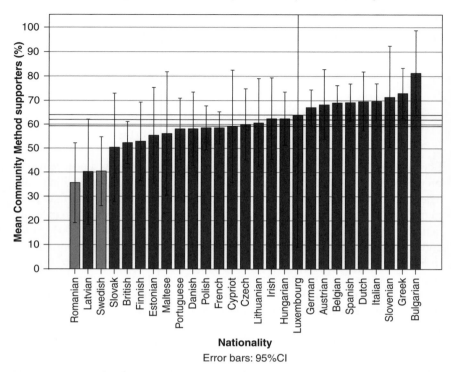

Fig. 5.1 Support for the Community Method by nationality

Note: n = 1,824, with n ≥18 for each nationality (except Luxembourg, n = 6). The vertical bars represent the mean value by nationality and the error bars the 95 per cent confidence intervals. The lighter coloured bars at the lower end highlight which nationalities have support profiles that are significantly below that of the overall mean. The overall mean is shown by the central horizontal line, with the 95 per cent confidence interval either side.

(Figure 5.1), which show that the degree of support for the CM may vary significantly according to the nationality of officials: it is significantly higher among Bulgarians than among Romanians, who, despite being regional neighbours entering the Commission at the same time, are at the extremes. Some well-established views are re-affirmed by the analysis: Italians, Greeks and Belgians tend to be more favourable to the CM than, say, the British or Swedes. We see there an echo of the findings in Chapter 4, in which 'supranationalists' dominated in the former nationalities and 'intergovernmentalists' in the latter.

Making sense of these differences is difficult. Size does not appear to be a decisive factor: there are large and small states among the countries whose officials appear most supportive, as well as among more sceptical ones. There appears to be a grouping of Southern countries at the positive end, but to speak of a North-South cleavage would be far-fetched, given the degree of support recorded in the Benelux countries or in Germany. In contrast, while

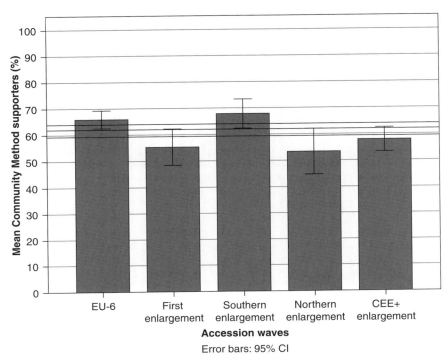

Fig. 5.2 Support for the Community Method by wave of accession

Note: n = 1,824. The vertical bars represent the mean value by date of accession and the error bars the 95 per cent confidence intervals. The overall mean is shown by the central horizontal line, with the 95 per cent confidence interval either side.

new member countries appear in both groups, officials from the founding states—with the possible exception of the French—are much more likely to be CM supporters. On the whole, those from the 'old' EU-15 countries are more supportive of CM than those from the newer EU-12 accession countries by an average margin of 5.5 per cent[3]. This appears to confirm the findings of Chapter 9, which show a greater adherence to the view that national governments should play a key role in the Union amongst officials from those newer countries. Yet it would be wrong to conclude from this that the longer one has been a member of the club, the more one is inclined to accept its rules. When disaggregated by the various waves of accession, the results do not show any clear trend (Figure 5.2). While officials from the six founding states and Greece suggest above-average support, the pattern of support is not significant and neither does it reveal a consistent decline over time, with some new

---

[3] p = 0.043; 95CI: 0.1–10.8 per cent.

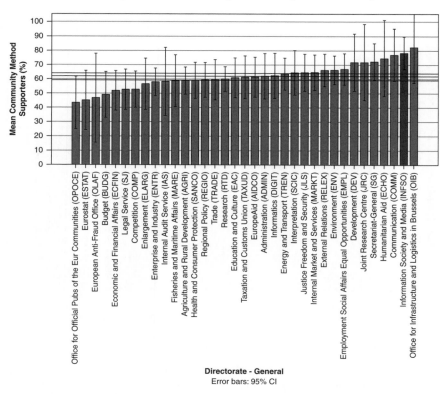

Fig. 5.3 Support for the Community Method by Directorate-General

Note: n = 1,751, excluding n < 12 for any DG. The vertical bars represent the mean value by DG and the error bars the 95 per cent confidence intervals. The darker coloured bar at the higher end highlights the DG which has a support profile that is significantly higher than that of the overall mean. The overall mean is shown by the central horizontal line, with the 95 per cent confidence interval either side.

members, such as Bulgaria and Romania, polarized within the same accession wave (2007).

We also tried to identify to what extent people's experience in the Commission could affect their support for the CM. To this end, we used three variables: the directorate-general in which they are active, the length of their stay in the institution and their level of seniority. It is known that the Commission's role may vary greatly from one area to the other, and it could be envisaged that this factor might influence officials' views of the world. Figure 5.3, however, reveals a high degree of homogeneity across the various Directorates-General (DGs) within the Commission,[4] with only DG

---

[4] p = 0.268.

Information Society and Media (INFSO) showing significantly higher support than the overall average. Support for the CM appears highest in some generalist DGs, the activities of which span the whole range of sectors in which the EU is active (Communication, Secretariat-General, Office for Infrastructure and Logistics), yet this appears to be contradicted by the lower than average attitude in the legal service, in Eurostat, or in the Office for Official Publications (OPOCE). Even when the Directorates are grouped into seven functional types (spending, regulatory, internal, external, legislative, spending and regulatory, and spending and legislative), there is no noticeable difference in their relative support for the CM.[5] It is, however, interesting to note that in the sectors in which legislative production has been high in the last decade (Grossman and Brouard 2009), such as internal market, environment, and justice, the mean of support is above average (65, 65 and 66 per cent, respectively). In contrast, it is below average in DG Trade and DG Competition, yet the Commission enjoys important prerogatives in those two areas. However, the size of the confidence intervals, resulting from smaller samples within DGs, makes it difficult to identify a clear pattern of behaviour. Of course, the horizontal mobility encouraged by the Kinnock reforms is likely to weaken the possibility of DGs retaining a distinctive culture.

Moving on to consider the second set of hypotheses concerning the professional experience of these officials, we have investigated the effect of seniority and length of service, as well as any prior experience of working in a national administration. In order to rule out the possible confounding effect of age, we have analysed individual age and the age cohort in relation to the level of CM support. As it turns out, there is no discernible relationship, either for age[6] or age group.[7]

Probably as a result of the positive relationship between age and level of seniority,[8] there is no discernible relationship between an official's current position and commitment to the CM,[9] as can be seen in Figure 5.4. Similarly, length of service has no discernible relationship at all with support for the CM, whether considered in absolute years[10] or in quartiles.[11] To sum up, officials' experience in the Commission does not appear to influence significantly their perception of the institution's role.

On the other hand, our data lend support to the idea that prior work in a national administration makes it less likely than an official will consider the upward transfer of authority to the supranational level in a positive fashion, although the relationship appears rather weak.[12] Supporters of CM were, on average, 4.7 per cent[13] less likely to have had experience in national civil services than other officials. On the whole, therefore, our data appears to

---

[5] $p = 0.546$.   [6] $p = 0.488$.   [7] $p = 0.435$.   [8] $p < 0.001$.   [9] $p = 0.226$.
[10] $p = 0.842$.   [11] $p = 0.286$.   [12] $p = 0.044$; phi = 0.047.
[13] 95CI: 0.1–9.3 per cent.

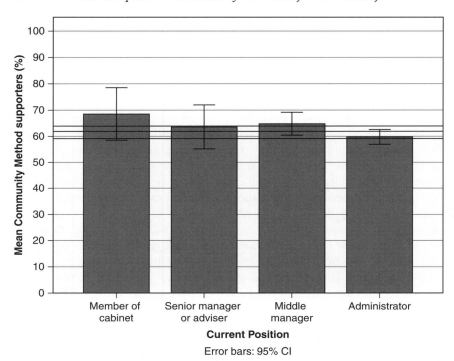

Fig. 5.4 Support for the Community Method by seniority

Note: n = 1,846. The vertical bars represent the mean value by level of seniority and the error bars the 95 per cent confidence intervals. The overall mean is shown by the central horizontal line, with the 95 per cent confidence interval either side.

give some sustenance to the view that officials' perspectives are more frequently shaped by their national origins than by their experience within the Commission (see Chapter 4).

Our third set of hypotheses concern officials' economic and socio-cultural ideology, as well as their commitment to integration as an ideal in its own right. The evidence from our survey is that CM supporters are less economically liberal than other officials on economic issues by 0.23 points on an 11-point scale,[14] whilst acknowledging that both groups are marginally to the right of centre (in relation to point 5 on the scale), at 5.40 and 5.63 respectively (Figure 5.5). However, the heterogeneity of this belief reveals a very wide 95 per cent confidence interval for the difference of between 0.04 and 0.42 scale points.

----

[14] p = 0.018.

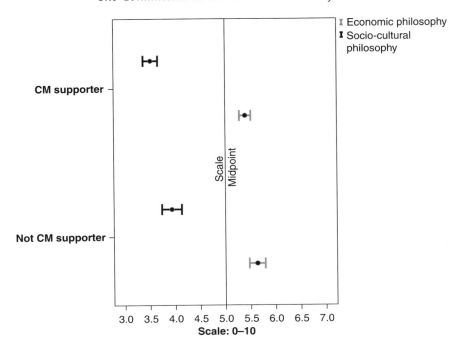

Fig. 5.5 Support for the Community Method by economic and socio-cultural philosophy

Note: The error bars show the mean and the 95 per cent confidence intervals for each scale: (a) Economic philosophy: 0 (a greater role for government) to 10 (a greater role for markets) [n=1,782]; (a)Socio-cultural philosophy: 0 (more liberal) to 10 (more conservative) [n = 1,783].

Turning to socio-cultural philosophical beliefs, we find CM supporters to be more socially liberal than other officials, in this case by a larger margin of 0.42 scale points,[15] with a 95 per cent confidence interval ranging from 0.18 to 0.66 points. On these issues Figure 5.5 shows both groups are clearly to the left of centre (in relation to point 5 on the scale), at 3.51 and 3.93 respectively. Thus, in relation to our original propositions, our evidence would appear to refute the view that the CM supporters are more likely to be free marketeers, while offering tentative support for the view that they value the regulatory powers of the Commission in compensating for the loss of such powers at national level. Nonetheless, as we suspected, this variable has not had a major influence on our findings. Our data does lend more support to the view that more socially libertarian officials are less concerned by the necessity of protecting national interests.

[15] $p = 0.001$.

Table 5.1. Personal and national characteristics supporting the Community Method

	Model 1			Model 2		
	B (SE)	Wald	Odds ratio (95% CI)	B (SE)	Wald	Odds ratio (95% CI)
Personal						
Commitment to	0.728	45.45***	2.072	0.674	37.946***	1.963
Europe (ref cat: no)	(0.108)		(1.676:2.561)	(0.109)		(1.584:2.432)
Socio-cultural	−0.061	9.32**	0.941	−0.067	10.876**	0.935
philosophy index	(0.020)		(0.905:0.978)	(0.020)		(0.899:0.973)
Economic philosophy	−0.066	6.89**	0.936	−0.053	4.275*	0.949
index	(0.025)		(0.891:0.983)	(0.026)		(0.902:0.997)
National						
Protestantism				−0.438	5.035*	0.645
(proportion)				(0.195)		(0.440:0.946)
Index of multi-level				0.014	6.853**	1.014
governance				(0.005)		(1.004:1.025)
Reduction in -2LL	63.77***			77.147***		
Nagelkerke R^2	0.048			0.058		
Hosmer and	0.803			0.989		
Lemeshow test (sig)						
n (unweighted)	1794			1794		

*** $p < 0.001$; ** $p < 0.01$; * $p < 0.05$.
NB Model 1 considers the personal characteristics only, while Model 2 adds the national characteristics.

The commitment to Europe, as a reason for choosing a career in the Commission, reveals a stronger link with CM supporters (76.1 per cent) than the others (63.1 per cent), an excess of 13 per cent, with a 95 per cent confidence interval of between 8.7 per cent and 17.4 per cent. Interestingly, this initial motivation is largely unrelated to ideological positions on economic or socio-cultural issues.

By building these various possible explanations of why some officials do or do not support the CM into a multivariate analysis using multi-level linear modelling of individuals nested within countries, we are able to identify the key variables (see Appendix 8). It turns out that the organizational level (DG) does not add at all to the model, whether the DGs are looked at individually or grouped by type of activity. In contrast, country-level variables do indeed contribute to our understanding. The key individual variables concern values, notably socio-cultural values,[16] and a 'commitment to building Europe'.[17]

[16] One scale point increase in socio-cultural conservatism decreases the odds of being a CM supporter by 6.5 per cent (95 per cent CI: 2.7 per cent to 10.1 per cent), holding all other variables constant.

[17] Those whose reasons for joining the Commission included wishing to build Europe have increased odds of being a CM supporter of 96.2 per cent (95 per cent CI: 58.5 per cent to 142.9 per cent), holding all other variables constant.

Those more to the left on economic and socio-cultural issues are more likely to support the CM,[18] as are those who joined the Commission in order to build Europe, where the odds of CM support are almost doubled. At the country level, additional explanation is given by the proportion of Protestants within the country, which reduces the support for the CM,[19] and the index of multi-level governance, where greater exposure to such structures increases CM support.[20] In other words, it would appear that national experience of multi-level governance arrangements and a lower proportion of Protestants are both contributory factors in support for the CM. These findings largely echo those of Chapter 4.

HOW SPECIAL IS THE 'COMMUNITY METHOD' PARTY?

Having established that, as expected, the number of 'faithful believers' in the CM was fairly high, we attempted to identify more clearly what membership in this group entails. First, do supporters of the CM hold different views from other officials on the evolution of the Union? What is their assessment of the impact of enlargement or that of the Kinnock–Prodi reforms on the functioning of the institution? Second, what preferences do they have as regards the future of the EU? What is, according to them, the most desirable distribution of authority between the EU and its member states or between the institutions? In answering these and related questions, we now consider support for the CM as the independent variable to see how well it explains differences in attitude or belief.

The decline of the Commission

First, we looked at the views of officials concerning the evolution of the Union. While, as noted above, our survey identified a clear disenchantment as regards the evolution of the Commission's political power, it was clearly more

---

[18] One scale point increase in economic support for markets decreases the odds of being a CM supporter by 5.2 per cent (95per cent CI: 0 per cent/9.9 per cent), holding all other variables constant.

[19] A one per cent increase in the proportion of protestants in a country shows a 0.36 per cent decrease in the odds of support for CM (95 per cent CI: 0.05 per cent to 0.56 per cent), holding all other variables constant.

[20] A one scale point increase in the index of multi-level governance in a country shows a 1.4 per cent increase in the odds of support for CM (95 per cent CI: 0 per cent to 2.4 per cent), holding all other variables constant.

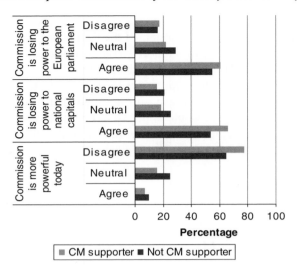

Fig. 5.6 Perceptions of the changing power of the Commission by support for the Community Method

Note: 1,515 ≤ n ≤ 1,525. The horizontal bars represent the percentage of agreement, neutrality, or disagreement for each question.

pronounced among CM supporters (77.7 per cent) compared to other officials (64.8 per cent)[21] (Figure 5.6; bottom question). Both groups agree, with similar majorities of nearly 50 per cent (allowing for neutral opinions), that there is today a greater focus on policy management and coordination rather than on policy conception. The main drain of power leakage is generally identified as being in the direction of the national capitals. Here again, CM supporters tend to be more radical: 65.9 per cent of them agree, compared to 53.6 per cent of other officials[22] (Figure 5.6). The difference is smaller as regards the European Parliament: 60.5 per cent of CM supporters assess the Commission as having lost ground to the Parliament, an opinion shared by 55.2 per cent of the others (Figure 5.6).[23]

What are the elements behind this negative assessment? We explored three types of possible sources of the Commission's weakening: enlargement, which has long been expected to complicate relations with the Council, as well as the internal organization of the Commission; administrative reform, often described as imposed on the institution (Georgakakis 2010); and changes in the Commission leadership.

Our survey confirms that enlargement is regarded as a disruptive element by a majority of officials. There seems to be no major disagreement between

---

[21] p < 0.001; Cramer's V = 0.159.   [22] p < 0.001; Cramer's V = 0.134.
[23] p = 0.317.

the 'CM party' and the rest on this assessment. In both groups, about three quarters of the respondents agree that a 27-member college makes coordination more difficult, although the CM supporters express more positive endorsement.[24] Likewise, there are no noticeable differences in opinion about the weakening of the Commission's *esprit de corps* as a result of enlargement, held by 61 per cent of officials,[25] or that the consequences of enlargements for an official's career prospects were not handled equitably, also held by a similar proportion.[26]

Concerning administrative reform, the situation is similar. On the whole, our respondents are fairly critical of what has been achieved, as is shown in more detail in Chapter 8. While they are fairly uncertain as regards the impact of recent reforms, only minorities appear convinced that they (23.3 per cent) or their unit (29.2 per cent) have become more efficient. Negative assessments tend to dominate: personnel management has not improved (49.7 per cent); resources are not better matched to policy priorities (48.0 per cent); almost two-thirds of our respondents consider that the new tools have been applied in a formalistic way and over 70 per cent believe that they have led to more red tape. There is only one issue, the situation of women, concerning which there is a clear majority (58.2 per cent) who believe that the situation has been improved. But our two groups generally agree on this gloomy picture of officials the situation; in some cases CM supporters are even slightly more positive than other officials. In other words, their assessment of the Commission's loss of authority does not seem to have been prompted by their view of the recent administrative reforms.

Moreover, dissatisfaction with the Kinnock–Prodi reforms is not to be equated with a negative assessment of the internal functioning of the institution. While a relative majority overall (41.8 per cent, excluding those with no opinion) consider that coordination between DGs does not work effectively, supporters of the CM are more likely to consider that officials work first for the Commission itself, rather than for their DG.[27] Both groups recognize that the Secretariat-General has gained ground in recent times, without this appearing as a source of major concern; nor are they particularly critical of the *cabinets'* role.

By contrast, there are clear divergences between the two groups' views on leadership. One set of our questions related to respondents' appraisal of the performance of various presidents and we observe clear differences of opinion at this level, except in relation to the Prodi Commission. The Santer Commission came in for the most criticism from CM supporters, arguing that it was

---

[24] p = 0.008; Cramer's V = 0.091.　　　[25] p = 0.217.
[26] p = 0.131.　　　[27] p = 0.006; Cramer's V = 0.096.

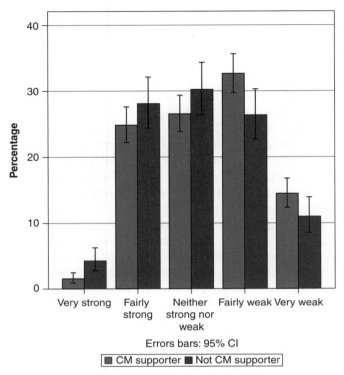

Fig. 5.7 Views on how well the Barroso Commission defends the Commission in the EU system by support for the Community Method

Note: n = 1,499. The vertical bars represent the percentage of agreement or disagreement and the error bars the 95 per cent confidence intervals.

weak in relation to setting a policy agenda (56.0 per cent against 43.7 per cent),[28] managing the house effectively (75.8 per cent against 66.8 per cent),[29] and defending the Commission in the EU system (67.7 per cent against 54.2 per cent).[30] As to the Barroso Commission, 47.1 per cent of CM supporters were of the opinion that it was fairly or very weak in defending the Commission in the EU system, against 37.4 per cent of other officials who thought so (Figure 5.7).[31] In contrast, both groups concur on a more balanced assessment of its ability to effectively manage the Commission or to set the Union's political agenda. Unsurprisingly, CM supporters were more positive about the Delors Commission, both in terms of setting a policy agenda (99.5 per cent vs 95.6 per cent)[32] and delivering on policy priorities (97.6 per cent against 95 per cent).[33] This does suggest that, while all officials

[28] p = 0.039.   [29] p = 0.014.   [30] p < 0.001.
[31] p < 0.001; Cramer's V = 0.117.   [32] p = 0.001.   [33] p = 0.038.

have fond memories of the Delors era, it is even more passionately seen as the golden age by those who support the CM.

Views about the future

Having defined the group of supporters of the CM by their vision of the functioning of the EU institutional system, we might expect them to have particular views about the future direction of European governance. Several elements are worth mentioning in this respect. First, CM supporters, unsurprisingly, would welcome transfers of authority to the European level in several areas (with the notable exception of agriculture where, like other officials, they would favour a degree of decentralization). This is a general trend amongst Commission officials, as was seen in Chapter 4. There is even agreement between the groups on the hierarchy of priorities, with foreign policy, development, and asylum and immigration heading the list. However, it is worthy of note that in every single policy area the CM supporters wish to have significantly more decision-making at the EU level than do other officials,[34] from + 0.39 scale points for competition and development policies to + 0.78 for foreign and security policy (on an eleven-point scale). By considering the difference between desired and perceived authority for each policy area, as in Figure 5.8, we can see that there is broad agreement about the rank order, whilst CM supporters are consistently desirous of more authority at the EU level, significantly so for all policy areas except trade and competition.

Supporters of the CM also appear well disposed towards the idea that the College of Commissioners should one day become the government of the EU. Figure 5.9 shows how strongly CM supporters, in contrast to other officials, show a distinctly positive view of the Commission's role in this regard.[35] The total of favourable opinions in their ranks reaches 47.4 per cent, against 26.3 per cent amongst other officials. Yet, even in the pro-CM group, support for this option is not clear-cut since the level of negative opinions is fairly high (37.1 per cent). In contrast, a strong majority (70.3 per cent) of the members of that group (against 55.9 per cent of other officials) consider that the Commission's role as policy initiator is made more important by the enlargement of the EU,[36] as shown in Figure 5.9. Having had to come to terms with an ever more assertive parliament in the last two decades, it could be expected that Commission officials would not be so positive about sharing the Commission's sole right of legislative initiative with the European Parliament. Indeed, a majority (57.8 per cent) are against such a development versus 32.4 per cent in favour. Figure 5.9 shows that there is only a marginal

---

[34] $p < 0.001$.   [35] $p < 0.001$; Cramer's V = 0.201.
[36] $p < 0.001$; Cramer's V = 0.174.

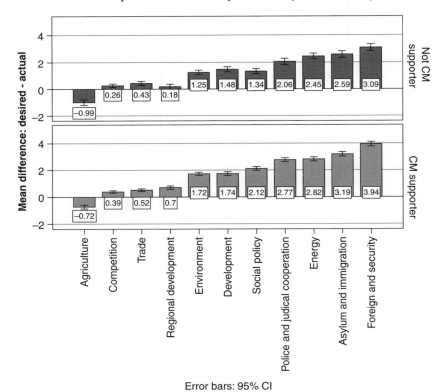

Fig. 5.8 Mean difference between desired and perceived distribution of authority between member states and the EU in various policy areas by support for the Community Method

Note: n varies between 1,574 and 1,624. The vertical bars represent the mean value on a scale from 0 (exclusively national/sub-national) to 10 (exclusively EU). The error bars represent the 95 per cent confidence intervals around the mean for each policy area.

difference between our two groups on this issue, with more difference being displayed within each group.

To summarize, it appears that CM supporters are more likely than other officials to support transfers of authority to the EU and that they are eager to see one of the Commission's strategic assets, its right of initiative, consolidated. None of these findings are particularly surprising. Yet they should not be seen as an unqualified call for greater centralization, nor as a self-interested plea. Over a third of CM supporters do not subscribe to the ideal of the Commission as the government of Europe, and a similar number would welcome greater powers being vested in the European Parliament, although only 12 per cent hold both positions. In the minds of those at least, the

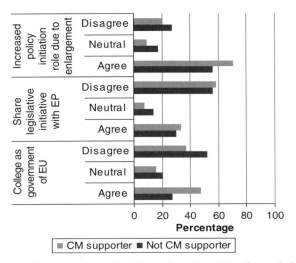

Fig. 5.9 Opinions of where power should reside in the EU and its role by support for the Community Method

Note: 1,718 ≤ n ≤ 1,752. The horizontal bars represent the percentage of agreement, neutrality, or disagreement for each question.

CM should not be associated with a centralization of authority in the hands of the Commission.

In the official discourse, the Commission's institutional privileges are justified by its duty to remain neutral and serve the general interest, the collegiality principle being a key element in this respect. This view finds a clear echo amongst supporters of the CM, for whom services have the responsibility to support politically-agreed positions of the College; yet there is weak evidence that they (89.0 per cent) are more likely than others (84.6 per cent) to hold this view.[37] They also display a relative distaste for state-based considerations at all levels of activity. Thus, asked what they thought about the need to ensure that posts be distributed on a geographically balanced basis, they were more likely to disagree (51.9 per cent) than were other officials (40.6 per cent).[38] They were also more likely (54.6 per cent, against 45.4 per cent for other officials)[39] to find it problematic for officials to manage dossiers of particular interest to their member state. Quite logically, over two thirds of them are hostile to the idea of having one Commissioner per member state, preferring a smaller and more efficient College. While this feeling is widely shared among the officials polled in our survey, CM supporters were even stronger opponents.[40]

[37] p = 0.044; Cramer's V = 0.079. [38] p < 0.001, Cramer's V = 0.120.
[39] p = 0.001, Cramer's V = 0.106. [40] p = 0.007; Cramer's V = 0.092.

CONCLUSION: A CITADEL UNDER SIEGE

There is little doubt that the post-Maastricht period has been a difficult one for the Commission, which has lost ground to the Council and the Parliament— the other corners of the 'institutional triangle'. This has long been the dominant view amongst observers of the EU scene and our survey has shown that it is shared by a vast majority of Commission staff. Considering the events in the ensuing months since the survey, and particularly the way the Union's response to the economic and financial crisis was managed, there is little reason to believe that their view will have changed. Yet awareness of the Commission's declining influence does not appear to have caused a change of paradigm, since support for the CM has remained quite high.

In some respects, these might appear as 'non-findings' since, according to a widespread view of bureaucratic politics, bureaucrats are expected to defend views that serve their own interest. Yet one should not forget that the Commission has seen momentous changes over the last two decades. It has witnessed the emergence of powerful rivals and has been subject to major reforms, while at the same time its membership has been changed by the recruitment of nearly 20 per cent of its staff from the new member countries. In these circumstances, it was far from sure that the average world view within the institution would have remained unchanged.

For supporters of the CM, that system has demonstrated its effectiveness and needs to be consolidated, rather than amended. Others may theorize the emergence of new forms of governance, but, for the average Commission official, the operating system crafted by Monnet and his followers still appears better suited to the needs of the twenty-first century Union than any of its rivals. That view, which features equally highly among newcomers and in the newer generation, cannot therefore be dismissed too lightly as a 'thing of the past'. However, the picture that results from our survey is more complex than it might seem at first sight. Even staunch supporters of the CM are cautious about the idea of transforming the Commission into a fully fledged 'government of Europe'. Similarly, while wary about the European Parliament, they are not systematically hostile to an expansion of its role.

Like many of their colleagues, supporters of the CM consider that enlargement has weakened cohesion within the Commission, and they have a fairly negative assessment of the impact of the Kinnock–Prodi reforms. Yet it is mostly in relation to their evaluation of their leadership's ability to defend the Commission in the EU system that a clear difference with other officials appears. Altogether, these elements may suggest that, should the Commission decide to be bolder and more assertive in its relations with other institutions, this attitude would find a positive echo in the Berlaymont building. Whether this can happen, and what response it would elicit from the national capitals is, needless to say, quite another story . . .

6

Leadership in the Commission

The role that the founding treaties entrusted to the European Commission has ensured that leadership of the organization has continued to be a constant preoccupation of practitioners and scholars. Other international organizations exist to find areas where states can identify and negotiate mutually beneficial acts of cooperation (see Keohane 2002: 27–38). In those bodies, which are invariably intergovernmental, the permanent administration is typically no more than a secretariat.[1] By contrast, the signatories to the Treaty of Rome intended the Commission to play a continuous role in policy initiation and enforcement. That it has not always been able to do so effectively is partly due to external influences over which the Commission has little control. The treaties certainly did not provide for 'the emergence of uninhibited leadership' (Hayward 2008: 2) by the Commission. Moreover, member governments have repeatedly asserted and reasserted their power.[2] However, the ambitions, choices, and capacities of the Commission President have also been a key factor. Thus, the Commission's weaknesses have unsurprisingly been implicated in recent diagnoses of 'leaderless Europe' (Cini 2008; Dimitrakopoulos 2008; Hayward 2008).

This chapter examines the leadership of the Commission through the eyes of its officials. Using responses to the online survey, it looks at how officials assess the performance of four Commission Presidents from Jacques Delors to José Manuel Barroso. It then focuses on the Barroso Presidency. Against the background of the 2004 and 2007 enlargements, Barroso spoke about the need for strong presidential leadership in an expanded College of twenty-seven that, for the first time, was composed of one Commissioner per member state (Spinant 2006; see also Peterson 2008a, 2008b). Drawing on data both from the online survey and elite interviews, the chapter investigates the extent to which this ambition has been achieved. It provides insights into the working

---

[1] On leadership in international organizations, see Claude (1956); Cox and Jacobson (1973); Young (1991); Barnett and Finnemore (1999); Janning (2005); Tallberg (2006); Deese (2008).
[2] For example, in the 1965 'empty chair' crisis, the rise of European summitry from 1969, and rounds of treaty reform since the Maastricht IGCs. See Kassim and Menon (2003, 2004).

and style of the Barroso Presidency, and examines the attitudes of officials, *cabinet* members and fellow Commissioners towards what emerges from the findings as a new model Presidency.

The chapter begins with a brief discussion of political leadership and the Commission. The second section offers a short overview of the powers of the Commission Presidency and how the office has developed. The third reports the ratings of Commission Presidents and tests hypotheses about the pattern of evaluation. The Barroso Presidency is examined in a fourth section. The strengthening of the Presidency since 2005 is highlighted and the ambivalent attitudes of officials towards this development, especially senior managers, are explored. The final section considers the merits and the 'perils' of a presidentialized Commission.[3]

POLITICAL LEADERSHIP AND THE EUROPEAN COMMISSION[4]

The functions entrusted to the Commission have inevitably directed attention toward the capacity of the organization to play a leadership role.[5] The leadership of the organization has attracted no less scrutiny. The two are intimately connected, as both practitioners and observers have long recognized (see for example Coombes 1970; Jenkins 1989; Delors 2004; Spence 2006). Although this chapter focuses on leadership of the Commission, it is premised on the assumption that how the Commission is led influences to a large degree its role and effectiveness within the EU system more generally.

Political leadership has proved an elusive concept for scholars,[6] but recent analyses of prime ministerial government have developed an approach that combines insights from agent-centred and structuralist perspectives (see Elgie 1995, Helms 2005).[7] This 'interactionist' approach suggests that leadership is contingent on interaction between the personal attributes of the leader and

---

[3] The allusion is to Linz's (1990) seminal article.

[4] We are grateful to Miriam Hartlapp and Gary Marks for their helpful suggestions for this section. They, of course, share no responsibility for its content.

[5] See, for example, the discussion in Coombes (1970: ch. 4) and Hayward (2008: 1–27).

[6] As one commentator observes warily; 'It is almost ritual for the authors of books and articles on leadership to make two statements at the beginning of their works. The first statement goes like this: "Many scholars have studied leaders and leadership over the years, but there still is no clear idea of what 'leadership' is or who leaders are". The second statement usually takes the form of several paragraphs summarizing the popular theories of leadership: great man, traits, group, behaviorist, and situational' (Rost 1991:13). For analyses of leadership, see MacGregor Burns (1978); Rose and Suleiman (1980); Blondel (1987). For useful reviews, see Kellerman (1986); Elgie (1995, ch. 1); Helms (2005: ch. 1).

[7] The interactionist approach is discussed and set out in Elgie (1995: ch. 1).

environment (Elgie 1995: 7)—a view that has much in common with studies of the Commission Presidency that highlight the importance of internal and external resources and constraints (see, for example, Endo 1999; Spence 2006). 'Personal attributes' include ambitions and style. These can vary significantly. Some leaders have a small number of specific goals, others a long list of general aims. The ambitions of some are far-reaching, radical, and transformative. Other leaders are simply concerned to keep the ship of state on an even keel or to implement modest changes. The level and scope of a leader's ambitions influence priority-setting, which has implications for the mobilization and investment of resources, including personal political capital. Leaders also differ in terms of style. They can be dogmatic or pragmatic, assertive or responsive, active or passive. Leaders learn on the job, adjusting and altering aims and leadership style over time.

'Environment', according to the interactionist approach, encompasses three elements: 'institutional structures, historical forces and societal demands' (Elgie 1995: 13, 192). As for the first, the structure of the College, the resources of the Commission Presidency, and relations with other actors and levels of government are the key elements.[8] The second—historical forces—highlights the extent to which the choices available to the Commission today are shaped by its previous actions. The appointments member governments make and their preparedness to develop policy at the EU level are also influenced by inferences based on the Commission's past performance. In terms of societal demands, as an executive body in an international organization, the Commission is relatively remote. It has little direct contact with EU citizens. Instead, the views of domestic publics tend to be channelled via national governments, the European Parliament, and interest groups. These elements constitute the environment within which the Commission works. They can operate either as resources or constraints on the Commission.

THE INSTITUTIONAL ENVIRONMENT[9]

The College

The College is the Commission's supreme decision-making body. The College makes decisions collectively for the Commission on a day devoted to the

---

[8] The party system and the distribution of power within political parties are less important in the case of the European Commission, although they have become more relevant as the powers of the European Parliament have grown. See Chapters 2, 3 and 4 for discussions of partisanship in the Commission.

[9] Space constraints do not permit a detailed consideration of historical forces and societal demands.

purpose. This power, moreover, cannot be delegated to other groups or individuals within the organization.[10] The principle of collective responsibility, which Cassese and della Cananea (1992: 80) contend is 'implicitly required by Article 163 of the Treaty', was 'later specified by Article 1 of the internal rules of procedures, adopted on 9 January 1963' (see Coombes 1970: 181–5). The organizational implications are well described by Michelmann (1978: 16):

> Even relatively trivial matters, which would be routinely decided by senior civil servants at the national level, are at least formally decided by the commission. Decisions within the commission are made by majority vote, although every attempt is made to attain unanimity, at least on important matters, and any commissioner can stall action on a decision. The upward funnelling of all matters, and collective decision-making, are devices to assure that few, if any, decisions can escape the attention of any Commissioner or his political advisers, and that consequently any action that may be interpreted as being rashly unfair or biased can be attacked by other nationalities.

It follows from the way in which collective responsibility has been defined as an organizational principle in the Commission that all departments have a right to be consulted on all policy proposals and that all proposals are submitted to the College for a final decision. As well as these operational implications, collective responsibility has a symbolic importance (Dimitrakopoulos 2008). By recognizing the right of all Commissioners to participate in decision-making across the full range of EU action, and not only the areas for which they hold portfolio responsibilities, it underlines the organization's claim to represent the general interest of the Union, transcending narrow interests including those of the member governments who nominated the Commissioners.

Collective decision-making can, however, take a variety of different forms (see Andeweg 1993).[11] Power within an executive body can be distributed

---

[10] Even mechanisms that have been introduced to expedite business, such as the division of the agenda into A points, for agreement without discussion—unless any member of the Commission wants to open the issue—and B points, which are discussed, and the written procedure, where the job of drafting a text is delegated to an individual Commissioner, which is then circulated to all members of the College, have been designed so as to preserve the principle of collective responsibility.

[11] 'The *collective* character of the government does not entail any specific distribution of power within the cabinet: it merely states that not one person (an individual minister or the prime minister) takes the decisions, but that all ministers are part of the process. Collective government is indeed the assumption that underlies the constitutional or customary rule of collective responsibility: it is largely concerned with the consequences of the involvement of ministers, whether such an involvement has been large or small, substantial or perfunctory. The collegial character of the government is based on the principle that all ministers should have an equal say in the decision-making process. This corresponds to a different concept, that of collegial government, which is assumed by the principle of "one man, one vote" within the cabinet. The idea is present, whether or not matters are decided by votes and notwithstanding the

equally ('collegiality'), exercised by 'an inner cabinet' ('oligarchy') (Andeweg 1993: 28) or concentrated in the hands of a single individual ('monocracy'). As shown below, there has been considerable variation in the Commission since 1958. The same is not true, however, in relation to where decisions are taken and the actors who are involved. In contrast to national executives, where prime ministers can choose where in the cabinet system a particular issue is to be handled and which of his or her colleagues cansit on the relevant cabinet committee, Commission decisions can only be taken by the full College. There is therefore limited scope for segmented decision-making or fragmented *cabinets* in the Commission (Andeweg 2003: 47).

The Commission Presidency

Despite the organization's commitment to collective decision-making, expectations of leadership were quickly directed at the Commission Presidency, and the incumbent of this office soon came to personify the Community. The post came to be seen as 'fundamental to the operation of the Commission and to the coherence of the EU per se' (Spence 2006: 27). At the same time, for most of the Commission's history—and certainly until the early 1990s—the President has been little more than a *primus inter pares*, or 'first among equals', and weak in comparison to prime ministers at national level (Kassim 2012). The task is daunting—to balance 'effective chairing of College, collegiate consensus, and leadership of policy orientation', without being able to exercise 'managerial control' nor to 'impose policy positions on his peers' (Spence 2006: 27–8).

In examining the powers of the office, it is useful to distinguish between resources of three kinds: *procedural* resources, which give influence over where, when, and how decisions are taken within a collective decision-making context; *political* resources, which concern powers, formal and informal, that attach to the office and the personal legitimacy of the incumbent; and *administrative* resources, which relate to the size of the personal office, powers of appointment within the administration, and wider prerogatives concerning the administration as a whole.

The President's procedural resources derive less from the EEC treaties than from the logistical necessities arising from the organization of the Commission's work, the institutionalization of the office by its first incumbent, Walter Hallstein (see Noël 1992; Loth et al. 1998), and the Commission's internal rules of procedure. The treaties entrusted important functions to the Commission, but did not differentiate the role of the Commission President from

---

fact that in most countries where cabinet government exists the prime minister has the casting vote in the event of a tie' (Andeweg 1993: 25–6. Emphasis is in the original).

other members of the College (Cini 2008). The powers granted to the President under the College's Rules of Procedure are important, but limited. Certainly, they give 'no monopoly over procedural weapons' (Spence 2006: 28). Significantly, the Commission President has only one vote—the same as other members of the College—and the rules of procedure provide for formal decisions to be taken by simple majority.

The Commission President convenes and chairs meetings of the College, establishes its agenda, and approves its minutes. But members of the College may request the addition of an issue to the agenda and can call for discussion of a particular dossier to be postponed. The minutes of College meetings, moreover, must be countersigned by the Secretary-General.

The President also has the power to establish College subcommittees and to decide on their composition, but cannot delegate decision-making authority to these formations.[12] Subcommittees have typically been used as a mechanism to affirm collegiality, and to improve the work of the College, rather than as an instrument to advance the Commission President's agenda (Coombes 1970: 124). Indeed, the main channel through which the President can influence the policy agenda is the weekly meeting of 'special *chefs*' that precedes the Monday meeting of the *chefs de cabinet* (the 'hebdo', from the French for 'weekly': *hebdomadaire*). It prepares the weekly Wednesday meeting of the College. 'Special *chefs*' is always chaired by a member of the President's *cabinet*, while the Secretary-General presides over the hebdo.

Historically, the Commission President had few *political* resources that distinguished him from other members of the College.[13] Like other Commissioners, he was appointed by common accord of the member governments.[14] He had neither the legitimacy that a popular mandate bestows[15] nor, since he was neither a party leader nor the head of a coalition, any of the resources—electoral mandate, party discipline, or formal coalition agreement—that prime ministers can mobilize to hold sway over their ministerial colleagues. As member governments decided on the allocation of portfolios, the President was not owed any sense of personal obligation on the part of

[12] Unlike a British Prime Minister (see Hennessy 1989, 2007), the Commission President cannot use procedural power to create sub-groupings that would enable him to bypass opposition in the College.

[13] Responsibility for representing the Commission externally was an important exception granted by the rules of procedure. The President receives the accreditation of ambassadors from non-EU states and is a member of the European Council, and also represents the Commission in meetings concerned with EU external relations as well as in bilateral meetings with the governments of third countries.

[14] It is worth recalling that prior to the Treaty of European Union 'member states were obliged to go through the formal renomination procedures halfway through the four-year term of the Commission in order for President to continue in office' (Spence 2006: 31).

[15] On whether the Commission President should be elected, see Hix (2002a, 2008). See Majone (2002) for a discussion of the 'perils of parliamentarization'.

fellow Commissioners.[16] Indeed, as Coombes (1970: 252) observed several decades ago, there was very little to hold the College together.

The political resources commanded by the office have changed significantly since the early 1990s (Table 6.1). The 1992 Treaty on European Union gave the nominee for President a voice in the nomination of other members of the College.[17] It also granted Parliament the right of approval over the member governments' nominee for Commission President (Westlake 1998). In 1997, the Amsterdam Treaty underlined the Commission President's pre-eminence: 'The Commission shall work under the political guidance of its President' (Art. 219 TEC). Over time, the method by which the Commission President is appointed changed in ways that conferred a stronger personal mandate. First, the 2001 Nice Treaty added the power to allocate portfolio responsibilities and, with the prior approval of the College, to appoint Vice-Presidents from within the College or to require that a Commissioner resign.[18] The Lisbon Treaty retained these provisions and extended them in respect of the appointment of the High Representative.[19] It also stipulated that the European Council must take account of the results of the preceding elections to the European Parliament in selecting their Presidential nominee, a move intended to align the choice of the heads of state and government with the expressed will of European citizens.[20]

The administrative resources of the office have also been limited. While the President's *cabinet* played a part in the selection of officials to the two most senior grades in the Commission services, A1 and A2 (Coombes 1970) under the old system (see Chapter 2), it was constrained by the geographical quota and other *cabinets*, backed by 'their' permanent representations and national capitals, who often fought fiercely to ensure nationals were fairly represented in the higher echelons of the organization.[21] Although the President's *cabinet* has tended to be larger than those of his colleagues— important, since the Commission President must oversee the work of the

---

[16] Spence (2006: 19) cites the following quotation from Delors: 'Il y a toujours un exercice difficile de repartition des portefeuilles, puisque . . . le président de la Commission n'est que le primus inter pares' ['The allocation of portfolios is always a problem, as the Commission President is only a *primus inter pares*'] (Delors 1994: 221).

[17] The requirement for 'common accord' among member governments remained, however (see Article 158 TEC as amended by Article G(48) TEU).

[18] Article 217(2–4) TEC.

[19] See Art. 17 TEU, Art. 248 TFEU and Article 81 para 1 TFEU.

[20] Art. 17(7) TEU.

[21] Note Delors's threat to Directors-General, recorded by Ross (1995: 121) and cited by Spence (2006: 138)—'If I could hire and fire here, I'd go after at least five or six of you . . . In a government, I'd be able to remove people. But here you are all barons, it is hard to shake you up . . . But I'll get you nonetheless'. This incident is telling, since it is often reported that Delors made use of the Article 50 procedure—which allows a generous pay-off for senior staff—to remove top managers during his Presidency.

Table 6.1 Constitutional resources of Commission Presidents, 1958–2004

	Mandate	Power over appointment of members of the Commission	Power to allocate portfolios among members of the Commission	Power to require resignation of members of the Commission	Power to re-shuffle portfolios	Formal status vis-à-vis members of the Commission	Prior nomination	Relationship with Secretariat-General
Commission Presidents pre-Maastricht	Personal mandate; appointment by member governments	Little say; joint agreement of member governments	Minimal	No	No	*Primus inter pares*	Informal	Ranges from close to loose
Between Maastricht and Amsterdam	Personal mandate; appointed by member governments, after approval of nomination by EP	Some say; joint agreement of member governments and approved by EP	Limited	No	No		Informal	Range from close to loose
Between Amsterdam and Nice						Political guidance		
after Nice	Personal mandate; appointed by member governments, after approval of nomination by EP	Qualified: member governments must agree and European Parliament must approve	Yes	Yes	Yes		Formalized	Close partnership

entire organization—it is small given the range of the President's responsibilities and the collective staff of the other Commissioners' *cabinets*.

While the Secretariat-General, the body responsible for central coordination within the Commission, has been formally accountable to the Commission President (Endo 1999), it has traditionally been a guardian of collegiality, serving and supporting the College, rather than a personal service of the President's. Indeed, its head has been seen as the representative of the services to the Commission's political leadership (Kassim 2006). The relationship between the President's *cabinet* and the Secretariat-General has been central to the functioning of the Commission, but the two bodies have been distinct and separate.[22] An important consequence is that the President has operated at some distance from interdepartmental coordination or arbitration, unlike prime ministers whose presence in these processes is assured by the action of, for example, the British Cabinet Office, the German *Kanzleramt* or the French *Secrétariat Général du gouvernement*. The Commission President has lacked an equivalent that would enable him to exercise oversight and control over the services.

Nor has the Commission President been able to take decisions over how the Commission is organized. The size of the College and its composition are delimited in the treaty and set by the unanimous agreement of governments meeting in an IGC,[23] while, the budgetary authority decides the number and grade of Commission officials that can be recruited. Historically, Commission DGs had to be created, merged, or split in order to accommodate the demands of member governments for particular portfolios. However, over time the Commission President has gained greater influence. The Treaty of Nice provided, for example, that the Commission President 'shall decide on [the Commission's] internal organisation in order to ensure that it acts consistently, efficiently and on the basis of collegiality'.[24]

---

[22] The same is true of the Legal Service and to a lesser extent the Spokespersons' Service. Though the Commission President has been the responsible Commissioner since 1967, it is understood that the Legal Service should be independent.

[23] Originally, the larger member states appointed two Commissioners and the smaller states one. As the Community grew from 6 to 9 (1973) to 10 (1981), 12 (1986), and 15 (1995), the size of the College grew from 9 to 13 to 14, 17 and 20 respectively. However, the Treaty of Nice, which came into force on 1 February 2003, removed the right of the governments of the larger states to appoint two members and permitted only one Commissioner per member state. With the 2004 enlargement, one Commissioner from each of the new member states joined the Commission to work alongside existing members. The Prodi Commission temporarily had 30 members. The first Barroso Commission had 25 members, which grew to 27 with the accession of Bulgaria and Romania in 2007. For arguments about the size of the College and its impact on the working of the organization, see Tindemans (1975) and Spierenburg (1979).

[24] Art. 217(1) TEC.

Especially before the changes introduced by the Maastricht Treaty, the Commission Presidency commanded few resources and was subject to significant constraints. The office, at least in formal terms, was weak (see Coombes 1970; Ross 1995; Peterson and Bomberg 1999; Kassim 2012). In fact, for one former President's biographer, it was 'an impossible job. Indeed, . . . hardly . . . a job at all' (Campbell 1983: 181). The ability of incumbents to keep colleagues in check,[25] orchestrate coherent policy programmes, or manage the house effectively was extremely limited. The constraints on the Commission Presidency had important implications for the internal working of the Commission. The absence of centralized political authority made coordination difficult between the *cabinets* and between the cabinets and the services. In most national systems, the proximity of central coordinating bodies to a powerful head of government strengthens their authority vis-à-vis line departments. In the Commission's case, the lack of such authority has been compounded by an insistence on the part of line DGs that the Secretariat-General is itself subject to the principle of collegiality. More broadly, as the Commission's responsibilities are core to the operation of the EU as a system characterized by institutional interdependence, the consequences of a weak Commission Presidency have been felt by actors and interests in Brussels and beyond.

Relations with other key actors

Relations with stakeholders within the EU political system are an important element of the institutional environment in which leadership of the Commission is exercised. The Commission is a 'multiply dependent' institution (Christiansen 1997) in three key respects. First, member governments and more recently the European Parliament appoint the Commission President and the other members of the College. Second, the EU budget is set by the Council and the Parliament. Third, in the performance of its main functions, the Commission cannot take action unilaterally. Its responsibility for setting EU goals is shared with the European Council and the Council of Ministers, legislative authority with the Council and the Parliament, and responsibility for policy implementation with member state administrations and the European courts.

Within this environment, the success of the Commission President is likely to be shaped by three key factors. The first is the calibre of nominees that member governments are prepared to select for the College (see Coombes 1970: 251–4; Spence 2006: 34–8; Peterson 2006b). The second is whether the

[25] The inability of Jacques Santer to request the resignation of the Commissioner (Edith Cresson) against whom allegations had been laid, allegedly because of opposition from the national capital of the individual concerned, or to prevent a fellow Commissioner (Ritt Bjerregaard) from writing a 'warts and all' insider's account of the Commission, are instructive.

Commission President can muster supportive majorities in the European Parliament. The third, and arguably the most important, is the willingness of member governments to take action at the EU. In particular, the Commission President's ability to persuade and to mobilize support among heads of state and government is likely to prove the main determinant of success.

COMMISSION LEADERSHIP IN HISTORICAL PERSPECTIVE

The twelve individuals, from Walter Hallstein to José Manuel Barroso, who have held the Commission Presidency have adopted very different strategies to the challenges it poses. They have taken up the office with very different ambitions. Each has had a distinctive leadership style, and has sought to mobilize differing resources. Moreover, the powers and definition of the office have varied over time, and each President has confronted conditions—institutional, historical, social—that have been more or less hostile to the EU and to the Commission.

A detailed investigation of each Commission Presidency is not possible, but, drawing on historical accounts,[26] it is instructive to highlight some contrasting cases. The Hallstein Commission was 'an intimate and cohesive team' (Coombes 1970: 253) that brought together several veterans of post-war integration. Walter Hallstein was an ambitious President, who sought to establish the Commission as equivalent to national administrations, and 'repeatedly referred to himself as the equivalent of a "European Prime Minister"' (Peterson 2006a: 504). Although he was personally involved in the main areas of policy, he permitted other Commissioners to take the lead in key domains, most notably, agriculture (Sicco Mansholt) and competition (Hans von der Groeben). Inside the Commission, Hallstein had a good working relationship with Emile Nöel, the Commission's first Secretary-General, who is credited with 'the Commission's rise to institutional maturity' (Lemaignen 1964: 69–70). Externally, Hallstein was an impressive performer (Noël 1998; von der Groeben 1998), but encountered fierce resistance from the French President, Charles de Gaulle, and resigned following the 'empty chair' crisis.

Delors was also a strong President. Like Hallstein, he led ambitious initiatives in major areas of policy, most notably the single market programme, budgetary reform, and economic and monetary union; but he also allowed other Commissioners to undertake notable policy changes. Delors's leadership style relied strongly on a powerful *cabinet* within the house and his ability to

---

[26] Such as Coombes (1970); Ross (1995); Spence (2006); Peterson (2006a); Kassim (2012).

persuade and convince his fellow members of the European Council. However, 'three propitious contextual variables: national receptivity to European solutions, international changes (especially German unification), and a favourable business cycle from 1985 to 1990' (Ross 1995: 234–7) were critical to his success.

Jacques Santer's more modest ambitions were captured by his promise to 'do less, but to do it better'. Although several important successes were achieved during his tenure and he was personally involved in initiatives to reform internal procedures and processes within the Commission, his Presidency illustrated the extent to which historical factors and societal demands can operate as constraints. He had been appointed to the office precisely because member governments had begun to be concerned about Commission-led expansionism under his predecessor.

Romano Prodi also recorded a number of notable achievements, but came ultimately to be viewed as a weak President. Although he was the first Commission President to benefit from the strengthening of the office under the Treaty of Amsterdam, and on entering office had spoken of the Commission as a 'European government', Prodi did not offer strong leadership to a College that included several imposing figures. Nor was he effective in the European Council, despite inside experience as a former Italian prime minister. Illustrating how the rating of a Commission President outside the institution can affect morale inside, the lack of support for the Commission in major national capitals led to reports that 'the Commission as a whole is losing heart' (Peterson 2006b: 97).

Table 6.2 shows that there have been four main models: active presidential, steered presidential, *primus inter pares*, and passive chair. Of the ten Commission Presidents, five have been passive chairs with limited ambitions, passive styles, collegial in the College, and modest in mobilizing resources. Two have been *primus inter pares*, with occasionally presidential styles on specific initiatives. Another two have been active presidential, with high ambitions, an interventionist style, and active in mobilizing resources. And only one—Jacques Delors—deserves association with the steered presidential model, defined by its heroic ambitions, a strongly presidential style, and very active—even aggressive—resource mobilization.

EVALUATING COMMISSION PRESIDENTS:
THE VIEW FROM THE INSIDE

The online survey solicited the opinions of Commission staff on the performance and achievements of four Commission Presidents.[27] One aim was to

---

[27] The survey was configured so that respondents were asked to rate only the Commission Presidents under whom they had served.

Table 6.2 Models of the Commission Presidency, 1958–2004

Type	Ambition: level and scope	Style	Autonomy extended to colleagues	Resources mobilized	Examples
Active presidential	High: general	Active: President launches major policy proposals; may intervene in portfolio areas	Allows other Commissioners to develop and promote initiatives	*Internal* Close working relationship between presidential cabinet and Secretariat-General. *External* Active use of power of persuasion in Council/European Council	Hallstein, Jenkins
Steered presidential	Heroic: general	Active: Strong presidential lead on major policies.	Allows other Commissioners to develop and promote initiatives	*Internal* Presidential cabinet plays steering role. Secretariat-General bypassed by personal networks of President and President's cabinet. *External* Active use of power of persuasion in European Council	Delors
Primus inter pares	Modest: general	Active: presidential lead on some areas	Allows colleagues to launch major initiatives	*Internal* Loose working relationship with Secretariat General. *External* Active in Council/European Council	Rey, Mansholt
Passive chair	Limited: introspective	Passive	Collegial	*Internal* President's cabinet is passive. Loose working relationship with Secretariat General. *External* Passive in Council/European Council	Malfatti, Ortoli, Thorn, Prodi, Santer

ascertain the extent to which the internal assessment of the leaders matched the evaluation in the scholarly literature. A second was to compare the performance of the four most recent incumbents of the office. Respondents were asked to assess each President in regard to setting a policy agenda, effectively managing the house, delivering on policy priorities, and defending the Commission. These four aspects of leadership are distinct, but complementary. The first points to the Commission President's effectiveness in articulating policy priorities, the second to the management of the Commission as an organization, the third to securing the passage of key policy initiatives, and the fourth to protecting the Commission's prerogatives, as well as its policy proposals, in the EU system. As indicators, the four dimensions embody an interactionist approach, as they combine the expression of personal attributes with the environment within which the leader operates.

Two findings from the descriptive statistics are noteworthy (see Figure 6.1). The first is that the ranking of Commission Presidents by Commission insiders largely coincides with assessments in the academic literature. Delors emerges as the strongest and Santer the weakest. Barroso is considered to be a strong President, and is second only to Delors, while Prodi is less strong, but not as weak as Santer. Second, respondents vary their assessments of the same individual across the four dimensions. Delors, for example, receives close to a 100 per cent rating for setting a policy agenda, delivering policy priorities, and defending the Commission, but only 44 per cent of respondents regarded his management of the house as fairly or very strong.

As it is unlikely that opinion in any of these instances was distributed uniformly or randomly across the Commission, a multivariate logistic analysis was undertaken to explore the characteristics (or roles within the Commission) of respondents who rated performance as strong in regard to each aspect of leadership. The aim was to examine the extent to which views on the strength of leadership are shaped by nationality (and having served in a national administration), length of service, current position (level of seniority), function of current DG, and governance belief (see Chapter 1). The explanatory variable is binary: a value 1 is given where respondents consider performance to have been strong (fairly or very); a 0 is given for all other responses.

Taking each incumbent in turn, the analysis (reproduced as an appendix) shows, first, that the Delors Presidency was rated as strong in all four dimensions by long-serving officials. Those officials working in spending and legislative DGs were more likely to view Delors as being strong in relation to defending the Commission. Supranationalists were more likely to regard Delors as being strong in relation to policy—both in managing the agenda and in delivering on priorities. Senior managers were less likely to rate Delors as strong in terms of his management of the house.

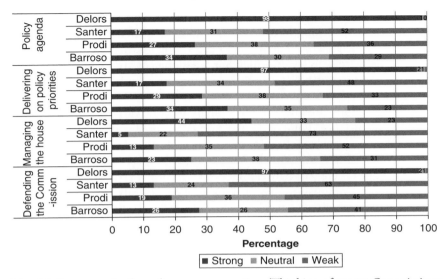

Fig. 6.1 Responses to the online survey question: 'Thinking of recent Commissions (detailed next), how would you rate their performance: . . .'

The descriptive statistics show that Santer is regarded as the weakest of the four Presidents. The minority (fewer than 20 per cent) who rated him as strong were more likely to be long-serving officials or those with *cabinet* experience. This relationship holds across all four dimensions. Those officials working in DGs that are primarily legislative were more likely to regard Santer as having been strong in managing the policy agenda. Middle managers were less likely to report Santer's management of the house as being strong.

Prodi was viewed as strong by up to a quarter of officials. Again, these officials were more likely to be long-serving. Those with *cabinet* experience or those working in administrative DGs were more likely to rate Prodi as strong in managing the house and delivering on policy priorities. However, officials from Scandinavian national administrations were less likely to regard Prodi as strong on these same dimensions. Senior managers were more likely to rate Prodi as strong in defending the Commission. Those officials working in spending and legislative DGs were more likely to view him as strong in relation to policy. Supranationalists were more likely to regard Prodi as having been strong in his management of the house.

Barroso was regarded as strong by up to a third of officials. He is viewed by senior managers and members of *cabinets* as strong in managing the house, delivering on policy priorities and defending the Commission. Those who entered the Commission during his Presidency rate Barroso as strong in terms of managing the policy agenda and defending the Commission. Officials from continental national administrations, however, are less likely to view Barroso as strong in relation to policy or managing the house. Officials working in adminstrative DGs are more likely to rate Barroso as strong in managing the house and those working in primarily spending or primarily regulatory DGs are less likely to agree that Barroso has been strong in defending the Commission or in delivering policy priorities. Supranationalists are more likely to view Barroso's handling of policy—both managing the agenda and delivering on priorities—as strong.

Reflecting more broadly on these analyses, the variables are pertinent and capture variance. Four particular points are noteworthy. First, position matters. It is noticeable that senior managers and *cabinet* experience are more likely to offer a high rating in all four cases. Second, DG is important. There are significant differences between DG types in how Presidents are rated for defending the Commission. Third, long-serving officials are more likely to recognize the strength of Commission Presidents. Interestingly, however, such officials do not rate Barroso as particularly strong, even though they recognize that he is stronger than either of his two predecessors. Finally, nationality is not an explanatory factor. Officials from the same member state do not appear to share the same assessments of Commission Presidents as their compatriots.

THE BARROSO PRESIDENCY IN FOCUS

As with prime ministers in a national setting, each incoming Commission President has a particular conception of the office he is assuming. Relations in the upper reaches of the organization are recast by each new incumbent. On taking office, Barroso insisted that the Commission needed 'presidential-style' leadership if it was to remain effective after enlargement. To avoid what Barroso termed 'fragmentation' or 'Balkanisation', the enlarged Commission needed 'a President that is seen by members of the Commission as a last resort and authority'.[28] In the light of the College's expansion to twenty-five (and later twenty-seven) members, he contended that the Commission could only function or be managed efficiently under strong, personalized authority.

Evidence from the online survey and interviews with Commissioners, *cabinet* members, and managers suggests that Barroso has largely succeeded in his aim of very significantly strengthening the Commission Presidency. To that extent, the data corroborates findings in the existing literature,[29] as well as in expert media

---

[28] Quoted in Spinant (2006: 2).
[29] This view is not uncontested. Trondal (2011), for example, has argued that the Presidentialization of the Commission is at best 'ambiguous' and that there remains a distinct 'lack of cohesion within the Commission as a whole'. Comprehensive administrative reforms, he contends, have 'not really changed the equation' on this front, and have resulted only in a 'marginal net increase in steering capacity'.

coverage.[30] Moreover, the changes he has introduced and the resources he has mobilized have led to the creation of a new model that is different from any of its predecessors. This new model Presidency has emerged principally as a consequence of entrepreneurship on the part of Barroso.

A more presidential Commission?

The EUCIQ surveys approached leadership from several perspectives. The online survey asked respondents to rate the Commission Presidents under whom they had served. In interviews, Commissioners were asked for their opinion of whether the College functions as a presidential or a collegial body. *Cabinet* members and middle and senior managers, meanwhile, were asked for their views on the role and status of the Secretariat-General. A full examination of responses on the Secretariat-General appears in Chapter 7, but those responses that bear on the Commission Presidency are discussed below.

As reported above, respondents to the online survey rated Barroso as strong on 'setting a policy agenda' and 'managing the house'. Importantly, these views were expressed especially strongly by *cabinet* members and senior managers, who have more direct contact with the Presidency than do more junior officials. In interviews, senior managers in particular testified that Barroso closely controlled the policy agenda at all levels of the policy process. *Cabinet* members highlighted how in meetings of 'special *chefs*', the President's *chef de cabinet* had shaped, delayed or effectively vetoed policy proposals. They reported that Barroso kept a much tighter rein on the Commission's policy programme than his immediate predecessors.

Of the five Commissioners interviewed, three characterized the College as presidential. They identified ways in which the President was able to control the agenda and otherwise to influence outcomes. In one interview with a Commissioner and a member of his cabinet, a comparison was drawn with experience of the Prodi Commission. Their observations are worth quoting at length:

> Commissioner: We have clearly a presidential system now, and a very strong one. And Barroso defends it even. He is fully aware of the problem. I've discussed it with him. I said, 'You have to establish a presidential system here', and he said, 'This is the only way our Commission of 27 can be organized. Otherwise, decision-making would be impossible'. He called it 'centralized decision-making, absent coordination'. Absent coordination means that his people, and the

---

[30] At the beginning of the second Barroso Presidency, one leading commentator offered a typical end-of-term evaluation for the first: 'He personifies and represents the Commission, and the gap between the president and the other commissioners is wider now perhaps than it ever has been. The very idea of a challenger to his status as *primus inter pares* now seems risible' (Taylor 2010: 12).

Sec-Gen coordinate or discuss things with just a very small number of Commissioners, a very small number. And of course, this is a problem for . . . collegiality. And you can see in this Commission, we normally do not have controversial points, or contentions . . . The President simply doesn't want that. Yeah? And he doesn't put it on the agenda, as long as there are still different views. So—

Interviewer: And that was different under Prodi, I suppose?

Commissioner: Yeah. Completely different. In this [Barroso] Commission there was never a vote. . . . Well, normally, a vote is not needed. . . . It does not happen. But here, the consensus in this Commission is achieved before the College meets. Before. The Prodi Commission, that was still normal, but at least two or three agenda points—yeah?—were on the agenda, where consensus was achieved during the meeting, and not before. . . . I mean, the reality, because in the majority of cases the Commissioner or the President are never involved, yeah? This is the matter and this then is solved at the level of *cabinet* members of the President, officials in Sec-Gen, and your *cabinet* members. I think that is the normal way—it is normally the exception if a Commissioner is involved. . . .

Member of the Commissioner's *cabinet*: I think there's been a fundamental change between the role of the President's *cabinet* under Prodi. I always felt that when we were dealing with the members of Prodi's *cabinet* their job was to make sure that what the portfolio Commissioner was wanting to do, fitted into the overall picture of what the Commission was doing. At the moment it's slightly bizarre. You have the impression that the member of Mr Barroso's *cabinet* that is following the work of a given Commissioner, is almost a kind of second Commissioner wanting to drive forward that interest, and so you have absurd situations where you have the President's *cabinet* on the top floor, the environment person in the President's *cabinet* supporting the Environment Commissioner's views, the industry person in the President's *cabinet* supporting the Industry Commissioner's views— . . .

—and it just all—it gets all messy, and you don't always have a clear view. And what happens in my view is that you have an incredible power now centralized on the Sec-Gen, who tends to be assimilated to the President's views and represents the President's views (interview 85).

Another Commissioner took a contrasting and mostly positive view of Presidentialization:

I've been in the [name of a member state] government . . . [and I disagreed with the Prime Minister] but he allowed me to pursue my policy. With Barroso it's not the case . . . [But] I can manage well. It's a College, so I . . . can manage to make my opinion known. And if I would like to [obstruct] . . . proposals that I don't like, I need to work a bit harder. The easiest way would be just [to] convince [the] President, but even if the President is not convinced, well, I could consult his colleagues . . . definitely [not] during the College; it's too late, but if I was really opposing to anything that he favours a lot, I could obstruct in preparing before. So, in a way I would say it's quite logical to [be] getting presidential, and I don't see any danger, and it makes [things] actually more efficient, as long as the president keeps the spirit of the College, and he keeps to his politics . . . I would say it's perhaps even a strength . . . I wouldn't like to have the . . . [College become a] second chamber of the European Parliament (interview 115).

A third Commissioner drew a contrast between how the College might work in an ideal world and its actual operation:

> To a great extent it's true, the President's will and directions [matter]. But it is also a collegial body . . . I think it would be better if we tried to reach consensus, but if not then it would be better to have voting, and have decisions by majority, if possible. This I would think it would be more democratic, because now, even if you place a reservation on something, it doesn't appear in print. It's a college decision. So, people don't know . . . who were against, who were in favour. And sometimes for the sake of reaching a consensus you compromise (interview 131).

The other two Commissioners interviewed took a slightly different view. For one, straightforwardly, the Commission was '*plutôt collégial*'—'rather collegial'. The other Commissioner saw the President as 'a mitigator, as a person not imposing something but rather supporting the approach of the college to reach a consensus' (interviews 101 and 67).

Testimony from interviews with *cabinet* members and Directors-General suggest that the President has been keen to ensure that he is personally linked with key legislative initiatives, such as the services directive and the REACH directive, rather than allowing them to be identified too closely with individual Commissioners. At the same time, insiders from the Barroso *cabinet* and the Secretariat-General, who were supportive of the President's ambition to centralize power, acknowledged that the aim had only partially been fulfilled and suggested that there may still be structural limitations to its realization:

> [N]ot all activities of the Commission are completely integrated into the President's own . . . agenda. . . . it's a presidential system, but that doesn't necessarily mean it's from the start top-down. . . . We don't have the capacity for that. The President's *cabinet* doesn't have the capacity for that. Even the Sec-Gen doesn't have the capacity for that. And there is room for the initiative of individual Commissioners and DGs, and which then leads to the situation where sometimes, for instance, in the Parliament, the president is criticized for not having prevented a certain Commissioner from coming with a certain initiative. But he doesn't see his role like that. . . . He wants [Commissioners] to come with ideas, because . . . he doesn't have the means to develop all the initiatives on his own. I mean, it's not that type of system. But then at some stage in the process of an initiative being worked out, then you look at how it fits in with the overall approach (interview 159).

Several interviewees speculated that the President's concern to maintain a tight grip over policy derived from concerns about what was necessary to make a 27-member College workable—thoughts that Barroso himself had aired on taking office. 'There's been a heavy centralization of what we do, but I think to myself that that's inevitable, given the size of the College' (interview 134). Others cited a conviction on the President's part that the Commission could only succeed if it worked cooperatively with the European Parliament and the Council. To that extent, he declared himself: 'a consensus-builder ... not an autocrat'. After barely avoiding a negative vote on his first Commission in 2004 over the Buttiglione affair,[31] Barroso took pains avoid embarrassment in the Parliament. He also remained true (too much so in the eyes of many within the Commission) to his determination to avoid provoking conflict with any of the larger EU member states, despite his pledge to fight 'economic nationalism', since failing to do so 'would be the end of the credibility of the European Commission'.[32]

Another characteristic of the Barroso era is the close relationship forged between the Commission Presidency and the Secretariat-General. The President sought explicitly to turn the Secretariat-General into an instrument of the Commission Presidency. As was observed in an interview with two senior officeholders:

> When Catherine arrived, she got a very clear mandate from the President, who as a former prime minister, like his predecessor but maybe more, and a different generation of prime minister, said, well, Catherine, I would like the Sec-Gen to be my service, and if I want to be a political president of the Commission, I need the Sec-Gen to be also a political part of this system (interview 159).

The same interviewees linked the Secretariat-General's new role and the need for greater intervention to the desire expressed by Barroso for the Commission to be more effective in its interactions with other EU institutions:

> After a request, a clear request from the President ... [Catherine Day] said, 'well, our work vis-à-vis the Council and the Parliament, in particular, should not just be a role of note-taker of the meetings we attend there. We should influence their work. We should listen to the political discussion out there, to the change of the composition of the Council'. The move from fifteen to twenty-seven member states was seen by the President and by Catherine as a major opportunity for us, for the Commission, to be a stronger player (interview 159).

Responses to the online survey appear to suggest that Barroso's ambitions—at least in terms of making the Secretariat-General an ally of the Commission Presidency—have been largely fulfilled. A plurality (37 per cent) disagreed with the proposition that the Secretariat-General is a 'neutral arbiter between the services in policy

---

[31] Barroso defended the Italian nominee for Commissioner, Rocco Buttiglione, even after he called homosexuality 'a sin' and declared that women 'belonged in the home' at his EP confirmation hearing. Eventually, Buttiglione stood down and a new team was voted in (see Peterson 2006b: 93).

[32] Barroso quoted in Spinant (2006: 2).

coordination'. Meanwhile, 59 per cent agreed that: 'The Secretariat General is becoming more political and more influential in the life of the Commission'.

Interviews with senior and middle managers provided further and more specific evidence. In response to the question 'Some respondents thought that the Secretariat-General is becoming too political in the life of the Commission. What is your view?', 47 per cent either agreed or strongly agreed.[33] When pressed, many confirmed that they viewed 'more political' to mean 'serving the Commission President'. The question, 'Some respondents thought the Secretariat-General focuses too much on procedure and not enough on policy content. What is your view?', also prompted some managers to express views on the President and the Secretariat-General. Most managers believed that the relationship had become closer:

> I think that this is a trend that the new Secretary-General would like to try. She would like to have a more, let's say, a more political body servicing the President . . . In the past, Secretariat General was more servicing the whole Commission, ensuring continuity . . . so now it might be changing (interview 8).

However, others thought that the Secretariat General was still caught mid-way between an old and a new role:

> It's not very clear what the role of the Secretariat General is. . . . It used to be a coordinating body focusing pretty largely on procedures. It is beginning to become more a prime minister's office, a large prime minister's office, trying to focus on policy. And the reality is probably somewhere in between those two. But it's not very clearly defined (interview 144).

Another senior official claimed that the Secretariat-General is 'becoming more political no doubt . . . [and] clearly transforming itself into the President's services . . . they are no longer the Commission's Secretariat-General' (interview 150).

A senior official from the Secretariat-General, who endorsed the President's new strategy, was concerned that the relationship between the Secretariat-General and the President's *cabinet* was not as close as it needed to be to make the arrangement a success:

> I think Catherine [Day] is really trying to turn this into a very modern organization, whereby barriers should not be an obstacle . . . So I think it is a good story. The one problem we are having here is . . . we really have to make an enormous effort to find out what the President intends to do. Not on the general basic political [orientation]—indeed that is clear, but I mean when I am organizing my work in the Council, I need to know what he is doing and what his staff is doing, and there I think . . . things can really improve (interview 60).

---

[33] Thirty five per cent either disagreed or strongly disagreed.

Strong support was expressed for this closer relationship. Many regarded close relations between the two as normal, since the Secretariat-General was in any case responsible to the Commission President:

> [The Secretariat-General is] serving the institution and it is the President who leads the institution so that's completely normal (interview 160).

> [I]f the Secretariat-General identifies with the President, it's normal. He's their line manager. Why wouldn't [they] identify with the President? (interview 142)

> [The Secretariat-General is] working for the Commission's President, are they not? I think it would be absurd to think of the Secretariat-General that was in some way independent and autonomous of the President of the Commission; absurd! (interview 139).

Some approved the relationship, because it promised to strengthen the Commission, especially given the record of the previous two administrations:

> Given that criticism of the Commission—the last two Commissions were too weak in political terms, . . . every effort and every contribution to counterbalance or to cultivate this aspect is positive (interview 116).

One interviewee felt that a close relationship was necessary for the Commission President to operate effectively within the European Council:

> In my view it [the Secretariat-General] would never be too political. It should be extremely active in the political sphere, because the . . . main interest of this institution is that the President is fully supported in its role as member of the European Council. That's the main interest . . . If our President is weak, all the rest will be weak. We need to ensure that everything works in order to give him the brightest ideas, the best products, and the top quality that we can deliver. In order to get there you inevitably need some political steer from the top, and the Secretariat-General can give that steer. . . . But of course this is the Commission so it will never become a Cabinet Office (interview 72).

Others were supportive because they wanted to see a more coherent policy programme put forward by the Commission or because they were concerned that the Commission should improve upstream coordination, and considered that this would only be possible if the Secretariat-General could ensure that proposed action by the services matched the priorities set by the President. In the words of one senior manager: 'I think I can only subscribe [to] the idea and the attempts to strengthen upstream coordination, and feel this is absolutely necessary' (interview 116). Similarly, according to a middle manager in the Secretariat-General:

> The President . . . sees the Secretary-General as his office, his department, there-fore—and he is a very political person. I mean, whether it's Barroso or not, it is a political role, but he sees it as such, and sees this as his department geared to drive forward the programme, which he has presented to the Parliament, and to the

Council, and that the Commission as a whole subsequently has presented (interview 53).

Some regarded a political role for the Secretariat-General as essential to the Commission's mission:

> I always privilege the political dimension for the Commission. And the Secretariat-General and Mrs. Day is the best proponent of that. It is to do the work to serve our political objectives . . . It seems to be, for me, a logical consequence of the institutional setup. If we confine ourselves [to] technical issues we will become irrelevant as an institution (interview 158).

At the same time, cautionary views were expressed by some interviewees. Although its orchestrating role at the centre of the Commission is indispensable many officials think that the Secretariat-General should leave the policy lead to Directorates-General, who, after all, are the technical experts. According to one middle manager in a large DG, with previous experience of working in the Secretariat-General:

> The Secretariat-General is the DG of the President, so I think it would be no news that there are some guidelines coming from there, but it's true that it shouldn't interfere too much in daily life, but rather [set out] the general guidelines. . . . [W]hen the Secretariat-General actually consulted the DGs, I found that positive (interview 56).

Regret was expressed by a few who lamented that the Secretariat-General had forsaken its historic role and was far too closely identified with the President. The views of one experienced senior manager were representative: 'I think the Secretary-General is losing its identity. The Secretary-General should be the guardian of the house. They decentralize too much. They do too little and I am afraid . . . [that a] private Secretariat is developing' (interview 49).

Another respondent considered that the Secretariat-General could best add value by concentrating on everyday coordination: 'I would prefer them to be a bit more—the oil in the machine so that everything works well, [so] that when there are conflicts, when there are differences in views, this is solved' (interview 56).[34] Such views were dismissed as outdated, however, by an official in the Secretariat-General. When informed that some respondents thought that the Secretariat-General was becoming too political in the life of the Commission, one senior manager retorted: 'And so there are those who are quite happy

---

[34] Another official, a long-serving senior manager, offered a more forthright view. When asked if he agreed that some respondents thought the Secretary-General was becoming too political in the life of the Commission, he replied: 'Just the opposite. They are nothing. They are not the guardian.' Recalling Emile Nöel and David Williamson, whom he described as 'Commissioners plus', he continued '[these guys] knew everything, [were] able to protect the Commission' and avoid 'political faults' (interview 49).

for us to be a notary. [Laughter] No. No, but those days are over. I think that is done' (interview 60).

A new model Presidency?

The changes towards which the data point have resulted in a Commission Presidency that is different from its predecessors. A new Presidential model has emerged. Barroso has become a pre-eminent President, but one that departs from the models incarnated by his predecessors. Whereas Hallstein and Delors relied on personal standing and authority, and in the case of the latter a powerful *cabinet* and personal networks throughout the Commission, Barroso's power has been rooted in the constitutional strengthening of the office, the appeal to centralized authority in an expanded College, and in the transformation of the Secretary General the annexation of a key organizational resource. The new model is 'presidential-organizational', where the Presidency is not *primus inter pares*, but pre-eminent. Barroso exercises close control over the College agenda and takes personal ownership of key policy initiatives. To an extent previously unseen, he runs the Commission through a close partnership with the Secretariat-General.

In terms of the types of Commission Presidency outlined above, the Barroso Presidency can be represented as shown in Table 6.3.

Explaining 'presidentialization' under Barroso

The political science literature suggests several ways in which a political office can be redefined. The first is as the intended result of deliberate 'constitutional engineering' (Sartori 1994). A second is unintended and the outcome of lower-level institutional change (see for example Poguntke and Webb 2005). A third method is through entrepreneurship, involving the mobilization of existing resources, by an individual post-holder. The Commission has been 'presidentialized' under Barroso largeky via the third route.

The first route was not open to the Commission, since treaty reform is largely in the hands of national governments.[35] Whilst the Commission Presidency was strengthened by a series of treaty changes introduced at Maastricht and after, the masters of the treaty did not intend to create a

---

[35] To some extent, Commission Presidents shaped debates at the margins as in the case, for example, of Santer's (little-noticed) success in convincing member states to embrace new (Amsterdam) Treaty provisions that the College be nominated 'by common accord with the nominee for President' and 'work under the political guidance of the President' (Peterson and Bomberg 1999: 52).

Table 6.3 A model of the Barroso Presidency

	Ambition: level and scope	Style	Autonomy extended to colleagues	Resources mobilized
Presidential-organizational	Modest and limited	Passive	Close control over College agenda, with active use of delay and veto. Personal ownership of policy initiatives	*Internal* Partnership between presidential cabinet and Secretariat-General. *External* Active use of power of persuasion in Council/European Council

strongly presidentialised Commission. Indeed, this outcome was one that, in the post-Maastricht ratification era and in the wake of Delors, they would have wanted to avoid. Rather, a critical mass of member states had two far more modest ambitions. The first was to reduce the democratic deficit. For reasons well explained elsewhere (Majone 2002; Rittberger 2005), the chosen solution has been to increase the Commission's accountability to the European Parliament. The second was to avoid problems of the sort that had led to the resignation of the College in March 1999. But reforms were pragmatic, incremental, and modest. They were not informed by a desire to engineer a radical reconfiguration of power within the College.

According to the second possibility, the redefinition of political offices is an unintended consequence of lower-level institutional change. Although there is some evidence of such institutional change, and it has contributed to the strengthening of the Commission Presidency since 2005, change of this kind has not been its cause. The lower-level change in question is the denationalization of *cabinets*, which has been evident both in terms of the composition of *cabinets* (see Egeberg and Heskestad 2010) and their functions (see Kassim 2012). The effect has been to make them more like the rest of the Commission, less like national outposts, and less likely to challenge the President.

Nor is there evidence that the processes that led to presidentialization more widely or their equivalents in national systems have been at work within the EU. Poguntke and Webb (2005) attribute presidentialization within parliamentary systems to the increase of leadership resources and autonomy within political parties and the executive, or to the rise of leadership-centred electoral processes. But the Commission President is not a party leader, nor is the Commission an elected body. Indeed, the EU is not a parliamentary system. Rather, the EU combines elements of both mixed government (Majone 2005) and the separation of powers (Hix 2005). To paraphrase Neustadt (1991: 29) in regard to the latter, parties in the Union have not combined what the treaties have kept separate—or at least not yet.

The change in the Presidency since 2005 has been effected largely by the actions of the new incumbent.[36] Barroso was the first Commission President to assume office after the 2004 'big bang' enlargement.[37] He came to the post with a particular conception of how the Commission would need to work in view of the College's expansion, and was the first Commission President to benefit from the strengthening of the office as the cumulative effect of successive treaty reforms. His powers over appointment, the distribution of portfolios, and resignation underlined his pre-eminent authority vis-à-vis his colleagues. Although he inherited the changes brought about by treaty reform and exploited the fact of enlargement, Barroso engineered the new relationship with the Secretariat-General and encouraged that body's new interventionism that has strengthened the office. Crucially, this new relationship provided him with a powerful new organizational resource that extended his reach into the services and thereby expanded his influence throughout the administration.

ATTITUDES TOWARDS PRESIDENTIALIZATION

The centralization of power within the Commission since 2005 is a significant and important development. It has implications for the Commission—not least because it responds to long-standing criticisms of weak leadership, fragmentation (see for example Spierenburg 1979), and a lack of control over decision-making and resource allocation—but also for the Union more broadly. Although there is much about the changes that is positive, there are also costs and risks. On the benefit side, presidentialization enables the organization to speak clearly with a single voice, diminishing the risk of sending out contradictory signals that may be politically damaging.[38] It also helps in attuning the political initiatives of the Commission to the prevailing climate, since presidential control makes it easier to dilute or delay initiatives, or to overrule colleagues who want to bring forward unpopular or badly-timed proposals. In addition, it clarifies issues of accountability, and significantly enhances the coordination capacity within the organization (see Chapter 7).

---

[36] The literature on political leadership, including Neustadt (1960), emphasizes the influence an incumbent can have on reshaping a political office.

[37] Commissioners from the ten new member states had joined the Prodi College on 1 May 2004.

[38] Once such incident arose early in the Barroso I Commission when Commissioners gave conflicting signals on the question of Ukraine's bid for EU membership. Cini (2008: 126) attributes this to 'a lack of cohesion arising out of Barroso's failure to instill a sense of collegiality amongst his commissioners'.

On the cost side, while concentrating power in the hands of a single individual may make decision-making more efficient, it carries the danger that the Commission's actions will be too ambitious or, more likely in an era of member state re-assertion, that they will not be ambitious enough. Barroso I, for example, was marked by caution,[39] understandably perhaps if the President was hoping to be reappointed to a second term. In any event, such caution may have had a negative impact on Commissioners, *cabinet* members, and senior officials. Individual Commissioners and their services may have felt inhibited and discouraged from proposing major initiatives. It may have dashed the hopes or ambitions of fellow Commissioners or led to a fall in morale within the services. There is also a normative dimension. One of the Commission's important claims to legitimacy is that it represents the general interest of the European Union. Collective or collegial decision-making is key to this claim, which may be weakened if excessive power is concentrated in the office of Commission Presidency.

Indeed, the data from interviews with Commission officials, *cabinet* members, and senior managers revealed an ambivalence about the presidentialization of authority within the Commission under Barroso. Although increasing presidential control was acknowledged, interviewees were divided on whether this centralization of authority was good or bad. Some respondents highlighted the benefits of a strong presidency. Some understood the necessity, but were concerned about the implications. Others, on various grounds, voiced disapproval. The Director-General of a large and powerful DG issued the following warning: 'I would say that the main risk I see now is a too big centralization in terms of policy shaping and that . . . the Directorate-General will not be asked enough their opinion on the policy content' (interview 133). A similar concern was voiced by another experienced Director-General: 'We are in the process of centralization. A bit too much. We were too much decentralized before. I hope we will find the right balance' (interview 15). Of course, some of these more negative opinions may reflect an expression of frustration towards the end of Barroso's first term (the online survey was conducted in 2008, the interviews in 2009), particularly on the part of Commissioners or senior managers whose policy ideas were blocked or otherwise remained unfulfilled. Nevertheless, the data registers a clear ambivalence within the organization.

A Barroso paradox?

In the light of the findings concerning the strengthening of the Presidency since 2005, it is tempting to construe the Barroso Presidency as a paradox. The

---

[39] See discussion of the 'Barroso paradox' below.

College over which Barroso presided, and which he came to dominate, was marked by a high level of ideological cohesion (Dimitrakopoulos 2008: 298–9; see also Taylor 2010) and he enjoyed the support of a notional majority in the Parliament. Yet neither the policy activism nor the flood of legislation that may have been anticipated under such circumstances materialized in practice. Such a paradox is, however, only apparent. First, Barroso's focus, reflected in the 2005 Strategy Paper he unveiled after taking office, was on effective implementation and management of existing EU policies. This was a logical choice following enlargement and the view that, after a decade of reform, the Commission itself was capable for the first time of truly monitoring implementation effectively. Second, Barroso might be credited with learning from his predecessor that '[t]he old Commission tactic of presenting a maximalist line in the hope that some of the Commission's agenda would ultimately be accepted often seems to backfire' (Cini 2008: 126).

Third, Barroso has often faced criticism for failing to stand up to large EU member states: '[t]he impression lingers . . . that Barroso is too politically cautious and too eager to trim his sails to the winds blowing from national capitals, especially Berlin, Paris and London' (Taylor 2010: 12). However, he has not been afraid to launch major policy initiatives. On climate change, regulation of financial markets, the Europe 2020 programme (designed to reinvigorate the internal market), repeated energy crises, and the Eurozone, Barroso showed genuine leadership without getting 'ahead' of key EU member states. Indeed, he has proved a far more effective political communicator and 'player' within the European Council than his two predecessors.

Fourth, the prospects for a 'new era of supranationalism' in the European Union of the twenty-first century are limited. The Union's diversity post-enlargement makes policy solutions more difficult to find. Moreover, '[c]hanges in the way that policy is made, with new and varied modes offering governments a flexible approach to European-level problem-solving, and the Europeanization of national polities' (Cini 2008: 127) have served to blur the distinction between intergovernmental and supranational policy-making. In short, it should not surprise us that Barroso chose the 'low' political road in trying to 'sow . . . the seeds of a credible approach for the Commission in what is a truly pragmatic strategy' (Cini 2008: 127).

CONCLUSION

The Commission Presidency historically has been an important, but weak, office. However, findings from the EUCIQ project suggest not only that Barroso has strengthened the office but that he has fashioned a quite different model of the Commission Presidency as compared to his predecessors. Although the change in the was made possible by a series of treaty reforms and enlargement, which occurred before he assumed the Presidency, Barroso seized the opportunity that they presented. His reconfiguration of the Presidency has had an important impact not only on the working of the College but on the Commission more generally, even if the response to the changes on the part of staff has been ambivalent.

It is unclear whether the change is likely to prove enduring. First, whoever succeeds Barroso may have a different conception of the Presidency. The changes that he has introduced may not have been so deeply institutionalized or accepted by the time that his term expires that they are irreversible. Second, much has depended on the willingness of other members of the Commission to buy into Barroso's view that leadership of a large College must be presidential. Future colleagues may not be as compliant. Third, the relationship between the Presidency and the Secretariat-General has worked effectively due partly to the personal relationship between José Manual Barroso and Catherine Day. Such a close partnership may not be possible in the future. Fourth, the EU as a political system is characterized by fluidity and improvisation. In the words of one senior manager:

> Power [in the Commission] is never with somebody for a very long time. It shifts all the time, and as soon as you see that it is somewhere visible too long, it's rebalanced somewhere else. So the automatic inner life of this organization is to ensure that there is always a fair balance between different interests, and that's basically the European idea. That's how we have always envisaged it, and here it works (interview 72).

There may be grounds, on the other hand, for thinking that presidentialization may prove to be enduring. First, with a College of twenty-seven or more members, each with an interest in each other's portfolios, strong 'brokerage' may be a functional necessity. Second, the more the Commission is under siege, the more do officials appreciate central authority.[40] Finally, it is useful to note one prominent commentator's observation:

> Like road signs or traffic lights, the European Commission is [now] a familiar presence whose value would be fully appreciated only if it did not exist. It plays a unique role in upholding the common rules that contribute to Europe's prosperity, but it is arguably the least loved European institution of them all (Barber 2009).

---

[40] We owe these points to an official from the Secretariat-General, who intervened in a discussion on an earlier version of this paper presented at the EUSA Biennial Conference, March 2011.

It is at least plausible that EU governments (will) in similar vein realize that the Commission is destined always to be essential, even if it is unloved. Under these circumstances, future candidates who look likely to replicate Barroso's style and agenda may be favoured.

7

Cabinets and Services: Coordination inside the Commission

Scholars and practitioners alike portray the Commission as a deeply fragmented administration, or even a 'multiorganization' (Cram 1994).[1] The Directorates-General (DGs) are feuding 'baronies', 'silos', or 'fiefdoms', quasi-autonomous and introspective institutions that pursue their own agendas and are fiercely protective of their turf.[2] The political level is little different. Commissioners form a 'government of strangers', with no shared background, ideology, or common fate to bind them. Meanwhile their *cabinets*, enclaves of the member states, are perpetually at odds. The *cabinets*, concerned principally to promote the interests of their Commissioner's home state, are in constant competition with each other and in a permanent stand-off with the services.

Internal coordination, according to these accounts, is problematic and ineffectual. DGs achieved considerable independence in agenda-setting, personnel policy, and resource allocation in the Community's formative years, and countervailing mechanisms proved difficult to establish (Coombes 1970, Michelmann 1978). For much of the organization's history, neither the College nor the Commission President has been sufficiently strong to make coordination effective. Although formally responsible for coordination, the Secretariat-General has been weak and concerned mainly with procedure (Kassim 2006). It has been constrained by the principle of inter-departmental equality and has lacked the proximity to the centralized political power that gives equivalent bodies at national level their authority. Ineffective horizontal and vertical coordination within the organization has had consequences not only for the Commission, but for the wider EU system (Kassim and Peters 2008).

---

[1] See *inter alia* Coombes (1970); Sasse et al. (1977); Abélès et al. (1993); Cini (1996); Page (1997); Stevens and Stevens (2001: 195); Smith (2004); Spence with Edwards (2006); Kassim (2006); Hartlapp et al. (2010); Hartlapp (2011); as well as insider testimony (Eppink 2007).

[2] Or, bluntly, in the words of an anonymous interviewee quoted by another researcher, 'quite simply, it's war' (McLaughlin 1995), cited by Greenwood and Cram (1995: 7).

Senior officeholders within the Commission have long been aware of these deficiencies. However, the Commission was only able to undertake the measures needed to address them in the 1990s.[3] Attempts to resolve problems associated with the *cabinets* were first undertaken by the Santer Commission, but real reform occurred under Prodi. The Prodi Commission also sought to improve interdepartmental coordination. Under Barroso, there has been a stronger political steer from the Commission Presidency and a concerted effort to give the Secretariat-General a more interventionist role in coordination (see Chapter 6). The extent to which these changes have improved intra-organizational coordination has not, however, been assessed hitherto.[4]

This chapter examines whether the traditional image still holds true or whether the Commission has succeeded in improving coordination. The evidence from both the online survey and the follow-up interviews points towards significantly improved coordination and suggests that the accepted wisdoms no longer obtain. First, relations between DGs appear to be more cooperative and not as hostile as widely depicted. Second, interdepartmental coordination seems less problematic and considerably more effective than previously contended. Third, the Secretariat-General is more prominent and more interventionist than it has been in the past, although there is some ambivalence about the perceived transformation of its status. Fourth, relationships both between the *cabinets*, and between the services and the *cabinets*, are more harmonious than traditionally has been construed.

The chapter makes two main arguments. The first is that the capacity for horizontal coordination within the Commission has been considerably enhanced in recent years. The second is that rules introduced since the late 1990s, notably those enforcing greater multinationality, have brought about a change in *cabinets*. Thus *functional* denationalization has accompanied the change in composition by nationality in the *cabinets* observed by Egeberg and Heskestad (2010).

This chapter is divided into four sections. The first reviews why coordination within the Commission is so crucial, the problems that have historically beset the organization, and recent attempts to address them. The second reports EUCIQ's findings about coordination between the services and the role of the Secretariat-General. A third addresses the role of the *cabinets* and how it has evolved, as well as how *cabinets* are perceived by the services and

---

[3] The 'Three Wise Men's report' (Biesheuvel et al. 1979) and the Spierenburg report (1979) criticized the Commission's 'rigid structures, failures of administrative coordination, and inadequate management' (Stevens and Stevens 2001: 183–4). However, the European Council did not follow its recommendations. For the argument that the Commission cannot undertake major reform without the support of the member states, see Kassim (2008).

[4] Hartlapp (2011: 182) observes, for example, notes that: 'We know little about the structures and rules in place to provide cross-sectoral coordination in the EU political system'.

vice versa, and the state of relations between them. The fourth section focuses on the College, and coordination at the top of the Commission.

THE COMMISSION AND THE CHALLENGE OF COORDINATION

The need for intra-organizational coordination arises from the task specialization that is a feature of all modern bureaucracies. Since decisions cannot be taken, implemented, or enforced by a single individual or administrative unit alone, it is unlikely that—in the absence of specific coordinating efforts—policy or action will be consistent or coherent, or that problems of 'duplication, overlapping, and redundancy' (Wildavsky 1979: 132) will be avoided. At the same time, given the effort that must be expended and the interdepartmental rivalries involved, coordination remains a perennial challenge for any organization (Jennings and Crane 1994; Peters 1998). For one commentator, 'No problem is more central to administration than coordination' (Kettl 2002: 163).

The need to coordinate is especially acute in the case of the Commission. It occupies a central position within the EU and is charged with legislative, management, and enforcement tasks that can only be accomplished through cooperation with multiple actors at EU level and in the member states. As the Commission is founded on the principle of collective responsibility, consultation must take place between the services, between the services and the *cabinets*, between the *cabinets*, and within the College. Intra-organizational coordination is also essential.[5] Although 'each sector is the responsibility of a different member of the Commission' (Commission 2004), the administration is 'one and indivisible' (Spence 2006: 148), its unity affirmed by Article 21 of the Rules of Procedure (Cassese and della Cananea 1992: 83). Since, like any public bureaucracy, the Commission is internally differentiated along functional as well as hierarchical lines (Gulick 1937), interaction takes place along horizontal and vertical axes.

In any institution, coordination is a perennial difficulty. In the case of the Commission, the task is especially challenging. First, multinationality presents a particular set of problems.[6] As well as the difficulties posed by multilingualism, officials and members of the Commission come from different national administrative traditions, with competing conceptions of the role, organization,

---

[5] Meanwhile, the Union must operate under close scrutiny with high (and, in an age of general public austerity, rising) pressures to ensure 'value for money' in a political climate of strong (and, again, by some measures increasing) Euroscepticism (see Kassim and Peters 2008).

[6] See Abélès et al. (1993); Shore (2000); and Hooghe (2001: 172).

and internal operation of public bureaucracy. Second, although 'the collegiate nature of the Commission makes co-ordination indispensable', the 'hierarchy and compartmentalisation of the DGs...militates against inter-service co-ordination' (Stevens and Stevens 2001: 212–13). Difficulties are further compounded by 'fragmentation at all levels, up to and including the level of political direction' (Stevens and Stevens 2001: 213).

Third, Commission Directorates-General (DGs) are powerful, introspective, and traditionally resistant to cooperation. Each is interested in 'its own responsibilities, defending and extending its turf' (Stevens and Stevens 2001: 196–205), and has its own mission, networks, and culture (Cini 1996; Smith 2004: 4). After developing a significant measure of organizational freedom early in the Commission's history, which Stevens and Stevens (2001: 196) argue can be traced back to continental traditions of ministerial autonomy, the independence of the Commission's DGs has been strengthened by a concentration of policy expertise and experience in each department. In contrast to many national administrations, identification with the DG has not been mitigated by loyalty to an overarching identity or centralized political authority (Abélès et al. 1993). The challenge is further accentuated by the dossier approach to decision-making within the organization, which personalizes policy responsibilities (Cini 1996: 153) and 'leads to an individualised approach to information' (Stevens and Stevens 2001: 177) and rigid hierarchies within DGs.

Interdepartmental coordination is exacerbated by a lack of cohesion within the College—a fourth factor. The College is a collective body, but it is different from cabinet governments in national systems in that it 'is never united by shared party political, national, or ideological affinities' (Peterson 2006b: 94). It is always a 'supercoalition'. At least until the Barroso Commission (see Chapter 6), an 'increasing politicisation of the College' (MacMullen 2000: 41) was arguably responsible for making the Commission's supreme decision-making body even more diverse and even less coherent. Finally, the breadth of EU policy competencies creates policy interdependencies that are difficult to manage, while the institutional environment in which the Commission functions, characterized by fluidity, procedural complexity, and institutional fragmentation, only adds to the difficulty of the task (Kassim and Peters 2008).

Neither the actors entrusted with coordination nor coordinating mechanisms, whether in the guise of inter-service groups,[7] inter-services consultation, weekly meetings of the Directors-General or their assistants, or the weekly meetings of the *chefs de cabinets*, special *chefs*, or even the College, have been a

---

[7] The Secretariat-General maintains a list of these groups and is responsible for their supervision.

match for these centrifugal pressures.[8] Weakness begins at the top. The Commission's central decision-making authority has been more an arena than an actor. *Cabinets,* moreover, were originally established on the French model as a private office to assist the Commissioners and 'as a general aid to both horizontal and vertical coordination' (Cini 1996: 112). Though they have played a key role in both—Pascal Lamy, Delors's *chef de cabinet,* for example, has described the *cabinet* system in the Commission as *'le jardinier de collegialité'* (quoted in Spence 2006: 61)—they have in addition been a source of disharmony and difficulty.[9] Illustrations are not hard to find. In the Delors era, the President's *cabinet* pursued the President's own agenda by circumventing formal lines of communication and coordination in the Commission and working directly through operatives in the services (see Ross 1995). Spierenburg (1979: 137) found that *'cabinets* shielded Commissioners from the services, usurped Directors General responsibilities, and launched proposals without consultation of responsible officials' (Spence 2006: 69).

Cabinets have typically been identified with specific member states. Usually younger than their interlocutors in the services, frequently hand-picked by a Commissioner's national capital, and often with little experience of Brussels, they sometimes engaged in a form of 'terrorism' by rewriting work done in the services to suit their member state's or Commissioner's agenda—or, in the words of one former Secretary-General, 'just for the fun of it' (Carlo Trojan, quoted in Ross 1995: 161). Many analysts have denounced the *cabinets* as agents 'of national affiliations and interests and a source of structural contradiction' (McDonald 1997: 51) within the Commission. The frustration of many in the services was summed up by an official in the Secretariat-General interviewed late in the Delors era: 'intergovernmentalism starts when proposals hit the *cabinets.* They're mini-Councils within the Commission' (quoted in Peterson and Bomberg 1999: 56). Interaction between the *cabinets* was less coordination proper than intergovernmental bargaining (Spence 2006: ch. 1).

At the heart of the Commission, the Secretariat-General has been responsible for intra-organizational coordination since the Commission's creation (Kassim 2006). As part of this responsibility, it has been the guardian of collegiality, ensuring that internal procedures are observed and maintaining the Commission's institutional memory. The part played by Emile Noël over three decades, first as Executive Secretary, then Secretary-General, in building

---

[8] The College meets on a Wednesday. Items that require a decision are discussed nine days before at the *chefs de cabinet* meeting. Controversial items are discussed at a meeting of the special *chefs,* chaired by a member of the President's *cabinet.*

[9] On *cabinets,* see Ritchie (1992); Cini (1996: 111–15); Donnelly and Ritchie (1997: 48–9); Page (1997: 125–9); Stevens and Stevens (2001: 236); and Peterson (2006: 95–6). For the Delors period, see Ross (1995). Hooghe (2001: 203) Spence (2006: 60–72) discuss the merits of the *cabinet* system.

the organization, ensuring the working of the machinery, and as a 'fixer' (Cockfield 1997), became legendary within the Commission.[10] The Secretariat-General has also traditionally charted the progress of legislative proposals and managed the organization's interactions with the Council, Parliament, and other actors. Over time, it has accumulated additional functions, such as direct responsibility for competencies that are new to the Union or for dossiers that are complex, sensitive, or controversial, as well as coordination of the Commission's input into treaty negotiations.

At the same time, for much of its history, the Secretariat-General has operated according to a narrow conception of its coordinating role. Though charged with responsibility for the Commission's programme, until the Kinnock–Prodi reforms this function consisted of little more than 'an annual opening of filing cabinets' (Ross 1995: 267–8, note 22). The Secretariat-General has been concerned primarily with enforcing the observance of procedure and the working of Commission machinery. It has only been involved to a limited extent in the internal negotiation of policy. For example, Hooghe (2001: 202), quotes a senior official's comment that the Secretariat-General 'can only concentrate on things when it becomes a political priority'. The traditional view within the organization was that the Secretariat-General added value where an overview concerned, but not necessarily in relation to the substance of policy.

Though indispensable, the Secretariat-General has also been weak (Kassim 2006, 2010a, 2010b, 2010c). While it has ensured that interested services are consulted ('input coordination'), it has lacked the authority to arbitrate or to coordinate contested issues in order to achieve coherent policy outcomes ('output coordination'). Unlike bodies with similar responsibilities at the national level, it has not benefited from the proximity to a strong political centre that would lend it the authority to arbitrate, intervene or impose solutions on policy DGs. Traditionally, DGs have resisted what they perceive as interference by the Secretariat-General on the grounds of departmental equality. Directorates-General recognized the claim of the Secretariat-General to be a *primus inter pares*, but only insofar as it applied to the enforcement of procedures. It was largely on the grounds of collegiality that senior officials opposed the more interventionist model that Carlo Trojan attempted to enact as Secretary-General between 1995 and 1999. His successor, David O'Sullivan, projected instead a conception of the Secretariat-General as 'a service at the service of the other services', which provided the rubric for a strengthening of the Secretariat-General as a coordination hub. As part of the reform, the Secretariat-General became the home for an enhanced, centralized capacity—

[10] On Noël, see Grant (1994: 102); Middlemas (1995: 222); Cini (1996: 104); Bossuat (2011).

Strategic Planning and Programming (SPP)—to govern priority setting and implementation across the organization (see Chapter 8).

The sections that follow examine the extent to which these accepted wisdoms hold true. Findings from the EUCIQ survey and interviews are reported respectively on interdepartmental coordination and the role of the Secretariat-General; the *cabinets*; the *cabinets* and the services; and the College. Drawing on insider testimony, they examine the degree to which change and reform over the past decade have improved intra-organizational coordination within the Commission.

COORDINATION BETWEEN THE SERVICES[11]

The dominant view within the academic literature is that DGs exhibit the same kind of 'possessive territorialism' (Stevens and Stevens 2001: 196) based on task specialization and competition for money, staff, resources, status, and reputation that characterizes many bureaucracies (Stevens and Stevens 2001: 202–5; see also 166–8). However, coordination is made especially difficult by '[h]ierarchical structures which discourage horizontal consultation at relatively junior levels' (Stevens and Stevens 2001: 213). The Commission suffers in particular from a weakness of coordinating actors and mechanisms (Coombes 1970; Spierenburg 1979).

Assessing the extent to which this image of the Commission is shared by its staff was one of EUCIQ's principal objectives. The online questionnaire asked, first, about the sharing of information within the Commission. The aim was to discover whether officials consider that the tendency is for individuals to hoard rather than to share information within the organization. It asked about attitudes towards information-sharing within the Commission in general, before asking more specifically about the experience of sharing information with colleagues in their unit, within their DG and between DGs. Officials were asked for their views on the following propositions:[12]

- 'information is power and people too often conceal it within the Commission'
- 'information relevant to my job is easy to obtain from colleagues within my unit'
- 'information relevant to my job is easy to obtain from colleagues within my DG'

---

[11] This section draws extensively on Kassim (2010b, 2010c).
[12] The available options were: strongly agree, tend to agree, neither agree nor disagree, tend to disagree, strongly disagree, not sure.

- 'information relevant to my job is easy to obtain from colleagues in other DGs'.

Respondents were then asked for their evaluation of coordination at different levels within the organization. Their responses were invited on the following statements:

- 'coordination works effectively in my unit'
- 'coordination works effectively in my DG'
- 'coordination works effectively between DGs'.[13]

The same questions about interdepartmental coordination were also included in the survey of middle and senior managers. In this case, an additional question was included. Interviewees were invited to elaborate on their answer—whether positive, negative or neutral—about the effectiveness of coordination. *Cabinet* officials, meanwhile, were asked for their views on the effectiveness of coordination within the DGs for which they were responsible and on the effectiveness of coordination in general within the Commission.

The expectation, based on academic commentary and practitioner testimony, was that the ratings on information sharing and coordination would be low. Whilst both processes are generally thought difficult for any organization, they are considered to be especially problematic in the Commission. Against this background, the online survey responses were surprisingly positive (Figure 7.1). Although information sharing and coordination were considered more effective at the unit level than at DG level, and more effective in turn at DG level than at interdepartmental level, even the lastr—the real test case— was rated more highly than the existing literature had suggested.

Thus, more than 90 per cent of respondents agreed or strongly agreed that information was easy to obtain within their unit. Close to 80 per cent of officials thought information flowed smoothly within their DG. The proportion dropped to just above 50 per cent when respondents were asked how easy information was to obtain from colleagues in other DGs. Yet this is a very positive rating for an organization as complex as the Commission. Since a further 20 per cent of respondents registered a neutral opinion, no less than 70 per cent of the Commission's staff do not regard information sharing within the organization as a problem. More generally, it was striking to find that officials were almost evenly split when asked if they agreed that 'information is power and people too often conceal it in the Commission' (see Figure 7.1).

The questions on coordination elicited a similar pattern (see Figure 7.2), but with lower levels of agreement in each case. On the question of whether coordination between DGs was effective, only 30 per cent tended to agree (and almost none agreed strongly). However, a further 25 per cent neither

---

[13] The available options were the same as for information sharing.

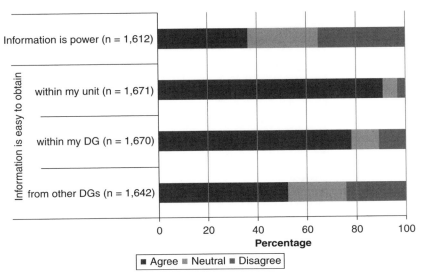

Fig. 7.1 Flow of information within the Commission

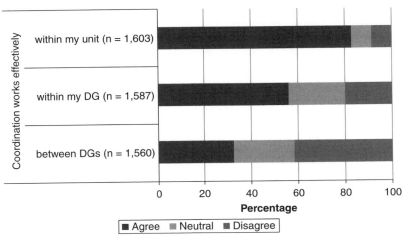

Fig. 7.2 Effectiveness of interdepartmental coordination

agreed nor disagreed. Although the 55 per cent of officials for whom interde-partmental coordination is effective (or who are neutral on the question) does not represent a large majority, the rating is considerably higher than might have been anticipated given the image of fragmentation and dysfunction projected in the literature.

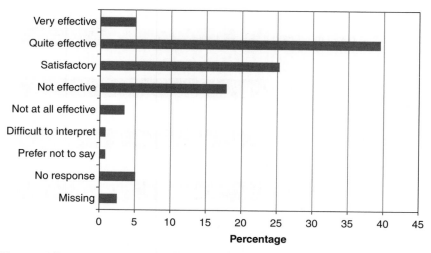

Fig. 7.3 Effectiveness of interdepartmental coordination (face-to-face interviews with middle and senior managers; n = 119)

Interviews with middle and senior managers suggested, moveover, that, while procedures were not always easy to navigate, could be cumbersome, and left room for improvement, interdepartmental coordination is less problematic than suggested by the existing literature. Forty-four per cent of the 119 interviewed considered it effective or very effective.[14] A further 25 per cent rated it satisfactory (see Figure 7.3). Only 20 per cent expressed the view that interdepartmental coordination was not effective or not at all effective.[15] *Cabinet* members, by contrast, were more negative in their assessment.[16]

---

[14] 'Much better now than it was 20 years ago' (interview 161) was one Director-General's assessment. A senior manager in the same DG agreed: 'I would say it has become more effective' (interview 14). In the words of a head of unit in an external-facing DG: 'we're on a constant improving trend' (interview 64).

[15] A minority expressed quite different opinions. For one head of unit in a sectoral DG 'Everything is wrong. Lots of inter-service groups. I would say that inter-service cooperation has not improved over the years' (interview 27). A middle manager in DG MARKT thought it was '[n]ot effective at all.' Nor was the same official impressed by the mechanisms for coordination in the Commission: 'I don't think they're very effective, no' (interview 126).

[16] Only 24 per cent of *cabinet* staff who completed the online survey tended to agree that inter-services coordination was effective, although a further 26 per cent neither agreed nor disagreed. (Fifty per cent either tended to disagree or strongly disagreed with the proposition.) The opinion of the 28 *cabinet* members interviewed face-to-face was similarly split. Although their views are, of course, important, *cabinet* members operate at a remove from inter-services coordination, do not necessarily have direct experience of the processes involved, and as a result of their responsibilities are likely to be more frustrated by the formal requirements of coordination. *Cabinet* officials (n = 28) also took a less than positive view of coordination *within* the DGs

The interviews provided an opportunity for middle and senior managers to offer more detailed reflections. They gave insights from a range of perspectives into how interdepartmental coordination works in the organization, how it has improved, and what problems remain. Those quoted below illustrate the range of opinion, but are not representative of the distribution of views.

A Director in a DG with responsibilities internal to the DG drew the following comparison between interdepartmental coordination in the Commission and in national administrations:

> If I compare it to a national administration, the cooperation between DG Budget and DG Internal Market or DG Competition is much better than the coordination between the [UK] Treasury and the DTI, or in France or in Germany or in small member states. If you look at it from a point of view of . . . sometimes conflicting, sometimes mutually supporting policy responsibilities, with political bosses on top of it, then what you find in national administrations is much less coordinated than we are. . . . [O]ur benchmark is higher, but we are very spoiled and we are never happy with the status quo (interview 72).

A middle manager in the Secretariat-General underlined the seriousness with which coordination had been taken not only by the Barroso Commission, but by its predecessors:

> I think that this is something which again has been taken very seriously by this Commission, but I think also predates it by some time, this attempt to get away from a silo approach to policy-making and ensuring that DGs share their experience and their knowledge, and also [to] ensure that their concerns are taken on board in any policy proposal (interview 107).

One long-serving official noted considerable improvement, which he attributed to two factors:

> I think that things are getting better now . . . for two reasons. . . . I think that President Barroso is right that everybody is working in this silo . . . and now in the modern world . . . there are . . . more interactions than was the case in the past between different policies. . . . And secondly, I think there is also another more managerial reason where now we have, with our internal reform ten years ago . . . more managers than there were in the past. . . . I would say that in the past at the level of Director General . . . we are closer to—I would say to state secretary type (interview 133).

Interviewees identified a number of factors that had served to improve interdepartmental coordination, including the use of information technology tools, such as SYSNET, which does not allow the lead DG to sign off a file until all interested services have had the opportunity to enter their view. It thereby

which they oversaw. Ten thought coordination was effective or very effective; six thought it satisfactory; and seven believed it not to be effective or not at all effective.

limits the extent to which individual DGs can 'game' the system by leaving the submission of a policy document until the last moment or otherwise attempting to limit the opportunities for other DGs to offer their comments. Among other factors cited are impact assessment, introduced at the same time as the Kinnock–Prodi reforms, which forces DGs to collaborate and reinforces the central role of the Secretariat-General (Radaelli and Meuwese 2010),[17] and cross-departmental networks that bring together officials with responsibilities in particular areas.[18] The role played by the Secretariat-General was also frequently cited. The comments of one insider were typical:

> [U]nder Catherine Day... and indeed, prior to her under David O'Sullivan as well,... there's been a big effort of coordination of legislative programming, which has been very effective, because in the old days, when I joined the Commission first, twenty years ago, every DG worked as a little kingdom of its own, and there was no coordination of policy; there was... a yearly legislative work programme, but it was sort of bits and pieces... Now, that has changed, and... this has been driven by [the] need to have good policy coordination (interview 162).

At the same time, a number of managers identified enduring impediments to effective coordination. According to one Director-General, interdepartmental coordination was '[m]uch better now than it was twenty years ago.' However, in his view, it is:

> [P]robably still not as good as it could be because of the natural bureaucratic resistance between different vertical silos... and... the single biggest obstacle of course remains the fact that we all report to a Commissioner who doesn't much want us to coordinate with other DGs (interview 161).

Others thought that DGs were the source of the main difficulties: '[DGs] tend to be protective and they tend to be self-promoting. I don't like it, but on the other hand, I can understand it. It's the nature of the people and the nature of the services to try and promote their own responsibilities and their own views.... I think that some of the services could be more cooperative' (interview 146). Coordination was destined to remain patchy for the same reason: 'DG's are little empires and you have no leverage' (interview 146).

---

[17] A middle manager in the Secretariat-General observed that coordination between DGs is 'something which we have tried to take to another level, again, with the impact assessment system. The impact assessment system... is supposed to provide the basis and the evidence for any policy that the Commission makes, and... every major legislative proposal has to have an impact assessment, and every impact assessment has to have a steering [committee] composed by the people from the relevant DGs' (interview 107).

[18] A middle manager in DG Employment, meanwhile, spoke enthusiastically about: 'groups in IT, in Human Resources, in Budget, which work together, with the assistance of the DG Human Resources... [N]ow there is the group of directors of resources who meet regularly, and... that improves also the coordination between the DGs' (interview 76).

For a head of unit in DG Internal Market, the lack of orientation from the College was an issue:

> I think there's also a need to have a stronger drive from the top on a political level in terms of coherent communication and what we stand for and what you want to communicate, and what the overall narrative is that the Commission wants to project on the EU project.... [I] understand that of course they want to profile themselves as individual members of the Commission and their portfolio, but it has to be part of a broader logic (interview 127).

In the view of a senior manager in the DG for Fisheries, the problem: 'is that we have too many Commissioners, and we have quite a number of Commissioners, and ours is probably an example, who have relatively small portfolios' (interview 81). Another senior manager thought that interference from the *cabinets* remained a problem:

> You have a proposal for . . . a directive, or for a paper, or whatever. You . . . get service consultations with the other DGs. That's concluded, you adapt your proposal, and then it moves up to the *cabinet* level . . . So then you have the two ways, either the *cabinets* tells us, okay, you do your work at the services level, I don't interfere, but I have the right of course to a different opinion. And then there is the other school who says, well, show me your job before you send it to the other services (interview 61).

A head of unit in DG External Relations considered that the right procedures were in place, but knowledge of how to use them was not as widespread as it should be: 'If the system is worked as it should, it's incredibly effective . . . , but the problem is that more and more people don't know or don't care about the procedures' (interview 151). According to a middle manager in the same DG 'we have the formal coordination mechanism through the inter-service consultation, with the different degrees of formality of them. But I think beyond that . . . a lot of the coordination should take place before you launch inter-service coordination, and . . . we need to improve on that' (interview 158).

The Secretariat-General

The role of the Secretariat-General was a matter of inquiry in its own right. The online questionnaire asked respondents whether they agreed or disagreed with the following propositions:

- 'The Secretariat-General is a neutral arbiter between services in policy coordination';
- 'The Secretariat-General focuses too much on procedure and not enough on policy content';

- 'The Secretariat-General is becoming more political and more influential in the life of the Commission'.

In face-to-face interviews, managers and *cabinet* members were asked two questions:

- 'Some respondents thought the Secretariat-General focuses too much on procedure and not enough on policy content. What is your view?' and

- 'Some respondents thought that the Secretariat-General is becoming too political in the life of the Commission. What is your view?'

In each instance, the interviewer recorded not only whether the respondent agreed or disagreed with the proposition, but also whether the interviewee expressed approval or disapproval.

Three findings stand out. First, as reported in Chapter 6, 38 per cent of the respondents to the online questionnaire disagreed with the proposition that the Secretariat-General is a neutral arbiter (see Figure 7.4). A somewhat larger proportion (49 per cent) agreed that: 'The Secretariat-General is becoming more political and more influential in the life of the Commission'. Similar views were expressed by managers in the interviews. The view that Secretariat-General had become more interventionist was widespread. The opinion expressed by a head of unit in DG Enterprise was not uncommon. While noting that much coordination activity is led by the individual DG in charge of a file, the same respondent added:

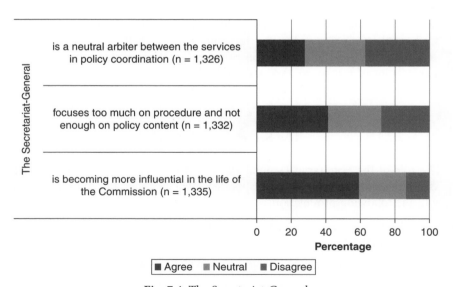

Fig. 7.4 The Secretariat-General

there is [an]other [kind of] coordination, which is centrally initiated by the Secretariat-General, and . . . I perceive that it is increasing. . . . [P]erhaps one of the more significant changes in the more recent past is that they work on substance. So they do not only formally coordinate . . . but they are trying to strongly influence the substance, the outcome of the coordination. This is relatively new (interview 52).

Second, officials had quite different views about whether the Secretariat-General had in fact become more interventionist in policy. This ambivalence was evident in responses to the online survey question on whether the Secretariat-General 'focuses too much on procedure and not enough on policy content'. Forty per cent agreed; 15 per cent disagreed; and 30 per cent neither agreed nor disagreed. Among the 119 managers interviewed, by contrast, 51 per cent agreed that the Secretariat-General focused too much on procedure over content, while 32 per cent disagreed.

The face-to-face interviews offered insights as to why opinion among staff appears divided. Some believed that there was little doubt that the Secretariat-General was now much more involved in policy. The view of a head of unit in DG Internal Market was typical:

There are two different layers that develop independently. . . . [T]he procedural layer has become more and more heavy. . . . But the Secretariat General, especially the present head . . . focuses on policy a lot . . . So [for] the internal market, the new document is written by the Secretariat-General (interview 158).

A similar view was expressed by a head of unit in DG Enterprise:

I think [the role of the Secretariat-General] has significantly changed. . . . I think there are more and more people aware . . . of the fact that on quite [a lot] of the key policy and legislative files over the last few years that Sec Gen has played a leading role: guiding, coordinating, whatever you want to call it . . . which is stronger than what we might have seen in the past (interview 127).

Other interviewees, however, thought that, despite its ambitions, the Secretariat-General had, for various reasons, yet to achieve a definitive shift towards a more interventionist policy role. In the words of one Director-General:

I think under Catherine Day they have tried very hard to move away from being only procedural to more coordination but . . . I don't see that yet and I don't think frankly they have the right people to do it yet. Most of the people there are still the people who want a more procedural sort of Secretary-General but my impression is that both Barroso and Catherine Day see the Secretary General as a . . . sort of Prime Minister's [or] President's office, laying down central policy guidelines. But it doesn't work like that (interview 132).

[Y]ou cannot probably change within very few years an institution or an entity or Sec Gen, which indeed for many years defined itself through reporting,

guardian of procedures, get at whatever all these lovely words are towards
a . . . more policy-oriented Secretariat (interview 127).

Indeed, a Secretariat-General insider conceded that it was not yet capable of
playing a more interventionist role: 'The problem however is that we simply
do not have all the in-house expertise to follow all the different policy areas
that are covered by the DGs. This is the main problem' (interview 60).

Third, there was ambivalence among middle and senior managers as to
whether the Secretariat-General should in fact focus on procedure rather than
policy. Thirty-four per cent of interviewees approved of the Secretariat-General's emphasis on procedure, whereas 33 per cent either disapproved or
strongly disapproved. The face-to-face interviews gave an insight into the
thinking on both sides. A head of unit in the Secretariat General explained:

> [W]hen you compare the Commission to ten or fifteen years ago, . . . [the]
> resources that are devoted to any particular area . . . has increased dramatically.
> And of course, one of the key issues is having twenty-seven Commissioners,
> because if you have a Commissioner in a policy area, by definition you have a
> need for activity, for visibility, for whatever. . . . [S]o in a body which is coordin-
> ating the actions of twenty-seven people I think you need a centre which is
> possibly stronger than it would have been when we had—you know, when the
> Commissioner for competition policy [who] also did personnel policy, budget,
> and consumer policy, which I think Karel Van Miert had at one stage. Inevitably,
> the amount of attention he could give to consumer policy was slightly less than
> the single Commissioner for consumer policy can give today. So, strong need for
> coordination, and I think that has to be the Secretariat-General (interview 107).

Others also welcomed the Secretariat-General's ambition to give the organization a stronger policy steer. One Director-General offered:

> I think that the Secretariat-General's role should be to look for policy coherence,
> so that what is done is coherent with what has been done before, has been done
> elsewhere in a related field. . . . Their role is also to observe that policies are in line
> with the President's and the house's overall priorities (interview 52).

Some wanted the Secretariat-General to move even further away from its
traditional role:

> [P]ersonally I feel that in coordinating the role of the Secretariat-General could be
> improved, because [it has become] very bureaucratic. It became a very heavy
> machine. They could do more coordination on policy, on the same issues, in
> order to create the common drivers for action other than coordinating the
> bureaucratic issues (interview 14).

Others, however, argued that, although there was a role for the Secretariat-
General in policy, the Directorates-General should retain their lead:

I would hope that the Sec-Gen will not develop into an institution that . . . is in the driving seat and dictates to us what kind of environmental policy we have to propose. That is not good. Coordination, fine. But the European Commission is what its DGs are doing and what kind of ideas they have. If they don't have any, I really don't think the Sec Gen would have better ones (interview 90).

[I]t's not something that I approve of. I think it's creating yet another layer. We started speaking about coordination. I would rather coordinate with a colleague that is in charge of agriculture or energy or whatever, than having to sit with someone who is in charge of nothing but coordination (interview 144).

[I]ts not their job to focus on policy content . . . it's the DGs', who are charged with policy . . . [it's their job] to make sure we don't go too far off the general strategy of the Commission (interview 125).

I wonder whether they should really focus on policy content, frankly. They should focus on policy harmonization and harmonization of the DGs' work. And that they're doing. I don't [think] they should get too much involved into the actual content of the policy (interview 43).

In summary, the main findings defy accepted wisdoms about the services and horizontal coordination in the Commission. DGs may be inclined to intro-spection, but information sharing within the organization appears not to be a problem. Similarly, inter-departmental coordination appears to be consider-ably less problematic than the literature contends, given the number of respondents who consider it to be effective or who are neutral on the issue. Finally, in the view of many officials, the Secretariat-General plays a more pronounced role in policy. However, there is considerable ambivalence within the organization about its more interventionist role.

CABINETS AND COORDINATION

Cabinets were established originally to provide the support necessary for Commissioners to carry out their collegial responsibilities. Over time, how-ever, they became seen as increasingly partisan 'national enclaves'.[19] These features of *cabinets* had three consequences: interaction between *cabinets* came to be driven by an intergovernmental logic; the identification of *cabinets* with particular national interests served only to (further) estrange them from the services; and third, *cabinets* intervened in personnel matters, often in

---

[19] Ritchie (1992: 103–4) argues that *cabinets* became identified as agents of national influence because they, rather than the Permanent Representations, were the main contacts for national capitals in the early days of the Community. See also Chapter 2 above.

association with the permanent representations, to advance the careers of compatriots in the services.[20] In short, rather than supporting collegiality, the *cabinets* came to be regarded as an impediment to it.

Both the online questionnaire and the survey conducted with *cabinet* members sought to test the characterization in the literature of *cabinets* as agents of national interests.[21] The online questionnaire invited respondents to record their views on whether *cabinets* were 'too preoccupied with developments in their Commissioners' home states'. Those who agreed with the proposition were a minority. A total of 30 per cent disagreed, and 32 per cent took a neutral view. Only a third agreed with the proposition. The responses suggest that the image of *cabinets* as instruments for the interests of member states is not widely shared by the people who work for the organization.[22]

The aim in the follow-up interviews was to gain an understanding of how *cabinet* members see the role of the *cabinets* in the Commission. There were two main areas of interest: the relative importance given to support of the Commissioner's portfolio and non-portfolio activities; and the priority attached to handling relations with the Commissioner's home member state. Interviewees were handed a list of possible roles and asked to indicate on a six-point scale how closely each described a role played by their *cabinet* (see Figure 7.5). A follow-up question asked whether any roles were missing from the list. When respondents suggested that something was absent, they were asked what should be added.

The image of the *cabinet* that emerges from the interviews with *cabinet* members is quite different from the picture presented in much of the literature. First, *cabinets* are centred on the portfolio of the Commissioner rather than supporting his or her non-portfolio responsibilities. A total of 28 respondents affirmed that portfolio support described the role either very closely (22) or quite closely (6). Managing the Commissioner's non-portfolio responsibilities was significantly less important. Twenty-seven of the 28 interviewees, meanwhile, highlighted oversight of the DG for which their Commissioner is responsible as a key role of the *cabinet*. Eleven members of *cabinet* indicated that this description fitted very closely and eight quite closely.

[20] Joana and Smith (2002: 119, fn 1) calculated that *cabinet* officials spent 10 per cent time of their time looking after the interests of their nationals.
[21] See Spierenburg (1979); Grant (1994); Ross (1995); Nugent (2001); Spence with Edwards (2006). Donnelly and Ritchie (1994), Peterson (2009); and Egeberg and Heskestad (2010) are exceptions.
[22] This impression was confirmed anecdotally in presentations of the provisional findings from the EUCIQ project to Commission officials. On more than one occasion, audience members commented that, in contrast to the 1980s and 1990s, no one refers to, for example, 'the German *cabinet*' or 'the French *cabinet*'.

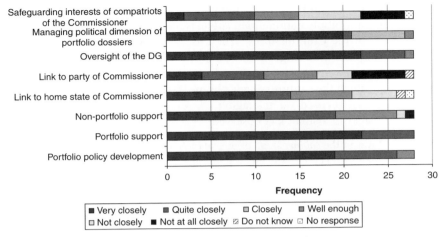

Fig. 7.5 The role and functions of *cabinets*

Note: Face-to-face interviews with members of cabinet (n = 28).

The twelve *chefs de cabinet* among the 28 interviewees were asked specific questions about their roles. Their responses also indicated that the work of the *cabinets* was directed more to management of the portfolio responsibility (monitoring developments in the services, managing the political dimensions of dossiers, and so on), including communicating with *cabinet* colleagues, than interacting with other *cabinets*. These findings suggest that the *cabinets* are more a private political office for their Commissioner than an instrument of collegiality.

Second, the identification of roles linked to the Commissioner's connections with his or her national capital and advancing the interests of nationals did not rate highly. Only half of the respondents considered that managing the Commissioner's relationship with his or her home state was a priority for the *cabinet*. In at least two cases—the Verheugen *cabinet* and the Piebalgs *cabinet*—the responsible official was not of the same nationality as the Commissioner (German and Latvian respectively). Only ten of the twenty-eight, moreover, considered that safeguarding the interests of the compatriots of the Commissioner was a function of the *cabinet*.

Functional Denationalization

Given the shift following the 2004 enlargement to one Commissioner per member state, it is curious that responses both to the online questionnaire and the surveys of *cabinet* officials suggest that *cabinets* are *less* national in orientation now than when (the larger) member states appointed two Commissioners. There is little or no evidence that interaction between the *cabinets* is informed by a new intergovernmental logic (Peterson 2008). Instead, the EUCIQ findings confirm the recent findings of other researchers that *cabinets* have undergone a process of denationalization. Egeberg and Heskestad (2010), for example, have found that following the introduction of rules requiring the recruitment of multiple nationalities, *cabinets* have ceased to be dominated by compatriots of the Commissioner. They use the term 'denationalization' to refer to changes in the composition of *cabinets*. The findings from EUCIQ, by contrast, suggest a *functional* denationalization. *Cabinets* serve less as a channel through which the Commissioner's home state pursues its interests than as a personal staff focused on managing the Commissioner's portfolio. As a middle manager in a small DG observed:

> [W]hen I was in the *cabinet* . . . all of the *cabinets* were much more linked to our member states. . . . [T]here was much more of a national agenda, and the composition of the *cabinets* was more of the Commissioner['s nationality] than others. Now, . . . there are more foreigners, and less of the same nationality as the Commissioner, and all sort of mechanisms where the Commission no longer has a free debate. Because there are 27, . . . you have to have that structure in the debate. There is definitely less opportunity for a Commissioner to take a higher profile on national interest (interview 166).

Three developments can explain the functional denationalization of *cabinets*. The first is the impact of rule changes on *cabinet* composition. When Romano Prodi became Commission President in 1999, he decreed that all *cabinets* had to have officials of at least three different nationalities, and that either a *chef* or deputy *chef* had to have a different nationality than the Commissioner. At least three (of, usually, six) *cabinet* officials had already to be Commission officials.[23] Rules on their composition made *cabinets* less national, but *cabinets* became more dossier-focused as Commissioners tended to appoint the required three Commission officials to their *cabinet* from the DGs working in the policy fields covered by their portfolio.

The expansion of the College as the result of the 2004 and 2007 enlargements is a second factor. With more constricted portfolios, Commissioners and *cabinets* focused more single-mindedly on the part of the work of the Commission for which they took a lead responsibility. Third, the range of Commission responsibilities has grown and individual portfolios have become more focused and more specialist than a decade ago.[24] In these

---

[23] Others were chosen more or less freely by the Commissioner and most were employed as Temporary Agents for the duration of the Commissioner's term in office. Commissioners were also urged to achieve gender balance in the composition of their *cabinet*. In theory, most *cabinets* continue to have six members. But the Commissioner's own Personal Assistant may be an 'AST-level' official (that is, serving in a non-administrative post), and hence, effectively, a seventh *cabinet* member. Barroso in his second Presidency had 12 *cabinet* members, while Baroness Ashton, as High Representative for Foreign Affairs and Vice-President of the Commission, had 11.

[24] The process continued under Barroso II. The rapid expansion of the Commission's work on police and judicial cooperation in the early 2000s, for example, led Barroso to create a new portfolio for 'Justice, Fundamental Rights and Citizenship'. He also created a new portfolio on 'Climate Action'.

circumstances, it is perhaps unrealistic to expect each individual *cabinet* to follow the work of the whole College. When, for example, in Competition Commissioner Karel Van Miert's *cabinet* (of nine officials), all worked exclusively on competition policy with the exception of one official who covered everything else, he was setting a trend.

THE CABINETS AND SERVICES: PARTNERS OR RIVALS?

The conventional wisdom is that the relationship between the *cabinets* and the services is one of permanent tension. This friction derives from a clash between the basic function of the two different layers of the organization— the one political, the other administrative (see Nugent 2001; Stevens and Stevens 2001: 229–37; Smith 2004; Spence 2006: 60–72)—and resentment on the part of the services that *cabinets* try to interpose themselves between the Commissioners and the administration. It is sharpened by the identification of each *cabinet* with a particular national capital, which introduces a further dimension of conflict, pitting the state-centric concerns of *cabinet* members against the commitment to the European ideal of permanent officials in the services.

To test whether this characterization held true, the online survey asked respondents to register their opinions on a series of propositions that addressed three main aspects of the *cabinets*, services, and their interaction: how the roles of *cabinets* and services are understood among Commission staff; how the services view the *cabinets*, and vice versa; and the effectiveness of coordination between *cabinets* and services. Similar questions were posed in the face-to-face interviews with *cabinet* members and with managers. With respect to the first, a plurality—more than 45 per cent of officials—disagreed that 'Commission officials work for their Directorate-General first, then for the Commission'. This finding runs counter to the view that officials identify most closely with the DG (see especially Abélès et al. 1993) and suggests instead that they owe their primary loyalty to the Commission.

The latter inference is supported by the finding that an overwhelming majority of survey respondents—more than three-quarters—agreed that 'it is the responsibility of the services to support the politically-agreed positions of the Commission'. Around one-third of officials agreed *strongly*. At the same time, however, a majority—more than 60 per cent—consider that a 'change in Director-General usually has a greater impact on the working methods of a

DG than a change in Commissioner'.[25] Although there is a widespread belief within the organization that the services should support the College, there is equally widespread a belief that the tone in each Directorate-General is set not by the political overlord, but by the senior manager.

Responses to both the online questionnaire and the surveys offer little or no support to the image of two levels of the Commission perennially at odds. The data suggest a strong degree of mutual respect in their relations, even if their values and preoccupations differ. Forty three per cent of the respondents to the online questionnaire agreed that the *cabinets* respect the expertise of the services. Only 19 per cent disagreed. No fewer than 88 per cent of the managers and 20 of the 28 *cabinet* members interviewed agreed with this proposition. There was, however, somewhat less consistency in views on how services perceive the *cabinets*. Forty-eight per cent of managers thought that the services understood the work of the *cabinets*. A majority of *cabinet* members took the opposite view.

In the face-to-face interviews, middle and senior managers expanded on the perceptions of *cabinets* that officials have within the services. One Director-General spoke of 'separate worlds' (interview 15); another described it as 'a completely different world' (interview 5). According to one middle manager, in an echo of the asymmetrical perception recorded in the responses to the survey: 'it's easier for the *cabinet* to respect the expertise of the Services than for the Services to accept the political dimension of the Commission or job' (interview 158). A middle manager in DG REGIO offered the following account:

> I think the vast majority of colleagues really don't know exactly what the *cabinet* does or what the Commissioner does, or how they work together. *Cabinets* and Commissioner is a bit of a mystery to them and so I don't think they do appreciate . . . the fact that the *cabinets* are usually very hard-working people with a very difficult job to do . . . coordinating with the DGs and making sure the key things are there on time, the speeches are there on time, that the quality is right and so on—it's a very difficult job (interview 16).

A head of unit in DG Development expressed a similar view:

> I don't think they have a clear understanding of what that work implies, which means that sometimes they underestimate the amount of stress and of pressure the *cabinets* are working . . . [under] . . . Now, then there is a . . . power relation-s[hip] that . . . creates other types of problems, but fundamentally I think that a better understanding of the pressure under which works the *cabinet* would help also our staff to work, to accept that they have to work sometimes on deadlines which are unreasonable (interview 89).

---

[25] A large segment of respondents to this question—around 20 per cent—either did not answer the question or replied 'don't know'.

By contrast, the Director-General of a large DG thought that the services were not so well-served:

> [T]here's a sort of learned disrespect, because they bring you trouble and they don't bring you any value added. And my feeling is that that trouble is not compressible. They are the messenger for many bits of bad news, mainly about additional work to be done too quickly. But the reason that that's not accepted in as professional [a] way as it should be is that [in] the other part of their role they don't really deliver as well as they could (interview 142).

Finally, views on vertical coordination were somewhat mixed. Thirty-nine per cent of respondents to the online survey agreed that coordination works effectively between the services and the College, while a further 31 per cent were neutral. Just under a third (30 per cent) disagreed with the proposition. When the issue was addressed in a less abstract form, the results were more positive. In face-to-face interviews with *cabinet* members and managers, interviewees were asked to rate the effectiveness of the working relationship between 'their' Directorate-General and its *cabinet* on a seven-point scale. *Cabinet* officials reported themselves especially satisfied with the working relationship they had with 'their' service: 54 per cent agreed that the relationship was 'effective'. In the managers' survey, agreement was even stronger. On a six-point scale, three-quarters of senior and middle managers judged coordination to be very effective, quite effective or satisfactory (see Figure 7.6).

The views of middle and senior managers in face-to-face interviews expressed a range of opinion.[26] Assessments of the working relationship between services and *cabinet* ranged from 'first class' (interview 113—the Director-General of a small internal service) to 'disastrous', the assessment of a senior manager in a major policy DG (interview 37).[27] For many: '[It] depends on the people . . . on the personalities' (interview 16), 'on the chemistry between the Directorate-General and the Commissioner, and in particular between the Directorate-General and say the *chef de cabinet*' (interview 79). Others considered experience inside the Commission invaluable. According to a head of unit in DG REGIO: 'it's not unusual and certainly not in this DG for members

---

[26] One middle manager—an outlier—declared: 'I deeply disapprove of that system, I should say. I think that the French administrative model is not appropriate. I would much prefer that the Directorate-General was the permanent Secretary, with his Commissioner in the office opposite. That's the way it should be' (interview 44).

[27] In this case, the interviewee attributed the poor relationship to the Commissioner. A head of unit observed similarly that his Commissioner: 'had his own private agenda, his own policy programme; he couldn't care less about the services. He said when he came to the Commission, "I'm the political master; you are there to serve me. I'm not here to serve you." And that's exactly how he treated us. So, whatever was there in terms of coordination was improvised, was reactive; was on the spot, was last minute, was not very well planned, was not very well organized. It was a mess' (interview 9).

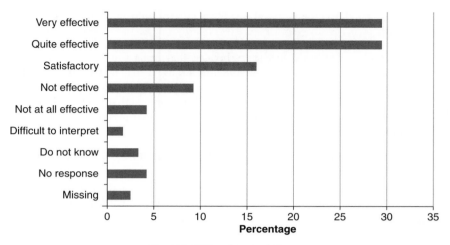

Fig. 7.6 DG–*cabinet* relations

Note: Face-to-face interviews with managers (n = 119).

of the *cabinet* to come from the ranks of the DG, so they will know stuff and they will know the people. That helps enormously' (interview 16).

Other interviewees highlighted the need to clarify responsibilities from the outset, including respect for the expertise of the services and the key role to be played by the Commissioner:

> [I]t depends on two or three features: One, is that there must be a written . . . contract, and written explicit understanding of who does what, and what the reporting requirements are, and what the transparency arrangements are. . . . We have that. And I think as a matter of process, all DGs and all *cabinets* would have that. Then there is a question of trust, which is the soft dimension . . . If there is no mutual trust, there is no possibility of actual teamwork. So, it's very important to draw the lines between who does what (interview 139).

> The best *cabinet* is a *cabinet* that fully recognizes the expertise of the service, and uses the expertise of the services to serve the policies of the Commissioner. They should . . . never, ever substitute for the expertise of the service. . . . [Some] think that they can go ahead on their own, and that's a major mistake (interview 144).

> I always say . . . that for me there are two necessary and sufficient conditions for an effective *cabinet*. The first is that the Commissioner first recruits them all, and the second is that he or she sees them every day they're in Brussels. And there are very few Commissioners who actually do both of those things (interview 142).

Somewhat different 'dos and don'ts' were identified by a head of unit in DG SANCO (Health and Consumer Protection):

> [I]t really depends on how you are treated. So, if you are considered as a slave, which is here to react to any solicitation, it is not appreciated. If you have the feeling that the *cabinet* fights for you . . . for your proposal, is understanding of your constraints, and tries to plan your work as well, fine (interview 95).

In summary, the EUCIQ data suggest that relations between the *cabinets* and the services are considerably more cordial than the existing literature suggests. In particular, vertical coordination is rated positively by both sides. The explanation lies, first, in a series of attempts from the late Delors period to improve the relationship, especially in curbing the tendency of the *cabinets* to intervene in the technical work of the services. These efforts culminated in the rule, enforced by the Secretariat-General, that incoming *cabinets* agree a written concordat with the Director-General of the services for which they are about to assume responsibility. These agreements set out commitments covering how information is to be communicated between the *cabinet* and the DG, how often meetings are to take place between *cabinet* members and officials, and who are the approved contact people in the DG. Second, the denationalization of *cabinets* has removed a key source of contention. *Cabinets* may still be political, but that logic is no longer compounded by the sense that *cabinet* members owe their ultimate loyalty to a source outside the Commission. Third, the Kinnock–Prodi reforms introduced greater clarity to the distinction between the work of the *cabinets* and that of the services.

COORDINATION AT THE TOP: THE COLLEGE

Collective decision-making by the College is both the beginning and the end of coordination. On one hand, it provides the rationale for horizontal and vertical coordination within the organization. On the other, the College is the supreme decision-making body in the Commission where final decisions, involving all Commissioners, are taken. Although the Commission's work has expanded dramatically since the late 1950s, each Commissioner is, in theory, responsible for following developments across the full range of portfolios, and not only their own. As discussed in Chapter 6, the adoption of collegiality as a foundational principle by the Commission was linked to its organizational myth: that it embodies and represents the general interest of the Community (Dimitrakopoulos 2008: 291–3).

Historically, coordination at the level of the College has been beset by difficulty. In tune with much of the existing literature, Smith (2003: 142) concludes his investigation of several Commissions with the observation that 'Colleges rarely become as cohesive as other parts of the EU's institutional arrangements'. The challenge begins with how members of the Commission are appointed—a process that is 'often a fraught and highly politicized exercise' (Peterson 2006b: 94). Commissioners have often not met each other prior to their appointment. The College is constructed through what Barroso has termed a series of 'blind date[s]' (quoted in Peterson 2006b: 93). Unelected on a manifesto or programme, 'Commissioners are not commissioned' as Page (1997: 119) puts it, 'by anyone to do anything in particular'.[28]

Moreover, it has often not been in the interest of member governments to appoint talented or popular figures. Often, individuals have been chosen to be Commissioners by political rivals in government who are happy for them be outside the national political arena. It is little wonder that, especially early in their mandates, Commissioners struggle to act as a coherent team with a single purpose,[29] and unsurprising that they are unable to muster a 'unified political purpose by which administrative action can be oriented and guided' (Stevens and Stevens 2001: 224).

Second, the College is large, and, it has been argued, artificially so, since its size has been determined less by the range of the Commission's responsibilities and more by the claims of the member states over appointment rights. Concern about whether such a large body could work efficiently or harmoniously, especially given the diverse origins of its membership, was expressed as early as late 1970s (in the 1979 Spierenburg Report) and voiced repeatedly thereafter. From the 1996 Inter-Governmental Conference (IGC) through to the Lisbon Treaty, various models for reducing the number of Commissioners were examined. A decision at Amsterdam (1997) to reduce the number to one per member state was confirmed at Nice (2000). The Nice principles were re-affirmed in the (2004) Constitutional Treaty, but amended by the subsequent IGC to the effect that one Commissioner per member state would persist until 2014, after which the number of Commissioners would be equivalent to two-thirds the number of EU member states. The Lisbon Treaty initially preserved this arrangement, but following its rejection in the first Irish referendum, the principle of one Commissioner per member state was re-introduced. Asked whether the result was an over-large and inefficient College, a leading MEP was blunt: 'it is far more important for the Commission to be legitimate than efficient' (quoted in Peterson and Birdsall 2008: 57).

Third, the ability of Commissioners to supervise the services is often limited, sometimes for structural reasons beyond their control. Not only does managing the services for which Commissioners are responsible form only one among many tasks (see Joana and Smith 2002), but a single Commissioner may often be responsible for several DGs or 'a single DG may answer to more than one Commissioner' (Cini 1996: 110). Especially worrying, perhaps, is the complaint made by an outgoing Commissioner in the

[28] Peter Mandelson, a self-described 'British politician who was well networked on the Continent', knew only two of the 27 Commissioners with whom he served when he was appointed to the College in 2004 (Spence 2006: 47).

[29] The position is well described by an official quoted by Hooghe (2001: 202): 'If you have a College of twenty politicians of different political colours, different national origins, put together without any natural political cohesion, you should not blame the DGs for want of unity. It starts there.'

aftermath of the resignation of the Santer Commission that 'Commissioners cannot in practice supervise the actions of their directorates-general' (Committee of Independent Experts 1999: 125, para. 7.9.7).

Fourth, coordinating mechanisms have been generally ineffective. The absence of a 'concentration of power at the centre of the Commission' (Kassim 2004c: 65; see also Chapter 5)—a key instrument for achieving coordination elsewhere—has already been discussed. Some Presidents, including Hallstein, have attempted to use formal or informal groupings of Commissioners to improve cooperation at the political level in the hope that this would encourage positive habits at lower levels of the organization—an approach also recommended by Spierenburg (1979). However, the idea of working parties, or groups of Commissioners, was ignored by Delors, 'partly implemented under Santer, toyed with by Prodi and rejected by Barroso' (Spence 2006: 50).

Ineffective coordination among Commissioners has been consequential, not only for the functioning of the College, but also for the working of the Commission more generally. The Spierenburg Report of 1979 posited that 'poor coordination among Commissioners and their lack of encouragement of senior officials had led to a dearth of coordination among Directors General and a resulting growth in the power and role of the *cabinets*' (Spence 2006: 50). Somewhat more dramatically, in the early days of the Barroso I Commission, Peter Mandelson (2005) contended that the resignation of the Santer Commission had had an important impact on power dynamics within the organization:

> [M]y guess is that power within the Commission has inexorably shifted to the Services. . . . [I]t was the Directors General who kept the Commission show on the road . . . Priorities have not been set by Commissioners who take an overall political view. They have been set by individual Services with their own entirely legitimate, but focused set of interests and concerns.

In short, the College has not been up to the task of defining 'the mission of the institution [or creating] an organization that is adequate to fulfil it' (Coombes 1970: 247).

Although there was no direct question about coordination within the College in either the online questionnaire or face-to-face interviews, opinions on this topic, as well as on leadership within the organization, were ventured by respondents on the functioning of the College in answers to questions about the role of the Secretariat-General. Moreover, as reported in Chapter 6, Commissioners were asked specifically about the working of the College and the extent to which it could be considered presidential or collegial.

This evidence from these sources suggests that, largely as a result of a strengthening of the Commission Presidency under Barroso, the political leadership of the organization has risen to meet the challenge posed by Coombes (1970). Under Barroso, the Commission has been able to define a political mission for the organization and to ensure conformity with his programme—an achievement arguably rivalled only by Delors and Hallstein among his predecessors. In an environment that is no longer conducive to an expansionist agenda, Barroso has mobilized the formal powers that have gradually been attached to the office, forged a close relationship with an interventionist Secretariat-General, and secured the acquiescence of his colleagues in his call for strong leadership in an expanded College.

The testimony of three insiders—respectively, a head of unit in the Secretariat-General, the Director-General of a medium service, and the Director-General of a small operational department—offers confirmation of these developments:

> [Barroso's] aim [is] to have a more Presidential method of work, where the programme of the Commission [is] presented to the Parliament and the Council . . . and then coordination . . . ensures that the programme and the aims that were set out at the beginning of five-year period [are] meshed, and of course, the Secretariat-General kind of does all this coordination. . . . The programme of the President . . . then becomes the programme of the Commission . . . [The] Sec-Gen oversees the implementation of the realization of this programme, and coordinates, putting the bits together so that in the end you have . . . initiatives that . . . are coherent . . . Barroso, himself, would claim that as a very positive fact that he's never had to go to the Commission [for a vote]. And that's why; because it's properly coordinated and balanced . . . [C]oordination is driven by not just his *cabinet*, but by the Secretary-General (interview 53).

> [W]e have a president who is quite—quite omnipresent if I may say so . . . which is positive. I think we have a stronger Secretariat-General now, which we have got a need for . . . and we have developed also because it was the wish of the President, but we have developed a much more [positive] attitude in coordination on a number of issues . . . There is one agenda. It is very clear (interview 15).

> [At the time of Barroso's appointment] it was very . . . important for the Commission to survive as a strong policy leader in Europe because the Commission was under siege. It had [paid] . . . so much attention to improving internal and inter-institutional functioning that its policy role had been slowed down a little bit. So . . . [the aim was to make] the Commission . . . a political actor on the map. And it has changed also the functioning of the Secretariat-General. It has developed from a regulatory centre to a policy centre [and] taken up the coordination of every political file. They have prevented the DGs from coming up with hobby horses. They trimmed down the action programme of the Commission to the real political priorities (interview 134).

CONCLUSION

Coordination has been a perennial problem for the Commission. However, findings from both the EUCIQ online questionnaire and the interviews suggest, first, that the image of the Commission as deeply fragmented is no longer accurate. Horizontal and vertical relations work more effectively than described in either official reports Spierenburg (1979), insider testimony (Jenkins 1989; Brittan 2000; Eppink 2007), or the academic literature (Coombes 1970; Michelmann 1978; Stevens and Stevens 2001; Spence 2006). The EUCIQ data point to more effective interdepartmental coordination, even if problems remain, as well as better—if not entirely harmonious—relations between the *cabinets* and the services. They also suggest a more interventionist Secretariat-General and stronger political leadership on the part of the Commission President.

A second argument concerns the role of *cabinets*. The evidence from EUCIQ shows that, as a result of the rules introduced by Prodi and Barroso, *cabinets* have not only become more 'European' and less national in composition, but they have also undergone a process of functional denationalization. *Cabinets* focus more on work associated with their Commissioner's dossier and less on imperatives emanating from national capitals—especially furthering the careers of their nationals in the Commission. Most seem to have amicable relations with 'their' services. There is evidence in the EUCIQ data of considerable mutual respect between *cabinets* and the services, even if on balance officials in the service understand less well the world in which the *cabinets* operate. It would not be surprising if *cabinets* and their Commissioners interfere significantly less in the work of the services in response to impulses from their home member state than they did in the past.

Venturing further, interview testimony in particular suggests that, according to the typology developed by Joana and Smith (2004: 31–2), Commissioners are 'accountants' who mostly focus on the work associated with their portfolio. It is unclear how many are 'European idealists', operating more or less independently of their national governments. But Commissioners who are 'pragmatic' defenders of national interests look to be a dying breed. Certainly, it appears that 'ideologists' who seek 'to influence a wide range of EU policy on the basis of their respective value systems' (Joana and Smith 2004: 31) are a thing of the past.

Finally, it certainly does not follow that life within the College or in the services is not intensely competitive or even conflictual. Nor should there be a rush to discount the view of one EU ambassador who claimed that 'the *cabinets* will always channel impulses from national capitals, and they probably always will' (quoted in Peterson 2006b: 91). Rather, the picture that emerges from the EUCIQ data is of a more harmonious, less fragmented, and more policy-focused Commission than previous accounts have proposed.

8

The Commission and Administrative Reform

Under the Prodi Presidency (1999–2005) the European Commission introduced a series of far-reaching administrative reforms.[1] The proximate cause was the demand by the European Council, following the resignation of the Santer Commission in the face of allegations of mismanagement and maladministration, to overhaul the Commission's administration (Schön-Quinlivan 2011: 59–63). However, the mandate gave senior officeholders the opportunity to address long-standing problems in the organization. Whereas earlier reform efforts had been modest and narrowly targeted, the measures announced by the former Italian Prime Minister and the programme enacted by the reform Vice-President, Neil Kinnock, were comprehensive in scope and aimed at fundamental change. Advanced under the slogan of modernization, their proclaimed goal was to transform the Commission into a twenty-first-century administration. The reforms were undoubtedly a milestone event for the Commission. They were a major preoccupation within the organization and attracted considerable attention from outside it throughout the Prodi mandate.

The views of bureaucrats towards a reform are likely to affect its prospects of success (Gains and John 2010). They also give an insight into staff morale. This chapter focuses on the attitudes of Commission officials to the Kinnock–Prodi reforms.[2] It examines, first, how officials in general and managers in

---

[1] For discussion of the Kinnock–Prodi reforms, see Schön-Quinlivan (2011); the special issue of *Journal of European Public Policy* edited by Bauer (2008a), and the special issue of *Public Policy and Administration*, edited by Levy and Stevens (2004). See also Metcalfe (2000); Kassim (2004a, 2004b); Levy (2006); Bauer (2007); Barzelay and Jacobsen (2009).

[2] Although the Kinnock–Prodi reforms are the principal focus of this chapter—the 'big bang' reform had been implemented by the end of the Prodi Commission and the Barroso Commission indicated that it did not plan any continuation—further measures were adopted. What many officials referred to as 'the reform of the reform' saw, for example, revision of the Career Development Review (CDR) (Ban 2008a) and an overhaul of staff appraisal procedures, as well as change to some internal controls. In an attempt to secure the Commission's first Declaration of Assurance from the European Court of Auditors (Commission 2005; Barzelay et al. 2011),

particular assess the elements of the reform programme. Although on balance more officials are negatively than positively disposed, there is significant spread and variation in their views. A second aim is to explain why individual officials hold the views that they express.[3] Three hypotheses are tested against the EUCIQ data: a utility-maximization hypothesis, which anticipates that the views of individual officials will vary according to whether they consider the reform will help them to do their job better; a socialization hypothesis, which suggests that officials interpret any proposed changes in terms of a worldview that they developed in a formative period before joining the Commission; and a preferred governance hypothesis, based on the conception of the European Union (supranational, state-centric, or pragmatic) that an official prefers.[4] The utility variables fare best, but national background—a socialization variable—is also important.

Before describing and examining the views expressed by officials, some contextualization of the reforms is necessary. The chapter thus begins with an introductory section that offers a brief outline of previous reform efforts, then describes how the Kinnock–Prodi reforms came about, what they sought to achieve, and how.[5] It also compares the reforms implemented by the Commission to reform programmes undertaken by public administrations elsewhere. As well as showing how the Commission's position relative to national bureaucracies has changed over time, it locates member state administrations in regard to staffing and financial management practices, and thereby provides a reference point for the testing of certain socialization variables undertaken below.

ADMINISTRATIVE REFORM IN THE EUROPEAN COMMISSION

A short history of administrative reform

Although nothing on the scale of the Kinnock–Prodi reforms had previously been attempted within the organization, a number of Commissioners and

Barroso also sought to improve budget execution in liaison with the member states, which required some procedural changes.

[3] The more general question of what drives EU officials is an important one. There is little systematic data on what motivates supranational bureaucrats, whether they have working ethics or attitudes different to staff of national administrations, and what implications their motivational characteristics may have either in view of policy-making or organizational change. From this perspective, the behavioural causes of opposition or acceptance of Commission officials towards the Kinnock–Prodi reforms is of considerable importance.

[4] For the theories of bureaucratic behaviour on which the first two are grounded, see Chapter 1. For a discussion of preferred conceptions of EU governance, see Chapter 4.

[5] For accounts of pre-Prodi reform initiatives, see especially Stevens and Stevens (2001: 181–94); Bauer (2007); Schön-Quinlivan (2011).

senior officeholders had sought to address problems that had long been recognized (Stevens and Stevens 2001: 181–6; Bauer 2007, 2008a; Kassim 2008; Schön-Quinlivan 2011: 26–9) (see Table 8.1). That these efforts were sporadic reflected the low priority generally attached to administrative issues within the Commission. Their limited effectiveness, by contrast, was explained partly by poor leadership. Failure of communication had enabled the staff unions to exploit uncertainty within the organization about the proposed measures and to mobilise opposition against them (Stevens and Stevens 2001: 181–6). In addition, since both staff policy and financial management are regulated by legislative acts, any major reform requires the active engagement of the Council of Ministers and the European Parliament. Neither body, however, has shown much interest in the internal management of the Commission and, in the absence of external pressure, would-be reformers inside the Commission have struggled to muster the resources necessary to undertake meaningful change.

Despite these difficulties, reform attempts were made in the 1980s and 1990s in both areas. In personnel policy, these efforts were directed at the Commission's career structure, which was regarded as overly rigid and out of date. Improving the mobility of officials so that resources could be more effectively matched to areas where they are needed, and cultivating management skills, which were underdeveloped and undervalued within the organization, were also key objectives. Particular attention was paid to promotion procedures, which were regarded as especially problematic (see, for example, Stevens and Stevens 2001: 98–104, 108–14). Historically, promotion between grades had been based on a performance assessment, which in accordance with the Staff Regulations was prepared for each official by his or her line manager every two years. Since officials were entitled to view the reports and could resort to litigation if they considered an evaluation to be unfair, assessors tended to use only the top two marks. As a result, the reports were insufficiently discriminating and reports were insufficiently discriminating and did not generally provide a robust basis on which to assess achievement. The system did not reward merit, nor did it create incentives for continuing high performance.

Financial management became an increasing concern in the wake of the Single European Act. The size and complexity of the EU's budget had grown considerably, and with it the Commission's responsibilities in the administration and oversight of spending programmes. Internal procedures and processes had failed to keep pace with the increased volume of transactions, evaluation and audit systems were underdeveloped, and staff lacked experience and expertise in handling financial matters (Laffan 1997). At the same time that national bureaucracies were becoming increasingly attentive to performance budgeting and policy evaluation (see below), the Commission operated an outdated system of *ex ante* centralized expenditure authorization that had been borrowed from the French administration in the 1950s. One of the important characteristics of this model was the way in which it separated

Table 8.1 Reform Initiatives of the European Commission, 1979–2001

Initiatives		Year		Structures	Process	Personnel reporting and promotion	Career structure	Managerial skills	Human resource management	Finance	Ethics	
Jenkins/Spierenburg		1979	Spierenburg Report	X	X	X		X				Follow up: reform of DG structures, portfolios and organigrams
		1980	Ortoli Report: Report on Implementation of Spierenburg report		X	X						
Delors/Hay		1986	Commission's decision on Modernization Policy		X	X						
		1987	Programme for creating awareness of Management Questions—Seminars for Personnel		X			X	X			
		1989			X	X		X	X			

(continued)

Table 8.1 Continued

Initiatives		Structures	Process	Personnel reporting and promotion	Career structure	Managerial skills	Human resource management	Finance	Ethics
Set of Management Measures: Management, Mobilization- and Information Programme									
	1994 Schmidhuber memorandum							X	
Santer/Likaanen	1995 Sound Efficient Management (SEM 2000)		X					X	
	1997 Modernization of Administration and Personnel Policy (MAP)			X					
	1997 Designing the Commission of Tomorrow (Decode): Caston Report (1998) Williamson Group (1998)		X	X				X	
Prodi/Kinnock	2001 Reforming the European Commission, White Paper	X	X	X	X	X	X	X	X

Source: own compilation based on Heisserer (2008), Schön-Quinlivan (2011), Stevens and Stevens (2001).

policy and spending responsibilities. Officials from the operational Directorates-General were required to seek clearance from DG Financial Control each time they needed funding approval for a proposed action. Such a division of labour did not encourage officials working in policy to consider the budgetary implications of their activities and therefore to take responsibility for their cost or value for money—a defect underlined by the Committee of Independent Experts Second Report (1999b).

The Commission's success in tackling these issues was distinctly mixed. Most initiatives were modest in their ambition. Some, for example, the proposals contained in the Spierenburg Report (1979), regarded as the seminal critique of the organization's shortcomings, were not carried through. Others, such as those based on the 'Caston Report'—an internal working paper that proposed reform of personnel management and career development (Stevens and Stevens 2001: 192)—were blocked or diluted in the face of strike action. Even those which achieved some degree of success, most notably Sound and Efficient Management 2000 (SEM 2000) and Modernization of Administration and Personnel Policy (MAP 2000)—initiatives to improve financial and personnel management implemented under the Santer Commission (Bauer 2001: ch. 3, 2002, 2008; Stevens and Stevens 2001: 186–94; Kassim 2004b; Schön-Quinlivan 2008)—were not well managed. They were poorly explained at the political level, and tended to be identified with a single Commissioner rather than the College as a whole. None received the active support of the Council or Parliament.

Administrative reform under Prodi: the background

Romano Prodi was nominated Commission President in the wake of the crisis precipitated by the resignation of the Santer Commission (1995–9) with a mandate to reform. Jacques Santer had long been mired in a confrontation with the European Parliament after MEPs had levelled allegations of mismanagement, nepotism, and corruption against the Commission (Topan 2002). At the insistence of the European Parliament, he had conceded the demand for creation of a Committee of Independent Experts to investigate these charges. On the eve of the publication of the Committee's first report, the College decided to resign rather than to face a vote of confidence in the European Parliament which it feared it would lose.

Prodi immediately committed himself to acting to restore confidence in the Commission, and agreed to implement whatever recommendations the Committee of Independent Experts might put forward in their second report. One of his first actions was to invite Neil Kinnock, a survivor of the Santer Commission and a reforming leader of the British Labour Party (Westlake 2001), to become Vice-President in charge of reform. The reform programme that Kinnock defined and implemented addressed a broader range of concerns than outlined either by the European Council or the Committee of Independent Experts (Kassim 2008).

A comprehensive reform

Prodi himself introduced a number of reforms, many of which anticipated recommendations that later appeared in the Committee of Independent Experts' second report. The measures included codes of conduct governing EU Commissioners and their relations with their departments; new rules for senior appointments, designed to strengthen the Commission's independence and to limit outside interference; a five-year limit on the length of time a Director-General could remain in the same position; and a reduction in the size of *cabinets* and an increase in their multinationality (see Chapters 2 and 7). Most of the measures, however, were prefigured in a reform White Paper (Commission 2000, 2 parts), which identified the areas where change was necessary, set out ninety-eight actions, and served as a blueprint for the reforms.[6] The text was drafted by a task force, which both looked at other bureaucracies to get a sense of current practice and sought to draw on the experience of Commission officials,[7] and was adopted by the College on 1 March 2000.[8]

The White Paper proposed general measures to create within the Commission a 'Culture based on Service', founded on the principles of independence, responsibility, accountability, efficiency, and transparency. It set out standards for the conduct of officials and their interaction with citizens, and extended further access to EU documentation. The remaining actions were directed towards three areas. The centrepiece of the reforms was the creation of a machinery designed to enable the Commission to set clear priorities and to allocate financial and human resources more efficiently. The Secretariat-General assumed responsibility for Strategic Planning and Programming (SPP), which would begin modestly but would then gradually extend and expand. The aim was nothing less than the orchestration and monitoring of activity at all levels of the organization to carry out the implementation of multiannual objectives set by the President and discussed by the College. These priorities would then be translated into work programmes for each Directorate-General and into specific actions for each unit. Activity-Based Management (ABM), a modern budgetary tool linking the allocation of financial, personnel, and IT

[6] Measures relating to personnel policy were negotiated in a working group chaired by Niels Ersbøll, a former Secretary-General of the Council Secretariat, and in which management and the staff unions were both represented.
[7] See Kassim (2004a).
[8] For comparison between the recommendations called for by the second report of the Committee of Independent Experts (1999b) and the reform programme, see Kassim (2008).

resources to a ranking of organizational priorities, was introduced as a key part of the new apparatus. The new system became fully operational in 2005.[9]

Second, financial management and control underwent a complete overhaul. The aim was to decentralize responsibility to name services and individual post-holders in order to improve efficiency and accountability within the organization. The system of centralized *ex ante* control was abolished and direct responsibility for the approval of expenditure devolved to budgetary authorizing officers in the services. Financial control and audit were separated, responsibility for both transferred from DG Financial Control to the individual services, and new structures created centrally and inside each Directorate-General to oversee financial management. Directors-General assumed accountability for financial management and control within their respective services, as symbolized by the personal assurance statement that each would be required to approve as they signed off the annual activities report. To support them in carrying out their new responsibilities, but also to oversee their work, a new Central Financial Service was created, connected to the services through a network of directors. Auditing was also reorganized. Auditing functions were devolved to specialist units in the Directorates-General, while a central Internal Audit Service with Commission-wide responsibilities was established to set standards and to monitor the services.

The changes in personnel policy—the third area—were no less far-reaching. The reforms revised procedures relating to professional underperformance,[10] and strengthened equal opportunities policy. They also introduced a code for whistle-blowers, measures to improve career development and training opportunities, and a range of family-friendly policies and allowances. The most radical changes concerned the career structure and promotion procedures. Although they fell short of full career linearization, the reforms introduced a system organizing staff into two grades, administrators (ADs) and assistants (ASTs) (see Chapter 2).

As well as removing the rigidities that had made it difficult for officials to move between categories under the old system, the new structure aimed to ensure that staff remained motivated throughout their career. Under the old system, officials often faced career bottlenecks once they had reached the highest

---

[9] Once priorities were established and resources allocated, the Commission could then distinguish between the core responsibilities, which it would retain, and other tasks that could be delegated to outside agencies. The decentralization of decision-making and a simplification of administrative procedures were also to be achieved under the heading of better priority-setting and more effective resource allocation.

[10] It was widely recognized that the procedures for managing and disciplining underperforming staff were somewhat elusive. By way of illustration, Coull and Lewis (2003: 3) observe that 'only one member of staff has ever been formally sacked by the Commission for poor performance—on that occasion it took over 9 years to end legal debate which went all the way to the European Court of Justice, and where both sides were funded by the European Union'.

grade that they could reasonably expect to achieve—A4, in the case of administrators. As they would continue to move up a step—and to receive the corresponding pay increase—every two years, it was considered that the organization 'failed to provide these staff with the right incentives to ensure they remained motivated' (Coull and Lewis 2003: 4) for the remainder of their career, which could be well over ten years. The new career system is more continuous and, with fewer steps in each grade, was intended to ensure 'that an official recruited at a low grade in the new system can, through proven merit, reach a much higher level of pay and responsibility than under the old' (Coull and Lewis 2003: 4). The new pay structure removed some of the anomalies that existed under the old system, in order to reward performance rather than seniority and to ensure that officials on the first step of a higher grade would be paid more than the highest step of the lower grade. At the same time, the entry level for administrators was set at two grades lower than for their counterparts recruited prior to the reforms: A5 rather than A7. ADs recruited at entry level after 1 May 2004 would have to negotiate more steps and thereby embark along a more prolonged career path than entry level officials recruited before this date (see Chapter 9).

The reforms also overhauled promotion procedures, linking them to a new system of appraisal, the Career Development Review (CDR), and the introduction of job descriptions for all posts. The complexities and administrative cost of the CDR (European Commission 2002; European Commission DG Personnel and Administration 2007; see Ban 2008b for detailed analysis), as well as other problems in its design, proved so controversial that Siim Kallas, the Commissioner for administration, and Claude Chêne, the Director-General of DG ADMIN, initiated a reform in 2007. A revised system, the 'new CDR', was introduced in 2009.

In the CDR's first incarnation, individuals were scored annually by their Head of Unit on a scale of 1 to 20 in regard to three criteria: performance relative to objectives, demonstration of abilities, and conduct.[11] The Director-General then awarded between 0 and 10 priority points to each official. To prevent grade inflation, a points ceiling equivalent to around two-and-a-half times the number of staff was set for each DG. The Director-General was not permitted to award high scores to a small number of employees and other measures were introduced to prevent grade inflation over time.[12]

---

[11] A target of 14 merit points was set for each Directorate-General and, in order to correct for possible inflation, scores were averaged across the Commission as a whole.

[12] Each DG had a promotion committee, including staff representatives, that could also award up to two additional priority points from a quota of points equal to the number of staff of the DG times a quarter (European Commission 2002). These points were generally awarded in recognition of extra service to the institutions (such as serving on a selection board).

The points awarded to each official were cumulative and collected in a so-called 'sac à dos'. After two years in a grade, an official became eligible for promotion. Promotion would follow, provided that the accumulated points met the defined threshold. In practice, however, it would usually take an official at least three or four years to collect the necessary points. One consequence was that it would take officials who joined the Commission after 1 May 2004 considerably longer to be promoted than colleagues recruited before this date. Moreover, since the number of posts and their level of seniority depended on budgetary resources, the thresholds for promotion would not be known until the budget was set.

The reformed CDR preserved the system of appraisal, but with a qualitative performance rating—1A, 1B, II, III, or IV (Commission 2007)—based on an assessment of merit, level of responsibilities, and language use. Whilst an evaluation meeting between supervisor and appraisee would focus on perform-ance and future goals, points were to be allocated by a meeting in each DG of the Director-General, Deputy Director-General, and Directors, within a three-point range.[13] At the same time, the Director-General was able to award a small number of additional promotion points to recognize outstanding performance over time. Other points (including priority points and points in the interest of the institution) were eliminated. Whilst the accumulation of points was retained, the number of points needed for promotion in all but the top grades was fixed in advance. The result was a shorter and more streamlined process, even if certain aspects continued to attract criticism.[14] Indeed, as the 'new CDR' proved no less workable, Maroš Šefčovič, the Commissioner for inter-institutional relations and administration in the second Barroso Presidency, took the decision to replace it, and the CDR was effectively abolished in January 2012.

Commission reform in comparative context

The Kinnock–Prodi reforms can usefully be compared to the changes under-taken by governments and several international organizations in the 1980s and 1990s.[15] Despite differences in their ambitions, the scope and content of the programmes they implemented, and the extent to which they were suc-cessful, reformers across the globe followed a similar 'trajectory of modernization

---

[13] A set formula determined how points were to be divided within each grade and functional unit, and the per DG quota was lifted.

[14] The fixed distribution quota—8 per cent in 1A and 22 per cent in 1B—provoked particular criticism (Ban 2008a). See also the websites of the staff unions: Confédération Syndicale Europé-enne at <http://www.conf-sfe.eu/index.htm>; Fédération de la Fonction Publique Européenne at <http://www.ffpe-bxl.eu/fr/accueil_286.php>; Renouveau & Démocratie at <http://www.renou-veau-democratie.eu>; Solidarity, Independence, Democracy at <http://sidtu.org/tiki-index.php>; TAO-AFI at <http://tao-afi.org>; and Union Syndicale at <http://unionsyndicale.eu>.

[15] For reform of national administrations, see Pollitt and Bouckaert (2004); Ongaro (2009). For international administrations, see Bauer and Knill (2007); Balint et al. (2008).

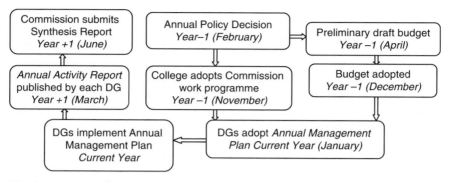

Fig. 8.1 Strategic planning and programming

Source: European Commission <http://ec.europa.eu/atwork/cycle/index_en.htm>, accessed 10 January 2013.

and reform' (Pollitt and Bouckaert 2004: 65–102). Later referred to under the rubric of the 'new public management',[16] the reforms were premised on the view that the traditional civil service was outdated, inflexible and introspective, and that a new model of administration was necessary.[17] With the aim of increasing efficiency, improving responsiveness to citizens, and cutting costs, governments of varying complexion sought to reduce the size of the public sector, to introduce new methods of service delivery, and to increase the autonomy of senior managers. Personnel policy and budgetary processes were particular targets of the new emphasis on performance.

Human resources reforms typically encompassed changes in recruitment procedures, career development, pay systems, and social security benefits.[18] They eroded, and in some cases brought an end to, the privileges, rights, and protections traditionally extended to civil servants. They also brought about a shift from the career-based civil service model to a more open position-based system where posts are open to both internal and external applicants,

---

[16] Christopher Hood describes its core features as 'the idea of a shift in emphasis from policy making to management skills, from a stress on process to a stress on output, from orderly hierarchies to an intendedly more competitive basis for providing public services, from fixed to variable pay and from a uniform and inclusive public service to a variant structure with more emphasis on contract provision' (1995a: 94). NPM has generated a vast literature. Key readings include: Hood (1991, 1995b); Peters and Wright (1996); Minogue et al. (1998); Lane (2000); Barzelay (2001); Christiansen and Lagreid (2002); OECD (2011); and Pollitt and Bouckaert (2011). For post-NPM developments, see Christiansen and Lagreid (2007). Most observers agree that NPM does not offer a template or blueprint but, as Pollitt and Bouckaert (2004) suggest, is more a 'theme' than a uniform model.

[17] Since much of NPM is concerned with direct service delivery, the extent to which it can apply to international administrations, such as the Commission, is a moot point. A further obligation is that the continued emphasis on hierarchy within the Commission disqualifies the Kinnock–Prodi package as an NPM-style reform.

[18] For discussion of NPM-style changes in personnel policy in public administrations, see OECD (2005a, 2005b, 2011).

especially in senior roles where the new emphasis on management requires access to specialist skills and knowledge. Whereas, historically, public servants had been rewarded on the basis of seniority, governments introduced performance assessment and performance-related pay as part of a new performance management regime.

In budgeting, the reforms centred on a shift from inputs to outputs. Departments and managers are judged by how well their programmes perform rather than the extent to which they comply with administrative controls or procedures. It has transformed budgeting from 'a situation where budgets were mainly a process by which annual financial allocations were incrementally adjusted, legalized, and made accountable to legislatures' (Pollitt and Bouckaert 2004: 67) to a position where planning, operational management, and performance management are integrated in the budgetary process.[19] Budgets include an element of performance assessment, to the extent that in some countries performance affects future funding. As part of this change, accounting systems have been increasingly adapted to deliver performance-management information. A transition has been undertaken from cash-based systems, which offer few incentives for efficiency, to double-entry bookkeeping, which is close to the private sector model, and beyond to accrual-accounting, where 'governments report commitments when they are incurred (rather than when the cash is actually disbursed)' (Pollitt and Bouckaert 2004: 7).[20] Public sector auditing has also followed a reform trajectory. Traditional audits were focused on recording procedural compliance, but ministries and other governmental bodies are increasingly required to supply performance and evaluation information with their accounts. In some countries, departments undergo full performance-auditing.[21]

The Kinnock–Prodi reforms shared many features of the new public management approach.[22] Attempting to bring the Commission into line with prevailing standards of public management, they sought to make it a more efficient and accountable administration through improved performance-management systems. The new personnel policy aimed to encourage performance and to reward merit. SPP sought to enshrine a concern with outputs and to improve performance by target-setting, steering from above and better management. The changes in financial management and control, meanwhile, introduced performance measurement into budgeting, control, and audit procedures. They were accompanied by the introduction of new monitoring

---

[19] For performance budgeting, see OECD (2007, 2008a).
[20] On accrual accounting, see Blöndal (2003, 2004); Schick (2007).
[21] On performance auditing, see OECD (1996).
[22] Despite the qualification noted above, the reform rhetoric was undoubtedly coloured by NPM with its emphasis on modernization and the creation of a more 'steerable', 'manageable' Commission.

tools (performance indicators and audit), evaluation, and performance measures, including job descriptions.

Assessing the extent to which these ambitions have been realized, still less whether the reforms have been successful, is beyond the scope of the current volume.[23] It is useful, however, to consider the impact of the reforms on the Commission and on how the organization compares to other administrations, as well as to assess the magnitude and direction of the change. For this purpose, Figures 8.2a and b show respectively the Commission's pre-reform and post-reform positions in regard to staff policy, while Figure 8.3 depicts how it relates in respect to budgeting and auditing. The position of national administrations has been plotted using OECD data.

Figures 8.2a and b illustrate the shift in the position of the Commission as a result of increased emphasis on performance assessment. They also show how selected national administrations have changed position over the same period. Figure 8.3 shows that the Commission is not an outlier in regard to its budgeting and auditing procedures and practices. Contrary to how it is depicted in some of the literature, many of its practices approximate to current norms. It follows that the Commission should no longer be considered an antiquated continental bureaucracy. Whatever their other consequences, the Kinnock–Prodi reforms succeeded in bringing the Commission closer into line with prevailing practices in public administration.

Furthermore, the changes to the CDR, the adjustment of internal control procedures in pursuit of the Commission's first ever Declaration of Assurance from the European Court of Auditors (Barzelay et al. 2011), and the changes to the Staff Regulations proposed in summer 2011 suggest that administrative reform has become normalized within the Commission. Although it still arouses passions,[24] change is no longer a no-go area. In the wake of the Kinnock–Prodi reforms, as in other administrations it has become part of the everyday life of the organization.

COMMISSION OFFICIALS AND ADMINISTRATIVE REFORM

The Kinnock–Prodi reforms were distinguished from earlier initiatives not only by their breadth (see Table 8.1) but also by the strategy and approach taken. Reform was a high and visible political priority, measures were adopted

---

[23] In his comments on an earlier version of this chapter as a discussant on the panel, 'The European Commission of the twenty-first century: new perspectives on a core institution', Council of European Studies Conference, Barcelona, 24–26 June 2011, Guy Peters suggested the Kinnock–Prodi reforms are better interpreted as 'NPM laid upon layers of legalism' than as the replacement of one administrative model by another.

[24] See the responses of the trade unions to the CDR reform; for example, TAO-AFI, Union Syndicale, Renouveau and Democratie, and Solidarity, Independence, Democracy.

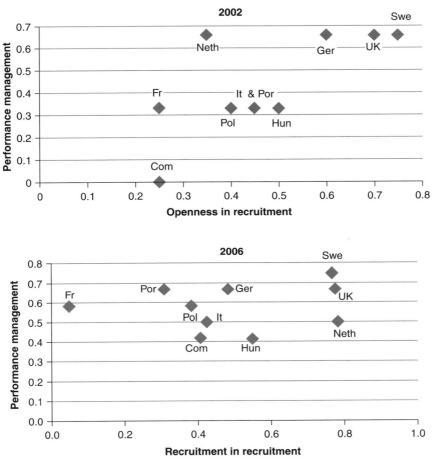

Fig. 8.2a and b Human resource management in Commission and selected EU countries

Source: Commission (authors' own calculation); OECD (2003, 2009).

and owned by the College as a whole, and considerable effort was invested in explaining the measures to staff and in keeping them updated.[25] The leadership recognized that it would be problematic if a significant number of employees, especially those at senior or middle management level, were to oppose organizational change that the leadership believed necessary, and sought strenuously to carry staff along.

The opinion of Commission officials on the Kinnock–Prodi reforms was gauged in the EUCIQ online survey. A series of general questions was posed to

---

[25] Bearfield (2004) offers an insider's view of the communications strategy that was part of the reform effort.

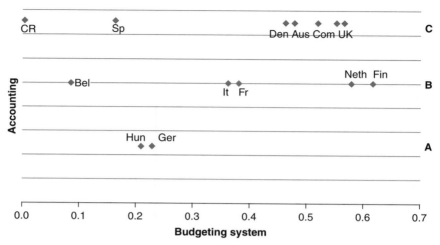

Fig. 8.3 Budgeting and accounting in Commission and selected EU countries

Source: Commission (authors' own calculation); Pollitt and Bouckaert (2004); CESifo DICE (2007).

all staff, and a second set of more detailed questions addressed to middle and senior managers.[26]

The attitudes of Commission officials towards reform

In a question to all officials, respondents were asked for their views on particular aspects of the Kinnock–Prodi reforms and their impact. A mixture of positive and negative propositions was used in framing the questions in order to check on the consistency of responses and capture any nuances in view. The results are summarized in Figure 8.4. The top three bars indicate responses to questions that suggested a negative impact ('more red tape', 'applied in a formalistic way', and 'the negative effects outweigh any general benefits'), whereas the questions in the bottom four bars focus on potential benefits ('more efficient', 'more effective', 'more efficient', and 'better match between resources and policy'). As Figure 8.4 shows, there was significant variation in the attitudes expressed. More than half of officials agree that the new rules led to more red tape or are applied in a formalistic way. Although more than a quarter agree that their unit or service has become more efficient or that personnel management has become more effective, more than one-third of officials disagree.

[26] In the absence of comparative longitudinal data, it is not possible to determine whether the views of Commission staff are atypical at this point in the reform trajectory or whether the pattern of views is normal for an organization at the same stage following the implementation of 'big bang' reform.

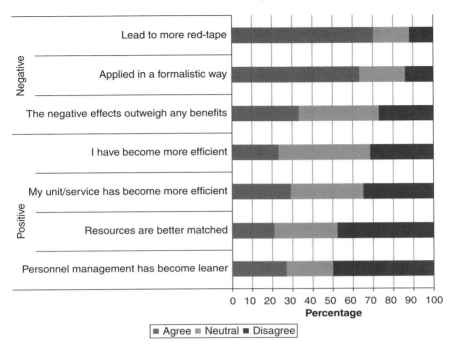

Fig. 8.4 Attitudes to the reforms

The variation of opinion is an important finding, since it is often supposed that bureaucrats are conservative and likely to oppose change (Putnam 1973; Suleiman 1974; Kellner and Crowther-Hunt 1980). However, as Figure 8.4 also shows, more officials are negatively disposed to the reforms than hold positive views—a surprising finding given that in 2008, when the online survey was conducted, the changes introduced had been in place for several years. At the same time, nearly a third of respondents neither agree nor disagree with the propositions put to them. That such a large number of officials take a neutral stance on a programme that has affected not only how the Commission operates, but their working conditions and career prospects is also somewhat surprising.[27]

Further examination shows that on each aspect of the reforms negative assessments outweigh the number of positive opinions, if only sometimes by a small margin, and that some interesting differences between administrators and managers emerge. Table 8.2, which is based on the same data, offers a more fine-grained picture. A mean of 2.0 indicates a neutral assessment. For questions where agreement with the proposition indicates a negative disposition to the reforms mean is greater than 2.0 in each case, and is less than 2.0 where agreement with the question indicates support for reform. Overall,

---

[27] Thirty per cent of officials did not answer the question.

Table 8.2 Assessment of the Kinnock–Prodi reforms

		Mean	Median	Mode	St Dev	N
All officials						
Negative	The new tools and rules lead to more red-tape	2.82	3	3	0.97	1285
	The new tools and rules are applied in a formalistic way	2.63	3	3	0.92	1253
	The negative effects on me outweigh any general benefits	2.12	2	2	1.12	1221
Positive	My unit/service has become more efficient	1.90	2	2	1.02	1184
	I have become more efficient in my day-to-day work	1.87	2	2	0.93	1244
	Personnel management has become leaner and more focused	1.65	2	1	1.07	1237
	Resources are better matched to policy priorities	1.60	2	1	1.01	1245
Administrators						
Negative	The new tools and rules lead to more red-tape	2.71	3	3	0.95	728
	The new tools and rules are applied in a formalistic way	2.58	3	3	0.91	702
	The negative effects on me outweigh any general benefits	2.37	2	2	1.09	707
Positive	My unit/service has become more efficient	1.82	2	2	1.01	650
	I have become more efficient in my day-to-day work	1.86	2	2	0.93	690
	Personnel management has become leaner and more focused	1.58	1	1	1.04	685
	Resources are better matched to policy priorities	1.56	2	1	1.01	691
Middle and senior managers						
Negative	The new tools and rules lead to more red-tape	2.97	3	3	0.98	557
	The new tools and rules are applied in a formalistic way	2.69	3	3	0.92	550
	The negative effects on me outweigh any general benefits	1.78	2	2	1.06	513
Positive	My unit/service has become more efficient	2.00	2	2	1.03	534
	I have become more efficient in my day-to-day work	1.88	2	2	0.92	554
	Personnel management has become leaner and more focused	1.73	2	1	1.11	551
	Resources are better matched to policy priorities	1.65	2	1	1.01	554

Note: The answer scale ranges from strongly agree (= 4) to strongly disagree (= 0); N = number of respondents.

officials are not overly enthusiastic about the Kinnock–Prodi reforms or their impact.

The views of middle and senior managers deserve particular attention. The Kinnock–Prodi reforms were intended to strengthen, expand, and support the role of managers within the organization.[28] Given the emphasis of the reforms on strengthening management and equipping managers with better tools, it would be disappointing—and even damaging—if senior managers (that is, Directors-General, Deputy Directors-General, and Directors), or middle managers (Heads of Unit) either disliked the reforms or were sceptical as to whether they had actually enabled them to carry out their responsibilities more effectively. The findings of earlier studies have not been encouraging (Bauer 2008b, 2009b) in this respect. Based on fieldwork conducted in 2006, Bauer reported that middle managers were especially negative: a majority were unambiguously opposed to the measures introduced. Complaints about the amount of red tape were commonplace. One official expressed the following view that was far from uncommon: 'Kinnock is a disaster and a 300 per cent bureaucracy increase with form-filling accounting for 80 per cent and substance just for 20 per cent. . . . [I]t is paperwork that nobody reads'. Another spoke of the 'control mania' inside the Commission which 'creates a culture of fear', and loss of sight of 'political priorities' and 'political function', such that the organization's 'original mission is forgotten'.[29] The 'real problem is that process has become an aim in itself'; there are 'lots of words, declarations, announcements which lead to nowhere, there is no increase in productivity'. Positive assessments were few and far between, and usually qualified: 'l'ésprit est bon, [mais] la mise en oeuvre moins car elle crée un surplus de la bureaucratie. . . . parfois amène à la diminution de l'effectivité' ['The idea's a good one, but how it's been put into operation, less so, as it creates a whole heap of bureaucracy . . . often leading to less efficiency']. (All cited in Bauer 2008b, 2009b).

The online survey (2008) and interviews (2009) made it possible both to compare the views of managers with other administrators and to examine the extent to which, if at all, the views of middle and senior managers had changed in the two to three years since Bauer conducted his fieldwork. As Table 8.2 shows, managers generally have more positive views towards the benefits of reform than administrators. Although managers are more likely than administrators to think that the reforms have created more paperwork, they also believe that the measures introduced have resulted in greater efficiency.

An additional set of questions in the online survey was put exclusively to middle and senior managers. They concerned elements of the reforms more specifically directed at managers. The results are shown in Figure 8.5. Asked

---

[28] The impact on middle managers was not unintended. A study of the likely consequences was set out in a Commission working document, 'In Praise of Middle Management' (interview 82).

[29] See Bauer (2008b).

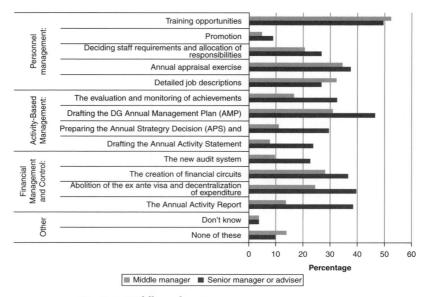

Fig. 8.5 Middle and senior managers
Which of the following has improved your capacity to do your job?
Note: n = 624.

whether the aspects in question have enhanced their abilities to do their job, senior managers express a more positive view than middle managers on all but one aspect of the reforms. Nearly 50 per cent of senior managers show their support for the Annual Management Plan, and close to 40 per cent affirm that elements including the abolition of the *ex ante* visa, the annual activity report, the creation of financial circuits, and annual appraisal have enabled them to do their job more effectively.

Finally, middle and senior managers were asked in follow-up face-to-face interviews about their views on the reforms. These questions were posed:

- In the survey, we asked a number of questions about rules and procedures within the Commission following administrative reform. We are interested in the extent to which the rules that govern the running of the house enable you as a middle/senior manager to carry out your responsibilities effectively. To what extent do the staff rules help or hinder you in achieving the goals of the unit/directorate/DG?[30]

- To what extent do the systems governing financial management and planning help or hinder you in carrying out your responsibilities as a Head of Unit/Director/Director General?[31]

---

[30] Respondents were given the following options: Extremely helpful; Quite helpful; Neither a help nor a hindrance; Something of a hindrance; Not at all helpful; Don't know; Prefer not to say.
[31] Respondents were given the following options: Extremely helpful; Quite helpful; Neither a help nor a hindrance; Something of a hindrance; Not at all helpful; Don't know; Prefer not to say.

- Do the financial management rules and procedures strike the right balance between accountability and efficiency?[32]

- What single rule or procedure would you change to help you carry out your job more effectively?

Overall, the responses showed that the spread of views among managers was broader than might have been anticipated. Those interviewed were more positive about financial management and strategic policy and planning than about the staff rules. Only 18 per cent said that the staff rules were quite helpful or extremely helpful; 27 per cent that they were 'something of a hindrance'; 22 per cent that they were neither a help nor a hindrance; and 28 per cent thought that the staff rules were not at all helpful. On financial management, respondents were more positive: 31 per cent thought that the systems and procedures introduced by the reforms were either quite helpful or extremely helpful; 18 per cent neither a help nor a hindrance; and 38 per cent either something of a hindrance or not at all helpful.

The individual responses prompted by the questions offer interesting insights into the reasoning behind these aggregate figures. For this reason, they are examined in some detail below.

Managers and the Kinnock–Prodi reforms

A number of managers seized the opportunity to offer an overall assessment of the reforms.[33] Many were very positive about the reform programme and its impact:

> I think that they have been strong and [the reform] works quite well (interview 51).

> I think the reform ... was amazing ... [T]he Commission has done an enormous job in reforming itself (interview 46).

> [S]ome of the more important aspects of it are now entered into our ways of thinking. You need proper planning. You need to have proper work programmes; staff need to know what they're meant to be doing. Staff need to be able to be appraised each year on the basis of what they think themselves; they need more, and managers need to manage people (interview 82).

---

[32] Respondents were given the following options: Yes, very much so; Yes; In some respects yes; In some respects no; No; Not at all; Don't know; Prefer not to say.

[33] Several ventured explanations for the reform. One interviewee saw it as a necessary response to a hostile climate: 'some of our member states do not trust us, so ... you have [to have] a system which is ... watertight' (interview 142). Another was convinced that it was a (British) plot: 'the staff rules are a big disaster, absolute disaster. [S]ome of us see [them] as a winning strategy to weaken the institution and to render it far less competitive than it was. This is as if they did it on purpose you know' (interview 129).

Many, however, could not see past the 'red tape':

> I would be surprised if you haven't heard this before. We are overburdened and overrun by these rules.... We don't see the forest for all the trees (interview 127).

> The system has become increasingly complex ... I know so many colleagues who are just [coordinating] themselves to death, filling in papers which nobody reads (interview 70).

> [T]he number of stupid things you can't imagine (interview 57).

One concern was that the volume of paperwork stopped the Commission from working on policy initiation: 'There's certainly important progress in there, in terms of accountability and procedures. But I am sometimes worried that it kills the scope for policy innovation' (interview 126).

More widespread, however, was the sentiment that disproportionate weight was borne by middle management. Middle managers could not get on with their 'proper job'.[34] According to one interviewee: 'the charge on the heads of unit is huge.... [T]rying to separate or divide the work between the head of unit and a deputy head of unit in terms of management, administration, and policy, that that would be a huge, huge improvement' (interview 76). Another lamented: '[Y]our role as the head of unit is 100 per cent administration.... [T]he amount of time taken by rules and applying the rules and applying the procedures is too much.... [I]t was understandable that the Commission reformed itself, and it was needed also, but the pendulum has simply gone too far in the direction of rules and constraints and procedures' (interview 52). One Director-General reflected: 'I ask myself nowadays what still drives these young people to want to become the head of unit' (interview 128).

The views expressed by managers on whether they were helped or hindered by personnel policy were mixed. Some considered that the reforms had achieved a real advance:

> Definitely, definitely a help. I can compare it to the situation before administrative reform, which was somewhat chaotic and unregulated.... [M]any of the new rules and the new guidelines and the new kinds of training and expertise have been a great change compared to before (interview 2).

> [I]n general they have improved the management, just like having very basic things which did not exist before, like a job description, or the procedures have become more transparent. I've been in human resources, and when I arrived it was very, very unclear (interview 76).

---

[34] One official who had been involved in the reform and in the drafting of a document on middle management recalled that the response to the concern that: 'the bureaucracy, and procedures, and paperwork associated with the reform would cost half of the middle managers' time' had been 'Well, managers should be doing all these things.' The official's response: 'Yes, but maybe not in such a bureaucratic and time-consuming way' (interview 82).

Others, however, were negative: 'I think they're a big stumbling block' (interview 3).

For a small minority the reforms were either wrong-headed or, alternatively, had not gone far enough:

> The staff rules are not helpful, and not modern in terms of providing anything that would be remotely related to effective personal underpinning for a Directorate-General that wants to react in a way that a business would react. . . . [T]he rules are constraints rather than part of a system that facilitates efficient and effective work. . . . I am highly critical of where we are in terms of our HR policy, because I find the system is slow (interview 138).

> The whole cultural attitude that permeates that world is thirty years out of line with what we would need to be truly modern . . . [W]e manage very well, but it's usually despite the system, not because of the system. . . . [W]e have great staff . . . but once they're in through the door, the thing that keeps them motivated is the work, not the HR policies that we are supposed to be applying (interview 138).

> [T]here are many issues that deserve a fresh look: recruitment, promotion, staff assessment, the flexibility of the allocation of staff between departments, too many levels of management, granting some management responsibility to officials at a junior level, mapping out satisfying career paths for officials other than by hierarcichal promotion. And there are many, many issues that affect the efficiency and morale of the staff that deserve to be looked at (interview 151).

Among the changes to personnel policy, the CDR was the most controversial. Even those who welcomed the new system were less than unequivocal in their support:

> [I]t is problematic. Still, as I experienced, you need the one or the other system in an institution like this to have career development and promotions organized (interview 116).

> [T]he staff reporting system is a pain in the neck . . . I have an extremely big unit, and . . . it takes basically two weeks to run them through this process . . . [I]t's in the end, a good instrument. But it takes an enormous amount of time (interview 52).

Some interviewees were critical because, even in its amended form, the CDR did not allow managers to reward merit or to motivate staff. According to one head of unit: 'The [new] CDR has failed completely' (interview 98). For a Director in DG Research and Innovation it was, 'a disaster, this CDR, the last one because we . . . [managers] do not have the power to reward . . . those who work very hard' (interview 81). A senior manager in the DG felt the same way: 'I find it awful [for] two reasons. First, . . . I am given the responsibility to assess colleagues, full responsibility, without being given the tools . . . Second thing is that since we are bound by these averages per grade, per unit, per directorate, the conflicts you create . . . between colleagues are very high' (interview 57).

The length of the reporting cycle was also a problem: 'the staff apprai-sals . . . take almost a year . . . [T]he staff appraisals for 2009 . . . have not yet been concluded. [A]s a head of unit, we are supposed to do the staff appraisals within a very short period—four weeks, . . . according to a very strict and rigid timescale—time schedule . . . [W]e are now in September . . . and nobody knows so far whether he or she got a promotion . . . It puts a huge burden on . . . the head of unit to do the appraisal, and creates a lot of frustration . . .' (interview 73).

Others thought that it imposed an excessive burden on managers. One middle manager complained that: 'it takes us from our core tasks in my view . . . and . . . makes us have to work long, late hours, unnecessarily . . . [T]hey're not adding anything to the job' (interview 53). Another elsewhere in the organization thought that: 'the staff assessment system . . . is grossly over-engineered, all these thousands and thousands of pages of self assessment that nobody's ever going to read apart from one person. That really is a very, very heavy burden on the system' (interview 44). Further criticisms were directed at the link that CDR had forged between appraisal and promotion, which some managers thought problematic, and at the complex points system for scoring staff:

> '[A]n evaluation . . . has nothing to do with a promotion' (interview 114).

> '[I]t is supposedly designed to reflect the individual merit. However, it is accom-panied with implementation rules for grading that prevents the organization as a DG to . . . give merit to people' (interview 121).

> 'Development" was meant to be the keyword, instead of which we've gone to a situation where development is completely forgotten about by all participants . . . [The whole process] has become focused on numbers . . . [I]t's based on . . . number crunching, and it's not working at all (interview 82).

The CDR was not the only element of personnel policy to draw criticism. Although many managers agreed in principle with the introduction of com-pulsory mobility for officials in 'sensitive posts', they thought that four or five years was too short. For one head of unit, it was the 'part of administrative reform, which causes the most grief'. Although 'the idea is good', the service was 'losing experience' and 'language abilities' due to the forced rotation of staff (interview 2). A middle manager in DG Information Society and Media also complained about the disruption: it 'cannot be very healthy and very efficient' (interview 54).

Specific criticism was directed at arrangements concerning contractual agents:

Contractual agents have a mandate of three years maximum. We just had to let go of a contractual agent who was doing a brilliant [job]. He was well-versed in that, and well-experienced. And since his departure, quality of service has been reduced. So yes, that is a hindrance (interview 126).

[T]he rules applying to contract agents as we call them and these are known not to be good—limited to three years and it is really not good (interview 151).

[O]f course we shouldn't create the power where you [become] a European civil servant for life. But on the other side I think the three-years period is very short (interview 49).

A lot of people now are contractual agents, and they're here for three years. So where the future is for them, us, especially an area like this where you train somebody. We spend a year maybe training them to know how to do the job. And then they have two years with us, and they're gone. That's a problem (interview 79).

Managers were considerably more positive overall in regard to the financial management reforms. For many, under no illusion about why they were introduced, the reforms were necessary:

This organization suffered a tremendous image blow because of perceived mis-management.... I think in financial management we have managed to set up a framework of rules within which ... risk is now manageable, transparent, and accountable, and people are made accountable for their financial work. In my view this has been a success. Now, inevitably that leads to a burden of work and a complex set of rules, but I prefer to have that protection against the reputational risk that you run if you just do what you like (interview 72).

The rules governing the financial management, day-to-day management, they are complicated.... I could live without most of them, but I am convinced that as a large institution and as a manager of money, the Commission needs rules, even if they are complicated. That also would be the case in a private enterprise, but in a private enterprise, it matters somewhat less to bring assurances that the system protects the money which is spent.... [O]ne needs to have guarantees for the sound management on a day-to-day basis, so rules are complicated (interview 124).

Other interviewees welcomed the reforms, because they put the Commission on a surer footing:

There's been a big improvement there—a very big improvement over the last ten years ... [R]igour was introduced, uniformity was introduced, rules that people can understand, training ... My staff are mainly working on project manage-ment ..., and there's been a vast improvement in performance.... We are now delivering exactly what we say we will deliver ... [T]hat's really a success story, which I think is now recognized in development circles.... [T]he financial rules were essential ... for us to achieve those objectives (interview 45).

[F]inancial management is something that we have always been weak in for many years and I think it was clear that we had to do something about it, and then something about it was done definitely. I think that the systems of managing money in the Commission have become tremendously safe, transparent, documented according to the rules; 150 checks and balances (interview 128).

I think it's a major advance for the institution to have much better rules on financial management and much better procedures for the annual planning and annual reporting. I think they're quite heavy procedures [and] they're still capable of improvement. . . . But on the whole I think it makes for a much more effective, modern institution. And gives a much better assurance that the budget is properly managed. [T]he Commission can present itself as one of the more advanced organizations in terms of how it manages its affairs. And I think that's important for its credibility. I think this is a major advance. You pay a price in terms of a certain amount of time you've taken up with operating these procedures, but I think it's critical (interview 122).

Yes, they help me. In fact, they help me a lot. Especially when I was head of the financial team, because with that, people understand better really again, the personal responsibility they have (interview 93).

I think they help me . . . the procedures are still flexible enough to be able to do the things that you should be doing, and stop you from doing what you shouldn't be doing (interview 46).

For several interviewees, however, the benefits of the new procedures were qualified by the weight of the rules, even where they assumed that the rules would be simplified over time:

I was heavily involved in the reform. Though . . . as we were doing it, I said we are over-engineering and our successors will certainly have to make adjustments . . . [W]e . . . had to cover all aspects . . . of the organization . . . [W]e were under such pressure from the Court of Auditors, from the Cocobu [Committee of Budgetary Control] in the Parliament and from other people, to show that we had built in braces and safety nets and checks and balances that inevitably . . . we over-engineered and I certainly was conscious as we were doing it (interview 150).

[T]he rules are now clear after all the reform . . . We went too far maybe . . . [but] now the procedures are clear . . . Yeah, and we have a lot of responsibility because we have to sign a lot of financial applications (interview 81).

The financial management systems have become extremely complicated, excessively complicated, and some simplification is, I think, called for but it's much better than it was ten years ago so I mean most of us remember the old system really shouldn't complain but we've had to invest vast resources. . . . I have a hundred people doing nothing but financial management at this DG, people doing it, people checking on people doing it, people auditing, people checking, a whole system. It's important because mistakes are extremely expensive politically and but maybe some readjustment, some perhaps some decentralization or in some cases even recentralization going back to some sharing of the burden would be appropriate (interview 131).

For a large number, however, the rules were simply too bureaucratic:

I think the Commission really overdid it to a degree of paralysis. And this is recognized because I realize now in the last one or two years that things get a bit more reasonable (interview 77).

It is extraordinarily rigid . . . it treats an expenditure of fifty thousand euros in the same way as an expenditure of fifty million euros. It treats services . . . who administer agricultural subsidy in the same way as the service who are on a yearly budget of eight million euros (interview 14).

[W]e are stymied at every turn almost, in trying to do anything effective. It's despite, not because of the rules that we managed to achieve final outputs (interview 44).

Financial management in the Commission is a nightmare. . . . It's a system which basically delegates . . . Whoever signs has the responsibility of what he is signing. But the whole system is built to insure that that responsibility, in fact, is meaningless because we have so many checks and balances in the system that there is no chance that he is signing something stupid. So it's all on an *ex ante* sort of procedure, which is extremely, extremely cumbersome and very, very demanding (interview 43).

Similar views were expressed by interviewees on the new auditing systems and structures:

[E]very time we have an audit, they always find things that they say oh, you should have done this, you should have done that or the other. Nothing is ever perfect, and everything should be checked to the nth degree. It's never, never enough (interview 79).

[F]inancial-management verification takes an extraordinarily disproportionate amount of time, energy, and resources, and this is in the end is what is going to suffer in the Commission, and partly it is inertia, partly it's cowardice of polit-icians, partly it's hypocrisy of member states, and partly it's a voluntary action of member states, including the UK. Someday soon the Commission will become . . . a pure administrator . . . (interview 37).

[A] lot of resources have been liberated for auditing . . . We have the internal audit capability. We have the internal audit service. We have the court of auditors. And it's like they are looking for work. It's like we spend more time auditing what we do than we're actually doing things. It's just everybody's just spending a lot of time on making sure that the money is well spent. . . . [T]here are so many auditors, there are so many audits, that it has gone too far (interview 76).

Others disliked the new architectures because they saw them as predicated on a 'presumption of corruption' (interview 44) or 'guilt' (interview 61). These officials called for a different approach and a system based rather on *ex post* control and 'punishment' (interview 61).

There was some variation of opinion among interviewees, which often self-consciously reflected the size of budget and the type of expenditure that they managed personally. For DGs with a small budget and indirect management, such as Employment and Social Affairs, the rules appeared not to weigh too heavily. A middle manager mostly engaged in 'shared management' averred that 'it certainly does strike a right balance' for the service concerned, but recognized that 'it really is a completely different ballgame compared to direct financial management, which is more risky in many ways than what we do' (interview 2). This view was confirmed by a manager in DG REGIO which in his words 'spends 35 billion euro a year'. For the official concerned, the financial procedures imposed 'a very heavy burden. [L]inked to the fact ... that we are in a context of shared management with the member states ... [and] the Commission ... [has] ultimate financial responsibility according to the treaty, ... a number of tricky issues ... need to be resolved, which come from this imbalance between shared management, programme management on one side, but ultimate responsibility for what happens financially on the other side' (interview 139). Similarly, in the view of a senior manager in an operational service in which 'financial management is core business ... [t]he rules are very cumbersome. That has something to do also with the collective responsibility of the college. . . . Here everything is collective so every financing decision that we take, even if it is two million, has to go in a written procedure to the whole college. And then secondly the [financial] rules are exaggeratedly detailed' (interview 133).

On whether the financial rules had struck the right balance between accountability and efficiency, some interviewees were emphatic:

> No. No, no, no, no. No, no, no. We lost that battle (interview 82).

> No. Absolutely not (interview 61).

> No, absolutely not, no. They're so obsessed with accountability that they generate massive inefficiency (interview 44).

> [M]aybe a little too much for accountability (interview 81).

Others offered a reflection on why the Commission found itself with such difficult rules and pointed to the consequences, intended and unintended, on the behaviour of officials:

> [W]e could do a bit more on efficiency. It is probably a bit biased to accountability. But the problem is, you see, . . . the policy risk appetite of those that give us the money, right? . . . You become risk averse because you don't want to get into trouble (interview 149).

> I think we have developed a culture of financial management and particular controls, where both in relation to our client countries and also in relation to internal controls and what we can do and not do, I think accountability and controls have taken over, and actually sometimes maybe is reducing effectiveness. And sometimes, I think the complexity of what we have to do, doesn't match the risk that we actually face in certain cases, you know, risk of mismanagement or

losing funds or these kind of things. There are limits there. You can cover yourself with a certain level of risk up to a certain level, and beyond that, you don't get much more in risk by adding complexities and they are just now controls . . . I think we are much too fundamentalist, if you like, in this reaction, which leaves us, you know, with some inefficiencies in place because of complex, too complex rules, too detailed rules, too many things that we cannot do, because . . . we are risk adverse (interview 123).

That depends, I think. One would certainly reflect whether smaller projects, for example, are really worth the effort that are linked to setting them up, making applications, and run them through the whole process . . . [For] a smaller project . . . in the order of 50,000 euros I would think twice whether this actually is really worth the effort, even if as such it would be useful (interview 52).

One interviewee expressed frustration at the limited discretion available to Commission officials in camparison to civil servants at the national level:

In particular if you compare with a similar . . . level of responsibility . . . in a member state agency, it's completely different. You have people in member states' offices in the delegations, for instance, that can sign off checks up to €200,000. The level of the individual responsibility for the Commission, I think it's €50. . . . [W]e are under much higher scrutiny because of the member state press, basically, than member states apply to their own systems. And in spite of that, I think we're doing a great job, frankly (interview 43).

Some were philosophical:

[I]f you need to be accountable to 27 member states plus one parliament, it's more complicated than in a member state. So I think probably efficiency could be higher, but then the accountability is more complex than it is in a member state (interview 64).

The right balance [in an organization like this] means that there is more emphasis on accountability than on efficiency (interview 72).

Finally, in contrast to the somewhat negative views they expressed on financial management and control rules, managers were positive about Strategic Planning and Programming (SPP). They believed in the principle and thought that it had considerably improved in practice since its introduction:

I think this is really good . . . very positive' (interview 52). 'I have introduced some of this planning stuff and I am still a believer. I think they are . . . necessary for [a] public sector organization with accountability for good stewardship' (interview 149).

'Every year, we have our team and we devote half a day to go through this one and that, try to look at what is important for us next year, and what do we have the tasks in, and our indicators, and so on (interview 123).

A small number endorsed the principle, but were less impressed with the way in which SPP had been implemented:

It's a necessary evil. I mean, it's a process whereby we are all required to make our priorities explicit in a relatively standardized way. It's not in my view the most effective, because it's too bottom-up (interview 141).

The basic idea is good, but it's not been working well (interview 127).

Explaining the attitudes of Commission officials towards reform

When and why do officials give the reform measures a positive or a negative evaluation? Three sets of hypotheses are tested against the data from the online survey. The first two are grounded in two standard theories concerning the behaviour of bureaucrats, outlined in Chapter 1. The third is derived from a finding reported in Chapter 4 concerning the beliefs of officials. According to the first, officials are utility-maximizers, who undertake an individual cost–benefit calculation in regard to proposed action or changes that are likely to affect them. When opportunity structures change, individual preferences adapt to the new circumstances (March and Olsen 1989: 160).

A second theory is based on the core assumption that preference formation is an endogenous process and that individuals develop preferences by internalizing norms and values from their social environment, often early in their lives (Converse 1964; Wildavsky 1987; Rohrschneider 1994; Johnston 2001; Loveless and Rohrschneider 2011). This sociological approach holds that officials are influenced by group dynamics, especially in their formative years, and that they develop attitudes that are shaped by norms and ethics within the environment at home, in education, or at work. Socialization is usually equated with 'group dynamic' effects; that is, the way in which the norms and values of the in-group are adopted by a (new) individual. The process by which norms are inculcated is usually considered to be automatic. The norms can be associated with nationality, social class, university education, or training in a particular discipline (Checkel 2005, 2007; Zürn and Checkel 2005).

A third possible explanation, based on the ideological dispositions of Commission officials, is suggested by the findings reported in Chapter 4. Officials are found to harbour three very different preferred visions of the EU system: one group has a preference for a supranationalist or federalist model, in which the Commission becomes the government of Europe; a second considers that the member states should remain the central pillars of the European Union; and a third prefers a Europe where the Commission plays its traditional roles of policy initiator and guardian of the treaties. If these views are fundamental dispositions, it may be that they shape other attitudes, especially those linked to the way that the European Union functions.

These three theories suggest three sets of hypotheses. First, hypotheses derived from the utility maximization view suggest that an exogenous change is likely to have consequences for the individual that are concrete and relatively easy to identify. In the current case, the implications of an organizational reform for an individual will lie in the professional opportunity structure it creates. More precisely, an official's preference will be shaped according to whether they perceive organizational change as enabling them to do their job and as better for their career prospects.

Since the reforms introduced by the Prodi Commission produce and redistribute professional costs and benefits vertically, it follows that the higher the hierarchical position that an official occupies, the more positive should be his or her evaluation of the reforms. According to the logic of the reforms, managerial information has to be produced at lower levels and transmitted upwards to provide the basis for improved decision-making at the top. Although some of the rank and file see the new process as giving them a clearer understanding of the goals of their part of the organization and of the expectations for their own performance, in general, officials at the lower echelons 'pay the price' in terms of greater coordination and more information production or worse career prospects. Top managers enjoy greater steering capacity, because they have more effective management tools and an improved informational basis for their policy decisions. A similar argument can be made with respect to the redistribution of power among DGs and services. The expectation is that officials working in management DGs, such as the Secretariat-General, will be more positively disposed towards the reforms than spending DGs. In addition, since the reforms have restructured career progression within the organization, officials who feel disadvantaged by the new ways of doing things are unlikely to have much sympathy for the recent organizational changes.

Second, hypotheses derived from the sociological theory focus on a number of key formative experiences. Individuals from countries where NPM-style reforms have been implemented, and where during their formative years they have had the opportunity to become familiar with the principles of this approach or the rhetoric surrounding it, may have a more positive view towards the reforms than officials from countries where NPM is more recent or does not inform the design of the administration. Moreover, the Commission reforms introduce concepts familiar from business administration. It may be anticipated, therefore, that officials with experience in the private sector are likely to be more in favour of the reforms than those who have worked in public administration not influenced by NPM principles. In short, those individuals who are familiar with NPM concepts and principles should have fewer problems to their application within the Commission.

A third series of hypotheses derive from the finding that officials tend to have one of three preferred visions of the EU. It builds on the findings reported in Chapter 4, as well as earlier research, which revealed a 'supranationalist' narrative of the Kinnock–Prodi reforms, according to which the Commission has been weakened by an Anglo-Saxon assault that has left it less able to

Table 8.3 Explanatory approaches and hypotheses

Approach	Hypothesis	Argument
Socialization hypotheses	H1 Administrative traditions	Individuals from NPM forerunner countries like the reforms, those from NPM laggards dislike the reforms
	H2 Years of experience	The longer the years of experience, the greater the acceptance of reform
	H3 Experience in private sector	Work experience in the private sector should lead to greater support for reform
	H4 Economists	Education in economics may lead to greater support for reform
	H5 Senior manager	The higher the rank, the greater support for reform
Utility hypotheses	H6 Middle manager	The higher the rank, the greater support for reform
	H7 DG type	Working in DGs assumed to benefit from the reforms should lead to greater support for reform acceptance
	H8 State centrists	Should be supportive of reforms
EU Ideology hypotheses	H9 Institutional pragmatists	No clear pattern of support or opposition
	H10 Supranationalists	Supranationalists show less support for reform

pursue its pro-integrationist mission (Bauer 2008b). From this view, the reforms are a perfidious strategy of deliberate over-bureaucratization that seeks to paralyse the Commission and distract staff from engaging in integrationist projects (for discussions of this view, see Kassim 2004a, 2004b; Schön-Quinlivan 2008; Georgakakis 2010).

State centrists, by contrast, are likely to have a different view. They can be expected to favour the 'instrumental' Commission that the reforms promised. From this reading, the purpose of the reforms is concerned with promoting good management, not policy entrepreneurship aimed at bringing about a federal Europe. Institutional pragmatists are an intermediate category. They can be expected neither zealously to support nor to oppose the reforms. Rather they appreciate the benefits that they have brought to their daily life.

Explaining where officials stand on the reforms

Officials' attitudes were modelled using the responses given on a five-point Likert scale by all officials to the seven general questions on reform. A factor analysis revealed a single component, 'attitude to reform', underlying the responses. Unlike answers to the individual questions, 'attitude to reform' is a continuous variable, which made it possible to run a multivariate regression analysis. The results are presented in Table 8.4. In testing the hypotheses

Table 8.4 Regression model: dependent variable, attitude to reform

		All	Pre-2000	Post-2000
H1	National administration—Scandinavian	−0.066	−0.032	−0.161
	National administration—Continental north	*−0.323*	*−0.378*	−0.241
	National administration—Continental south	*−0.218*	*−0.245*	−0.13
	National administration—former Communist	0.069		0.026
H2	Length of service (years)	0.027	−0.008	−0.184
	Length of service in Commission in years—squared	*−0.001*	0	0.008
	Entered Commission under the Barroso presidency	*0.535*		0.113
H3	Worked in private enterprise or liberal professions—career before entering Commission	−0.065	−0.062	−0.045
H4	Economics or business—subject of main degree	0.108	0.135	0.073
H5	Current position—senior management or adviser	*0.298*	*0.291*	*0.497*
H6	Current position—middle management	0.122	0.113	0.285
	Current position—member of cabinet	−0.129	−0.02	0.113
	Has Cabinet experience	0.148	0.097	−0.021
H7	Management DG—admin, budget, anti-fraud, internal audit or Sec Gen	*0.307*	*0.442*	−0.002
	Current DG—primarily spending	*−0.301*	−0.206	*−0.444*
	Current DG—primarily regulatory	−0.073	−0.115	0.046
	Current DG—primarily legislative	*−0.314*	−0.268	−0.426
	Current DG—primarily external	−0.07	0.024	−0.346
	Current DG—spending AND regulatory	*−0.344*	*−0.435*	−0.173
	Current DG—spending AND legislative	*−0.273*	−0.287	−0.207
H8	EU governance beliefs—state-centrists	*−0.265*	*−0.317*	−0.169
H9	EU governance beliefs—institutional pragmatists	−0.077	−0.068	−0.131
H10	EU governance beliefs—supranationalists	*−0.193*	−0.156	*−0.316*
Controls	Female	−0.034	−0.097	0.053
	Law—subject of main degree	0.052	0.165	−0.157
	Politics, international relations or other social science—subject of main degree	0.05	0.002	0.106
	Studied outside country of citizenship	0.011	0.038	−0.062
	Worked in national civil services—career before entering Commission	−0.087	−0.046	−0.103
	Worked in another international organisation—career before entering Commission	−0.01	−0.017	0.062
	Worked in party politics, trade union or social movement—career before entering Commission	−0.184	0.162	*−0.764*
	Worked in education or research—career before entering Commission	−0.002	−0.017	−0.037
	Worked in journalism or PR—career before entering Commission	−0.264	−0.263	−0.167
	Other or prefer not to say—career before entering Commission	0.144	0.086	0.326
	Constant	0.197	0.545	*1.237*

outlined above, care was taken to distinguish between officials who joined the Commission before the reforms (that is before 2000), and therefore with experience of the *status quo ante*, and officials who joined after 2000.

The testing of the three sets of hypotheses showed strongest support for the utility variables, in particular for the hypothesis that the more senior an official the more likely he or she is to be positive about the reforms. Senior managers, especially those recruited after 2000, are strongly positive about the reforms.[35] In regard to DG function, officials in management DGs are more likely to express positive views,[36] while those in spending DGs are strongly negatively disposed towards the reforms, though this applies more to post-2000 recruits.

The socialization variables fare less well, though two findings are significant. The first is that, with respect to national origins, although Anglo-Saxons and Scandinavians do not exhibit strong views either way, both continental north (especially) and continental south are negative: this is particularly noticeable for the pre-2000 recruits. Second, there is only mixed support for the ideological variables. Whilst as expected supranationalists take a negative view, the institutionalist pragmatist view is not supported. Moreover, although it was anticipated that state centrists would be supportive of the reforms, they appear in fact to be negatively disposed.

Overall, an individual's position in the Commission as an organization (in terms of hierarchy and function) is a strong predictor of an individual's opposition or support of the reforms. Socialization variables (national background and years of experience) complement but do not dominate this picture. The ideological predictors have no systematic relevance. The main finding of the statistical analysis is that the individual attitudes of Commission officials towards management change can best be explained by the utility model, which emphasizes the rational calculation of individual costs and benefits. Hierarchical rank and organizational function are the best predictors for acceptance of management change. Socialization variables do less well. Most interestingly, the data show very clearly that the acceptance of the reforms is *not* driven by 'outside socialization' or 'EU ideology'. (see also Bauer 2012; for an alternative view, see Ellinas an Suleiman 2011).

---

[35] A possible objection is that managers may feel more inclined to defend organizational decisions because of their greater responsibility for administrative policies or their proximity to decision-making processes. However, there was no indication in the face-to-face interviews that managers felt obliged to defend the reform, as the quotations from the interviews cited above illustrate. On the contrary, the frankest statements often came from staff in the higher ranks of the organization. Hooghe (2001) makes a similar observation about her experience in an earlier project.

[36] If we also include DG Administration in this group, the effect disappears. This indicates that officials in DG Administration see the reform more critically. This fits the interpretation offered that the Kinnock–Prodi reforms empowered DG Budget, but reduced the influence of DG Administration.

CONCLUSION

The measures introduced by the Prodi Commission were a 'big bang' reform that sought to shift the Commission away from the antiquated combination of Roman-German and Roman-French features that had marked it since the late 1950s. The changes moved the organization in the direction of performance management, characterized by multi-annual planning, performance indicators and audits, and resource-for-results (Pollitt and Bouckaert 2004; Balint et al. 2008; Schön-Quinlivan 2008). As shown in this Chapter, the Commission is no longer an outlier in terms of its human resources practices or budgeting and financial management, operating according to practices that have long been abandoned by national administrations, but has been brought into convergence with current management styles. Such a development highlights the extent to which the Commission can be considered a normal bureaucracy.

A decade after the reform process began, Commission officials are less than enthusiastic about the measures. However, although on balance they are negatively disposed to reform, there is little trace of the fierce condemnation of the reforms that was recorded in earlier work, also often based on qualitative studies and small-scale quantitative research (Kassim 2004a, 2004b; Levy 2006; Bauer 2008b; Ellinas and Suleiman 2008, 2011; Georgakakis 2010). The pathologies of the reforms—'audit fury', unresolved issues about how best to manage decentralization—and the frustration of staff who have to cope with paradoxes of organizational change (Wright 1997) are still evident.[37] As noted above, these were themes that ran through the interviews.

At the same time, the passing of time and establishment of new routines seem to have assuaged earlier worries and reservations. Commission officials, however grudgingly, have become reconciled to the new systems, suggesting that a process of normalization has taken place. In the words of one interviewee: 'We will have to live with that. We learn to live with that' (interview 114). The variation of views among officials is best explained by the position that they hold in the hierarchy. Directors-General, arguably the category of official that has most benefited from the reforms, are the most positive, while senior managers are also relatively positive. Nationality is also important. Officials from member countries that have enacted NPM-style change tend to have a positive view of the Kinnock–Prodi reforms.

Finally, the Kinnock–Prodi reforms mark a watershed in the organization's history. Compared with the relative inertia of the preceding four decades, organizational change now appears to have become a routine part of the Commission's activities. The Commission has entered a phase where a level

---

[37] See also Balint et al. (2008).

of managerial experimentation that would have been inconceivable in the late 1990s is now a regular feature. Whether the outcome has been that the Commission has become a more professional and a more efficient administration is a different matter. It is clear, however, that the Commission is a different organization, and one that is closer to 'best practice' in national administrations.

9

The Enlarged Commission

The enlargements of 2004 and 2007 changed the face of Europe. Arguably, they constitute the most ambitious and important achievement in the history of European integration (see Lamy 2004). We know that enlargement has had a profound effect on the way that the states that acceded in the 2000s— collectively, the 'EU-12'—are governed. A large body of work has emerged focusing on the process of enlargement, and how and why it happened.[1] Its impact on EU policy has also been covered quite thoroughly.[2] Yet, despite notable exceptions,[3] our knowledge of what impact the EU's two latest enlargements have had on its institutions—including the Commission—is still in its infancy.

Much of the literature written close to or during the period of the EU-12 enlargements predicted that the accession of twelve new member states would act to fragment the Commission and make it less single-minded. Some works suggested a perhaps surprising degree of continuation of business as usual (see Dehousse et al. 2006), as seemed to be the case in the Council (see Hagemann and De Clerck-Sachsse 2007). Still others predicted that enlargement would make the Commission younger, more liberal and female, and perhaps more 'post-national' and representative of Europe as a whole, if not necessarily more coherent or integrated (see Gravier 2008; Peterson 2008; Peterson and Birdsall 2008; Ban 2010).

The Commission's own (2011) analysis of the effects of (the 2004) enlargement on the house is breathtakingly self-congratulatory. It is full of claims that the recruitment of around 4000 new officials—expanding the size of the administration by 16 per cent—took place 'without major disruptions or conflicts'. The way in which enlargement was handled constituted 'a great success for the Commission' (16), even 'an historic achievement' (6).

---

[1] See Sedelmeier (2000, 2002, 2005); Sjursen (2002); Nugent (2004); Vassilou (2007); Smith (2011).

[2] See Johnson and Rollo (2001); Gnesotto (2002); Missiroli (2002); van den Hoven (2004); Elsig (2010); Heidbreder (2011).

[3] Best et al. (2008; Crespy and Gajewska (2010); Heidbreder (2011); Hosli et al. (2011); Ban (2013).

The report, however, is silent on the attitudes of Commission officials towards the 2004 enlargement. The EUCIQ data suggest that many officials are ambivalent or even negative about the impact of enlargement on the Commission. We find strong feelings about the way that the process of enlargement was handled in terms of its effect on careers in the Commission: not well. Only somewhat less strongly held is the view that enlargement made the Commission a more difficult organization to manage. If there is any residual institutional pride or satisfaction arising from the way in which the Commission facilitated the EU's historic achievement—or from how 'member state governments delegated extraordinary competences to the Commission that were without precedent in earlier enlargements'[4] (Heidbreder 2011: 4)—it is not readily visible in our findings.

Nevertheless, many officials from the older member states—the 'EU-15' for the purposes of this chapter—declared themselves impressed by the calibre and enthusiasm of colleagues recruited from the EU-12. There is evidence in our data (and in other sources) to suggest that the most recent enlargements *have* made the Commission a younger and more economically liberal and female administration. Perhaps the most striking difference we found separating EU-12 officials from their colleagues is that a significantly smaller share of the former cite 'commitment to Europe' as the reason why they joined the Commission. As such, officials from the newest member states more often appear to be utility maximizers.

What remains an open question—and one that we cannot answer—is how far and how quickly EU-12 officials will become *socialized* to the Commission. That is, will their views 'bend' over time in the direction of those that are mainstreamed within the house? An alternative possibility, of course, is the opposite: that the recent enlargements have changed the mainstream in terms of the views of its officials.

The question of how socialization occurs, and with what effects, must be considered in the light of what is perhaps our most dramatic finding about the effect on the Commission of the recent enlargements. It may be, in a sense, no finding at all. By over-weighting officials from EU-12 member states in our survey sample—so as to make possible meaningful comparisons between them and EU-15 officials (see Figure 9.1)—we incurred, strictly speaking, significant data loss. Viewed another way, we uncovered a considerable 'opinion deficit' amongst EU-12 officials. The point is illustrated by responses to a question about whether *cabinets* were 'too preoccupied by developments in their Commissioner's national capital' (see Figure 9.2). More than one-third of

---

[4] As Heidbreder (2011: 4) notes, the Commission was given powers to supervise compliance with EU standards in the 12 accession states including 'criteria [that] went beyond the Commission's competences under the [EU's] formal legal framework . . . The Commission was therefore involved in policies in the candidate states of which it had no say in the member states'.

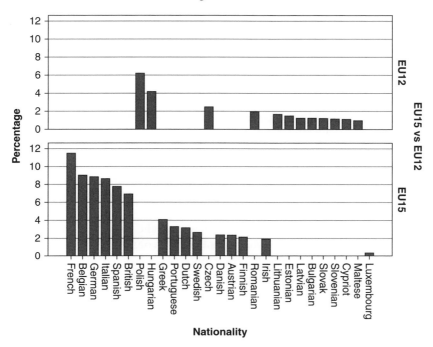

Fig. 9.1 EU-12 vs EU-15 officials in survey sample

Note: n = 1824 (EU-12 = 455; 25%).

As of early 2011, a total of 19.7 per cent of Commission officials were listed as holding the nationality of an EU-12 country. See <http://ec.europa.eu/civil_service/docs/europa_sp2_bs_nat_x_dg_en.pdf> (accessed 4 February 2011).

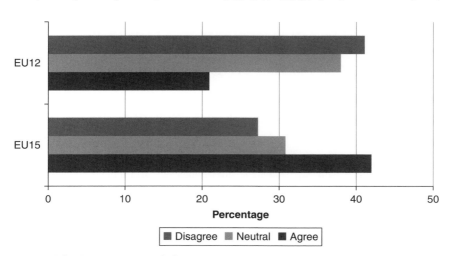

Fig. 9.2 The EU-12 opinion deficit

The *cabinets* are too preoccupied by developments in the national capital of their Commissioners.

Note: n = 1,316.

EU-12 officials answered 'don't know'. Similarly, only two-thirds of all EU-12 respondents gave a clear answer to a question about whether 'coordination works well between the services and the College (including *cabinets*)'. Nearly 40 per cent of those EU-12 officials that did answer chose 'neither agree or disagree'.

Thus, a very large share of officials from the new member states are still learning the ropes and often do not hold clear or strong views.[5] As such, there appears to be considerable scope for socialization of EU-12 officials and room to shape their views and attitudes in the direction of those that predominate amongst longer-serving officials.[6] In any case, we have a large enough sample of both EU-15 and EU-12 officials both to make meaningful comparisons between them and to draw conclusions about the impact of enlargement on the Commission.

An underlying research question into which the impact of enlargement translates in this context is: to what extent are newcomers different (or similar) *because* they are EU-12 officials? Or are differences more attributable to other cohort effects: age, gender, nationality, type of DG and so on? Our data strongly suggest that EU-12 officials are a diverse group but they *are*—perhaps paradoxically—different. The 'split' between them and their EU-15 colleagues is a statistically more powerful determinant of views than any other split in the data representing cohort effect. Put simply, the Commission has been changed, in significant ways, by enlargement, even if the permanence of that change remains open to question.

ENLARGEMENT: THE BIG PICTURE

Learning from previous enlargements

Work on the effect of previous enlargements on the Union's institutions, such as it is, does not offer us many clues about the institutional effects of the 2004

---

[5] Predictably, the vast majority of EU-12 respondents to the survey—89.5 per cent—joined the Commission in 2004 or later and are relatively junior officials ('administrators'): 85.5 per cent compared to 57 per cent of EU-15 respondents. An obvious question is whether EU-12 officials are really distinctive or simply new to the administration, and similar to other— including EU-15—newcomers. Although the survey sample includes a large cohort of (455) EU-12 officials, it contains (unsurprisingly) only 45 EU-15 officials who joined the Commission in 2004 or later. Extensive comparison between 'post-enlargement' EU-12 and EU-15 officials is thus not (statistically) meaningfully.

[6] One Director-General with long experience of multiple very senior posts suggested that any new divisions created by the 2004 and 2007 enlargements were 'no different from those created by the 1973 enlargement . . . the EU creates loyalties, it even brainwashes officials over time'. Non-EUCIQ interview, conducted by one of the authors, 29 November 2011.

and 2007 enlargements. To illustrate the point, the most recent, previous enlargement—extending membership to Austria, Finland and Sweden in 1995—brought three relatively rich states with modern and professional civil services into the fold. It seemed to impact the EU's institutions primarily in three ways. First, it made English the *lingua franca*. Second, if the Commission itself is anything to go by, it made the EU's institutions slightly more female in terms of gender balance.[7] Third, ministers and officials in the Council and all of its offshoots could no longer be sure they would be able to see the face of the speaker in Council meetings (see Peterson and Bomberg 1998; Peterson and Jones 1999). Generally, however, the EU digested Nordic enlargement with little difficulty, and its institutional impact was quite limited.

Moreover, as in the cases of all previous enlargements, 1995 saw the EU extend membership to only a few states—as opposed to the twelve that joined in the 2000s. Generally, past accession states were closer to the existing EU in terms of levels of economic development and professionalism of national administrations than were the states that joined in 2004 and 2007. The Mediterranean enlargements of the 1980s did admit states that were, at the time, considerably less modernized than the rest of the then European Community, and thus might hold the most promise for meaningful comparison. But we are aware of no existing research on their impacts on the Community's institutions.

Views of Enlargement: the EUCIQ Data

A logical place to start an analysis of EUCIQ's findings on the EU-12 enlargements is with results from questions that asked officials to specify the impacts enlargement has had on the Commission. Responses to a series of such questions are summarized in Figure 9.3. To ensure that their meaning and purpose were clear, these questions were introduced with the phrase: 'We are interested in your views on how the 2004 and 2007 enlargements have affected the Commission and its work'.

The first statement presented (1 in Figure 9.3 below) was that 'enlargement has strengthened *esprit de corps* within the Commission's administration'. Nearly two-thirds (around 61 per cent) disagreed, although considerably more than half of this cohort only 'tended' to disagree. However, a notably higher share of EU-15 officials disagreed strongly (26 per cent) or 'tended to disagree' (around 40 per cent) compared to EU-12 officials (around 10 and 30 per cent respectively). As was the case for many questions in the survey, a large share of EU-12 officials—more than a third in this case—neither agreed nor

---

[7] Almost exactly 60 per cent of all officials recruited from Austria, Finland and Sweden in the first post-accession round of recruitment were women (see European Commission 2011: 9).

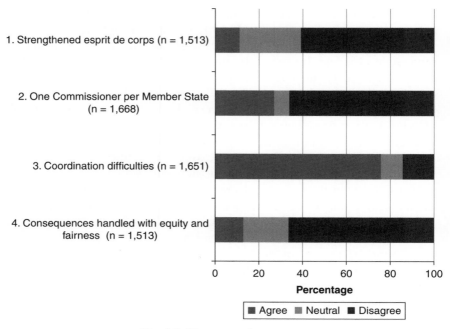

Fig. 9.3 Views on enlargement

disagreed. But those who took a clear view were considerably more positive about the effect of enlargement on the cohesion of the Commission.

A second statement (2 in Figure 9.3) sought to gauge views about the size of the College: 'it is more important to have one Commissioner per member state than to have a smaller and more efficient College'. Again, a very large share of officials—almost exactly two-thirds—disagreed. Here, there was no perceptible difference between the views of EU-15 and EU-12 officials. Our finding thus debunks any notion that officials from new member states are more concerned than others about ensuring their country always has a Commissioner.

Third, officials were presented with the statement: 'a 27 member College makes coordination more difficult' (3 in Figure 9.3). An overwhelming major-ity of respondents—more than three-quarters—agreed. A *very* large share of EU-15 (79 per cent) agreed, strongly or otherwise. The overall EU-12 share was somewhat lower (67 per cent). But this result, when viewed next to the previous statement on the size of the College, appears to demonstrate that most officials want a smaller and (therefore) more efficient College, with an overwhelming majority of EU-15 officials bemoaning the now historically large size of the College.

Fourth, survey respondents were asked to react to the claim that 'the consequences of enlargement for career development have been handled with equity and fairness' (4 in Figure 9.3). Almost exactly two-thirds of respondents disagreed. Interestingly, the response that produced the largest differential between officials from new and older member states was 'strongly disagree': 37 per cent for EU-12 officials versus 29 per cent for their EU-15 counterparts. These results appear to disconfirm the notion that EU-15 officials feel the most hard done by as a consequence of enlargement because promotion or career advancement has often been blocked by the need to recruit officials from the new member states. If anything, we might hypothesize that the changes to the staff salary scale that made salary increases considerably more incremental on the precise day (1 May) that 10 new states joined in 2004 appears to have left EU-12 officials particularly sore. Generally, however, it seems clear that most Commission officials think the consequences of enlargement for career development were badly handled.

As such, it would appear that a clear majority of Commission officials would not agree that enlargement represents, in the words of Jacques Delors, *'le bonheur de la fin de la guerre froide'* ['delight at the end of the cold war],[8] at least insofar as it has impacted on the life of the Commission. Most officials want a smaller Commission, believe an overlarge College causes coordination problems, and think the EU-12 enlargements have negatively affected career development. And most EU-15 officials appear, in particular, to believe that enlargement has made the Commission a less unified, commodious institution with a strong sense of *Mannschaftsgeist*.

A NEW BIFURCATION?

Is there a new bifurcation in the Commission between EU-12 and EU-15 officials? The survey found interesting differences of view between officials from older and new member states. They included:

- Officials' motivation for pursuing a career in Brussels. When asked why they decided to pursue a career in the Commission, a significantly higher share of EU-12 officials reported that they were motivated by reasons other than a 'commitment to Europe', such as job stability, promising career prospects, or quality of the work (see Figure 9.4). The proportion of EU-15 officials who cited 'commitment to Europe' was the same

---

[8] The comment was made by Delors during exchanges with his audience following an address in Berlin entitled 'Where does Europe Stand Today?' on 28 January 2011. The event was hosted by the German Green Party of the European Parliament.

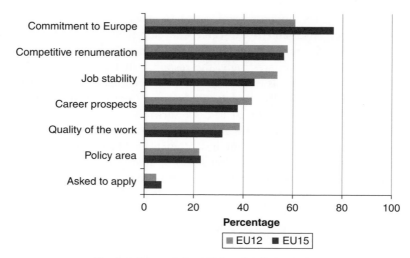

Fig. 9.4 Reasons for joining the Commission
Note: n = 1, 786.

(75 per cent) for the very few officials recruited since 2004 as for those recruited in earlier years—thus suggesting that what most often determines whether or not being committed to Europe was a motivator is whether or not an official hails from a newer member state.[9]

- Officials' preferences on the Commission's role in the EU system. The survey found a considerably smaller share of EU-12 officials—only about one-third—were attracted to the idea that the College of Commissioners should act as a 'government of Europe' (see Figure 9.5). In contrast, just over 42 per cent of EU-15 officials expressed support for the idea. When asked whether EU member states—not the Commission or European Parliament (EP)—should be the central players in the Union, nearly 40 per cent of EU-15 officials strongly disagreed, compared with only about a quarter of EU-12 respondents.[10]

- Views of officials on the Community method. Elsewhere in this volume (Chapter 5), the strength of officials' commitment to the Community method is defined by two simple criteria: disagreement with the idea that 'member states—not the Commission or EP—should be the central players in the European Union' and opposition to the view that 'the Commission should primarily focus on managing existing policies, rather

---

[9] One manager commented that: 'officials from the older member states have different views on the role of the Commission, the future of EU, commitment to Europe . . . Many of the new member states sometimes do not want to give up their newly discovered independence, do not want a new Soviet Union . . . . it is sad: at least the people joining the Commission should be more committed' (interview 144).

[10] The precise totals were EU-15 = 39.4 per cent; EU-12 = 26.3 per cent; 48.9 per cent of EU-12 officials 'tended to disagree', compared with 40.9 per cent of EU-15 officials.

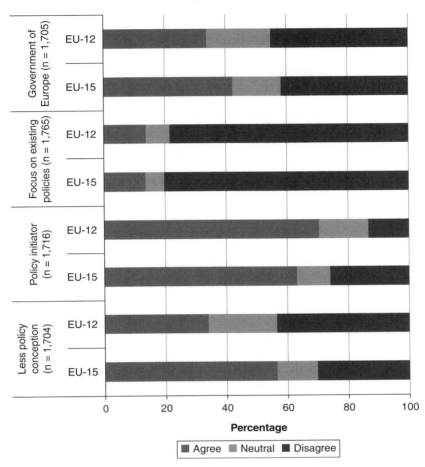

Fig. 9.5 Views on the Commission

than developing new ones' (see Figure 9.5). The data generally confirm a strong bias in favour of the Community method so defined: a large share of all respondents (62 per cent) disagreed with the first statement and opposed the second. However, a careful analysis of the data suggests that EU-12 officials are less committed to the traditional way of doing EU business and the powerful role it reserves for the Commission. This finding is reflected in response to questions (other than those on which the analysis of Chapter 5 is based) that could be interpreted as gauging commitment to the Community method. For example, only 15 per cent of EU-12 respondents strongly disagreed that the Commission should share its right of initiative with the European Parliament, compared with 26 per cent of their EU-15 counterparts.

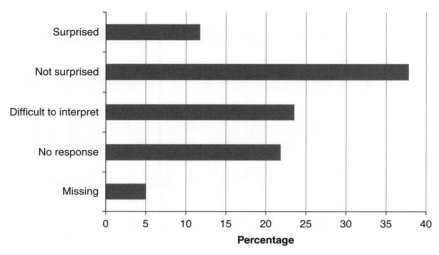

Fig. 9.6 EU-12 less committed to Community Method: does this surprise you?
Note: Face-to-face interviews with managers, n = 119).

The project's interviews with managers allowed an opportunity to see whether relatively senior officials were surprised at the finding that their EU-12 colleagues appeared less committed to the Community method. Considerably more managers were *not* surprised at this finding than were (see Figure 9.6). The comments of two interviewees were typical: '[It is] not surprising, they have an understandable historical reticence and hostility to the idea of any overarching external government influence and power. There is no shortage of instances of politicians saying that we didn't shake off Moscow to replace it with Brussels' (interview 59). '[This result reflects] a lack of communication, understanding and explanation of the importance of the community method to the new member states' (interview 62).

Do managers notice 'any other differences between officials from the EU-15 and those from the recent enlargement that you are made aware of in your day-to-day work'? More than half from our sample of 119 *did* say they were aware of differences (see Figure 9.7). But the two most often mentioned types of differences were somewhat innocuous: first, the relative youth of EU-12 officials and, second, their linguistic prowess, which tended to be more in English or German than in French. One manager identified the main difference as: 'The linguistic thing. The vast majority of the people coming from the new member states don't have French (with the exception of the Romanians, and therefore there are more Romanians amongst them). If anything these new member states have German as a reference language rather than French' (interview 123). Another highlighted the difficulties that arose for many EU-12 officials of 'the prevalence of the French language. It is a huge

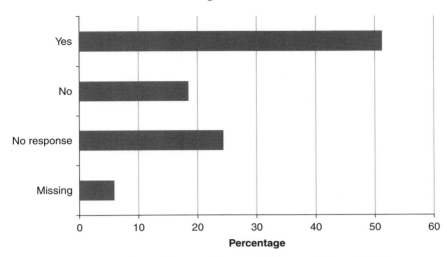

Fig. 9.7 Are there differences between EU-12 and other officials?

Note: face-to-face interviews with managers, n = 119.

disadvantage for people do not speak this as a first language. [Our] resource documents and meetings are all in French' (interview 109). One (Belgian) Head of Unit was unusually blunt: 'We are totally different animals. I do see a unique feature of those colleagues who are from new member states: they developed their career under a communist system. They saw the EU as a solution to their problems, not as a solution to a common problem' (interview 156).

Nevertheless, it may be easy to overestimate both how bifurcated the Commission has been made by enlargement and the durability of its effect on the house. As we have seen (in Chapter 4), EU-12 officials are less likely (30.2 vs 38.6 per cent) to be 'supranationalists', and slightly more likely (14.8 vs 12.8 per cent) to be 'state-centric' compared to their EU-15 colleagues. But EU-12 officials are *more* likely—by a very small margin (30.0 to 28.9 per cent) to be 'institutional pragmatists'. Considerably more must be classified as 'other' (25.1 against 19.7 per cent of EU-15 officials), whose views do not fit neatly into the other three typologies.

Moreover, the Commission may be flexible enough, first, to 'digest' enlargement fairly quickly and, second, to re-discover its *esprit du corps* within a relatively short time. The first point is illustrated by the very similar responses of EU-12 and EU-15 officials to one of the questions used to gauge commitment to the Community method: 'some think the Commission should primarily focus on managing existing policies, rather than developing new ones. What do you think' (see Figure 9.5 above; 'focus on existing policies')?

To illustrate the point about how quickly the Commission might be able to digest enlargement, we might look to reactions to the suggestion that 'the

Commission's role is evolving in the direction of more policy management and coordination, and less policy conception'. EU-12 officials were considerably *less* likely to agree (see Figure 9.5 above; 'less policy conception'). It may well be that they have so little experience that many have trouble coming to a judgment on any question concerning the evolution of the Commission's role. But this result suggests that a strong plurality of EU-12 officials retain a vision of the Commission continuing to set the policy agenda for the Union as it has done traditionally.

We even find what we might consider to be conflicting evidence on the question of how committed EU-12 officials are to the Community method. When asked to comment on the statement 'the more member states the EU has, the more important is the Commission's role as policy initiator', officials from the new member states were actually more likely to agree than their EU-15 colleagues (see Figure 9.5 above; 'policy initiator'). In fact, EU-12 respondents were considerably more decisive in response to this question—with nearly 70 per cent in agreement—than they were on almost any other question in the survey.

Another indicator of how quickly EU-12 officials are likely to become integrated into the house takes us back to the analysis of personal networks presented in Chapter 3. Are officials from newer member states more likely to rely on their fellow nationals as members of their own personal networks compared to their EU-15 counterparts? The survey evidence suggests the answer is clearly *no*. As we saw in Chapter 3, one of the main reasons for questioning the 'myth of nationality' thesis is that, of survey respondents who answered for three members of their network, nearly 60 per cent reported that at least one of their most important personal contacts in the Commission shared their own nationality.

However, EU-12 officials are considerably more likely *not* to have fellow nationals in their network: almost exactly half report no fellow national in their personal network, as opposed to 36 per cent of EU-15 officials.[11] As such, it appears that officials from the newer member states are networking primarily with officials of other nationalities, particularly those from EU-15 states who are likely to be more experienced. One interviewee—a Director (and thus a manager of many officials)—claimed that many EU-12 officials 'are easily integrated. I have members here from all areas. The differences are between the very young and older ones. Older ones have more difficulties to adapt. The young ones already have a network before they get here, [and] their network

---

[11] Of course, most EU-12 officials are from smaller member states and it is difficult to control for this contingency. There is an interesting exception to our general findings on networking with fellow nationals: around 12 per cent of Bulgarian and Romanian officials reported having *exclusively* fellow nationals as members of their personal network.

may play a role at [the] start. They know how to integrate the quickest way possible' (interview 66).

In fact, of all network contacts reported by EU-12 officials, exactly two-thirds were with EU-15 officials. This share is considerably smaller than the percentage of EU-15 officials whose contacts are from older member states: a massive 97 per cent. Generally, it appears that officials who were asked about their personal networks (administrators only) network mostly with EU-15 officials who are likely to have more experience of the house. True, EU-12 officials are more likely than officials from older member states to network with other EU-12 officials. But most of the time they network with their EU-15 counterparts. Enough do so to suggest that socialization and integration into the Commission could happen quite quickly, or at least that newer officials engage in personal networks that could be effective conduits for socialization and integration.

To summarize, EU-12 officials tend to hold different views from their EU-15 counterparts on a number of questions. But evidence that enlargement has created a new and sharp bifurcation in the Commission is ambiguous. We find few reasons to think that such a split is permanent, even if we interpret some of the data as suggesting that one existed in late 2008. First, while EU-12 officials are different, they rarely show themselves to be different in ways that preclude socialization or integration into the house. Second, the most common reason given by EU-12 officials for their decision to join the Commission is 'commitment to Europe', even if they are considerably less likely to cite this reason compared to their EU-15 counterparts. We might well conclude that this result is unsurprising when we consider that remuneration, the quality of work, and the professionalism of administrations (public and private) in the EU's newer member states often falls considerably short of what is on offer by joining the Commission. Bureaucracies remain highly politicized, weak, and far short of meritocracy in many EU-12 states. To illustrate, one of Ban's (2012: 210) Hungarian interviewees comments: 'With every change of government, we may change employees completely, even heads of unit. There is no continuity, no stability'. One likely, even logical effect is that competent, talented, non-partisan officials, especially those with an international bent or policy-specific passion, are driven to Brussels.

Finally, it is impossible not to at least ask the question: are officials from the newer member states more *realistic* about where the Commission and EU currently stand? At a time when the College seems further away than ever from becoming a 'government of Europe', the tendency for EU-15 officials— far more often than their EU-12 counterparts—to cling to this preference as their favoured role for the Commission might be taken as evidence of wishful, 'old school' thinking. Recruits from the newer member states generally appear to be pragmatic, careerist, and utility maximizers—yet still committed to the Commission's traditional prerogative of setting the EU's policy agenda.

'CLONES OF OURSELVES'? THE BACKGROUND OF EU-12 OFFICIALS

When first approached about the idea of the present study, a very senior Commission official commented on the 'interesting backgrounds' of EU-12 officials: 'there are lots with degrees from Bruges or the US (United States). It makes us wonder if we are bringing in "clones of ourselves"'.[12] In fact, data from both the survey and interviews suggest that, in a number of respects, the cadre of officials from the newer member states is distinctive. If they have reinforced any existing feature of the Commission, it is that they have made an already cosmopolitan administration even more so.

The point is illustrated by the considerable share of EU-12 survey respondents who studied abroad as part of their main educational degree programme. More than 70 per cent of officials from the newer member states studied in a country other than that of their nationality (see Figure 9.8). Nearly half did so for more than one year. Both totals are considerably higher than for EU-15 respondents.[13]

Nevertheless, there is evidence in the data to suggest that many EU-12 officials might still be focused on their home countries. Unsurprisingly, a

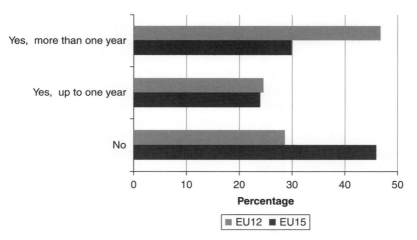

Fig. 9.8 Officials who studied abroad

Note: n = 1, 821.

---

[12] Non-EUCIQ interview conducted by one of the authors, 5 July 2006.
[13] It might be noted that very similar shares of EU-12 (7.9 per cent) and EU-15 officials (6.2 per cent) reported having more than one nationality.

smaller share of respondents from new member states reported themselves to be in management jobs (21.6 per cent) than was the case for EU-15 officials (29.9 per cent). The primary function of most EU-12 respondents (52.1 per cent) was 'implementation', compared with 41.5 per cent of EU-15 officials. Logically, the Commission is likely to have hired many officials from the new member states to oversee implementation of EU policies in their home countries. The interviewee mentioned at the outset of this section put it this way: 'one of the most striking effects of enlargement is how much more difficult but critical it is to monitor implementation. There are now far more geographically responsible units in services monitoring specific groups of member states'.

The hunch that many officials from the newer member states are involved in the monitoring of implementation in their home countries finds support in the large share of surveyed EU-12 officials—nearly half—who report previous experience in a national (or regional or local) civil service.[14] In contrast, only just over one-third of EU-15 officials surveyed had such a background.[15] Here we find the most striking difference—besides having studied abroad—in the backgrounds of EU-12 and EU-15 officials. By way of comparison, there is no perceptible difference in the likelihood that either category of official will have private sector experience.[16]

Thus, the 'clones of ourselves' thesis is not borne out in the EUCIQ data in any straightforward way. Particularly given that the 'legacies of Communist regimes' (Hughes et al. 2004: 31) have persisted in many EU-12 countries—in the form of weak, politicized and relatively unsophisticated civil services—it makes sense that officials recruited from these countries to the Commission are likely to be more cosmopolitan and worldly than many of their national counterparts. Studying abroad is a logical route to acquiring such sophistication. Yet, at the same time, with the EU-12 enlargements the Commission has to monitor implementation of EU policies and standards in states that naturally have more difficulty doing so properly and legally than do more long-standing Union members. It therefore needs officials who know these states and their administrations well (see Chapter 2). Both in terms of background and

---

[14] Ban (2012: 24) notes that regional and local government officials in accession states were rarely involved in accession negotiations. Thus, they were 'less likely to be socialised in the same way' as national civil servants to the EU and Commission. All of the EU-12 officials she interviewed who joined the Commission from government positions came from national civil services.

[15] The precise totals were EU-12 = 48.4 per cent; EU-15 = 35.8 per cent.

[16] Compare 63.3 per cent of EU-12 officials with private sector experience with 62.2 per cent of EU-15 officials.

current function, it appears that a large share of EU-12 officials we surveyed help meet that need.

YOUNGER, MORE FEMALE AND LIBERAL?

The main effects of the 2004 and 2007 enlargements on the Commission appear to be that they have produced an administration that is younger, more female, and more economically (but not socially) liberal. In point of fact, perhaps the most striking difference between EU-12 and EU-15 survey respondents is how much younger is the former group compared to the latter. No fewer than 44.3 per cent of EU-12 officials reported themselves to be 31 years old or younger, compared with only 2.6 per cent of EU-15 officials.[17]

Moreover, two-thirds of all officials recruited (at all levels) in the subsequent five years from states that joined in 2004 were female. The Commission's own statistics suggest that being young and being female go together in the administration. For instance, of the relatively small number of officials aged 31 or younger (around 2100), almost three times more were female (1521) than were male (553) by 2011. The survey data also corroborate figures compiled by the Commission that show enlargement has brought a disproportionately high number of women into the house, including not only young officials but also a considerable number in management positions (see Ban 2012).[18] A total of 59 per cent of EU-12 respondents to the survey were women, compared to 41 per cent of EU-15 respondents. As of late 2012 a majority of all officials—52.4 per cent—were female, compared to 46.6 per cent in 2004.[19]

Interestingly, considerably fewer EU-12 officials surveyed thought 'it is possible for women to advance their careers on an equal footing' compared to EU-15 officials (see Figure 9.9). One possible explanation is that proportionately more of these officials are female and thus in stronger position to know! Alternatively, it may be that EU-12 officials simply could not compare

[17] Data shares based on number of officials were born in 1976 and after.
[18] The share of female middle managers recruited to the Commission in 2005–10 was 31 per cent for all EU-10 officials recruited to this level compared with 29 per cent for EU-15 officials. The gap for newly-recruited female senior managers was considerably wider: 33 per cent of all EU-10 recruits versus 24 per cent of EU-15 recruits (European Commission 2011: 8–9).
[19] What the Commission's statistics also do not tell us is what percentage of female officials hold 'AST'—that is, administrative or secretarial, not policy-making posts, or are involved in interpretation or translation. It might be noted that the EUCIQ survey sample did not include any AST officials, interpreters or translators. The source for figures in late 2012 is: <http://ec.europa.eu/civil_service/docs/europa_sp2_bs_nat_x_grade_en.pdf> (accessed 9 October 2012).

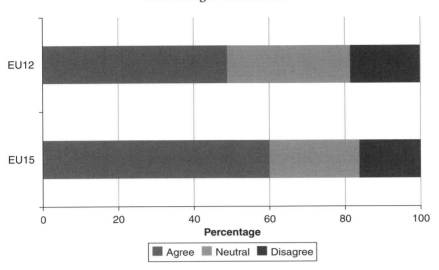

Fig. 9.9 It is now easier for women to advance their careers: EU-15 vs EU-12

Note: n = 1, 249.

the time when they were surveyed with earlier eras in terms of how easy or difficult it was for women to advance their careers.

After a slow start and with considerable differences between different states, the pace of recruitment from the newer member states picked up considerably in the latter half of the 2000s. Between September 2007 and February 2011 (a period of 40 months), the number of EU-12 officials working for the Commission increased by two-thirds. Meanwhile, the number of EU-15 officials fell (presumably mostly because of retirements) by 6 per cent. A few months after the 2004 enlargement, the Vice-President and Commissioner for Administrative Reform, Neil Kinnock, estimated that enlargement would lower the average age of Commission officials by two years once the administration hit its target for pace of recruitment.[20] The survey data suggest this figure may have been an underestimate, although the Commission's own statistics are more ambiguous: they show that the average age for all officials only fell from 45.5 to 44.5 years between 2004 and 2010.

However, enlargement has clearly brought to the Commission many young managers. By 2011, the average age of middle managers recruited from states that joined in 2004 was 45, against 52 for the EU-15. For senior managers, the figures were 51 against 57 for the EU-15 (European Commission 2011: 10–11).

Is the Commission also more liberal—as well as younger and more female— as a result of enlargement? If studying economics or business and working in core economic policy areas are viewed as indicators of economic philosophy,

---

[20] Non-EUCIQ interview conducted by one of the authors, 24 June 2004.

Table 9.1 Subject of main degree

Subject	EU15	EU12
Law	24	25
Economics or business	27	37
Politics, international relations, or other social science	15	15
Arts or humanities	4	7
Mathematicss, computing, engineering, physical or life science	29	17
EUCIQ sample size	1,336	440

Table 9.2 EU-12 and EU-15 officials in 'market enhancing' DGs

	Total EU-12 officials in all DGs	Total EU-12 officials in Market Enhancing DGs*	Total % of state's officials in Market Enhancing DGs*
BGR	149	34	22.8
CYP	88	12	13.6
CZE	302	76	25.2
EST	80	21	26.3
HUN	403	109	27.0
LTU	136	32	23.5
LVA	80	17	21.3
MLT	48	8	16.7
POL	852	209	24.5
ROM	242	59	24.4
SVK	186	38	20.4
SVN	96	19	19.8
Total EU-12	2,662	634	23.8
Total EU-15	14,991	2,604	17.4

Note: Market Enhancing DGs are: Competition, Economic and Financial Affairs, Enterprise and Industry, Internal Market, Taxation and Customs Union, Trade.

Source: Distribution of officials and temporary agents by Directorate-General and nationalities (all budgets) September 2008.

the answer appears to be 'yes'. The survey data suggest that EU-12 officials are considerably more likely than officials from older member states to have studied economics or business as the subject of their main degree (see Table 9.1). Moreover, the Commission's own data show that EU-12 officials are disproportionately recruited to Directorates-General that are centrally concerned with economics. Compared to the situation in 2007, when 13.9 per cent of all officials from new member states worked in five 'economics DGs' (see Peterson and Birdsall 2008: 69), the share had increased to 14.9 per cent by 2011 (see Table 9.2).[21]

---

[21] In fact, the share of all EU-12 officials in these five DGs had increased even more, from 10.7 per cent in 2007 to 12.1 per cent. What is clear more generally is that these DGs are growth areas in terms of the number of Commission officials employed in them. It should be noted that the

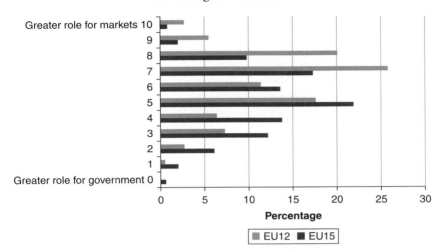

Fig. 9.10 Economic philosophy

Note: n = 1,769.

Of course, we have a considerably sharper indicator of economic philosophy in the form of the survey question that asked officials to place themselves on an eleven-point continuum ranging 'a greater role for government' (0) to 'a greater role for markets' (10). In response to this question, EU-12 officials reported themselves to be considerably more liberal than their EU-15 colleagues (see Figure 9.10). Nearly two-thirds (64 per cent) of EU-12 survey respondents placed themselves on the liberal side of this scale, compared to less than half (43 per cent) of EU-15 respondents.[22] The mean score for EU-12 officials was 6.22, compared to 5.22 for EU-15 officials.

Yet, the picture changes when the survey's data on philosophical views about social and cultural issues ('expanded personal freedoms' vs 'traditional notions of family, morality and order') are examined. On this question, a majority (55 per cent) of EU-12 officials place themselves on the liberal side of an eleven-point continuum (see Figure 9.11). However, this figure must be compared to the considerably higher share (69 per cent) of EU-15 officials who locate themselves on the liberal side. The mean for EU-12 officials is 4.21, compared to 3.51 for their EU-15 colleagues. The gap is thus considerably less wide than it is on economic philosophy, if still statistically significant. Generally, then, enlargement appears to have made the Commission (considerably)

definition of 'market-enhancing' DGs is different from that employed in the earlier (Peterson and Birdsall 2008) study.

[22] These figures—and those in the following paragraph—are based on the share of officials who chose to place themselves between 6 and 10. See Chapter 4 or the appendices for the precise wording of this question as well as that on 'socio-cultural' philosophy.

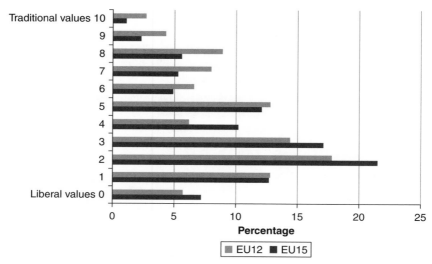

Fig. 9.11 Socio-cultural philosophy
Note: n = 1, 771.

more liberal in terms of economic philosophy but (slightly) more conservative on social and cultural issues.

Of course, even if the Commission has become more economically liberal as a consequence of enlargement, it does not mean that enlargement has made the EU more liberal in general. There is little evidence that enlargement has 'liberalized' other EU institutions. For example, Elsig (2010) argues that enlargement has, on balance, made the Council of Ministers more protectionist because of the economic profile of most EU-12 states, their lack of coherent business lobbies, and the Council's increasing reliance on informal decision-making. However, it seems beyond dispute that the 2004 and 2007 enlargements have made the Commission younger, more female, and economically liberal in outlook.

IS THERE A 'TYPICAL' EU-12 OFFICIAL?

We have painted a portrait of how enlargement has changed the Commission in broad brush strokes. No doubt many in EU-12 administrative, diplomatic, and academic circles would protest that the newest EU member states are a diverse group in terms of administrative traditions, cultural backgrounds, and social attitudes. To illustrate the point, we saw in Chapter 4 that differences between officials in terms of how they think of EU governance very much depends on their nationality and whether they come from a state that is unitary or decentralized, Protestant or not, big or small. Some EU-12 states are highly centralized (the Baltic states), others are not (the Czech Republic). The 2004 and 2007 enlargements made the Union considerably more Catholic, as it brought into the EU some overwhelmingly Catholic states (Poland, Lithuania, Malta). But others are almost entirely non-Catholic (Cyprus, Bulgaria).[23] Most EU-12 states are small, but Poland is a large state of 38 million and Romania (22 million) ranks as the seventh largest amongst all 27 member states.

We find (see Figure 4.5) that Hungarians and Slovenians are 'supranationalists' more often than is the mean for the EU-27. Maltese and Slovenians are *the* most likely among all nationalities to report themselves as 'institutional pragmatists'. Latvians and (especially) Slovaks are more often 'state-centric' than anyone besides the British and Swedes. It would thus be easy to conclude that we cannot generalize and identify the characteristics of a typical EU-12 official beyond saying that they are younger, more likely to be female, and are more economically liberal (and slightly more socially conservative).

But rather than leaving the matter there, it is worth considering if there are differences between nationalities from the newer member states on what may be the most dramatic difference of attitude that we have uncovered: commitment to Europe as a motivator for joining the Commission. Although the sample sizes are rather small—ranging from 113 Poles to 18 Maltese—we do indeed find considerable differences between EU-12 nationalities on this score (see Figure 9.12). Corroborating Ban and Vandenabeele's (2009) findings, Bulgarians are as likely to report being motivated to join the Commission by a commitment to Europe as EU-15 officials do. For Cypriots, it is only slightly less so. In contrast, clear majorities of Latvian and Slovak officials eschew this choice, which is the case for no nationality among the EU-15.

If our sample of EU-12 officials reveals distinct views and attitudes between different nationals, does it contain evidence that there are similarities between officials who might be grouped together into meaningful categories? Is there, say, a typical Baltic or south-eastern or *mitteleuropäischer* official? The data suggest considerable ambiguity, with only very broad similarities and plenty of exceptions.

To illustrate, similar shares of Hungarians, Slovenians, Bulgarians and Cypriots hold supranationalist views of EU governance (see Figure 4.4). Considerably fewer Czech or (especially) Slovak officials do. Majorities of Czech and Hungarian officials were motivated to join the Commission by a 'commitment to Europe'. But only a minority of Slovaks were. Latvians and Estonians have state-centric views of EU governance, while considerably fewer Lithuanians do. Most Baltic state officials cited commitment to Europe

---

[23] For the political system, religious composition and population of all 27 EU member states, see the interactive map at <http://e-uprava.gov.si/e-uprava/en/evropa.euprava> (accessed 27 July 2012).

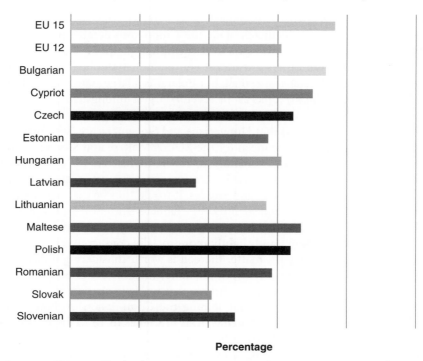

Percentage

Fig. 9.12 EU-12 officials: 'commitment to Europe' as motivation for joining by nationality

Note: n = 1,786, EU 12 = 455.

as a reason for choosing a career in the Commission. Yet, Latvians are outliers: they are less likely than any other nationality of official to say this commitment was a motivator for them.

At the same time, there is evidence in our data to suggest that EU-12 officials are a more distinctive group of officials than those grouped by (say) size of home member state,[24] gender, type of DG, age, and so on. Figure 9.12 presents a multivariate analysis using binary regression analysis of data from three questions and answers:

   a. Was 'commitment to Europe' listed as primary reason for joining the Commission?

----

[24] Large states were considered to be Germany, France, the UK, Italy, Poland, and Spain. All others were considered to be small member states.

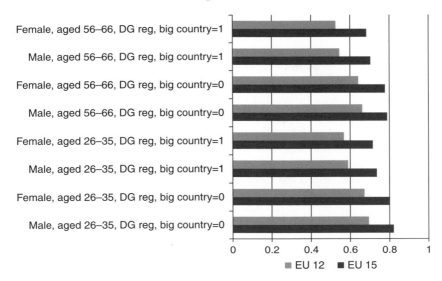

Fig. 9.13 Multivariate analysis: EU-12 vs EU-15: probability that official cited 'commitment to Europe' as reason for joining the Commission

    b. Is the Commission 'more powerful today' than it ever before?

    c. Did officials rate President Barroso as strong in terms of 'defending the Commission within the EU system'?[25]

As can be seen from Figure 9.13, there is significant variation between EU-12 and EU-15 respondents in all cases where we have combined different categories of official. Put simply, there are major differences between the views of officials from the newer member states and all other Commission officials. The 'split' between EU-12 and EU-15 officials is a more powerful determinant of responses to these—and many other—questions than any other split.

There is no question that the 2004 and 2007 enlargements added considerable diversity to the Commission's cultural mosaic. We do find some patterns in terms of beliefs and attitudes that make EU-12 officials distinctive as a group. However, when we drill down to examine the details of specific nationalities, we find much to make us cautious about generalization. These enlargements near-doubled the number of EU member states and increased the EU population by just over a quarter. It did not make the Commission a proportionately more diverse administration. But it did not fall far short.

---

[25] We report full findings in response to the latter two questions in Figure 9.15.

CONCLUSION

How and how much has the Commission changed as a consequence of enlargement? It will be impossible to answer this question definitively until many years after the publication of this book. Moreover, this question really is two distinct questions. First, what will be the consequences of enlargement on the EU's institutional *system*, of which the Commission is a part? To answer this question, we must know the impacts of enlargement on the Parliament and Council, because how and how much they change impacts on the Commission (at least indirectly). Second, how has the influx of new officials from the EU-12 changed the Commission itself?

The EUCIQ data can lead us to make reasoned hunches about the answer to this second question. In particular, we can judge (first) how 'bifurcated' the Commission is post-enlargement and (second), how officials of all stripes think the consequences of enlargement have been handled within the house. But, ultimately, we must leave the first question unanswered—because we cannot judge based on our data how much the 'big bang' enlargements changed the EU's institutional system.

We can, however, turn to other sources that offer at least partial answers to the second question. The first is the Commission's own evaluation (European Commission 2011). As we have seen, the company line within the house is that the 2004 and 2007 enlargements were digested by the Commission with ease and skill. In many respects, such claims can be justified. After all, the recruitment target after the 2004 enlargement was three times higher than it was for Mediterranean enlargement in the 1980s or northern enlargement in the 1990s. Post-2004 recruitment was eased by the suspension of the Commission's staff regulation that clearly states that 'no posts shall be reserved for the nationals of any specific member state', as well as the embrace of the pragmatic principle that the Commission's 'services were free to recruit nationals from the 10 member states whenever they saw a candidate fit for a post' (European Commission 2011: 3). In fact, the Commission *overshot* its target for the EU-10 (officials from states that joined in 2004) recruitment by 14 per cent overall. Crucially, in political terms, it overshot its recruitment target by 30 per cent at the most senior levels (European Commission 2011: 3–5). As would be expected, the report extols the virtues of post-2004 recruitment for the Commission's gender balance and age profile.

Yet, as we have argued, the report lacks credibility insofar as it breathes not a word about the change in the staff salary scale that took effect on 1 May 2004, which will mean that EU-12 officials (and others who joined after that date) will require far longer to advance on the Commission's salary scale. The Commission report is also almost completely silent on the adverse effects of the post-2004 recruitment strategy on EU-15 officials. It acknowledges that the recruitment strategy:

> led to certain restrictions to the recruitment of nationals from the 15 old member states. Nevertheless . . . the recruitment policy did not jeopardise the recruitment of EU-15 nationals, which kept a reasonable pace over the period, so that in the long-term no major geographical imbalances will appear (European Commission 2011: 7).

The EUCIQ data suggest that many EU-15 officials would dispute this claim, including those who may have had promotion to management level delayed or blocked because of the need to recruit EU-12 officials to more senior positions. Almost exactly two-thirds of EU-15 survey respondents disagreed that the 'consequences of enlargement for career development were handled with equity and fairness'. As we have seen, even more—69.3 per cent—of EU-12 officials disagreed, many (more than a third) 'strongly' (see Figure 9.3).

A second source is Gravier's (2008) analysis of recruitment to the Commission after the 2004 enlargement. She stresses that the move to suspend the Commission's staff regulation to get sufficient numbers of EU-10 officials into post defied multiple decisions of the European Court of Justice that held that 'geographical balance is but a secondary consideration' in recruitment to the Commission (Gravier 2008: 1029). As such, she concludes that 'the 2004 enlargement was perceived to be an exceptional one', which by any account it certainly was (Gravier 2008: 1034).

But Gravier certainly does not portray the post-2004 recruitment as trouble-free. First, levels of recruitment from some member states lagged well behind targets (see Chapter 2). By spring 2007, for example, only 61 per cent of the Czech target had been met and (strikingly) only 52 per cent of Poland's. The result was considerable discontent in Prague and especially Warsaw. When Poland's Prime Minister, Jaroslaw Kaczynski, made his first visit to Brussels in 2006 the slow pace of recruitment of Poles to the Commission was the first issue he raised in a meeting with the Polish Commissioner, Danuta Hübner (Peterson and Birdsall 2008: 58).

Moreover, we find evidence in the EUCIQ survey data of a clash of views between EU-15 and EU-12 officials about the favouritism shown to the latter in post-2004 recruitment. While exactly half of EU-12 survey respondents agree that 'posts in the Commission should be distributed on the basis of geographical balance', a majority (53 per cent) of EU-15 officials *disagree*, and more than one-fifth do so strongly (see Figure 9.14). The gap is even wider when we compare EU-12 totals with EU-15 officials recruited in 2004 or later: although the sample size is small, nearly 60 per cent of the newest EU-15 officials disagree (23.4 per cent 'strongly'). Here, more than almost anywhere else, we find a truly bifurcated Commission. At the same time, Commission officials are united as in few other areas on the 'equity and fairness' with which

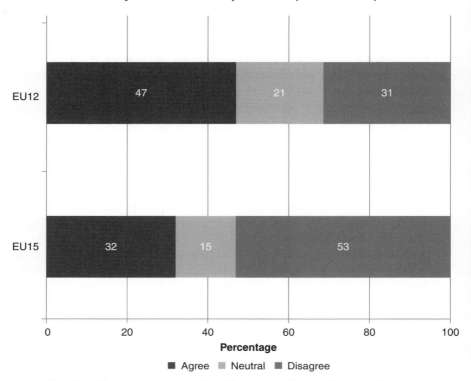

Fig. 9.14 Views on the geographical balance in the distribution of posts
Note: n = 1,665.

the career implications of enlargement were handled: overwhelming majorities report themselves unhappy with the results.

A third and particularly notable source is Ban's (2013) monograph that specifically focuses on the process of 'enlarging the Commission'. Her analysis is mostly upbeat, offering 'a generally positive report, with most new staff integrating successfully and being well-accepted in the organization', although 'the picture is more mixed for those entering at management levels' (Ban 2013: 12). At the same time, she finds evidence of considerable friction between the Commission and officials in the new member states during the accession negotiations, with the former treating the latter as 'second-class citizens'. She even highlights speculation that this friction carried on into post-accession recruitment, quoting Polish interviewees as claiming 'we were treated as barbarians' during the accession negotiations, leading afterwards to a 'reticence to hire Poles. That's what we see' (Ban 2013: 24).

Ban's portrayal of relatively backward civil services amongst newer EU member states casts our findings about what motivated EU-12 officials to join the Commission in a particular light. Maybe it should come as no surprise that EU-12 officials are more often motivated by job stability,

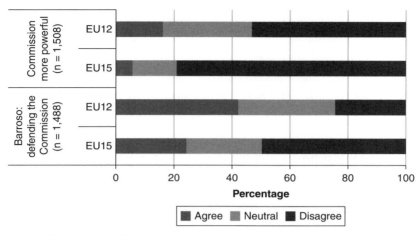

Fig. 9.15 The power of the Commission and rating Barroso

promising career prospects, or competitive remuneration to join the administration. A 'commitment to Europe' might well be expected to be a less
powerful motivator.

Again, however, Ban's (2013) assessment is generally positive. It gives
sustenance to the claim that enlargement has changed the Commission mostly
because EU-12 officials have breathed fresh life into the administration (see
also Peterson and Birdsall 2008). So do EUCIQ survey data collected in
responses to two questions about the Commission's position and recent
performance. One sought reactions to the statement that 'the Commission is
more powerful today than ever before'. Although nearly one-third of respondents from newer member states 'neither agreed nor disagreed' (and another
quarter 'did not know'), only 12 per cent strongly disagreed—compared with
nearly one-third of EU-15 officials (see Figure 9.15).

Moreover, EU-12 officials were considerably more positive about José
Manuel Barroso's performance as President (which perhaps, itself, reflects
how EU-12 officials tend to be economic liberals). For instance, a considerably
larger share of EU-12 officials credited him with effectively 'defending the
Commission in the EU system' (see Figure 9.15 for general results). Thus, we
find substantive evidence to sustain the view, often shared in interviews, that
officials from the new member states are less jaded and cynical and more
positive about where the Commission stands.

As a final point, it is important to remember that enlargement is not
monocausal and that it has taken place concurrent with other changes (Peterson
2008), including the 'bedding down' of sweeping administrative reform (see
Chapter 8), the attempt (regardless of enlargement) to achieve more gender
balance in Commission (Ban 2010), and so on. But the headline finding from
our inquiry into how the EU-12 enlargements have changed the Commission

might be found in the answer—partial though it may be—we can offer to Heidbreder's (2011: 3) primary research question: 'under which conditions does the widening of the EU cause deepening within the EU'? Insofar as the Commission as an administration is concerned, our evidence suggests *not* under the conditions of the Union's most recent widening(s). We find little evidence that it has deepened the sense of mission or commitment to the European project within the Commission. Thus, we are frankly dubious about the claim made by Ellinas and Suleiman (2011: 923)—based on 188 interviews—that 'Commission managers favour deeper integration regardless of their national background or their organizational experience'. Notably, their only comment on enlargement is a highly tentative one: while it '*might* be pushing the Commission towards a more intergovernmental outlook . . . institutional and policy setbacks *might* moderate these effects, enhancing organizational solidarity and allowing the Commission to continue serving its integrative function' (Ellinas and Suleiman 2011: 942; emphasis added).

There is considerable support (with nuances) for the view that the initial impact of the 2004 and 2007 enlargements has been to create new divisions of view and perception within the administration. The Commission (European Commission 2011: 16) is not unreasonable in trumpeting its achievements in post-2004 recruitment or claiming that the administration is 'a truly European institution today'. But it cannot pretend that enlargement has not also caused resentment, complicated the Commission's work, and brought to Brussels a considerable number of officials who seem to be utility maximizers. How quickly or comprehensively they will be socialized, with views that 'bend' over time in the direction of mainstream views held within the house, remain open questions.

10

Conclusion: The Commission of the Twenty-First Century—What Kind of Administration?

The European Commission's recent history, and that of the European Union more generally, has been marked by a series of especially testing challenges. A protracted debate about 'the future of Europe' came to an end with the implementation of the Lisbon Treaty on 1 December 2009, producing a system arguably more complex and fragmented than the one it replaced. In the new settlement fundamental questions concerning legitimacy and accountability that had been posed at the Laeken European Council in December 2001, when the process began, remained largely unanswered.[1] Moreover, the 2004 and 2007 enlargements created a Union of substantial size but also considerable diversity. The accession of twelve new member states from Central, Eastern and Southern Europe was a historic milestone, but raised fears of institutional gridlock and inevitably complicated policy and policy-making. Furthermore, the economic and financial crisis that broke out after 2007 appeared at times to pose an existential threat to economic and monetary union—arguably the high point of European integration—which looked as though it might spill over to other parts of the European project.

Throughout the long debate about the EU's future, the responsibilities and powers of the Commission were frequently called into question. Reflecting on the decade-long discussion of the European constitutions, successive rounds of treaty reform, and other developments, many commentators argued that the Commission was in relative decline (see, for example, Kassim and Menon 2004, 2010; Kurpas et al 2008; Peterson 2012: 97). While the continued expansion of the European Council and the rise-and-rise of the European Parliament eroded its leadership role and its influence over legislation, 'politicization, enlargement,

---

[1] On the Lisbon Treaty, see Devuyst (2008); Piris (2010); Craig (2010); Laursen (2012). For the EU's institutional system after Lisbon, see Piris (2012: 25–31). On the EU and legitimacy, see Moravcsik (2002); Kohler-Koch and Rittberger (2007); Scharpf (2009); Enzensberger 2011.

and administrative reform' (Hooghe and Kassim 2012: 196; see also Bauer 2012) posed new and difficult challenges (Hooghe and Marks 2009; Piris 2012: 25–31). Yet the Commission continued to perform its traditional functions as policy initiator, guardian of the treaties, executive, and trade negotiator. Despite the EU's apparent fragility—arising from the Eurozone crisis (Hodson 2012; Tsoukalis 2011), its divisions over EU foreign policy, notably in Iraq (Peterson et al 2012), and its pereceived remoteness from many average Europeans (Enzensberger 2011; Hobolt 2012)—there are 'few signs that these changes have weakened the Commission's traditional role' (Hooghe and Kassim 2012, or 196–7)[2] or any doubt that the Commission remains an influential actor both inside the EU and beyond.

In spite of the central role that it plays in the EU system—and, indeed, the attention it has commanded since the creation of the European Communities—much about the Commission, however, is either not well known or understood. Its status, purpose, and composition have long been controversial and remain contested. Similarly, the motivation, behaviour, and beliefs of its officials, as well as its internal operation, continue to be keenly debated.[3] At the same time, hostile views about the organization and those who work for it have become ingrained in the public mind. In an era of general scepticism about bureaucracy, bureaucrats, and European integration the Commission is often considered to embody the most undesirable traits of all three.[4]

The present volume, and the project on which it is based,[5] put to the test competing perspectives in the academic literature, as well as the widely accepted wisdoms about the Commission and its staff. In addressing fundamental questions about the organization, its aim is to develop a better understanding of the people who work for the Commission, how it functions internally, and its response to major challenges. Unlike other studies, it examines the entire organization, draws on primary source material created by the research team, and approaches the analysis of the Commission from a comparative perspective. The overall ambition is to offer an appraisal of the European Commission as a twenty-first-century administration.

This concluding chapter considers the main findings reported in the volume. It offers an overview of the Commission as an administration, and outlines directions for future research. After considering the answers suggested by analysis of the source material in response to the questions outlined in Chapter 1 (and summarized below), it draws out the implications of the findings for a number of more general debates; namely, the importance of nationality in the Commission, the role of partisanship within the organization, the extent to

---

[2] See, for example, Kassim and Menon (2004, 2010); Kurpas et al. (2008).

[3] See, for example, Coombes (1970); Cini (1996); Nugent (1997); Page (1997); Shore (2000); Hooghe (2001); Stevens and Stevens (2001); Joana and Smith (2004).

[4] On attitudes to bureaucracy and bureaucrats, see du Gay (2000, 2005); on Euroscepticism, see Harmsen and Spiering (2004); Szczerbiak and Taggart (2008a, 2008b); Fuchs et al. (2009).

[5] For a description of the project, see Chapter 1. For further information, see <http://www.uea.ac.uk/psi/research/EUCIQ>.

which officials regard the Commission as technocratic and themselves as technocrats, and whether the Commission is best considered a singular or a *sui generis* administration. As well as offering a summary characterization of the Commission, the final section points to a number of problems that the organization may face in the future.

THE COMMISSION AS AN ORGANIZATION AND THE PEOPLE WHO WORK FOR IT

Much of the now voluminous literature on the EU is concerned with assessing the organization's power as an actor in policy, measuring its influence in decision-making processes, or reflecting on its wider role within the EU political system. These investigations are important and have generated many invaluable insights, but they have not always paid sufficient attention to the Commission's organizational features or the characteristics of its staff. Nor typically do they approach the Commission as an administration. Yet, as Coombes (1970) and others have contended, the organization of the Commission, how its various structures articulate and the functions that they perform, as well as the expertise and experience of the people who work for it, are important determinants of the Commission's ability to carry out the responsibilities entrusted to it. Since these tasks are central to the EU, the Commission's organization and the attributes of its personnel are likely to affect the functioning and administrative capacities of the Union more broadly.

The book began with four main questions: Who are the people who work for the Commission? How do officials navigate the organization? How do the various structures and parts of the Commission interact? What are the attitudes of officials to recent challenges? The popular understanding, as an answer to the first question, is that the Commission is peopled by career civil servants who are distant, arrogant, and remote, with little experience of life beyond the European bureaucracy. The picture offered by the academic literature is often no more sympathetic. Work that is grounded in a rational choice perspective proceeds from the assumption that Commission officials are budget-maximizers, bureau-shapers, or competence expanders (see, for example, Pollack 2003; Franchino 2007; see also Jupille 2004). An alternative viewpoint presents the Commission as a privileged caste (Page 1995), combining the aloofness of the Napoleonic model of bureaucracy (see Stevens and Stevens 2001) with the legalism of the German tradition (Balint et al. 2008, Shore 2000: 132–5).

Scholarship on the strategies that Commission officials adopt in order to get their job done—the second question—suggests that, as in many workplaces and organizations, individuals develop a range of personal contacts to seek advice, gather intelligence, and short-circuit formal procedures (Stevens and Stevens 2001). The prevailing view is that officials have responded to the emphasis on hierarchy and the intricacy of procedures within the organization by forging informal networks (see, especially, Abélès et al. 1993; Spence with Edwards 2006). Some authors go further. A number suggest that the Commission is criss-crossed by networks based on partisan affiliation (see, for example, Ross 1995), the old school tie in the form of a 'Bruges mafia' (see, for example, Schnabel 2002; Stares 2005), or nationality (Egeberg 1996; Hooghe 1999; Shore 2000; Laffan 2004). Few, however, have tested these theses against data drawn from across the organization.[6]

Claims in the literature about the internal operation of the organization— the third question—are, by contrast, somewhat contradictory. From one perspective, the Commission is depicted as a monolith. Formidable and impenetrable, it remorselessly pursues an expansionist agenda.[7] From the other, it is portrayed as a deeply fragmented organization, divided into fiefdoms, and riven by political and functional rivalries (see Coombes 1970; Cini 1996; Stevens and Stevens 2001; Hartlapp et al. 2010; Hartlapp 2011), that is scarcely capable of coherent action. Since, moreover, the Commission Presidency has historically had few and limited resources at its disposal (see, e.g. Coombes 1970; Campbell 1983; Ross 1995; Kassim 2012), and power has been widely dispersed within the organization (see Coombes 1970); Spierenburg 1979), leadership has been a precarious enterprise. Thus, of the eleven incumbents of the Commission Presidency between 1958 and 2004, it could be unequivocally claimed only of two—the first, Walter Hallstein, and the eighth, Jacques Delors—that they gave effective leadership to the Commission.

While the first three questions address issues that have been of long-standing concern, the fourth concerns two specific recent developments; namely, the implementation of a far-reaching programme of administrative reform by the Prodi Commission, and the 2004 and 2007 enlargements, which saw the Union grow from fifteen to twenty-seven member states. The literature on the reform is substantial—a testament to its historic significance—but coverage has typically been directed towards the circumstances that brought it about, and its design and content (see, for example, Kassim 2004a, 2004b). Until recently (Bauer 2008b; Ellinas and Suleiman 2007), little attention was paid to the attitudes of officials to the reform, still less its impact on the functioning of the institution. Similarly, aside from the concern with the impact of EU action on the 'new' member states, the scholarly literature on the 'big bang'

---

[6] Suvarierol (2007) is an important exception. She collected original data to test the widespread assumption that networks within the Commission are based on nationality.

[7] This view is to be found, for example, in the literature on EU competition policy and specifically the 1999 modernization of anti-trust (see, for example, Riley 2003a, 2003b; Wilks 2005; for an alternative interpretation of the same reform, see Kassim and Wright 2009).

enlargement has focused on the effects of expansion on the machinery or institutions of the EU (see Dehousse et al. 2006; Best et al. 2008; Dittmer-Odell 2010; Heidbreder 2011). However, it has not examined the views of officials from either the old or new member states on how the process was managed by the institution, nor reflected on the medium or long-term consequences of the recruitment of officials from ten post-Communist countries.

As well as adding to knowledge about the Commission, the findings reported in the preceding chapters challenge many accepted wisdoms and myths about Commission officials, and about leadership and coordination within the organization. They reveal a very different picture of the Commission and its staff from the images that have become dominant in the public mind or that feature prominently in the scholarly literature. They show that the Commission is stronger and better equipped to meet the challenges that confront the Union than is often thought. At the same time, they point to potential fault lines that may be a source of difficulties in the future.

Commission officials: backgrounds, career trajectories and beliefs

The view that Commission officials are a privileged elite, whose members have little experience of the world beyond university study and public administration, is widely held. The inference, seldom explicitly drawn, but strongly implied, is that its staff, and therefore the organization as a whole, lack the skills, expertise and imagination necessary to meet the challenges that confront the EU. The EUCIQ survey data show that such a belief is in large part mistaken. Although the online questionnaire did not enquire about social origins, it found that Commission officials are highly educated and cosmopolitan. No fewer than 70 per cent have postgraduate qualifications, while 58 per cent completed at least part of their studies in more than one country. To that extent, a substantial proportion of officials are likely to come from a background of relative privilege.

The belief that Commission officials know little of life beyond the ivory tower of European administration receives significantly less support, however. According to EUCIQ data, the overwhelming majority of officials—96 per cent, in fact—had worked before they joined the Commission. Only a handful moved to Brussels directly after graduating from university. In addition, even if there has been a recent increase in the percentage of officials with a civil service background (mainly due to the 2004 and 2007 enlargements), no fewer than a third of the Commission's staff are recruited from the private sector—a baseline that has not been breached in over three decades. While it is true that officials with business experience tend to be attracted to certain departments—notably the DGs for Administration,[8] Budget, Communications, Transport

---

[8] DG Administration (ADMIN) was renamed DG Human Resources (HR) under Barroso II.

and Energy,[9] Enlargement, Enterprise, Informatics, Information Society and Media, Market, Research and Innovation, the Legal Service, and the Joint Research Centre—the overall proportion of officials with such a background is considerably larger than the image of Commission officials as lifelong bureaucrats suggests.

The conception of the Commission as an administration of lawyers is a further myth that is challenged by the EUCIQ data. Often when the claim is made that the Commission is populated by law graduates, the portrayal is not value neutral (see, for example, Shore 2000: 132–5). Legal expertise can easily be taken to imply an overriding formalism, a preoccupation with procedure and process, and a concern to preserve the status quo rather than to think creatively about how to meet new and emerging challenges. When other educational backgrounds and professional experience are disregarded, the impression can be given that the Commission lacks the range of competencies necessary to carry out its responsibilities or to develop innovative solutions to problems that arise in different areas. Data from the online survey shows in fact that, among the administrative grade staff working in policy-related DGs, lawyers are outnumbered not only by economists but also by scientists. The depth and diversity of expertise at the Commission's disposal is far greater therefore than implied by the 'administration-of-lawyers' image.

In contrast to the educational and professional backgrounds of Commission officials, which have been an object of study, the career trajectories of officials have generally been of little interest beyond all but a small group of scholars. In addition, the few studies that have been undertaken have usually drawn on limited data.[10] Of the findings from the EUCIQ data reported in Chapter 2, three are especially noteworthy. First, commentators on the Commission usually report a low level of mobility (see, for example, Spierenburg 1979) and have interpreted this lack of movement between departments as problematic.[11] The EUCIQ data suggests, however, that, with 53 per cent of officials having served in more than one DG, horizontal mobility is higher than often thought.

A second finding bears on the character of the Commission and specifically on the extent to which Hallstein's ambition of creating a permanent career civil service to rival national administrations has been realized. Career-building offers an important metric of the extent to which this aim has been achieved. According to the EUCIQ data, evidence of career-building among middle and senior managers is mixed. While a substantial proportion have made their career within the Commission and been promoted from within, a

---

[9] DG Transport and Energy (TREN) was divided into DG Mobility and Transport (MOVE) and DG Energy (ENER) in 2010.

[10] Page (1997) is an exception.

[11] Levels of mobility and the extent to which it is regarded as beneficial either to the individual or the service varies considerably between administrations (see Bossaert et al. 2001).

significant number are external recruits. Many of the latter joined at the time of the 2004 and 2007 enlargements. They reflect the organization's need to have at its disposal expertise from all member states, As management posts are reserved to outside candidates, at each round of enlargement, career progression for officials already working in the organization is inevitably restricted.

Third, though not necessarily out of line with many national bureaucracies, the Commission's past record in the recruitment and promotion of women has been lamentable (Stevens and Stevens 2001: 108–15). Official Commission data from DG Human Resources from 2012 show that, although the gender balance has improved dramatically, women still tend still to be concentrated in the lower grades (see Chapter 2). Analysis of the EUCIQ data reveals however that, although there are still only a small number of women in middle and senior management posts, those who occupy those positions have reached them more quickly than their male counterparts. There are also striking differences between DGs in the extent to which the proportion of female managers reflects the proportion of women working in the DG (see Chapter 2).

A final myth challenged by the EUCIQ findings is that Commission officials are federalist inclined, wanting continually to extend the competencies of the Union and aspiring to a future where the Commission is the government of Europe. As Chapter 2 reports, the EUCIQ data shows that, at whichever point in the last three decades they were recruited, a majority of officials (between 66 and 76 per cent) cited 'building Europe' as a motivation for deciding to pursue their career in Brussels. However, competitive remuneration has always been an attraction for a significant proportion of officials (between 50 and 60 per cent). Commitment to a particular policy area, by contrast, has become an increasingly important motivation, rising from 16 per cent for officials who joined twenty-six or more years ago to 24 per cent of those recruited between 2002 and 2007. However, as Chapter 4 shows, the desire to 'build Europe' as a motivation for joining the Commission does not automatically translate into pro-federalism.

Indeed, the EUCIQ survey data offers little support for the idea that Commission officials are instinctively supranational. First, when asked what model of EU governance they preferred, only 36 per cent of officials voiced support for a supranational or federal EU in which the College of Commissioners is the 'government of Europe'. Thirty per cent are 'institutional pragmatists': they want the Commission to continue in its traditional role as policy initiator and guardian of the treaties. Fourteen per cent, meanwhile, are state centrists. These officials consider that the member states should remain the central pillars of the Union.[12]

Second, findings on how Commission officials are disposed to the further extension of the EU's decision-making authority are at odds with the widely

---

[12] State centrists are found in some unexpected places. As Chapter 4 shows, the Legal Service, DG SANCO and DG COMP are among DGs with the highest percentages.

held view that they are likely to be instinctively expansionist. Although, on aggregate, respondents would like to see greater EU authority in a number of policy areas,[13] their desire to centralize is measured and selective. Officials may think that there should be 'more Europe' in foreign policy, justice and security, and energy, for example, but they believe that power should be returned to the member states in agriculture. The latter result is noteworthy, since as the first common policy, the common agricultural policy has historically been regarded by supporters of European integration as sacrosanct.[14] More broadly, the pattern of differentiated preferences challenges the image of officials as competence maximizers. Close examination suggests that the views registered by officials on the question of competencies are driven by functional imperatives—centralization where scale economies can be reaped—and by personal and political values rather than a generalized or instinctive preference to maximize Commission power.

Leadership and coordination in the Commission

EUCIQ findings concerning the Commission's internal structures and operation also challenge conventional views. The first concerns the strength and leadership style of the Barroso Presidency. Officials consider Barroso to be stronger than either of his immediate predecessors, Romano Prodi and Jacques Santer, and rate Barroso second only to Delors in his defence of the organization. The degree to which leadership has been centralized around the person of the Commission President is remarkable. Historically, the Commission has been an institution where power is widely dispersed. Despite the expectations directed towards the office, the President has typically lacked the resources—procedural, political and administrative—to exercise strong leadership.[15] The exceptions—Hallstein and Delors—drew on more informal sources of authority, such as personal clout and standing, the ability to perform effectively in the European Council, and, in the case of Delors, respect from Paris and Bonn (Ross 1995; Endo 1999; Grant 2004; Kassim 2012). Against the background of a series of treaty reforms that have considerably enhanced the authority of the office since the Amsterdam Treaty, as well as the 2004 and

---

[13] They were asked where between the Union and the member states decision-making authority resides, and where it *should* reside, in eleven areas: agriculture, energy, social, development, regional development, competition, environment, foreign and security, defence, asylum and immigration, trade, and police and judicial cooperation.

[14] One veteran Director-General remarked following a presentation of results based on the EUCIQ survey that such a viewpoint would for most of his career have been regarded as heretical.

[15] For example, control over policy initiation, the legislative agenda, and cabinet subcommittees, powers of appointment and dismissal, and a sizeable administrative staff.

2007 enlargements, which increased the size of the College, and a climate in which the Commission has to demonstrate the value of its initiatives, Barroso has re-fashioned, re-positioned and significantly strengthened the Commission Presidency.

Second, the presidential leadership model developed by Barroso is distinctive. Barroso, together with the Secretary General, Catherine Day, has transformed the Secretariat-General from a service that supports the College to a service of the Commission President, and has supported a more interventionist role for the Secretariat-General in policy-making. Together with more effective coordination systems within the Commission, most notably strategic planning and programming, which is located in the Secretariat-General, these changes have strengthened the administrative resources available to the Commission President. As a result, Barroso has a more comprehensive and detailed grip on policy than his predecessors.

At the same time, officials are ambivalent about a stronger Presidency. Many interviewees recognized the benefits of a strong Commission President. As Chapter 6 shows, Commissioners, *cabinet* members, and senior managers accepted Barroso's argument on taking office that only presidentialized leadership could enable the Commission to play an active role vis-à-vis the member states and the European Parliament and that the expansion of the College to twenty-seven Commissioners necessitated concentration of authority. Others, however, were concerned about the decline of collegiality that has accompanied presidentialized leadership. A number of senior managers pointed to the negative impact on staff morale.[16]

A similar picture emerges in relation to coordination. As Chapter 7 shows, the image that recurs in the memoirs of former Commissioners and officials—and is repeated in the academic literature—is that of a fragmented institution, where the *cabinets* are in perpetual conflict, and where services battle with each other and with the *cabinets* (Coombes 1970; Spierenburg 1979; Ross 1995; Stevens and Stevens 2001; Spence with Edwards 2006). The EUCIQ findings suggest that this portrayal is outdated. First, according to both the survey data and interview responses, the close identification between *cabinets* and the home state of their Commissioner has faded. Across the Commission, the perception that *cabinets* are too preoccupied by developments in their Commissioner's national capital is relatively weak. *Cabinet* members do not consider that advancing the interests of their Commissioner's home state (or the careers of the Commissioner's compatriots in the Commission) is a part of the *cabinet's* responsibility. Thus, a process of *functional* denationalization has accompanied, or perhaps been caused by, rule changes that have compelled *cabinets* to become more multinational in their composition (Egeberg and Heskestad 2010).

[16] An important question was whether the new relationship between the Commission President and the Secretariat-General would endure when Barroso and Catherine Day no longer hold office.

Second, relations between the *cabinets* and the services are considerably more harmonious than the existing literature suggests (see, for example Ross 1995; Joana and Smith 2006; Spence with Edwards 2006). According to the EUCIQ data, *cabinets* generally respect the expertise of the services. Meanwhile, albeit to a lesser extent, the services appreciate the role played by the *cabinets*. This greater cordiality can be attributed partly to rule changes that compel incoming *cabinets* to sign a concordat with the services for which they are responsible, detailing, for example, how often meetings are to be held and through what channels *cabinet* members should contact officials in the services. Other factors include reduction in the size of the *cabinets*, denationalization, and the lowering of the grade at which *cabinet* members can re-enter the services on the expiration of their Commissioner's term of office—which has dramatically reduced the rate of *parachutage*.

Interdepartmental coordination, meanwhile, is also much more effective than the view presented by either insider or outsider perspectives in the existing literature—a third finding. Responses to the online survey show that, in moving from the smallest to the largest administrative division—the unit, the Directorate-General and the Commission as a whole—coordination and the sharing of information becomes increasingly less effective. Yet, a high percentage of officials regard coordination between the services as unproblematic. When the views of officials with experience in the private sector or a national administration were compared with those without such experience, no statistically significant difference in their evaluation was discovered. In the interviews, managers who had worked for several years in the Commission noted that interdepartmental coordination had improved, and attributed this to better IT tools, mechanisms such as impact assessment, and the more activist role played by the Secretariat-General.

Movement in the direction of a more proactive Secretariat-General did not win universal favour, however. Concern was expressed about the centralization of authority in the Secretariat-General, which some interviewees thought lacked both the staff numbers and the expertise to fulfil its new ambitions. Others expressed anxiety either that greater policy involvement on the part of the Secretariat-General had come at the expense of the performance of its traditional functions—for example, institutional memory, minute-keeping, and supporting the College—or that it had displaced the lead role of line DGs, with their specialist knowledge and relations with stakeholders.

Attitudes to change: administrative reform and enlargement

The final question concerns the views of officials on two recent, though quite different, challenges. The first is the administrative reform, led by Neil Kinnock and introduced by the Prodi Commission in 1999–2005, following the resignation of the Santer Commission (see Kassim 2004a; 2004b, 2008; Bauer 2008; Schön-Quinlivan 2011). The wide-ranging measures, adopted under the banner of modernization, aimed at improving planning, resource allocation, financial management, and accountability within the organization, as well as overhauling personnel policy. They were intended to bring the Commission more closely in line with practices and procedures that had become standard in other administrations at national and international levels.

The reforms were significant not least because they were the most radical to be adopted by the Commission since its creation in the late 1950s. They were also controversial inside the organization. Chapter 8 investigated attitudes on the part of officials towards the procedures and processes that were introduced by the reforms, and that had therefore been in operation for a number of years by the time that the EUCIQ online survey was administered (2008) and the interviews conducted (2009). The results showed greater diversity of opinion than the main theoretical perspectives in the comparative public administrations literature would anticipate. According to the traditional Weberian approach, as well as variants of historical institutionalism and sociological institutionalism,[17] bureaucrats are essentially conservative and are instinctively resistant to reform. The EUCIQ survey data, however, revealed a picture that is considerably more complex. Although on balance more officials were negative than they were positive about the reform, opinion was much more differentiated than the main theoretical perspectives would suggest. Moreover, analysis of the EUCIQ data showed that attitudes varied according to position and function. For example, senior managers considered that the tools introduced by the reforms enabled them to carry out their responsibilities more effectively. The reforms were popular among management DGs, but disliked by officials in spending DGs.

A more tentative conclusion is that the experience of the Kinnock–Prodi reforms removed an important taboo with respect to administrative change. In the past, management was regarded as a secondary concern in the Commission, significantly behind policy initiation, which itself was regarded as the organization's *raison d'être* and the most prestigious responsibility for its personnel. In addition, the staff unions had taken a confrontational stance to changes in working conditions or other aspect of personnel policy that Commissioners or senior officials had periodically proposed. The mobilization of opposition among staff had often been enough to force the dilution or abandonment by management of these initiatives. Commissioners and senior

[17] The Weberian orthodoxy is essentially a theory of bureaucratic power, according to which bureaucrats both want and are able to preserve the status quo (see, for example, Kellner and Crowther-Hunt 1980; Suleiman 1974; Putnam 1973). For approaches inspired by historical institutionalism or sociological institutionalism, see Brunsson and Olsen (1993); Christensen (1997); Capano (2003).

managers in the organization had tended to shy away from reform. The experience of the Kinnock–Prodi reforms, the continued development of strategic planning and programming, amendments to financial control and management, and the readjustment (and later the abolition) of the Career Development Review (CDR), suggest, however, that administrative change has become a continuous feature of life in the Commission rather than a one-off event or episode.[18]

Attitudes towards enlargement were also considerably more complex than anticipated. Hostility might have been expected among both serving and incoming officials. The first group would have found their career prospects worsened by an influx of officials from the EU-12, while the second may well have been resentful at the lower salaries and slower career progression on offer for staff recruited after 1 May 2004. Indeed, a first finding reported in Chapter 9 was that most officials did not consider that enlargement had been well handled by the Commission. The assessment of the impact of enlargement on the coherence of the organization was also negative, and officials were no more positively inclined to the principle of one Commissioner per member state. At the same time, in interviews, middle and senior managers expressed their appreciation of officials from the newer member states, whom they valued for their talents, energy, and vitality.

EUCIQ FINDINGS AND THE CLASSIC RESEARCH AGENDA

The findings from the survey and interviews are also (if to varying degrees) germane to a number of classic debates in existing scholarship on the EU institutions and the European Commission. These debates are broader than the questions that served as the starting point for the current study and typically cut across the themes addressed individually by the foregoing chapters. Four are considered here: nationality; partisanship; technocracy; and uniqueness, or the extent to which the Commission should be considered *sui generis*.

Nationality

Interest in the role and significance of nationality within the Commission has been long-standing (see, for example, Siotis 1964). But a failure to distinguish

---

[18] A further extension of this line of argument would be that the Commission is no longer an 'adolescent bureaucracy' (Mazey and Richardson 1993:2), but is now a mature administration.

between different understandings has often led to discussions to be conducted at cross-purposes. Nationality is used in two senses in this study. The first is as a demographic characteristic, which is classificatory. Used in this way, nationality is essentially passive and serves as a descriptive variable. Nationality can also be considered active; that is, as a factor that shapes attitudes or influences behaviour. Used in this second sense, it can be an explanatory variable.

Nationality has featured in one or both of these senses in each chapter. Thus, Chapter 2 considered nationality from the perspective of representation—whether nationals are present in the Commission in proportion to their member state's relative share of the total EU population—and examined the attitudes of officials towards nationality in a passive sense. It also investigated whether some member state nationals were promoted more rapidly than others.

Chapter 4 sought to classify adherents of different models of EU governance by nationality, but it also tested whether economic and cultural values, preferred models of EU governance, or attitudes towards the desirability of expanding EU competences in certain policy areas can be explained by nationality.[19] Chapter 5, meanwhile, sought to identify which nationals are most likely to adhere to the 'Community method', and Chapter 3 whether nationality is a key basis for the personal networks formed in the Commission. Chapter 7 investigated whether the defence of the national interests of the Commissioner's home state is a key objective of the *cabinets*. Nationality-based attitudes towards presidentialization and to administrative reform were similarly tested in Chapters 6 and 8 respectively. Nationality was also a central consideration in the enlargement chapter, where a key ambition was to explore similarities and differences among officials from old and new member states, as well as among the EU-12.

Three overall findings emerge from the analyses. First, officials believe that nationality is important, but only in a *passive* sense. In other words, they believe that it is important that nationals of all member states are present in the Commission's administration, but they do not expect that officials will act as agents or advocates of their home country once inside the organization (Chapter 2). Interviewees spoke of the need for the Commission to have at its command both knowledge of the political systems, and especially the administrations, of the member states and the range of linguistic skills needed to allow the organization to communicate with national officials in their mother tongues. Despite their commitment to diversity, interviewees echoed the views of near half the survey respondents in opposing the idea that a strict quota—the 'geographical balance' as historically understood and inscribed in the Staff Regulations—should be enforced in recruitment or promotion.

Second, nationality appeared *not* to be a major factor in Commission personnel policy, the functioning of key structures, or in the conduct of its

[19] Chapter 4 went a step further by defining nationality in terms of experience of specific models of domestic governance (see also Hooghe 2005).

officials. Although nationality was a consideration in recruitment as part of EU enlargement,[20] examination of the share of senior manager positions by nationality showed no evidence that member states are represented in proportion to their share of their population. Neither, as noted above, are *cabinets* considered to be either advocates of the member states or enclaves of national interest. Only a minority of officials in the services considered that *cabinets* were too preoccupied with developments in the national capitals, while members of *cabinets* did not themselves regard protecting the interests of their Commissioner's home state, maintaining links with the Commissioner's national capital, or advancing the careers of his or her compatriots within the administration as a priority.[21]

Furthermore, a majority of officials expressed confidence that nationality does not unduly influence the conduct of their colleagues. Just over a half of respondents to the online survey did not consider it a problem if officials were given responsibility for handling issues salient to their home state.[22] Interviewees asked to reflect on this response, meanwhile, pointed to rules designed to safeguard against the influence of the nationals of any member state becoming too influential in the Commission.[23] Some are longstanding, such as the prohibition on compatriots serving in the same portfolio area as Director-General and Commissioner or as senior officials occupying adjacent hierarchical positions. Others, including strict procedures governing financial management and control, were adopted as part of the Kinnock–Prodi reforms. Beyond these formal rules are informal taboos that censure officials who appear to be too closely identified with their home state.

As an explanatory factor, nationality was significant in a number of instances—a third finding. In several chapters, hypotheses were framed in terms of nationality, which was presented in Chapter 1 as a version of the socialization thesis (see below). For example, Chapter 4 shows that nationality shapes the model of EU governance that officials favour. State-centrists are most likely to come from larger (centralized) member states, while supranationalists tend to be from smaller and more decentralized member states.

---

[20] See European Commission (2011).

[21] Even the responsibility within *cabinets* for maintaining relations with the Commissioner's home state is no longer necessarily reserved for a compatriot of the Commissioner.

[22] In responding to the survey, 48 per cent opposed geographical balance, 35 per cent approved; 51 per cent did not consider it a problem if officials handled issues salient to their home country against 34 per cent who did.

[23] The question in the follow-up interviews was phrased as follows: 'We received a somewhat puzzling response to the two questions we asked in the survey about the role of nationality... Question a: "Some argue that posts in the Commission should be distributed on the basis of geographical balance. What is your view?" Answer: 48 per cent opposed such a distribution; 35 per cent were in support. Question b: "Some think that it is problematic for Commission officials to manage dossiers of special interest to their own member state. What do you think?" Answer: 34 per cent thought it problematic; 51 per cent did not consider it a problem'.

Nationality was also a factor, although only secondarily so, in explaining attitudes towards reform.[24]

In summary, the evidence from both the EUCIQ survey and the interviews is that nationality plays a relatively minor role in the life of the Commission. Though it continues to feature in a passive sense, recruitment is the only area where nationality appears to remain important otherwise. In traditional sites, such as promotion and the role and action of the *cabinets*, its influence is negligible. To that extent, the Commission can be qualified as a post-national administration.

Political partisanship

Though not generally considered to be as important as nationality, political partisanship is nevertheless thought to have played a role in some periods and in some areas of the life of the Commission. Accounts of the Delors Presidency vividly portray the importance of partisanship. Ross (1995), for example, points to a network of socialists mobilized by Pascal Lamy, Delors's *chef de cabinet*. Political affiliation was considered important in the composition of *cabinets* before 1999, when the larger member states appointed two Commissioners and often opted to balance the ideological ticket.

In the EUCIQ project, the issue of political partisanship and its significance was addressed in the interviews. The following questions were asked:

- 'Past studies of national civil services—particularly in Europe—have found that the party affiliation or party sympathy of top managers is often important. How important is the party affiliation or party sympathy of officials in the Commission?'[25]

- 'If you don't mind us asking, do you belong to a political party?'[26]

- 'How important is party affiliation for *cabinet* members?'[27]

- 'Our survey results suggest that officials in the Commission find the use of informal contacts important to get things done. We asked respondents to think about the persons they consult about work-related issues and

[24] Although Anglo-Saxons and Scandinavians do not exhibit strong views either way, officials from northern and southern continental member states were negatively disposed towards the reform (see Chapter 9). Neither was nationality a factor in explaining ratings of the strength of Commission Presidents (see Chapter 6).

[25] Respondents were offered the following options: Party affiliation is very important; It is important; Sometimes it plays a role, sometimes not; It is not very important; It does not play any role at all.

[26] Respondents could reply: No, never; In the past, not anymore; Yes, but I am not active; Yes, and I am still active.

[27] This question was asked only of *cabinet* members. The options were: Party affiliation is very important; It is important; Sometimes it plays a role, sometimes not; It is not very important; It does not play any role at all.

whether the link is based on . . . nationality, party affiliation, having worked together in the past, or sharing the same language, regional identity (e.g. Nordic) or education. Party affiliation came last. Does that surprise you?'[28]

- 'In your experience, is this [the importance of party affiliation] something that has increased or diminished over time?'[29]

The responses gave no indication that political affiliation is a significant factor in the life of the Commission. Few managers (fewer than 5 per cent of the 119 interviewed), though more *cabinet* members (43 per cent of the 28 interviewed), thought that party affiliation or sympathy was important or very important for senior managers.[30] A frequent refrain among officials was to paraphrase quotations cited in Chapter 2: 'I have no idea of the political leanings of my colleagues'. More considered it important for *cabinet* members (19 per cent of managers; 54 per cent of *cabinet* members). Meanwhile, party membership was also very low among officials that we interviewed. Fewer than ten per cent of managers and nine *cabinet* members of the twenty-five who answered the question indicated that they were members of political parties. Finally, neither managers nor *cabinet* officials were surprised that shared party sympathies did not feature more prominently as the basis of personal networks. In summary, political partisanship appears to play a negligible role in the life of the Commission. To that extent, the organization can be characterized as a post- or non-partisan administration.

While they do not affiliate with particular parties, however, officials do express ideological or philosophical views (see Chapter 4). In terms of their economic values, they tend to be pro-market rather than to favour government intervention, and on cultural issues situate themselves very close to the liberal end of the spectrum. There is evidence that ideological views are not randomly distributed within the organization. For example, individuals in social DGs are significantly more likely to be left of centre, and individuals in market DGs more likely right of centre. In addition, officials from the newer member states tend to have a distinctive ideological profile from those of the EU-15: they are more right-of-centre on economic issues, and more conservative on socio-cultural issues. Setting the agenda on policies is rarely value-free, and Commission officials are acutely conscious of this fact.

[28] The responses offered were: Yes; No; Don't know; Prefer not to say.
[29] The options were: Increased; Decreased; Stayed the same; Don't know; Prefer not to say.
[30] The different views expressed by officials compared to *cabinet* members and the different perceptions of the extent to which partisanship is relevant to the services on the one hand and the *cabinets* on the other is related to the broader theme of politicization. On this subject, and for a treatment based on EUCIQ data, see Bauer and Ege (2012). See also Wille (2011, 2010).

Technocracy

A common criticism levelled against the Commission is that it is a techno-cratic institution.[31] Technocracy in the purest sense is a system in which experts govern. As Radaelli (1999: 3) contends, however, there are few advo-cates of 'a government of scientists, or a Soviet of technicians'. However, with the rise of the importance of knowledge and expertise, as exemplified by the regulatory state, a technocratic mentality on the part of administrations can be nurtured and encouraged. According to Radaelli (1999: 4), a technocrat is

> fundamentally hostile to the openness of democracy, and suspicious of parlia-mentary institutions (Putnam 1976; see also Meynaud 1968). Political conflict is not considered a healthy component of democracy, but a consequence of ignor-ance. Rational analysis . . . produces efficient solutions that should be accepted by all people of good will.

Certainly, the Commission has a technocratic past. The European Coal and Steel Community (Featherstone 1994) was a technocratic project. Moreover, the Monnet method of *engrenage*—the close interaction of technical experts and interest groups working in tandem like the gears of a clock (Coombes 1970: 86–91)—envisaged little or no input from political actors or the wider populace.

Although technocracy was not a major theme of EUCIQ, a number of questions that bear on the issue were asked in the face-to-face interviews. The aim was to test the image of the Commission official as a technocrat,[32] and to examine the extent to which officials regard their work as technical or political. Managers were asked to give their responses to the following three questions:

- 'In policy-making it is essential for the good of the European Union that technical considerations are accorded more weight than political factors';
- 'In order to assess the work of the services properly, it is necessary to eliminate political considerations'; and
- 'The European Union should be judged on the basis of the effectiveness of its policies, rather than any other criteria.'

The responses to these questions suggested that most Commission officials do *not* conceive of their work as purely technical. Thirty-four per cent agreed with the first proposition, but over 60 per cent disagreed. Managers also reject the idea that the performance of the services should be judged on the basis of technical criteria alone. Fifty-three per cent disagreed that political consider-ations should be eliminated. However, over 80 per cent thought that the EU should be judged on the basis of its policy effectiveness.

---

[31] On the Commission and technocracy, see Featherstone (1994); Radaelli (1999); Wonka (2007).
[32] French President Charles de Gaulle famously pronounced the Commission to be a 'tech-nocratic, stateless, and irresponsible Areopagus' (Snyder 1968: 101).

These responses suggest that the self-image of the Commission's officials is nuanced. Officials tend to hold mildly positive views of politics.[33] Indeed, they believe that political considerations need to be taken into account in their work and that the services and the EU need to be judged according to political, as well as technical, criteria.

Is the Commission a sui generis or singular administration?

Whether the Commission is a unique organization among international administrations or compared with to national bureaucracies has long been contested (see, for example, Siotis 1964; Coombes 1970). Discussions in the academic literature often lack clarity as to the grounds on which the Commission is thought to be comparable to or distinct from other administrations.[34] Although the Commission may be different from national bureaucracies—in terms of its multinational composition, shadowing by member governments, distance from political authority, responsibility for policy initiation, and limited involvement in policy delivery on the front line—these are dimensions of variation that invite rather than limit comparison with other international administrations.[35]

Compared to national administrations, the Commission's powers and functions are unique. However, the current study has sought as far as possible to examine the Commission as an administration from a comparative perspective. A surprising paucity of systematic data on national administrations—comparative data on some aspects of personnel policy and of financial management and control collected by the OECD is an exception—has limited the extent to which direct comparisons could be drawn.[36] Hence, the book has sought to pursue its comparative ambition in three ways.

First, it has drawn on the literature on public administration to frame lines of enquiry. Thus, the book looks at the educational and professional backgrounds of officials, and at their values and beliefs. It also considers issues of hierarchy, coordination, and bureaucratic politics. In this way the findings speak to the broader literature.[37] Second, the book has grounded the hypotheses that it tests in general theories of administration, administrative behaviour, and political attitudes. In several chapters, candidate explanations are framed in terms of competing theories. As outlined in Chapter 1 these are

---

[33] Managers were asked whether they agreed or disagreed with the following proposition: 'The European Parliament and/or the Council of Ministers too often interfere with the work of the European Commission'. Eighty per cent disagreed.

[34] The issue can be posed as a question about any of the following aspects of the Commission: its powers and responsibilities; its internal organization; its staffing; or its personnel policy.

[35] See, for example, Bauer and Knill (2007); Trondal (2010: ch. 6).

[36] Though see Balint et al. (2008).

[37] Pollitt and Bouckaert (2004) is a model of research of this kind, as is Webb (2000), although it addresses an entirely unrelated topic.

socialization theory, which holds that 'individuals acquire attitudes by intern-alizing the values of the groups or institutions in which they live or work', and utility maximization, according to which 'attitudes reflect the desire to maximize utility'. Third, where possible, the Commission has been located relative to established ideal-types or national paradigms. This last exercise was especially important in assessing the extent to which the Commission has changed over time.[38]

In comparative terms, the Commission is a career-based, as opposed to an open, bureaucracy in regard to recruitment. Staff are promoted according to merit, but when new member countries accede to the EU, officials are recruited in significant numbers to management positions from outside the service. There are differences between DG types in terms of the educational and professional backgrounds of officials, and economic and cultural values: social policy-oriented DGs were significantly more social-democratic than DGs handling market integration.

Moreover, the Commission is an administration in which information flows relatively freely both between different levels and between specialized services. Information-sharing and horizontal coordination are—somewhat surprisingly in view of how the existing literature has depicted the organization–not viewed as problematic by officials. Finally, as Chapter 8 shows, the reforms undertaken by the Prodi Commission have aligned the Commission more closely with national administrations in terms of procedures and practices relating to financial management and audit control.

CONCLUSION: BEYOND THE MYTHS

This study has addressed a number of fundamental questions about one of the world's most powerful international administrations and the people who work for it.[39] It has investigated the backgrounds, beliefs, and careers of Commission officials, examined the operation, roles, and interaction of key structures within the organization, and explored staff attitudes and responses to the

[38] An initial 'normalization' hypothesis was that the Commission has become less singular and is more like other bureaucracies. However, the difficulty of establishing a reference point given the diversity of existing administrative models made such a thesis difficult to validate or falsify.

[39] The current study has not been exhaustive. First, there were questions that it did not ask: for example, how officials in a multinational organization negotiate linguistic and cultural differences in their daily work, or why Commission officials choose to remain in the organization rather than moving elsewhere. Second, some questions that were included did not yield data sufficiently robust to analyse. This was the case concerning questions about role definition, for example, following the work of Aberbach et al. (1981). Third, not all findings or analysis of the data could be reported due to limitations on space.

challenges of administrative reform and the 2004 and 2007 enlargements. Drawing on original primary source material, gathered through an online survey and structured programme of follow-up interviews, it offers a detailed portrait of an institution that not only affects the daily life of citizens in EU member states, but whose influence is felt far beyond. Though recognizing the connection between the two, the aim has been explicitly to consider the Commission as an administration rather than to assess its relative power and influence in EU decision-making.

The picture of the Commission that emerges from this volume is very different from the portrayal of the organization in much of the academic literature and, especially, from the image that has become entrenched in the public mind. The Commission of the twenty-first century is not populated by federalists, lifelong bureaucrats, or lawyers. It is not a fragmented body where determinedly introspective departments fiercely protect their turf, refuse to share information with their counterparts, or resist coordination and cooperation; where cabinets are bastions of national interest, seeking to advance the agenda of their Commissioner's national capital, and permanently at war with each other and the services; or where leadership is a near-impossibility. The organization has not been brought to a halt by enlargement; nor is it an antiquated bureaucracy that is unwilling or unable to embrace new administrative procedures and practices.

The Commission of the twenty-first century commands a workforce with an impressive range of subject expertise and professional experience. Officials may join the Commission because they want to 'build Europe', but material incentives and professional considerations are also important. Officials are not overwhelmingly supranational idealists or technocrats. Nor do their beliefs reflect an ingrained institutional credo that there should always be more Europe.

The Commission of the twenty-first century is not a fragmented institution. Power and authority is implanted firmly at the centre of the organization. It is not only that the centrifugal pressures described by Coombes (1970) and later writers have been checked, but that under the Barroso Presidency the Commission has been led from the top. The close relationship between the Commission Presidency and the Secretariat-General, moreover, has ensured that planning, resource allocation, and coordination have been more effective than under previous presidents. Furthermore, the functional denationalization of the *cabinets* has removed a major source of tension at the political level of the organization, as well as between *cabinets* and services.

Officials may not have been impressed by the way in which enlargement was managed, but they appreciate the talent, vigour, and enthusiasm of their colleagues recruited from the EU-12. Attitudes towards administrative reform are similarly ambivalent, but despite misgivings the implementation of the Kinnock–Prodi programme has brought Commission practices more closely in line with prevailing public management wisdoms, distancing the Commission even from the 'golden age' of Delors. In the modern Commission, neither nationality nor partisan affiliation has much day-to-day significance. To that extent, the administration is post-national and post-partisanal.

At the same time, the findings reported above do not suggest that the Commission is an administration without flaw or fault-lines. Indeed, they indicate that there are at least four issues that could develop into serious problems. The first is the extent to which larger member states are under-represented within the administration.[40] As discussed in Chapter 2, France, Germany, Italy, Poland, and the UK have fewer officials, especially in management positions, than their share of the total EU population would suggest. Given the importance of the responsibilities that it exercises, the impact that its decisions have within the member states, and the scrutiny under which it operates, the Commission could find itself in difficulty if key states are under-represented among its staff, especially if they happen to be the most populous and the most wealthy. It is true that in absolute terms, France, Germany, and Italy have the largest contingents among Commission personnel, and the UK is in sixth place (after Belgium and Spain), ensuring that the organization commands critical insider knowledge and expertise. Moreover, such malapportionment is not unusual in federal-type systems (see, for examples, Amoretti and Bermeo 2004). Even so, in a climate where the democratic deficit is increasingly salient, the under-representation of the member states in question could pose a problem for the Commissionand even call its legitimacy into question.

Second, the 2004 and 2007 enlargements have introduced a young, talented and dynamic cohort of officials into the Commission. At the same time, however, officials from the newer member states are less committed to the traditional conception of the European project. They hold more liberal economic values than their counterparts from the older member states, but are more socially conservative. As well as different aspirations and ambitions, they may have different expectations as to the EU's role and different policy preferences. The implications are potentially far-reaching. If the demographic balance of the Commission continues along the same path, ideological debates within the organization may become more intense and established Commission policy nostrums challenged or changed.

Third, gender balance remains a problem. The percentage of women within the organization has increased significantly in the recent past, and enlargement has made the Commission a more female administration. In addition, the small number of female managers have reached that position more rapidly than their male counterparts. However, women remain over-represented in the lower echelons and under-represented at the top. It is unclear whether or how that position is likely to change in the coming years.

---

[40] It is even greater in international general secretariats.

Fourth, officials are divided on the desirability both of a strong Commission President and of an interventionist Secretariat-General closely identified with the Commission Presidency. Although some officials support the idea of presidential leadership as the only way for the Commission to be effective when the College is twenty-seven (plus) strong and the member states are wary of Commission action, others express concern about the impact on morale, especially among senior managers, on the grounds that officials can no longer be entrepreneurs. Senior politicians may also be less inclined to serve in the College if they cannot be personally identified with policy success.

On the Secretariat-General, opinion was divided both on its close identification with the Commission President and on its more proactive role. For some officials, it is normal for the Secretariat-General to serve the Commission President, in the same way that other DGs are responsible to their Commissioners. However, others took the view that the Commission should be a collegial or, more properly, a collective body and that the Secretariat-General should be at the service of the College. On the question of the Secretariat-General's greater influence and interventionism, recognition of the need for improved coordination was mitigated by a strong sense that policy expertise and therefore policy ownership should reside with line DGs.

Any one of these issues could emerge as problematic. The difficulty for the Commission is that, as in many areas of its operation, its ability to address or to resolve them will be limited. The Commission is to a large extent a dependent institution (see Kassim 2008). The rules under which it operates and the resources allocated to it are decided elsewhere by other bodies or other actors, with their own priorities, attention cycle, and constituencies to serve.

These considerations aside, the preceding pages reveal an organization that is better equipped than is widely assumed or asserted to meet the challenges that confront the Union. It has proved robust in the face of transformations, internal and external, that have led to far-reaching change in its operation and composition. It has also shown itself to be adaptable to the changed circumstances of an environment that is markedly less conducive to and more sceptical of EU action than the era that began with the Single European Act and closed with the Maastricht Treaty. In uncertain times, there is no expectation that these attributes will be any less important.

Appendices

1. Online survey: 'The Commission of the Twenty-First Century. Views from the Inside'
2. Interview template for Commissioners
3. Interview template for *chefs decabinet* and members of *cabinet*
4. Interview template for middle and senior managers
5. List of interviews
6. Explaining perceptions of politicization in the Commission
7. Explaining variation in general desire for EU policy scope
8. Personal and national characteristics supporting the Community Method
9. Probability that Delors is considered strong in each of the following dimensions
10. Probability that Santer is considered strong in each of the following dimensions
11. Probability that Prodi is considered strong in each of the following dimensions
12. Probability that Barroso is considered strong in each of the following dimensions

Appendix 1. The Commission of the Twenty-First Century: Views from the inside. An independent survey of the European Commission

This survey is being conducted purely for the purposes of scientific research. It aims to be one of the most comprehensive surveys of the Commission in its history.

We are an international team of researchers based at universities in the EU. We are entirely independent of the Commission and work within the EU-CONSENT Network, partially funded through the Framework Six Research Programme.

The survey is strictly anonymous. You cannot be personally identified from your answers.

Some of our questions originated in previous surveys. They are included here to compare changes over time.

If you do not wish to answer any question, please tick 'prefer not to say' or 'don't know', as appropriate.

This survey is part of a long-term study, which will involve further surveys, interviews, and focus groups. Your completion of the survey in no way commits you to any further engagement. We will publish aggregated results only after we have completed the full study.

To protect privacy, the questionnaire has been designed to be completed in a single session. The programme will automatically disconnect and all data will be lost after 30 minutes of inactivity. Please contact us to know more.

NB: If you wish to ask us any questions before you respond to this survey, we would be pleased to hear from you. You would, of course, remain anonymous. Any queries that you might have would remain confidential. Please telephone us (from 10am-6pm WEST) at: UK + 44 (0)131 . . . or click here [send email to . . .].

PART I. YOUR BACKGROUND

We would like to ask you about what attracted you to work for the Commission, your background, and your career path.

1 Why did you choose to follow a career in the European Commission? (Please choose as many as are relevant).

- Job stability
- Promising career prospects
- Competitive remuneration
- Commitment to Europe
- Commitment to a particular policy area
- Quality of the work
- I was asked to apply
- Other: _____
- Prefer not to say

2 And in which year did you join the Commission?   _____

3 What is your educational background?

Highest educational qualification:
- *University (undergraduate) degree*
- *Postgraduate degree*
- *Other_____*
- *Prefer not to say*
Subject of main degree:
- *Law*
- *Economics*
- *Politics/International Relations*
- *Arts*
- *Physical Sciences*
- *Engineering*
- *Other _____*
- *Don't know/Prefer not to say*

4 Did you study in a country *other* than the country of your present nationality?

- *No*
- *Yes, up to one year*
- *Yes, more than one year*
- *Prefer not to say*

5 What career, if any, did you follow before you entered the Commission, and for how long?

(Please choose as many as are relevant and indicate the number of years for each)

Your career
- International organisation (non-EU)
- Civil service (national, regional or local)
- Trade union, social movement
- Political party, politics
- Liberal professions
- Private enterprise
- Education, research
- Journalism, public relations
- Other EU institution
- None
- Other
- Prefer not to say
- Member of cabinet

6

What position do you currently hold in the
Commission?

- Senior Management (Director
  General, Deputy Dir Gen,
  Director)
- Advisor (or Assistant to Director
  General)
- Middle Manager (Head of Unit)
- Administrator [or Principal
  Administrator]
- Other _____

[FOR ADMINISTRATORS ONLY]

What is your *primary* function at the current time?
Please tick the box that corresponds most closely.

O Steering jobs
O Relational jobs
O Implementation jobs
O Support jobs
O Prefer not to say

7   What year did you take up your current post?   _____

8   What positions have you previously held in the EU
     administration?

In the Commission: Member of
cabinet
In the Commission: Senior
Management
In the Commission: Advisor

(Please choose as many as are relevant. If you
previously worked in multiple other EU
institutions, please indicate (by numbering in the
boxes) the order in which you worked in each).

In the Commission: Middle Manager
In the Commission: Administrator
[or Principal Administrator]
In the Commission: Other
In the Council of Ministers
In the European Parliament
In another EU institution or body
In a European agency
None of the above
Other
Prefer not to say

If you selected 'other', please identify the organisation below
Please indicate the order in which you worked in each position, below. Please use '1' to indicate
your first job, '2' your second, et cetera.

In the Commission: Member of
cabinet
In the Commission: Senior
Management
In the Commission: Advisor
In the Commission: Middle Manager
In the Commission: Administrator
[or Principal Administrator]
In the Commission: Other
In the Council of Ministers
In the European Parliament
In another EU institution or body
In a European agency
Administration (ADMIN)

9

a) Which is your current Directorate-General/ service?

[QUESTION NOT ASKED OF CABINET MEMBERS]

Agriculture and Rural Development (AGRI)
Budget (BUDG)
Bureau of European Policy Advisors (BEPA) Cabinet
Communication (COMM)
Competition (COMP)
Development (DEV)
Economic and Financial Affairs (ECFIN)
Education and Culture (EAC)
Employment, Social Affairs, Equal Opportunities (EMPL)
Energy and Transport (TREN)
Enlargement (ELARG)
Enterprise and Industry (ENTR)
Environment (ENV)
EuropeAid (AIDCO)
European Anti-Fraud Office (OLAF)
European Personnel Selection Office (EPSO)
Eurostat (ESTAT)
External Relations (RELEX)
Fisheries and Maritime Affairs (MARE)
Health and Consumer Protection (SANCO)
Humanitarian Aid (ECHO)
Informatics (DIGIT)
Information Society and Media (INFSO)
Internal Audit Service (IAS)
Internal Market and Services (MARKT)
Interpretation (SCIC)
Joint Research Centre (JRC)
Justice, Freedom and Security (JLS)
Legal Service (SJ)
Regional Policy (REGIO)
Research (RTD)
Secretariat-General (SG)
Taxation and Customs Union (TAXUD)
Trade (TRADE)
Translation (DGT)
Other
Don't know
Prefer not to say

If you selected 'other', please indicate your department or organisation below. _____

b. And in which (other) DGs have you worked during your career?

Please indicate the designation (SG, REGIO, etc), or closest equivalent (since many names have changed).

Administration (ADMIN)
Agriculture and Rural Development (AGRI)
Budget (BUDG)
Bureau of European Policy Advisors (BEPA)
Cabinet
Communication (COMM)
Competition (COMP)
Development (DEV)
Economic and Financial Affairs (ECFIN)
Education and Culture (EAC)
Employment, Social Affairs, Equal Opportunities (EMPL)
Energy and Transport (TREN)
Enlargement (ELARG)
Enterprise and Industry (ENTR)
Environment (ENV)
EuropeAid (AIDCO)
European Anti-Fraud Office (OLAF)
European Personnel Selection Office (EPSO)
Eurostat (ESTAT)
External Relations (RELEX)
Fisheries and Maritime Affairs (MARE)
Health and Consumer Protection (SANCO)
Humanitarian Aid (ECHO)
Informatics (DIGIT)
Information Society and Media (INFSO)
Internal Audit Service (IAS)
Internal Market and Services (MARKT)
Interpretation (SCIC)

If you selected 'other', please specify this below.

Joint Research Centre (JRC)
Justice, Freedom and Security (JLS)
Legal Service (SJ)
Regional Policy (REGIO)
Research (RTD)
Secretariat-General (SG)
Taxation and Customs Union (TAXUD)
Trade (TRADE)

		Translation (DGT)
		Other
		None
		Don't know
		Prefer not to say
10	What is your (present) nationality?	*[Drop down menu]*
	Do you have more than one nationality?	Yes
		No
		Prefer not to say
11	What is your year of birth?	_____
12	What is your gender?	? Male
		? Female

PART II: YOUR PHILOSOPHICAL VIEWS

13. We would like to ask some questions concerning your philosophical views. We understand that the choices offered are simplifications, but they are useful for comparison. Please tick where you stand on a scale from 0 to 10

   (a) People often think of themselves in terms of their personal *philosophical stance on economic issues.* Some favour an *active role for government* on economic policy questions. Others look primarily to markets. Where would you place yourself in terms of *economic philosophy on a scale of 0–10 (below), where 0 represents a greater role for government and 10 a greater role for markets?*

   A greater role   *A greater role*
   for government   *for markets*
   0——1——2——3——4——5——6——7——8——9——10

   (b) *People often think of themselves in terms of their personal philosophical stance on social and cultural issues. Many people who consider themselves to be progressive/libertarian tend to favour expanded personal freedoms on (for example) abortion, same-sex marriage, and so on. People on the conservative/traditionalist side tend to favour more traditional notions of family, morality, and order. Where would you place yourself in terms of social-cultural philosophy on a scale of 0–10 (below), where 0 represents more liberal and 10 more conservative?*

   More liberal   *More conservative.*
   0——1——2——3——4——5——6——7——8——9——10

PART III—TODAY'S EUROPEAN UNION

14. *We are interested in your views about where power should reside in the European Union.*

	Strongly agree	Tend to agree	Neither agree nor disagree	Tend to disagree	Strongly disagree	Not sure
a. Some people want the College of Commissioners to become the government of the European Union. What do you think?	1	2	3	4	5	6
b. Some argue that member states—not the Commission or European Parliament—should be the central players in the European Union. What is your position?	1	2	3	4	5	6
c. Some want the Commission to share its sole right of legislative initiative with the European Parliament. What is your view?	1	2	3	4	5	6
d. Some think the Commission should primarily focus on managing existing policies, rather than developing new ones. What do you think?	1	2	3	4	5	6

15. *We are interested in your views on the Commission's role, and how it may be changing.*

	Strongly agree	Tend to agree	Neither agree nor disagree	Tend to disagree	Strongly disagree	Not sure
a) The Commission's role is evolving in the direction of more policy management and coordination, and less policy conception.	1	2	3	4	5	6
b) The more member states the EU has, the more important is the Commission's role as policy initiator.	1	2	3	4	5	6

16. *We are interested in your views on the distribution of authority between member states and the EU on a range of policies.*

Please start by giving us your assessment of the *actual* distribution in 2008.
Where is each policy decided?

	Exclusively EU	Exclusively national/sub-national
Agriculture	0—1—2—3—4—5—6—7—8—9—10	
Energy policy	0—1—2—3—4—5—6—7—8—9—10	
Social policy	0—1—2—3—4—5—6—7—8—9—10	
Development policy	0—1—2—3—4—5—6—7—8—9—10	
Regional development	0—1—2—3—4—5—6—7—8—9—10	
Competition policy	0—1—2—3—4—5—6—7—8—9—10	
Environmental policy	0—1—2—3—4—5—6—7—8—9—10	
Foreign and security policies	0—1—2—3—4—5—6—7—8—9—10	
Asylum and immigration	0—1—2—3—4—5—6—7—8—9—10	
Trade policy	0—1—2—3—4—5—6—7—8—9—10	
Police and judicial cooperation	0—1—2—3—4—5—6—7—8—9—10	

Where should this policy be decided?

	Exclusively EU	Exclusively national/sub-national
Agriculture	0—1—2—3—4—5—6—7—8—9—10	
Energy policy	0—1—2—3—4—5—6—7—8—9—10	
Social policy	0—1—2—3—4—5—6—7—8—9—10	
Development policy	0—1—2—3—4—5—6—7—8—9—10	
Regional development	0—1—2—3—4—5—6—7—8—9—10	
Competition policy	0—1—2—3—4—5—6—7—8—9—10	
Environmental policy	0—1—2—3—4—5—6—7—8—9—10	
Foreign and security policies	0—1—2—3—4—5—6—7—8—9—10	
Asylum and immigration	0—1—2—3—4—5—6—7—8—9—10	
Trade policy	0—1—2—3—4—5—6—7—8—9—10	
Police and judicial cooperation	0—1—2—3—4—5—6—7—8—9—10	

Appendices

17. *We would like to know your views on the recruitment of officials to the Commission and who should do specific jobs.*

	Strongly agree	Tend to agree	Neither agree nor disagree	Tend to disagree	Strongly disagree	Not sure
a) Some argue that posts in the Commission should be distributed on the basis of geographical balance. What is your view?	1	2	3	4	5	6
b) Some think that it is problematic for Commission officials to manage dossiers of special interest to their own member state. What do you think?	1	2	3	4	5	6

18. *We are interested in your views on how the 2004 and 2007 enlargements have affected the Commission and its work.*

What is your position on the following statements?	Strongly agree	Tend to agree	Neither agree nor disagree	Tend to disagree	Strongly disagree	Not sure
a) Enlargement has strengthened *esprit de corps* within the Commission's administration	1	2	3	4	5	6
b) A 27 member College makes co-ordination more difficult	1	2	3	4	5	6
c) It is more important to have one Commissioner per member state than to have a smaller and more efficient College	1	2	3	4	5	6
d) The consequences of enlargement for career development have been handled with equity and fairness	1	2	3	4	5	6

PART IV. YOUR EXPERIENCE OF
WORK IN THE COMMISSION

19. *We are interested in your responsibilities within the Commission and your view on your institutional environment.*
    Your unit/department

How many staff do you manage?	Total Number
[TO BE ASKED OF HEADS OF UNIT, DIRECTORS, DIRECTORS GENERAL]	☐ 0–5
	☐ 6–10
	☐ 11–15
	☐ 15–20
	☐ 20–25
	☐ More than 25
	☐ Don't know

20. *We would like to ask your view(s) on the flow of information within the Commission.*

What is your position on the following statements:	Strongly agree	Tend to agree	Neither agree nor disagree	Tend to disagree	Strongly disagree	Not sure
a) Information is power and people too often conceal it within the Commission	1	2	3	4	5	6
b) Information relevant to my job is easy to obtain from colleagues within my unit	1	2	3	4	5	6
c) Information relevant to my job is easy to obtain from colleagues within my DG	1	2	3	4	5	6
d) Information relevant to my job is easy to obtain from colleagues in other DGs	1	2	3	4	5	6

21. *We are interested in your views about how formal or informal are interactions within the Commission.*

What is your position on the following statements:	*Strongly agree*	*Tend to agree*	*Neither agree nor disagree*	*Tend to disagree*	*Strongly disagree*	*Not sure*
a) *To get its work done, the Commission must rely more on informal networks than formal hierarchies.*	1	2	3	4	5	6

b) *In your experience, what are the most important bases for informal networks in the Commission?*

Nationality
Ideology or party affiliation
Personal (e.g. previously worked in the same unit or team)
Language group

(Please choose THREE (3) & RANK in order of importance, i.e:

1. *Most important of all*
2. *2ⁿᵈ most important*
3. *3ʳᵈ most important*

Regional identity (e.g. Nordic, Mediterranean, etc)
Educational background (e.g. College of Europe)
Other
Not sure

[FOR ADMINISTRATORS ONLY]

22. *We would like to ask you about the people to whom you regularly turn for infor-mation or advice on professional matters (in person, phone, e-mail, and so on). We do NOT necessarily mean the Commission officials whom you are obliged to contact in carrying out your responsibilities or due to the regulations of the house, such as your manager or direct colleagues.*

Please note: we do not wish to know who may be part of your own professional network; we simply wish to know about the nature of networks in the commission generally.

Please think about three people to whom you turn for information or advice. We will ask you questions about each person individually.

[drop-down options to facilitate answering]	*Person 1*	*Person 2*	*Person 3*
How long have you known this person? (years)	Less than 1 year	Less than 1 year	Less than 1 year
	1 to 2 years	1 to 2 years	1 to 2 years
	2 to 3 years	2 to 3 years	2 to 3 years
	3 to 4 years	3 to 4 years	3 to 4 years
	4 to 5 years	4 to 5 years	4 to 5 years
	More than 5 years	More than 5 years	More than 5 years
	Not sure	Not sure	Not sure
On which issues do you usually consult this person? [indicate more than one if you'd like] Career issues; policy advice; procedural advice; other; not sure_____			
How did you first meet? Professional contact; national context; party political context; other _____			
Gender: M or F			
Age of this person: your age group, at least 10 years younger, at least 10 years older			
What is this person's country of nationality?			
Do you share the same mother tongue?			
Usual language of communication? Your's, their's, third language, it varies			
Ideological affinities: similar to yours, quite different, don't know			
What is this person's grade compared to yours: junior, senior, about the same			

PART V: THE COMMISSION AS AN ORGANIZATION

23. *We are interested in relationships between different parts of the Commission and categories of Commission official Please think generally; not just about your own— or your Commissioner's—Directorate General*

What is your position on the following statements:	Strongly agree	Tend to agree	Neither agree nor disagree	Tend to disagree	Strongly disagree	Not sure
a) Commission officials work for their Directorate General first, then for the Commission	*1*	*2*	*3*	*4*	*5*	*6*
b) A change in Director General usually has a greater impact on working methods of a DG than a change in Commissioner	*1*	*2*	*3*	*4*	*5*	*6*
c) It is the responsibility of the services to support the politically-agreed positions of the College	*1*	*2*	*3*	*4*	*5*	*6*

24. *We are also interested in your views on coordination*

What is your position on the following statements:	Strongly agree	Tend to agree	Neither agree nor disagree	Tend to disagree	Strongly disagree	Not sure
a) Coordination works effectively in my unit	1	2	3	4	5	6
b) Coordination works effectively in my DG	1	2	3	4	5	6
c) Coordination works effectively between DGs	1	2	3	4	5	6
d) Coordination works effectively between the services and the College (including cabinets)	1	2	3	4	5	6

25. *We are interested in the role of the Secretariat General.*

What is your position on the following statements:	Strongly agree	Tend to agree	Neither agree nor disagree	Tend to disagree	Strongly disagree	Not sure
a) The Secretariat General is a neutral arbiter between the services in policy coordination	1	2	3	4	5	6
b) The Secretariat General focuses too much on procedure, and not enough on policy content	1	2	3	4	5	6
c) The Secretariat General is becoming more political and more influential in the life of the Commission.	1	2	3	4	5	6

26. *We would like to ask your views on the role of cabinets in the Commission.*

What is your view on the following statements:	Strongly agree	Tend to agree	Neither agree nor disagree	Tend to disagree	Strongly disagree	Not sure
a) On the whole, the *cabinets* respect the technical expertise of the services	1	2	3	4	5	6
b) The *cabinets* are too preoccupied by developments in their Commissioners' national capitals	1	2	3	4	5	6

27. *We would like to ask your views on recent administrative reforms.*

Thinking of the administrative reforms implemented since 2000, what are your views on the following statements?	Strongly agree	Tend to agree	Neither agree nor disagree	Tend to disagree	Strongly disagree	Not sure
a) I have become more efficient in my day-to-day work	1	2	3	4	5	6
b) The negative effects on me personally—in terms of benefits and promotion—outweigh any general benefits to the house	1	2	3	4	5	6
c) My unit/service has become more efficient	1	2	3	4	5	6
d) Personnel management has become leaner and more focused	1	2	3	4	5	6
e) Resources are better matched to policy priorities	1	2	3	4	5	6
f) The new tools and rules are applied in a formalistic way, which means they have not produced their intended effects	1	2	3	4	5	6
g) The new tools and rules lead to more red-tape and increase the administrative load	1	2	3	4	5	6
h) It is now easier for women to advance their careers in the Commission on an equal footing	1	2	3	4	5	6

Thinking of administrative reforms, which of the following has *improved* your capacity to do your job?	Agree	Neutral	Disagree

a) *Personnel management:*
i)   Detailed job descriptions
ii) Annual appraisal exercise
iii) Deciding on staff requirements and the allocation of responsibilities
iv) Promotion
v)   Training opportunities

b) *Activity-Based Management*
i)   Drafting the Annual Activity Statement
ii) Preparing the Annual Strategy Decision (APS) and Commission Work Programme
iii) Drafting the DG Annual Management Plan (AMP)
iv) The evaluation and monitoring of achievements

c) *Financial Management and Control*
i)   The Annual Activity Report
ii) The abolition of the ex ante visa and the decentralisation of expenditure
iii) The creation of financial circuits
iv) The new audit system

None of these
Don't know

PART VI: THE COMMISSION IN HISTORICAL PERSPECTIVE

We are interested in your reflections on the institutional position of the Commission and its work.

28. *Please tell us your views on the position of the Commission relative to other EU institutions and its member states*

	Strongly agree	Tend to agree	Neither agree nor disagree	Tend to disagree	Strongly disagree	Not sure
a) The Commission is more powerful today than ever before	1	2	3	4	5	6
b) The Commission is losing power to national capitals	1	2	3	4	5	6
c) The Commission is losing power to the European Parliament	1	2	3	4	5	6

29. *We would like your views on the development of the Commission over the past twenty years.*

[Respondents presented only with Commission(s) under which they have served (as indicated by response to question 2)]

Thinking of recent Commissions (detailed next), how would you rate their performance in:	Very strong	Fairly strong	Neither strong nor weak	Fairly weak	Very weak	Not sure

The Barroso Commission
- Setting a policy agenda
- Effectively managing the house
- Delivering on policy priorities
- Defending the Commission in the EU system

The Prodi Commission
- Setting a policy agenda
- Effectively managing the house
- Delivering on policy priorities
- Defending the Commission in the EU system

The Santer Commission
- Setting a policy agenda
- Effectively managing the house
- Delivering on policy priorities
- Defending the Commission in the EU system

The Delors Commission(s)
- Setting a policy agenda
- Effectively managing the house
- Delivering on policy priorities
- Defending the Commission in the EU system

Thank you for responding to our survey. Please share any views you may have below on the questionnaire itself.

If you would be interested in further participation in this research project, please provide your e-mail address. This information will not be linked to your answers to this questionnaire to preserve your anonymity.

Appendix 2 *The Commission of the twenty-first century: views from the inside. Template for interviews with members of the Commission*

Date:		Respondent:	
Interviewers:		Interview number:	

THE COMMISSION OF THE 21ST *CENTURY: VIEWS FROM THE INSIDE*

Template for interviews with members of the Commission

Introduction

Thank you for agreeing to be interviewed. We are a team of University professors working on an independent research project. Our structured programme of interviews forms the second part of a project that we began last autumn. The first consisted of a survey that was administered to a sample of around 4000 respondents and was completed by than 2000 officials. We now are conducting interviews to help us interpret our data and find out why officials responded to our questionnaires as they did and to follow-up particular issues. We aim to interview a cross-section of *cabinet* members, as well as around 200 middle and senior managers, and a number of Commissioners.

Your anonymity is guaranteed. All responses will be treated as confidential, no comments or remarks will be attributed to a particular individual, and it will not be possible to identify the source of any of the material in our published findings.

YOUR BACKGROUND [Interviewer to append CV from Commission website]

- Your current position:
- Nationality:
- Subject of highest educational qualification:
- Professional background:
- Year of birth:
- Year of entry into Commission:
- Previous positions in the Commission:
Gender:M/F

Motivation and the role of Commissioner

1. Why did you decide to become a Commissioner?
2. Before taking up your post, what ambitions did you hope to achieve over your term?
3. How closely do you consider the following descriptions capture the job of a Commissioner? [Please hand respondent Commissioner Form Q3-see below]
4. How would you weigh the relative importance of your portfolio and your non-portfolio responsibilities?
5. In your view, what does a Commissioner need in order to be successful?
6. Some people argue that the College is a presidential body; others that it is collegial. What is your opinion?
7. What has surprised you most about how the College works?
8. How important is nationality in the work of the College?
9. How often does the College take a formal vote?
10. How could the working of the College be made more effective?
    The Commission as an organization
11. What surprised you most about the working of the Commission as an organization?
12. In our survey, most respondents said that a change in Director General was more significant for their work than a change in Commissioner. Does that surprise you?
13. What changes—political, structural, procedural—would make the Commission work more effectively?
14. Some people argue that the Commission is in decline: increasingly eclipsed by the European Council, constrained by the European Parliament, and ignored or circumvented by the member states. What is your view?
15. What are the main challenges facing the Commission?
    Reflections
16. Would do you consider your main achievements?
17. Would you do it again?

COMMISSIONER FORM Q3

Question: How closely do you consider the following descriptions capture the job of a Commissioner? Please tick all that apply.

	Very strongly	Quite Closely	Closely	Not very closely	Not at all closely
Policy entrepreneur					
Representative of the European Commission					
Representative of the European Union					
Member of a government of Europe					
Portfolio manager					
Manager of a department/ departments					
Conduit for the representation of views from the country you know best					

Appendix 3 The Commission of the twenty-first century: views from the inside. Template for interviews with members of cabinets

Date:		Respondent:	
Interviewers:		Interview number:	

THE COMMISSION OF THE 21ST CENTURY: VIEWS FROM THE INSIDE

Template for interviews with cabinet members

Introduction

Thank you for agreeing to be interviewed. We are a team of University professors working on an independent research project. Our structured programme of interviews forms the second part of a project that we began last autumn. The first consisted of a survey that was administered to a sample of around 4000 respondents and was completed by more than 2000 officials. We now are conducting interviews to help us interpret our data and find out why officials responded to our questionnaires as they did and to follow-up particular issues. We aim to interview around 200 middle and senior managers, *cabinet* members, and Commissioners.

Your anonymity is guaranteed. All responses will be treated as confidential, nothing will be attributed, and it will not be possible to identify the source of any of the material in our published findings.

YOUR BACKGROUND *[Only ask these questions if respondent has not completed prior to the interview]*

- Your current position:
- Nationality:
- Subject of highest educational qualification:
- Professional background:
- Year of birth:
- Year of entry into Commission:
- Previous positions in the Commission:
- Gender: M/F

I. THE CABINETS

Q1   Can I begin by asking why you decided to join a cabinet?
Intro   We should like to ask you about the functions and responsibilities of cabinets.
Q2a   Here is a list of roles that could be used in relation to cabinets. Could you tell us how
         closely they describe the role of your cabinet? [Hand over FORM CABS Q2a - see below]
Q2b   Are there other role descriptions missing from the above list? YES/NO
Q2c   If so, what are they?

Q3a	EITHER FOR CHEFS DE CABINETS

EITHER FOR CHEFS DE CABINETS
Here is a list of questions relating to the responsibilities of chef de cabinets. Could we ask you to rank the top three in order of your priorities? [Hand over FORM CHEF DE CABINETS Q3a - see below]

    1   2   3

Q3b   Are there any important roles functions or roles that should be added to the list?
OR: FOR OTHER CABINET MEMBERS
Here is a list of responsibilities of typical cabinet members. Could you tell us *how much time* you spend on each? [Hand over FORM CABS Q* - see below]

Q3b*   Are there any important responsibilities that should be added to the list?

Intro   We should now like to ask you some questions about the organization and operation of your cabinet

Q4a   How are responsibilities shared and divided within the cabinet?

Q4b   What procedures are in place to coordinate the work of cabinet members?

Q4c   Do members of the cabinet work directly with the Commissioner or is work generally channelled via the chef de cabinet?

II. THE COMMISSION IN THE COMMUNITY SYSTEM

Intro   In the survey, we asked respondents which conception of the Commission they preferred. Three models emerged:
1. The Commission as policy initiator and guardian of the treaties
2. The Commission as an administration serving the Council and the Parliament
3. The Commission as the government of Europe

Q5   Which one do you personally support? ANSWER: 1 2 3

Q5a   Why?

Q5b   Which do you think the Commission will be closest to ten years from now?
ANSWER:. . . . . .1. . . . . .2. 3

III.   NATIONALITY

Intro   We received a somewhat puzzling response to the two questions we asked in the survey about the role of nationality. [Hand over FORM Q6 - see below]
Answer: 34% thought it problematic; 51% did not consider it a problem.

Q6a   Are you surprised by these results? How would you explain the difference?

Q6b   The result on dossiers concerning the home state was a reversal of what we found in 1996 and 2002. Do you think that there has there been a change of mind about nationality in the Commission?
- Yes
- No
- Don't know
- Prefer not to say

IV. THE COMMISSION AS AN ORGANIZATION

Working relationships within the Commission

Intro   One of our interests is in the effectiveness of coordination inside the Commission.

Q7a   How effective is coordination the DG(s) that your cabinet oversees?
- Very effective
- Quite effective
- Satisfactory
- Not effective

Q7b   Do you think that coordination between DGs is effective?

- Very effective
- Quite effective
- Satisfactory
- Not effective
- Not at all effective
- Don't know
- Prefer not to say

Q7c   Could I press you on why you think this is so?

Q7d   What makes a good working relationship between cabinet and services? Please identify two features on each side. [SKIP IF PRESSED]

Q7e   The working relationship between a Directorate-General and its cabinet is an important one. How would you describe the working relationship between your cabinet and the services?

Q7g   In your experience, do the cabinets respect the expertise of the services?

- Yes
- No
- Don't know
- Prefer not to say

Q7h   In your experience, do the services respect the work of the cabinets?

- Yes
- No
- Don't know
- Prefer not to say

Q7i   What could be done to improve coordination between cabinets and services in the Commission?

Q7j   Some respondents thought the Secretariat General focuses too much on procedure and not enough on policy content. What is your view?

ANSWER

Agrees?	Approves?
Strongly agree	Strongly approves
Agrees	Approves
Has not noticed a change	Neutral
Disagrees	Disapproves
Strongly disagrees	Strongly disapproves
Don't know	Don't know
Prefer not to say	Prefer not to say

Q7k   Some respondents thought that the Secretariat General is becoming too political in the life of the Commission. What is your view?

ANSWER

Agrees?	Approves?
Strongly agree	Strongly approves
Agrees	Approves
Has not noticed a change	Neutral
Disagrees	Disapproves
Strongly disagrees	Strongly disapproves
Don't know	Don't know
Prefer not to say	Prefer not to say

V. *Intro*	COMMISSION RULES AND PROCEDURES We should like to ask your view about rules and procedures within the Commission following administrative reform.
Q8a	Do you think that the systems of planning, programming and financial management work effectively? Yes No Don't know Prefer not to say
Q8b	[ASK CHEF DE CABINETS ONLY] How effectively do you think the staff rules enable the house to manage human resources?
Q8c	What single rule or administrative procedure would you change to help you do your job more effectively? [SKIP IF PRESSED]

VI. *Intro*	THE COMMISSION IN COMPARATIVE PERSPECTIVE *Politicization* One of the aims of our project is to place the Commission in comparative perspective. Our penultimate set of questions concerns the balance between politics and administration.
Q9	Cabinets by definition are involved in policy making. This inevitably involves contact with the world of politicians and of politics. Could we ask how much you like the political side of your work? • I like it very much • I like it, but have some reservations • It's part of the job • I do not like it that much • There is no political side
Intro	Past studies of national civil services have found that the party affiliation or sympathy of top managers is often important.
Q10a	How important is party affiliation for officials in the European Commission? • Party affiliation is very important • It is important • Sometimes it plays a role, sometimes not • It is not very important • It does not play any role at all
Q9b	How important is party affiliation for cabinet members? • Party affiliation is very important • It is important • Sometimes it plays a role, sometimes not • It is not very important • It does not play any role at all
Q10c	If you don't mind us asking, do you belong to a political party? • No, never • In the past, not anymore. • Yes, but I am not active. • Yes, and I am still active

Intro   We would like to ask some questions concerning your philosophical views [Hand over
          FORM Q11 - see below].
WRAPPING UP
Finally, is there any important aspect of the cabinet's life that we did not ask you about today that
we should have asked about? Is there anything that we have missed?

*Thank you very much for your time and thoughtful answers. If you are interested in
knowing when our published findings are available, please let us have your card and we
will email you. Thank you once again.*

FORM CABS Q2A

Q2a Here is a list of roles that could be used in relation to cabinets. Could you tell us
how closely they describe the role of your cabinet? [Please tick all that apply].

	Very closely	*Quite closely*	*Well enough*	*Not closely*	*Not at all closely*	*Don't know*
Developing policies in the Commissioner's area of portfolio responsibilities						
Providing support for the Commissioner's portfolio responsibilities						
Providing support for the Commissioner's *non-portfolio* role as a member of the College						
Providing a link to the Commissioner's home state						
Helping the Commissioner manage his or her links to a political party						
Assisting the Commissioner in overseeing the Directorates-General for which he or she is responsible						
Managing the political dimensions of dossiers falling within the Commissioner's areas of responsibility						
Safeguarding the interests of the Commissioner's compatriots in appointments and promotions						

FORM CHEF DE CABINETS Q3A

Q3a Here is a list of questions relating to the responsibilities of chef de cabinets. Could we ask you to rank the top three? Please tick boxes as relevant

	1	2	3
Providing policy advice to the Commissioner			
Supervising the work of the *cabinet*			
Linking the cabinet to the services for which the Commissioner is responsible			
Communicating with other *chefs de cabinet*			
Representing the Commissioner in political events			

FORM CABS Q*

CABINET MEMBERS
Here is a list of questions relating to the responsibilities of cabinet members. Could you tell us how much time you spend on each?

	A great deal	A lot	Quite a lot	Not very much	Not at all
Monitoring policy developments in the services in my areas of responsibility					
Taking responsibility for the political dimension of dossiers					
Preparing for the hebdo or chef du cabinet					
Communicating with officials in the services					
Communicating with my colleagues within the cabinet					
Communicating with my counterparts in other cabinets					
Meeting interest group representatives					

FORM Q6

We received a somewhat puzzling response to the two questions we asked in the survey about the role of nationality. Are you surprised by these results? How would you explain the difference?

Question a: 'Some argue that posts in the Commission should be distributed on the basis of geographical balance. What is your view?'Answer: 48% opposed such a distribution; 35% were in support

Question b: 'Some think that it is problematic for Commission officials to manage dossiers of special interest to their own member state. What do you think?'
Answer: 34% thought it problematic; 51% did not consider it a problem.

Appendices

FORM Q11

Q11a   People often think of themselves in terms of their personal philosophical stance on economic issues. Some favour an active role for government. Others look primarily to markets. Where would you place yourself on a scale of 0-10 (below), where 0 represents a greater role for government and 10 a greater role for markets?

A greater role   A greater role
for government   for markets
0——1——2——3——4——5——6——7——8——9——10

Q11b   People often think of themselves in terms of their personal philosophical stance on social and cultural issues. Many people who consider themselves to be progressive tend to favour expanded personal freedoms on (for example) abortion, same-sex marriage, and so on. People on the conservative side tend to favour more traditional notions of family and order. Where would you place yourself on a scale of 0-10 (below), where 0 represents more liberal and 10 more conservative?

More liberal 0——1——2——3——4——5——6——7——8——9——10 More
conservative

Appendix 4 The Commission of the twenty-first century: views from the inside. Template for interviews with middle and senior managers

Date:		Respondent:	
Interviewers:		Interview number:	

THE COMMISSION OF THE 21ST *CENTURY:* *VIEWS* FROM THE INSIDE

Template for interviews with middle and senior managers

Introduction

Thank you for agreeing to be interviewed. We are a team of University professors working on an independent research project. Our structured programme of interviews forms the second part of a project that we began last autumn. The first consisted of a survey that was administered to a sample of around 4000 respondents and was completed by more than 2000 officials. We now are conducting interviews to help us interpret our data and find out why officials responded to our questionnaires as they did and to follow-up particular issues. We aim to interview around 200 middle and senior managers, and *cabinet* members.

Your anonymity is guaranteed. All responses will be treated as confidential, nothing will be attributed, and it will not be possible to identify the source of any of the material in our published findings.

YOUR BACKGROUND [*Only ask these questions if respondent has not completed prior to the interview*]

- Your current position:
- Nationality:
- Subject of highest educational qualification:
- Professional background:
- Year of birth:
- Year of entry into Commission:
- Previous positions in the Commission:
- Gender: M/F

I. TODAY'S EUROPEAN UNION

Intro   In the survey, we asked respondents which conception of the Commission they preferred. Three broad models emerged from the responses:
1. The Commission as policy initiator and guardian of the treaties
2. The Commission as an administration serving the Council and the Parliament
3. The Commission as the government of Europe

Q1a   Which one do you *personally* support? ANSWER: 1 2 3

Q1b   Why?

Q1c   Which do you think the Commission will be closest to ten years from now?
ANSWER: . . . . 1 . . . . 2 3

II. YOUR ROLE IN THE COMMISSION
Roles

Q2a   Here is a list of roles that middle or senior officials may consider to be part of their job. It has proven useful in comparative studies to describe how national or international public servants perceive their role. [Hand over FORM Q2a - see below].

Q2b   Staying with this list, how well in your view do these descriptions fit your role as a middle/senior manager? Is there anything that you would add?
- Very well
- Well
- Satisfactory
- Not well
- Not at all well
- Don't know
- Prefer not to say

Alternate Q2b* (for ½ of officials)
Here is a list of roles that has been used in relation to middle or senior officials in the Commission. Are there any with which you decidedly do not identify? Could you rank the top three in order of your priorities? [Hand over FORM Q2b* - see below]

Q2b*   How well in your view do these role descriptions fit the Commission? Is there anything missing?
- Very well
- Quite well
- They're satisfactory
- Not well
- Not at all well
- Don't know
- Prefer not to say

Q2c   We would like to ask your views on the role of Commission officials more generally. [HAND FORM Q2c TO RESPONDENT – see below]. What is your position on the following statements?

III. NATIONALITY *[SKIP IF PRESSED]*

Intro   We received a somewhat puzzling response to the two questions we asked in the survey about the role of nationality. [Hand over FORM Q3 – see below]

Q3a   Are you surprised by these results? How would you explain the difference?

Q3b   The result on the handling of dossiers by officials that concern their home country was a reversal of what we found in 1996 and 2002. Do you think that there has been a change of mind about nationality in the Commission?
- Yes
- No
- Don't know
- Prefer not to say

I. TODAY'S EUROPEAN UNION

IV. THE COMMISSION AND ENLARGEMENT *[SKIP IF PRESSED]*

Intro   We found significant differences in the views expressed by officials from the EU-15 and those from countries that joined the Union in 2004 and after, especially relating to their motivation for choosing a career in the Commission [Refer to FORM Q4a – see below – and point to significant statistical difference in levels of commitment to Europe and job stability]

Q4a   What do you think lies behind these differences?

Q4b   Officials from the new member states were also less likely to be strongly supportive of the Community method than officials from the EU-15, and less likely to want the Commission to be the government of Europe. Does this surprise you?

Q4c   Are there any other differences between officials from the EU-15 and those from the recent enlargement of which you have become aware in your day-to-day work?

V. THE COMMISSION AS AN ORGANIZATION

Coordination

Intro   One of our interests is in the effectiveness of coordination inside the Commission.

Q5a   How effective is coordination within your DG?
- Very effective
- Quite effective
- Satisfactory
- Not effective
- Not at all effective
- Don't know
- Prefer not to say

Q5a   [If no elaboration is offered, ask] Could I press you on why you think this is so?

Q5b   How effective is coordination between DGs?
- Very effective
- Quite effective
- Satisfactory
- Not effective
- Not at all effective
- Don't know
- Prefer not to say

Q5c   [If no elaboration is offered, ask] Could I press you on why you think this is so?

Q5d   The working relationship between a Directorate-General and its cabinet is an important one. How effective is that relationship between your Directorate General and its cabinet?
- Very effective
- Quite effective
- Satisfactory
- Not effective
- Not at all effective
- Don't know
- Prefer not to say

Q5e   In your experience, do the cabinets respect the expertise of the services?
- Yes
- No
- Don't know
- Prefer not to say

Q5f   In your experience do the services appreciate the work of the cabinets and the role they play?

I. TODAY'S EUROPEAN UNION

ANSWER
Yes
No
Don't know
Prefer not to say

The Secretariat General

Intro   In the survey, we asked a series of questions about the Secretariat General

Q6a   Some respondents thought the Secretariat General focuses too much on procedure and not enough on policy content. What is your view? [We want to know whether the respondent agrees or disagrees with the proposition *and* whether they approve or disapprove]

Agrees?	*Approves?*
• Strongly agree	• Strongly approves
• Agrees	• Approves
• Has not noticed a change	• Neutral
• Disagrees	• Disapproves
• Strongly disagrees	• Strongly disapproves
• Don't know	• Don't know
• Prefer not to say	• Prefer not to say

Q6b   Some respondents thought that the Secretariat General is becoming too political in the life of the Commission. What is your view?

Agrees?	*Approves?*
• Strongly agree	• Strongly approves
• Agrees	• Approves
• Has not noticed a change	• Neutral
• Disagrees	• Disapproves
• Strongly disagrees	• Strongly disapproves
• Don't know	• Don't know
• Prefer not to say	• Prefer not to say

Systems and procedures

Intro   In the survey, we asked a number of questions about rules and procedures within the Commission following administrative reform. We are interested in the extent to which the rules that govern the running of the house enable you as a middle/senior manager to carry out your responsibilities effectively.

Q7a   To what extent do the staff rules help or hinder you in achieving the goals of the unit/directorate/DG? [if asked, we mean by 'staff rules' the Statut plus rules relating to hiring new staff, promotions, performance, appraisal and any other rules relating to HR]
         • Extremely helpful
         • Quite helpful
         • Neither a help nor a hindrance
         • Something of a hindrance
         • Not at all helpful
         • Don't know
         • Prefer not to say

Q7b [If no elaboration is offered, ask] What draws you to this conclusion?

Q7c To what extent do the systems governing financial management and planning help or hinder you in carrying out your responsibilities as a Head of Unit/Director/Director General?
- Extremely helpful
- Quite helpful
- Neither a help nor a hindrance
- Something of a hindrance
- Not at all helpful
- Don't know
- Prefer not to say

Q7d Do the financial management rules and procedures strike the right balance between accountability and efficiency?
- Yes, very much so
- Yes
- In some respects yes, in some respects no
- No
- Not at all
- Don't know
- Prefer not to say

Q7e What single rule or procedure would you change to help you carry out your job more effectively?

VI. THE COMMISSION IN COMPARATIVE PERSPECTIVE
Politicization

Intro One of the aims of our project is to place the Commission in comparative perspective. The next questions are about the balance between politics and administration.

Q8 [Q TO ASK OF DIRECTORS GENERAL AND DIRECTORS ONLY]
Senior managers in the Commission by definition are involved in policy making. This inevitably involves contact with the world of politicians and of politics. Could we ask how much you like the political side of your work?
- I like it very much
- I like it, but have some reservations
- It's part of the job
- I do not like it that much
- There is no political side

Intro	Past studies of national civil services—particularly in Europe—have found that the party affiliation or party sympathy of top managers is often important.
Q9a	How important is the party affiliation or party sympathy of officials in the Commission?

- Party affiliation is very important
- It is important
- Sometimes it plays a role, sometimes not
- It is not very important
- It does not play any role at all

Q9b   How important is party affiliation for cabinet members?

- Party affiliation is very important
- It is important
- Sometimes it plays a role, sometimes not
- It is not very important
- It does not play any role at all

Q9c   If you don't mind us asking, do you belong to a political party?

- No, never
- In the past, not anymore.
- Yes, but I am not active.
- Yes, and I am still active

Intro   We would like to ask some questions concerning your philosophical views [Hand over FORM Q10- see above. Same questions as Q11].

FORM Q10

People often think of themselves in terms of their personal philosophical stance on economic issues. Some favour an active role for government. Others look primarily to markets. Where would you place yourself on a scale of 0-10 (below), where 0 represents a greater role for government and 10 a greater role for markets?

A greater role   A greater role
for government   for markets
0——1——2——3——4——5——6——7——8——9——10

Q11b   People often think of themselves in terms of their personal philosophical stance on social and cultural issues. Many people who consider themselves to be progressive tend to favour expanded personal freedoms on (for example) abortion, same-sex marriage, and so on. People on the conservative side tend to favour more traditional notions of family and order. Where would you place yourself on a scale of 0-10 (below), where 0 represents more liberal and 10 more conservative?

More liberal 0——1——2——3——4——5——6——7——8——9——10 More
                                                        conservative

VII. NETWORKS IN THE COMMISSION

Intro	Our survey results suggest that officials in the Commission find the use of informal contacts important to get things done. We asked respondents to think about the persons they consult about work-related issues and whether the link is based on [FORM Q11 – see below] nationality, party affiliation, having worked together in the past, or sharing the same language, regional identity (e.g. Nordic) or education.
Q11a	Party affiliation came last. Does that surprise you?
	• Yes
	• No
	• Don't know
	• Prefer not to say
Q11b	In your experience, is this something that has increased or diminished over time?
	• Increased
	• Decreased
	• Stayed the same
	• Don't know
	• Prefer not to say
Q11c	We find that long-serving officials [from the EU-15] are *more* likely to say that party affiliation is the base of their networks than recent recruits. Does this correspond to your experience?
	• Yes
	• No
	• Don't know
	• Prefer not to say
Q12a	Just over half of respondents indicated that networks were based on nationality. Does that surprise you?
	• Yes
	• No
	• Don't know
	• Prefer not to say
Q12b	In your experience, is this something that has changed over time?
	• Increased
	• Decreased
	• Stayed the same
	• Don't know
	• Prefer not to say
Q12c	We find that senior officials are *less* likely to say that nationality is an important base for their informal networks than middle/junior officials. Does this sound right or odd in your experience?
	• Right
	• Odd
	• Don't know
	• Prefer not to say

VII. NETWORKS IN THE COMMISSION

Q13   An overwhelming majority of officials (about 80%) said that personal
               contact—that is, having worked in the same unit, or being on the same
               training or induction course—is the most important basis for their network.
               Is this figure higher or lower than you would expect?
               • Higher
               • Lower
               • About the same
               • Don't know
               • Prefer not to say

WRAPPING UP
Finally, is there any important aspect of the Commission's life that we did not ask you about

Thank you very much for your time and thoughtful answers. If you are interested in knowing when our published findings are available, please let us have your card and we will email you.

Thank you once again.

FORM Q2A

Here is a list of roles that middle or senior officials may consider to be part of their job. The list has proven useful in comparative studies to describe how national or international public servants perceive their role. Are there any with which you decidedly do not identify? Could you rank the top three in order of your priorities?

	Ranking	Not relevant
Solving technical policy problems and applying specialized knowledge		
Fighting for or representing the interests of a social group, class or cause, or protesting against injustice		
Focusing on legal processes or legalistic definitions of one's responsibilities		
Mediating or resolving conflicts of interest and political conflicts		
Representing the European Union		
Protecting the interests of specific clientele groups or constituents		
Focusing on the political or partisan aspects of the job		

FORM Q2B*

Here is a list of roles that has been used in relation to middle or senior officials in the Commission. Could you please rank the top three in order of your priorities? Are there any with which you decidedly do not identify?

	Ranking	Not relevant
Mediate conflicts in the Council, between Council and Parliament		
Mediate conflicts between national interests		
Identify policy problems and devise new policies		
Defend the Commission's prerogatives vis-à-vis Council and Parliament		
Fight public interventionism and overregulation		
Provide expertise in a specific policy area		
Combat pure market ideology and promote social values		
Respect divergent national interests		
Be accessible for fellow nationals		
Promote a positive working environment in the DG		

FORM Q2C

We would like to ask your views on the role of Commission officials more generally. What is your position on the following statements?

	Strongly agree	Agree	Disagree	Strongly disagree
a) 'In policy-making it is essential for the good of the European Union that technical considerations are accorded more weight than political factors.'	1	2	3	4
b) 'In order to assess the work of the services properly, it is necessary to eliminate political considerations'	1	2	3	4
c) 'The European Union should be judged on the effectiveness of its policies rather than any other criteria'	1	2	3	4
d) 'The European Parliament and the Council of Ministers too often interfere with the work of the European Commission'	1	2	3	4

FORM Q3

We received a somewhat puzzling response to the two questions we asked in the survey about the role of nationality. Are you surprised by these results? How would you explain the difference?

Question a: 'Some argue that posts in the Commission should be distributed on the basis of geographical balance. What is your view?'
Answer: 48% opposed such a distribution; 35% were in support
Question b: 'Some think that it is problematic for Commission officials to manage dossiers of special interest to their own member state. What do you think?'
Answer: 34% thought it problematic; 51% did not consider it a problem.

FORM Q4A

Question: Why did you choose to follow a career in the European Commission? (Please choose as many as are relevant).

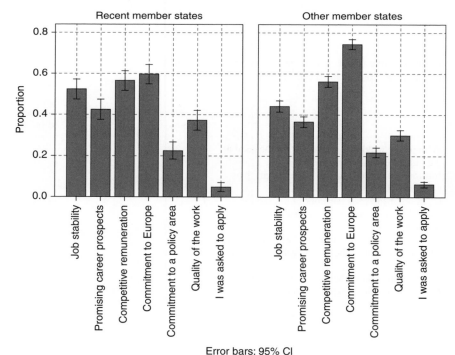

Error bars: 95% CI

Enlargement and motivation for joining the European Commission

Appendix 5 List and dates of interviews and number of interviews per DG

Interview number	Date on which interview was conducted
1	01/09/2009
2	01/09/2009
3	01/09/2009
4	01/09/2009
5	01/09/2009
6	02/09/2009
7	02/09/2009
8	02/09/2009
9	02/09/2009
10	02/09/2009
11	02/09/2009
12	03/09/2009
13	03/09/2009
14	03/09/2009
15	03/09/2009
16	03/09/2009
17	03/09/2009
18	09/09/2009
19	09/09/2009
20	09/09/2009
21	09/09/2009
22	09/09/2009
23	09/09/2009
24	10/09/2009
25	10/09/2009
26	10/09/2009
27	10/09/2009
28	10/09/2009
29	10/09/2009
30	11/09/2009
31	11/09/2009
32	11/09/2009
33	15/09/2009
34	15/09/2009
35	15/09/2009
36	15/09/2009
37	16/09/2009
38	16/09/2009
39	16/09/2009
40	16/09/2009
41	16/09/2009
42	16/09/2009
43	17/09/2009
44	17/09/2009
45	17/09/2009
46	17/09/2009
47	17/09/2009
48	17/09/2009
49	17/09/2009

Interview number	*Date on which interview was conducted*
50	18/09/2009
51	18/09/2009
52	18/09/2009
53	18/09/2009
54	18/09/2009
55	18/09/2009
56	21/09/2009
57	21/09/2009
58	22/09/2009
59	22/09/2009
60	22/09/2009
61	22/09/2009
62	22/09/2009
63	22/09/2009
64	23/09/2009
65	23/09/2009
66	23/09/2009
67	23/09/2009
68	23/09/2009
69	28/09/2009
70	28/09/2009
71	28/09/2009
72	28/09/2009
73	29/09/2009
74	29/09/2009
75	29/09/2009
76	29/09/2009
77	29/09/2009
78	29/09/2009
79	29/09/2009
80	29/09/2009
81	30/09/2009
82	30/09/2009
83	30/09/2009
84	30/09/2009
85	30/09/2009
86	30/09/2009
87	06/10/2009
88	06/10/2009
89	06/10/2009
90	06/10/2009
91	06/10/2009
92	07/10/2009
93	07/10/2009
94	07/10/2009
95	07/10/2009
96	07/10/2009
97	07/10/2009
98	08/10/2009

Interview number	*Date on which interview was conducted*
99	08/10/2009
100	08/10/2009
101	08/10/2009
102	09/10/2009
103	09/10/2009
104	09/10/2009
105	09/10/2009
106	09/10/2009
107	09/10/2009
108	06/10/2009
109	06/10/2009
110	06/10/2009
111	06/10/2009
112	08/10/2009
113	08/10/2009
114	08/10/2009
115	08/10/2009
116	08/10/2009
117	08/10/2009
118	08/10/2009
119	09/10/2009
120	09/10/2009
121	09/10/2009
122	21/10/2009
123	21/10/2009
124	21/10/2009
125	21/10/2009
126	22/10/2009
127	22/10/2009
128	22/10/2009
129	22/10/2009
130	27/10/2009
131	27/10/2009
132	05/11/2009
133	05/11/2009
134	05/11/2009
138	23/11/2009
139	24/11/2009
140	24/11/2009
141	24/11/2009
142	24/11/2009
143	24/11/2009
144	25/11/2009
145	25/11/2009
146	24/11/2009
147	24/11/2009
148	24/11/2009
149	24/11/2009
150	24/11/2009
151	25/11/2009
152	25/11/2009
153	25/11/2009
154	25/11/2009
155	25/11/2009

Interview number	Date on which interview was conducted
156	27/10/2009
157	27/10/2009
158	28/10/2009
159	28/10/2009
160	28/10/2009
161	28/10/2009
162	28/10/2009
163	29/10/2009
164	29/10/2009
165	29/10/2009
166	29/10/2009

Directorate-General	Number of interviews
ADMIN	5
AGRI	7
AIDCO	4
BARROSO	2
BEPA	1
COMP	7
DIGIT	1
EAC	6
ECFIN	3
ECHO	3
ELARG	4
EMPL	10
ENTR	8
ENV	5
HR	7
IAS	1
INFSO	6
JLS	2
MARE	5
MARKT	7
MULTILINGUALISM	2
OLAF	2
REGIO	6
RELEX	6
RTD	8
SANCO	8
SG	7
TAXUD	6
TRADE	5
TREN	6
DEV	3
BUDG	5
DGT	1
SDME	1
CDMA	1
COMM	2
Other (incl. Blanks)	5
Total	158

Appendix 6 Explaining perceptions of politicization in the Commission

	B	std.error	p-value
Party membership	0.274	0.297	0.358
Left/right ideology	0.110	0.050	0.030
Current position	−0.367	0.204	0.076
Delors recruit	0.567	0.310	0.071
Interregnum recruit	0.237	0.365	0.517
National politicization	0.099	0.055	0.077
Constant	−1.000	0.589	0.093
R^2	*0.164*		
Adj. R^2	*0.107*		

Note: n = 100; party membership: a value of 1 when the official has been a member of a political party (self-reporting); current position: 1 if a director or director-general, and 0 if a head of unit; national politicization: see Chapter 4, footnote 17 for details on operationalization.

Appendix 7 Explaining variation in general desire for EU policy scope

	B	std.error	p-value
Current position	−0.209	0.127	0.101
Gender	0.003	0.072	0.972
EU-12	−0.279	0.128	0.030
Supranationalists	1.157	0.109	0.000
Institutional pragmatists	0.674	0.111	0.000
Others (fence-sitters)	0.819	0.118	0.000
Left/right ideology	−0.033	0.018	0.058
Liberal/conservative ideology	−0.031	0.014	0.025
Country size	−0.003	0.000	0.007
Protestantism	−0.435	0.175	0.013
Governance efficacy	−0.153	0.103	0.137
Multilevel governance	0.001	0.005	0.809
Spending DGs	0.039	0.086	0.648
Regulatory DGs	−0.038	0.098	0.701
Legislative DGs	−0.108	0.104	0.296
Internal DGs	0.041	0.129	0.750
External DGs	0.300	0.122	0.014
Constant	6.955	0.237	0.000
R^2	*0.137*		
Adj. R^2	*0.126*		

Note: n = 1,678 current position: same operationalization as in Table A; gender, EU-12, supranationalist, institutional pragmatist, others, left/right, liberal/conservative, country size, governance efficacy, multilevel governance: see ch 1 for operationalization; Protestantism: see note 2 for detailed operationalization. DGs: see Chapter 4, footnote 10 for details on operationalization.

Appendix 8 Personal and national characteristics supporting the Community Method

	Model 1			Model 2		
	B (SE)	Wald	Odds ratio (95%CI)	B (SE)	Wald	Odds ratio (95%CI)
Personal						
Commitment to Europe (ref cat: no)	0.728 (0.108)	45.45***	2.072 (1.676:2.561)	0.674 (0.109)	37.946***	1.963 (1.584:2.432)
Socio-cultural philosophy index	−0.061 (0.020)	9.32**	0.941 (0.905:0.978)	−0.067 (0.020)	10.876**	0.935 (0.899:0.973)
Economic philosophy index	−0.066 (0.025)	6.89**	0.936 (0.891:0.983)	−0.053 (0.026)	4.275*	0.949 (0.902:0.997)
National						
Protestantism (proportion)				−0.438 (0.195)	5.035*	0.645 (0.440:0.946)
Index of multi-level governance				0.014 (0.005)	6.853**	1.014 (1.004:1.025)
Reduction in -2LL	63.77***			77.147***		
Nagelkerke R^2	0.048			0.058		
Hosmer and Lemeshow test (sig)	0.803		0.989			
n (unweighted)	1794			1794		

*** p < 0.001;   ** p < 0.01;   * p < 0.05
Notes: The multilevel modelling, carried out using MLwiN (v2.02) with Markov Chain Monte Carlo methods to allow Bayesian estimates, shows that no additional variance is found between countries once adjustment is made for the fixed variables, implying that a logistic regression would offer an equivalent analysis. The table shows the results of the hierarchical logistic regression run in SPSS (v17). Model 1 considers the personal characteristics only, while Model 2 adds the national characteristics.

Appendix 9 Probability that Delors is considered strong in each of the following dimensions

	Delors	Policy agenda	Managing the house	Delivering policy priorities	Defending the Commission
H1	National administration—Scandinavian	−0.62	0.32	−0.36	−0.26
	National administration—Continental north	−0.35	0.11	−0.23	0.00
	National administration—Continental south	−0.58	0.21	−0.37	−0.35
	National administration—former Communist	−0.13	0.56	0.03	0.08
H2	Length of service (years)	1.10	0.66	1.06	1.08
	Length of service in Commission in years—squared	−0.02	−0.01	−0.02	−0.02
H3	Worked in private enterprise or liberal professions—career before entering Commission	0.48	0.02	0.27	0.29
H4	Economics or business—subject of main degree	0.20	−0.26	0.35	0.02
H5	Current position—senior management or advisor	0.39	−0.89	0.39	0.48
H6	Current position—middle management	0.30	−0.14	0.26	0.14
	Current position—member of cabinet	0.39	−0.08	0.67	0.42
	Has Cabinet experience	0.51	0.40	0.37	0.62
H7	Current DG—admin, budget, anti-fraud, internal audit or sec gen	0.30	−0.29	0.51	0.67
	Current DG, primarily spending	−0.01	−0.44	0.13	0.08
	Current DG, primarily regulatory	0.30	−0.04	0.52	0.38
	Current DG, primarily legislative	0.41	−0.07	0.45	0.38
	Current DG, primarily external	0.56	−0.24	0.76	0.74
	Current DG, spending AND regulatory	0.41	0.11	0.37	0.17
	Current DG, spending AND legislative	0.77	0.27	0.60	0.94
H8	EU governance beliefs—state-centrists	−0.26	−0.07	−0.44	−0.39
H9	EU governance beliefs—institutional pragmatists	0.21	−0.22	0.14	0.13
H10	EU governance beliefs—suprantionalists	0.62	−0.01	0.64	0.40

	Delors	Policy agenda	Managing the house	Delivering policy priorities	Defending the Commission
Controls	Female	−0.13	−0.06	−0.14	−0.17
	Law—subject of main degree	0.16	0.42	0.20	0.09
	Politics, international relations or other social science—subject of main degree	0.79	0.24	0.65	0.36
	Studied outside country of citizenship	−0.10	−0.10	−0.02	−0.17
	Worked in national civil service—career before entering Commission	0.44	0.25	0.29	0.29
	Worked in another international organisation—career before entering Commission	0.06	−0.18	−0.05	0.06
	Worked in party politics, trade union or social movement—career before entering Commission	0.75	−0.47	0.76	0.64
	Worked in education or research—career before entering Commission	−0.17	−0.21	−0.16	−0.13
	Worked in journalism or PR—career before entering Commission	0.09	−0.55	0.22	0.19
	Other or prefer not to say—career before entering Commission	0.50	−0.02	0.52	0.24
	Constant	−12.82	−8.77	−12.63	−12.37

Appendix 10 Probability that Santer is considered strong in each of the following dimensions

	Santer	Policy agenda	Managing the house	Delivering policy priorities	Defending the Commission
H1	National administration—Scandinavian	−0.23	−1.24	−0.01	0.51
	National administration—Continental north	0.06	0.41	0.18	0.55
	National administration—Continental south	−0.15	−0.45	−0.45	−0.09
	National administration—former Communist	−17.04	−14.48	−3.02	−16.17
H2	Length of service (years)	0.33	0.78	0.45	0.41
	Length of service in Commission in years—squared	−0.01	−0.02	−0.01	−0.01
H3	Worked in private enterprise or liberal professions—career before entering Commission	0.15	0.28	0.37	0.12
H4	Economics or business—subject of main degree	−0.13	0.67	0.20	0.17
H5	Current position—senior management or advisor	0.32	−1.12	0.36	0.20
H6	Current position—middle management	0.15	−1.63	−0.11	−0.13
	Current position—member of cabinet	−0.51	−1.64	−0.35	−1.22
	Has Cabinet experience	0.86	1.76	1.34	0.91
H7	Current DG—admin, budget, anti-fraud, internal audit or sec gen	0.15	−1.00	−0.24	−0.64
	Current DG, primarily spending	0.13	−0.72	−0.15	−0.03
	Current DG, primarily regulatory	0.45	−0.21	0.48	−0.14
	Current DG, primarily legislative	0.94	0.33	0.22	0.49
	Current DG, primarily external	−0.37	−1.49	−0.37	−0.52
	Current DG, spending AND regulatory	0.05	−0.33	0.52	−0.09
	Current DG, spending AND legislative	0.66	−0.45	0.19	0.32
H8	EU governance beliefs—state-centrists	0.33	−0.05	0.68	0.32
H9	EU governance beliefs—institutional pragmatists	−0.27	−0.39	0.25	−0.31
H10	EU governance beliefs—suprantionalists	0.04	0.21	0.10	−0.07

	Santer	Policy agenda	Managing the house	Delivering policy priorities	Defending the Commission
Controls	Female	−0.10	−0.76	−0.79	−0.15
	Law—subject of main degree	0.16	0.90	0.51	0.63
	Politics, international relations or other social science—subject of main degree	−0.18	0.00	0.08	0.20
	Studied outside country of citizenship	0.17	−0.20	0.23	−0.18
	Worked in national civil service—career before entering Commission	0.51	0.29	0.41	0.04
	Worked in another international organisation—career before entering Commission	0.21	0.43	0.08	0.26
	Worked in party politics, trade union or social movement—career before entering Commission	−0.12	0.61	−0.20	−0.58
	Worked in education or research—career before entering Commission	0.21	−0.56	0.08	0.12
	Worked in journalism or PR—career before entering Commission	1.12	1.59	1.23	1.36
	Other or prefer not to say—career before entering Commission	0.31	−16.88	0.89	0.17
	Constant	−6.22	−9.41	−7.21	−6.58

Note: binary dependent variable. Takes value 1 if official agrees or strongly agrees and 0 otherwise (i.e. neutral, disagrees, strongly disagrees).

Appendix 11 Probability that Prodi is considered strong in each of the following dimensions

	Prodi	Policy agenda	Managing the house	Delivering policy priorities	Defending the Commission
H1	National administration—Scandinavian	−0.56	−1.44	−0.73	−0.43
	National administration—Continental north	−0.21	−0.38	−0.39	0.04
	National administration—Continental south	−0.27	−0.67	−0.32	−0.36
	National administration—former Communist	−0.98	−1.19	−1.14	−0.65
H2	Length of service (years)	0.15	0.19	0.15	0.12
	Length of service in Commission in years—squared	0.00	−0.01	0.00	0.00
H3	Worked in private enterprise or liberal professions—career before entering Commission	0.09	0.27	0.01	0.12
H4	Economics or business—subject of main degree	−0.19	0.39	−0.03	−0.01
H5	Current position—senior management or advisor	0.43	0.47	0.54	0.74
H6	Current position—middle management	0.17	0.17	0.10	0.39
	Current position—member of cabinet	−0.07	−0.74	0.07	0.92
	Has Cabinet experience	0.54	0.39	0.60	0.27
H7	Current DG—admin, budget, anti-fraud, internal audit or sec gen	0.06	0.82	0.60	0.33
	Current DG, primarily spending	0.31	0.16	−0.08	−0.29
	Current DG, primarily regulatory	0.28	0.02	0.10	0.08
	Current DG, primarily legislative	0.31	0.02	0.28	−0.09
	Current DG, primarily external	0.35	−0.57	0.23	0.12
	Current DG, spending AND regulatory	0.01	−0.16	0.27	−0.19
	Current DG, spending AND legislative	0.63	−0.10	0.61	0.04
H8	EU governance beliefs—state-centrists	−0.11	−0.23	−0.38	−0.32
H9	EU governance beliefs—institutional pragmatists	0.21	−0.28	−0.01	0.02
H10	EU governance beliefs—suprantionalists	0.19	0.52	0.10	0.06

	Prodi	Policy agenda	Managing the house	Delivering policy priorities	Defending the Commission
Controls	Female	0.31	−0.32	−0.08	0.22
	Law—subject of main degree	−0.26	0.22	0.28	0.24
	Politics, international relations or other social science—subject of main degree	−0.05	0.32	0.31	0.16
	Studied outside country of citizenship	0.20	0.19	0.29	0.24
	Worked in national civil service—career before entering Commission	0.01	0.09	0.02	0.10
	Worked in another international organisation—career before entering Commission	0.07	0.25	−0.28	−0.29
	Worked in party politics, trade union or social movement—career before entering Commission	0.97	−0.77	0.45	0.67
	Worked in education or research—career before entering Commission	−0.08	−0.22	0.22	0.10
	Worked in journalism or PR—career before entering Commission	−0.30	−0.69	0.31	−0.36
	Other or prefer not to say—career before entering Commission	0.00	−1.15	0.43	−0.57
	Constant	−2.88	−3.46	−2.68	−3.20

Note: binary dependent variable. Takes value 1 if official agrees or strongly agrees and 0 otherwise (i.e. neutral, disagrees, strongly disagrees).

Appendix 12 Probability that Barroso is considered strong in each of the following dimensions

	Barroso	Policy agenda	Managing the house	Delivering policy priorities	Defending the Commission
H1	National administration—Scandinavian	−0.07	−0.34	−0.14	−0.36
	National administration—Continental north	−0.43	−0.59	−0.64	−0.19
	National administration—Continental south	−0.45	−0.51	−0.86	−0.29
	National administration—former Communist	−0.34	−0.15	−0.69	0.17
H2	Length of service (years)	−0.03	−0.02	−0.01	−0.02
	Length of service in Commission in years—squared	0.00	0.00	0.00	0.00
	Entered Commission under the Barroso presidency	0.48	0.14	0.43	0.49
H3	Worked in private enterprise or liberal professions—career before entering Commission	0.00	−0.02	−0.09	−0.04
H4	Economics or business—subject of main degree	0.23	−0.02	0.05	0.07
H5	Current position—senior management or advisor	0.46	0.85	1.03	0.60
H6	Current position—middle management	0.07	0.22	0.15	−0.04
	Current position—member of cabinet	0.76	1.45	1.56	1.17
	Has Cabinet experience	0.14	0.14	0.25	−0.44
H7	Current DG—admin, budget, anti-fraud, internal audit or sec gen	0.17	0.75	0.15	0.32
	Current DG, primarily spending	−0.34	−0.20	−0.21	−0.60
	Current DG, primarily regulatory	−0.35	−0.08	−0.32	−0.51
	Current DG, primarily legislative	−0.04	0.17	0.27	−0.20
	Current DG, primarily external	−0.09	0.07	0.01	−0.02
	Current DG, spending AND regulatory	−0.09	0.08	0.01	−0.05
	Current DG, spending AND legislative	0.01	−0.01	0.09	−0.56
H8	EU governance beliefs—state-centrists	0.20	0.15	0.31	0.15
H9	EU governance beliefs—institutional pragmatists	0.23	0.19	0.17	−0.05

	Barroso	Policy agenda	Managing the house	Delivering policy priorities	Defending the Commission
H10	EU governance beliefs—suprantionalists	0.46	0.27	0.40	0.17
Controls	Female	0.20	−0.18	0.17	−0.11
	Law—subject of main degree	−0.10	−0.25	−0.07	−0.23
	Politics, international relations or other social science—subject of main degree	0.10	−0.07	−0.08	−0.12
	Studied outside country of citizenship	−0.03	0.36	0.03	−0.09
	Worked in national civil service—career before entering Commission	0.29	0.09	−0.06	0.08
	Worked in another international organisation—career before entering Commission	−0.24	0.01	−0.31	−0.14
	Worked in party politics, trade union or social movement—career before entering Commission	−0.13	−0.12	−0.58	−0.01
	Worked in education or research—career before entering Commission	0.11	0.07	−0.13	−0.02
	Worked in journalism or PR—career before entering Commission	−0.07	0.46	0.30	−0.66
	Other or prefer not to say—career before entering Commission	0.08	−0.25	0.19	0.05
	Constant	−0.84	−1.25	−0.50	−0.87

Note: binary dependent variable. Takes value 1 if official agrees or strongly agrees and 0 otherwise (i.e. neutral, disagrees, strongly disagrees).

References

Abélès, M., I. Bellier, and M. McDonald (1993) *Approche Anthropologique de la Commission Européene* (Brussels: Commission of the European Communities).

Aberbach, J., R. D. Putnam, and B. A. Rockman (1981) *Bureaucrats and Politicians in Western Democracies* (Cambridge, Massachusetts: Harvard University Press).

Aberbach, J. D., and B. A. Rockman (2006) 'The Past and Future of Political-Administrative Relations: Research 'from Bureaucrats and Politicians' to 'In the Web of Politics'—and Beyond', *International Journal of Public Administration*, 29 (12): 977–95.

Alesina, A., and Spolaore E. (2003) *The Size of Nations* (Cambridge, Massachusetts: MIT Press).

Alford, J. R., C. L. Funk, and J. R. Hibbing (2005) 'Are Political Orientations Genetically Transmitted?', *American Political Science Review*, 99 (2): 153–67.

Amoretti, U. M., and N. Bermeo (eds) (2004) *Federalism and Territorial Cleavages* (Baltimore, MD: Johns Hopkins University Press).

Anderson, C. J. (1998) 'When in Doubt, Use Proxies: Attitudes toward Domestic Politics and Support for European Integration', *Comparative Political Studies*, 31 (5): 569–601.

Andeweg, R. (1993) 'A Model of the Cabinet System: The Dimension of Cabinet Decision-Making Processes' in J. Blondel and F. Müller-Rommel (eds) *Governing Together. The Extent and Limits of Joint Decision-Making in Western European Cabinets* (New York: St Martin's Press).

Ansell, C. K., C. A. Parsons, and K. A. Darden (1997) 'Dual Networks in European Regional Development Policy', *Journal of Common Market Studies*, 35 (3): 347–75.

Armstrong, J. A. (1973) *The European Administrative Elite* (Princeton NJ: Princeton University Press).

Balint, T., M. W. Bauer, and C. Knill (2008) 'Bureaucratic Change in the European Administrative Space: The Case of the European Commission', *West European Politics*, 31 (4): 677–700.

Ballinger, G., R. Cross, P. Gray, and E. Craig (2011) 'A Stitch in Time Saves Nine: Leveraging Networks to Reduce the Costs of Turnover', *California Management Review*, 53 (4): 111–33.

Ban, C. (2008a) *The Making of the New Eurocrats: Self-Selection, Selection, and Socialization of European Commission Staff from the New Member States* (Lyon: Ecole Normale Supérieure, Lettres et Sciences Humaines).

Ban, C. (2008b) 'Performance appraisal and promotion in the European Commission: the challenge of linking organizational and individual accountability'. Paper prepared for conference on Accountability and Governance in International Organizations, University of Konstanz, June 2008.

Ban, C. (2010) 'New Blood: the Interaction of Enlargement and Gender in the Changing Composition of the European Commission Staff,' paper presented at the Annual Meeting of the Council for European Studies, Montreal, Canada, 15–17 April.

Ban, C. (2010a) 'Reforming the Staffing Process in the European Union Institutions: Moving the Sacred Cow out of the Road', *International Review of Administrative Sciences*, 76 (1): 5–24.

Ban, C. (2013) *From Diversity to Unity: Management and Culture in an Enlarged European Commission* (Basingstoke: Palgrave Macmillan).

Ban, C., and W. Vandenabeele (2009) 'Motivations and Values of European Commission Staff', paper presented at the European Union Studies Association conference, Marina del Rey, US, 23–25 April.

Barber, T. (2009) 'Brussels leader's priority must be fighting threats to single market', *Financial Times* (16 September), 8, online at <http://www.ft.com/cms/s/0/8d894104-a258-11de-9caa-00144feabdc0.html#axzz29COJORQH>.

Barnett, M., and M. Finnemore (2004) *Rules for the World: International Organizations in Global Politics* (Philadelphia, PA: Temple University Press).

Barroso, J. M. (2011) *Un an après le traité de Lisbonne: un test de résistance réussi*, speech at the BEPA Conference Implementing the Lisbon Treaty.

Bartolini, S. (2005) *Restructuring Europe: Centre Formation, System Building and Political Structuring Between the Nation-State and the European Union* (Oxford: Oxford University Press).

Barzelay, M. (2001) *The New Public Management: Improving Research and Policy Dialogue* (Berkeley CA: University of California Press).

Barzelay, M., and A. S. Jacobsen (2009) 'Theorizing Implementation of Public Management Policy Reforms: A Case Study of Strategic Planning and Programming in the European Commission', *Governance*, 22 (2): 319–34.

Barzelay, M., R. Levy, and A-M. P. Gomez (2011) 'The Reform of Financial Management in the European Commission: A Public Management Policy Cycle Case Study', *Public Administration*, 89 (4): 1546–67.

Bauer, M. W. (2002) 'Reforming the European Commission: A (missed?) Academic Opportunity', *European Integration Online Papers*, 6 (8), <http://eiop.or.at/eiop/pdf/2002-008.pdf >.

Bauer, M. W. (2006) 'Co-managing Programme Implementation: Conceptualizing the European Commission's Role in Policy Execution', *Journal of European Public Policy*, 13 (5): 717–35.

Bauer, M. W. (2007) 'The Politics of Reforming the European Commission Administration' in M. W. Bauer and C. Knill (eds) *Management Reforms in International Organizations* (Baden-Baden, Nomos).

Bauer, M. W. (2008b) 'Diffuse Anxieties, Deprived Entrepreneurs: Commission Reform and Middle Management', *Journal of European Public Policy*, 15 (5): 691–707.

Bauer, M. W. (2008a) 'Special Issue: Reforming the European Commission', *Journal of European Public Policy*, 15 (5): 625–26.

Bauer, M. W. (ed.) (2009a) *Reforming the European Commission* (London: Routledge).

Bauer, M. W. (2009b) 'Impact of Administrative Reform of the European Commission: Results from a Survey of Heads of Unit in Policy-Making Directorates', *International Review of Administrative Sciences*, 75 (3): 459–72.

Bauer, M. W. (2012), Tolerant, If Personal Goals Remain Unharmed: Explaining Supranational Bureaucrats' Attitudes to Organizational Change. Governance, 25 (3): 485–510

Bauer, M. W., and J. Ege (2011) 'Commission Civil Servants and Politics: Depoliticized Bureaucrats in an Increasingly Political Organization', Arbeitspapier Humboldt-Universität zu Berlin.

Bauer, M. W., and J. Ege (2012) 'Politicization within the European Commission's Bureaucracy', *International Review of Administrative Sciences*, 78: 403–424.

Bauer, M. W., and C. Knill (2007) *Management Reforms in International Organizations* (Baden-Baden: Nomos).

Baylis, T. (1989) *Governing by Committee: Collegial Leadership in Advanced Societies* (New York: State University of New York Press).

Beach, D., and T. Christiansen (2007) 'Introduction: Political Agency in the Constitutional Politics of the European Union', *Journal of European Public Policy*, 14 (8): 1163–6.

Bearfield, N. D. (2004) 'Reforming the European Commission: Driving Reform from the Grassroots', *Public Policy and Administration*, 19 (5): 13–24.

Bellier, I. (1994) 'La Commission Européenne. Hauts Fonctionnaires et Culture du Management', *Revue Française d'Adminstration Public*, 70: 253–62.

Bellier, I. (2000) 'A Europeanized Elite? An Anthropology of European Commission Officials' in R. Harmsen and T. M. Wilson (eds) *Europeanization* (Florence: European University Institute).

Best, E., T. Christiansen and P. Settembri (eds) (2008) *The Institutions of the Enlarged European Union: Continuity and Change* (Cheltenham: Edward Elgar).

Beyers, J. (2005) 'Multiple Embeddedness and Socialization in Europe: The Case of Council Officials', *International Organization*, 59 (4): 899–936.

Biesheuvel, B., E. Dell, and R. Marjolin (1979) *The Three Wise Men Report: Report on the Operation of the Community Institutions* (Brussels: Official Publications Office of the European Community).

Blom-Hansen, J. (1997) 'A 'New Institutional' Perspective on Policy Networks', *Public Administration*, 75 (4): 669–93.

Blöndal, J. R. (2003) 'Accrual Accounting and Budgeting: Key Issues and Recent Developments', *OECD Journal on Budgeting*, 3 (1): 43–59.

Blöndal, J. R. (2004) 'Issues in Accrual Budgeting', *OECD Journal on Budgeting*, 4 (1): 103-19.

Blondel, J. (1987) *Political Leadership* (London: Sage).

Bomberg, E. (1998) 'Issue Networks and the Environment: Explaining European Union Environmental Policy' in D. Marsh (ed.) *Comparing Policy Networks* (Buckingham: Open University Press).

Boomgaarden, H. G., and A. Freire (2009) 'Religion and Euroscepticism: Direct, Indirect or No Effects?', *West European Politics*, 32 (6): 1240–65.

Borgatti, S. P., and R. Cross (2003) 'A Relational View of Information Seeking and Learning in Social Networks', *Management Science*, 49 (4): 432–45.

Börzel, T. (1998) 'Organizing Babylon: On the Different Conceptions of Policy Network', *Public Administration*, 76 (2): 253–73.

Börzel, T. (2005) 'Mind the Gap! European Integration between Level and Scope', *Journal of European Public Policy*, 12 (2): 217–36.

Börzel, T. (2010) 'European Governance: Negotiation and Competition in the Shadow of Hierarchy', *Journal of Common Market Studies,* 48 (2): 191–219.

Börzel, T. A., and T. Risse (2009) 'The Transformative Power of Europe: The European Union and the Diffusion of Ideas', KFG Working Paper 1 (Berlin: Freie Universität Berlin).

Bossaert, D., C. Demmke, L. Nomden, R. Polet (2001) *Civil Services in the Europe of the Fifteen* (Maastricht: European Institute of Public Administration).

Bossuat, G. (2011) *Émile Noël, premier secrétaire général de la Commission européenne* (Brussels: Emile Bruylant).

Bourtembourg, C. (1987) 'La Commission des Communautes Européennes: Son personnel' in S. Cassese (ed.) *The European Administration* (Paris: International Institute of Administrative Sciences).

Brass, D. (1984) 'Being in the Right Place: A Structural Analysis of Individual Influence in an Organization', *Administrative Science Quarterly,* 29: 518–39.

Brinegar, A., and S. Jolly (2005) 'Location, Location, Location: National Contextual Factors and Public Support for European Integration', *European Union Politics,* 6 (2): 155–80.

Brittan, L. (2000) *A Diet of Brussels: The Changing Face of Europe,* (Boston, MA: Little, Brown).

Brunsson, N., and J. P. Olsen (1993) *The Reforming Organization* (London: Routledge).

Burt, R. S. (1992) *Structural Holes: The Social Structure of Competition* (Cambridge, MA: Harvard University Press).

Callaghan, H. (2010) 'Beyond Methodological Nationalism: How Multilevel Governance Affects the Clash of Capitalisms', *Journal of European Public Policy,* 17 (4): 564–80.

Calvert, R., M. D. McCubbins, and B. R. Weingast (1989) 'A Theory of Political Control and Agency Discretion', *American Journal of Political Science,* 33 (3): 588–611.

Campbell, J. (1983) *Roy Jenkins: A Biography* (London: Weidenfeld and Nicolson).

Capano, G. (2003) 'Administrative Traditions and Policy Change: When Policy Paradigms Matter. The Case of Italian Administrative Reform During the 1990s', *Public Administration,* 81 (4): 781–801.

Caporaso, J. A. (1996) 'The European Union and Forms of State: Westphalian, Regulatory or Post-Modern?', *Journal of Common Market Studies,* 34 (1): 29–52.

Caporaso, J. A., and S. Tarrow (2009) 'Polanyi in Brussels: Supranational Institutions and the Transnational Embedding of Markets', *International Organization,* 63 (4): 593–620.

Cassese, S., and G. della Cananea (1992) 'The Commission of the European Economic Community: the Administrative Ramifications of its Political Development (1957–1967)', in E. V. Heyen (ed.) *Yearbook of European Administrative History,* vol. 4: *Early European Community Administration* (Baden-Baden: Nomos), 75–94.

CESifo DICE (2007) 'Report', *Journal for Institutional Comparisons,* 5 (3): 43–45

Checkel, J. T. (2005) 'Tracing Causal Mechanisms', *International Studies Review* 8 (2): 370–262.

Checkel, J. T. (ed.) (2007) *International Institutions and Socialization in Europe* (Cambridge: Cambridge University Press).

Chicowski, R. (2007) *The European Court and Civil Society: Litigation, Mobilization and Governance* (Cambridge: Cambridge University Press).

Chong, D. (2000) *Rational Lives: Norms and Values in Politics and Society* (Chicago, IL: University of Chicago Press).

Christiansen, T. (1997) 'Tensions of European Governance: Politicised Bureaucracy and Multiple Accountability in the European Commission', *Journal of European Public Policy*, 4 (1): 73–90.

Christiansen, T. (2002) 'The Role of Supranational Actors in EU Treaty Reform', *Journal of European Public Policy*, 9 (1): 33–53.

Christiansen, T., and Lagreid, P. (eds) (2002) *New Public Management: The Transformation of Ideas and Practice* (Guildford: Ashgate).

Christiansen, T., and Lagreid, P. (eds) (2007) *Transcending New Public Management: The Transformation of Public Sector Reforms* (Guildford: Ashgate).

Christoph, J. B. (1993) 'The Effects of Britons in Brussels: the European Community and the Culture of Whitehall', *Governance*, 6 (4): 518–37.

Cichowski, R. (2007) *The European Court and Civil Society* (Cambridge: Cambridge University Press).

Cini, M. (1996) *The European Commission: Leadership, Organisation, and Culture in the EU Administration* (Manchester: Manchester University Press).

Cini, M. (2007) *From Integration to Integrity: Administrative Ethics and Reform in the European Commission* (Manchester: Manchester University Press).

Cini, M. (2008) 'Political Leadership in the European Commission: The Santer and Prodi Commissions, 1995–2005', in J. Hayward (ed.) *Leaderless Europe* (Oxford: Oxford University Press), 113–30.

Claude, I. L. (1956) *Swords into Plowshares: The Problems and Process of International Organization* (New York: Random House).

Cockfield, A. (1997) 'Communication to the Conference "A tribute to Emile Noël"' (London: London Office of the European Commission).

Cohen, A., Y. Dezalay and D. Marchetti (2007) 'Esprits d'État, Entrepreneurs d'Europe', *Actes de la Recherche en Sciences Sociales*, 1 (166–167): 5–13.

Cole, A. (2008) 'Franco-German Relations: From Active to Reaction Cooperation' in J. Hayward (ed.) *Leaderless Europe* (Oxford: Oxford University Press).

Commission of the European Communities (1962) *Staff Regulations of Officials of the European Communities* (Brussels: Commission of the European Communities).

Commission of the European Communities (1979) *Bulletin of the European Communities November (11)* (Luxembourg: Office of Official Publications of the European Union).

Commission of the European Communities (2000) 'Reforming the Commission', COM(2000) 200, March 2000, http://ec.europa.eu/reform/refdoc/index_en.htm, accessed 10 January 2012.

Commission of the European Communities (2001) 'European Governance: A White Paper', COM (2001): 428 final, <http://europa.eu.int/comm/Governance/index_en.htm>.

Commission of the European Communities (2004) *Staff Regulations of Officials of the European Communities, 1.05.2004* ([Brussels]: Staff Regulations Unit, Commission of the European Communities).

Commission of the European Communities (2005) *A Roadmap to an Integrated Internal Control Framework. Communication from the Commission to the Council, the European Parliament and the European Court of Auditors,* COM(2005): 252 final.

Commission of the European Communities (2008) *Statistical Bulletin: The Personnel of the Commission* (Brussels: DG Personnel and Administration).

Committee of Independent Experts (1999a) *First Report on Allegations regarding Fraud, Mismanagement and Nepotism in the European Commission* (Brussels: European Parliament), <http://www.europarl.europa.eu/experts/1_en.htm>.

Committee of Independent Experts (1999b) *Second report on Reform of the Commission: Analysis of Current Practice and Proposals for Tackling Mismanagement, Irregularities and Fraud,* 10 September (Brussels: European Parliament) <http://www.europarl.europa.eu/experts/default_en.htm>.

Conrad, Y. (1992) 'La Communauté Européenne du Charbon et de l'Acier et la situation de ses agents. Du régime contractuel au régime statutaire (1952–58)' in E. V. Heyen (ed.) *Yearbook of European Administrative History,* vol. 4: *Early European Community Administration* (Baden-Baden: Nomos), 223–37.

Converse, P. E. (1964) 'The Nature of Belief Systems in Mass Publics' in D. E. Apter (ed.) *Ideology and Discontent* (London: Collier-Macmillan).

Coombes, D. (1970) *Politics and Bureaucracy in the European Community a Portrait of the Commission of the E. E. C* (London: Allen and Unwin).

Costa, O., R. Dehousse, and A. Trakalová (2011) 'Co-Decision and 'Early Agreements': an Improvement or a Subversion of the Legislative Procedure?', *Notre Europe,* 84, <http://www.eng.notre-europe.eu/media/CodecisionEarlyAgreements_CostaDehousseTrakalova_NotreEurope_Nov2011.pdf >.

Coull, J., and C. Lewis (2003) 'The Impact Reform of the Staff Regulations in Making the Commission a More Modern and Efficient Organisation: An Insider's Perspective', *EIPASCOPE,* 2003(3): 2–9, <http://aei.pitt.edu/5921/01/scop_3_1(2).pdf>.

Cox, R. W., and H. K. Jacobson (1973) *The Anatomy of Influence: Decision Making in International Organization* (New Haven: Yale University Press).

Craig, P. P. (2010) *The Lisbon Treaty: Law, Politics, and Treaty Reform* (Oxford: Oxford University Press).

Cram, L. (1993) 'Calling the Tune Without Paying the Piper? Social Policy Regulation: the Role of the Commission in European Community Social Policy', *Policy & Politics,* 21 (2): 135–46.

Cram, L. (1994) 'The European Commission as a Multi-organization: Social Policy and IT Policy in the EU', *Journal of European Public Policy,* 1 (2): 195–217.

Crespy, A. (2010) 'Contre «Bolkestein»: Le Parlement Européen entre Idéologie et Stratégie Institutionnelle', *Revue Française de Science Politique,* 60 (5): 975–5.

Crespy, A., and Gajewska, K. (2010) 'New Parliament, New Cleavages after the Eastern Enlargement? The Conflict over the Services Directive as an Opposition between the Liberals and Regulators', *Journal of Common Market Studies,* 48 (5): 1185–208.

Cronin, D. (2005) 'Cabinets still in pole position for top jobs', *European Voice,* 2 June, online at <http://www.europeanvoice.com/article/imported/cabinets-still-in-pole-position-for-top-jobs/52451.aspx> (accessed 8 October 2012)

Cross, R., S. P. Borgatti, and A. Parker (2001) 'Beyond Answers: Dimensions of the Advice Network', *Social Networks,* 23 (3): 215–35.

Cross, R., and A. Parker (2004) *The Hidden Power of Social Networks: Understanding How Work Really Gets Done in Organizations* (Boston, MA: Harvard Business School Press).

Crozier, M. (2009) *The Bureaucratic Phenomenon* (New Brunswick, NJ: Transaction Publishers).

Damgaard, B. (2006) 'Do Policy Networks Lead to Network Governing?', *Public Administration*, 84 (3): 673–91.

Daugbjerg, C. (1999) 'Reforming the CAP: Policy Networks and Broader Institutional Structures', *Journal of Common Market Studies*, 37 (3): 407–28.

De Jong, M. and J. Edelenbos (2007) 'An Insider's Look into Policy Transfer in Transnational Expert Networks', *European Planning Studies*, 15 (5): 687–706.

De Vries, C. E., and E. E. Edwards (2009) 'Taking Europe To Its Extremes: Extremist Parties and Public Euroscepticism', *Party Politics*, 15 (1): 5–28.

Deese, D. A. (2008) *World Trade Politics: Power, Principles, and Leadership* (London: Routledge).

Degenne, A., and M. Forsé (1999) *Introducing Social Networks* (London: Sage).

Dehaene, J.-L., R.v. Weizäcker, and D. Simon (1999) *The Institutional Implications of Enlargement: Report to the European Commission* (Brussels: European Commission).

Dehousse, R. (1997) 'Regulation by Networks in the European Community: the Role of European Agencies', *Journal of European Public Policy*, 4 (2): 246–61.

Dehousse, R., F. Deloche-Gaudez, and O. Duhamel (eds) (2006) *Élargissement: comment l'Europe s'adapte* (Paris: Presses de Sciences Po).

Dehousse, R. (2011) *The 'Community Method': Obstinate or Obsolete* (Basingstoke: Palgrave Macmillan).

Dell, E. (1993) 'The Report of the Three Wise Men', *Contemporary European History*, 2 (1): 35–68.

Delors, J. (1994) *L'Unité d'un Homme: Entretiens avec Dominique Wolton* (Paris: Odile Jacob).

Delors, J. (2004) *Mémoires* (Paris: Plon).

Derlien, H.-U. (2003) 'Mandarins or Managers? The Bureaucratic Elite in Bonn, 1970 to 1987 and Beyond', *Governance*, 16 (3): 401–28.

Derlien, H.-U., and R. Mayntz (1988) *Einstellungen der politisch-administraven Elite des Bundes* (Bamberg: University of Bamberg, Lehrstuhl für Verwaltungswissenschaft).

Devuyst, Y. (1999) 'The Community-Method after Amsterdam', *Journal of Common Market Studies*, 37 (1): 109–20.

Devuyst, Y. (2008) 'The European Union's Institutional Balance after the Treaty of Lisbon : "Community Method" and "Democratic Deficit" reassessed', *Georgetown Journal of International Law*, 39 (2): 247–325).

Dimitrakopoulos, D. G. (ed.) (2004) *The Changing European Commission* (Manchester: Manchester University Press).

Dimitrakopoulos, D. G. (2008) 'Collective Leadership in Leaderless Europe: A Sceptical View' in J. Hayward (ed.) *Leaderless Europe* (Oxford: Oxford University Press), 288–304.

Dittmer-Odell, M. (2010) 'Reassessing the Theoretical Relationship between Widening and Deepening in the Council of the European Union: Presenting and Evaluating a

Sociological Institutionalist Alternative in the Context of the 2004 Enlargement', PhD thesis, Birkbeck, University of London.

Dogan, M. (1975) *The Mandarins of Western Europe* (New York: Halsted Press).

Dolan, J., and D. Rosenbloom (eds) (2003) *Representative Bureaucracy: Classic Readings and Continuing Controversies* (Armonk, NY: M. E. Sharpe).

Donnelly, M., and E. Ritchie (1994) 'The College of Commissioners and their Cabinets' in G. Edwards and D. Spence (eds) *The European Commission* (London: Cartermill), 31–61.

Donnelly, M., and E. Ritchie (1997) 'The College of Commissioners and Their Cabinets' in G. Edwards and D. Spence (eds) *The European Commission*, 2nd edn (London: Cartermill).

Döring, H. (2007) 'The Composition of the College of Commissioners: Patterns of Delegation', *European Union Politics*, 8 (2): 229–50.

Dowding, K. (2001) 'There Must Be End to Confusion: Policy Networks, Intellectual Fatigue, and the Need for Political Science Methods Courses in British Universities', *Political Studies*, 49 (1): 89–105.

Drake, H. (2000) *Jacques Delors: Perspectives on a European Leader* (London: Routledge).

du Gay, P. (2000) *In Praise of Bureaucracy: Weber, Organization, Ethics* (London: Sage).

du Gay, P. (2005) *The Values of Bureaucracy* (Oxford and New York: Oxford University Press).

Dumoulin, M. (ed) (2007) *The European Commission, 1958–72 : History and Memories* (Luxembourg: Office for Official Publications of the European Communities).

Dunleavy, P. (1991) *Democracy, Bureaucracy, and Public Choice: Economic Explanations in Political Science* (Brighton: Harvester Wheatsheaf).

Dunn, J. A., and A. Perl (1994) 'Policy Networks and Industrial Revitalization: High Speed Rail Initiatives in France and Germany', *Journal of Public Policy*, 14 (3): 311–43.

Egeberg, M. (1996) 'Organization and Nationality in the European Commission Services.' *Public Administration*, 74 (4): 721–35.

Egeberg, M. (1999) 'Transcending Intergovernmentalism? Identity and Role Perceptions of National Officials in EU Decision-Making', *Journal of European Public Policy*, 6: 456–74.

Egeberg, M. (2001) 'How federal? The Organizational Dimension of Integration in the EU (and Elsewhere)', *Journal of European Public Policy*, 8 (5): 728–46.

Egeberg, M. (2004) 'Organising Institutional Autonomy in a Political Context: Enduring Tensions in the European Commission's Development', ARENA Working Paper 02/2004 (Oslo: ARENA Centre for European Studies, University of Oslo), <http://www.sv.uio.no/arena/english/research/publications/arena-publications/workingpapers/working-papers2004/wp04_2.pdf>.

Egeberg, M. (ed.) (2006a) *Multilevel Union Administration* (Basingstoke: Palgrave Macmillan).

Egeberg, M. (2006b) 'Towards an Organization Theory of International Integration', ARENA Working Paper 13/2006 (Oslo: ARENA Centre for European Studies, University of Oslo), <http://www.sv.uio.no/arena/english/research/publications/arena-publications/workingpapers/working-papers2006/wp06_13.pdf>.

Egeberg, M. (2006) 'Executive Politics as Usual: Role Behaviour and Conflict Dimensions in the College of European Commissioners', *Journal of European Public Policy*, 13 (1): 1–15.

Egeberg, M., and A. Heskestad (2010) 'The Denationalization of Cabinets in the European Commission', *Journal of Common Market Studies*, 48 (4): 775–86.

Elgie, R. (1995) *Political Leadership in Liberal Democracies* (Basingstoke: Palgrave Macmillan).

Ellinas, A., and E. Suleiman (2007) 'Reforming the Commission: Has the pendulum swung too far?', paper presented at the EUSA conference in Montreal, Canada, 17–19 May.

Ellinas, A., and E. Suleiman (2008) 'Reforming the Commission: Between Modernization and Bureaucratization', *Journal of European Public Policy*, 15 (5): 708–25.

Ellinas, A., and E. Suleiman (2011) 'Supranationalism in a Transnational Bureaucracy: The Case of the European Commission', *Journal of Common Market Studies*, 49 (5): 923–47.

Elsig, M. (2010) 'European Union Trade Policy after Enlargement: Larger Crowds, Shifting Priorities and Informal Decision-Making', *Journal of European Public Policy*, 17 (6): 781–98.

Endo, K. (1999) *The Presidency of the European Commission under Jacques Delors: The Politics of Shared Leadership* (Basingstoke: Macmillan).

Enzensberger, H. M. (2011) *Brussels, the Gentle Monster: Or the Disenfranchisement of Europe* (London: Seagull Books).

Eppink, D. (2007) *Life of a European Mandarin: Inside the Commission* (Tielt: Lannoo).

Erikson R. S., and K. L. Tedin (2003) *American Public Opinion*, 6th edn (New York: Longman).

European Commission (2000) 'Code of Good Administrative Behaviour for Staff of the European Commission in their Relations with the Public', <http://ec.europa.eu/transparency/civil_society/code/_docs/code_en.pdf>.

European Commission (2002) 'Reforming the Commission', archived at <http://ec.europa.eu/reform/2002/chapter02_en.htm#3>.

European Commission (2010) 'Communication to the Commission on the strategy on equal opportunities for women and men within the European Commission (2010–2014)', SEC (2010) 1554/3, Brussels, 17 December, <http://ec.europa.eu/civil_ service/docs/equal_opp/strategie_1554_en.pdf> (accessed 8 October 2012).

European Commission (2011) *The 2004 Enlargement and Commission Recruitments: How the Commission Managed the Recruitment of Staff from 10 New Member States —Situation at the end of the EU-10 Transition Period: Final Report* <http://ec.europa.eu/civil_service/docs/qabd_1946_eu-10_recruitments_en.pdf>.

European Commission DG Personnel and Administration (2007) 'Pers Admin, The Revision of the CDR and promotion system', European Commission intranet.

Falkner, G. (1998) *EU Social Policy in the 1990s: Towards a Corporatist Policy Community* (London: Routledge).

Falkner, G. (2002) 'EU Treaty Reform as a Three-Level Process: Introduction', *Journal of European Public Policy*, 9 (1): 1–11.

Favell, A. (2008) *Eurostars and Eurocities: Free Movement and Mobility in an Integrating Europe* (Oxford: Blackwell Publishing).

Featherstone, K. (1994) 'Jean Monnet and the 'Democratic Deficit' in the European Union', *Journal of Common Market Studies*, 32 (2): 149–70.

Feldman, S. (2003) 'Values, Ideology and the Structure of Political Attitudes,' in D. O. Sears, L. Huddy, and R. Jervis (eds.) *Oxford Handbook of Political Psychology* (Oxford: Oxford University Press).

Franchino, F. (2007) *The Powers of the Union: Delegation in the EU* (Cambridge: Cambridge University Press).

Fuchs, D., R. Magni-Berton, and A. Roger (2009) *Euroscepticism: Images of Europe among Mass Publics and Political Elites* (Opladen and Farmington Hills, MI: Barbara Budrich Publishers).

Fusacchia, A. (2009) 'Selection, Appointment and Redeployment of Senior Commission Officials', PhD thesis, Florence: Department of Political Science, European University Institute.

Gains, F., and P. John (2010) 'What do Bureaucrats Like Doing? Bureaucratic Preferences in Response to Institutional Reform', *Public Administration Review*, 70 (3): 455–63.

Gelleny, R. D., and C. J. Anderson (2000) 'The Economy, Accountability, and Public Support for the President of the European Commission', *European Union Politics*, 1 (2): 173–200.

Georgakakis, D. (2010) 'Do skills kill? Les Enjeux de la Requalification de la Compétence des Eurofonctionnaires', *Revue française d'Administration publique*, 133 (1): 61–80.

Georgakakis, D. (2010) 'Où en est l'Administration de la Commission Europeéenne? What is the European Commission's Administration currently up to?', *Revue française d'Administration publique*, 133 (1): 5–122.

Georgakakis, D. (2012) *Le champ de l'eurocratie: une sociologie politique du personnel de l'UE* (Paris, Economica).

Georgakakis, D., and M. de Lassalle (2007) 'Genèse et Structure d'un Capital Institutionnel Européen', *Actes de la recherche en sciences Sociales*, 166–7 (1–2): 38–53.

Georgakakis, D., and M. de Lassalle (2008) 'Where have all the lawyers gone? Structure and transformation of the top officials' legal training' *European University Institute Working Papers RSCAS* 2008/38.

Georgakakis, D., and J. Weisbein (2010) 'From Above and From Below: A political Sociology of European Actors', *Comparative European Politics*, 8 (1): 93–109.

Geri, L. R. (2001) 'New Public Management and the Reform of International Organizations', *International Review of Administrative Sciences*, 67 (3): 445–60.

Gibbons, D. (2004) 'Network Structure and Innovation Ambiguity Effects on Diffusion in Dynamic Organizational Fields', *Academy of Management Journal*, 47(6): 938–51.

Gnesotto, N. (2002) 'Terrorism and Enlargement: A Clash of Dynamics', *Institute of Security Studies Newsletter*, 3 (4): 1–6.

Grande, E., and A. Peschke (1999) 'Transnational Cooperation and Policy Networks in European Science Policy-Making', *Research Policy*, 28 (1): 43–61.

Grant, C. (1994) *Delors: Inside the House That Jacques Built* (London: N. Brealey).

Gravier, M. (2008) 'The 2004 Enlargement Staff Policy of the European Commission: The Case for Representative Bureaucracy', *Journal of Common Market Studies,* 46 (5): 1025–47.

Greenwood, J. and L. Cram (1995) 'European Industry Beyond the Single Market: How can we Understand European-Level Collective Action?', paper presented to the Fourth Biennial International Conference of the European Community Studies Association, Charleston, South Carolina, USA, May 11–14.

Grossman, E., and S. Brouard (2009) 'Quelles Sont les Priorités de l'Union Européenne?' in R. Dehousse, F. Deloche-Gaudez and S. Jacquot (eds) *Que Fait l'Europe?* (Paris: Presses de Sciences Po).

Gulick, L. H. (1937) 'Notes on the Theory of Organization' in L. H. Gulick and L.F. Urwick (eds) *Papers on the Science of Administration,* (New York: Institute of Public Administration).

Haas, E. B. (1958) *The Uniting of Europe* (Stanford, CA: Stanford University Press).

Hagemann, S., and D. De Clerck-Sachsse (2007) 'Old Rules, New Game: Decision-Making in the Council of Ministers after the 2004 Enlargement', *CEPS Special Report* (accessed 05/06/2007: <http://shop.ceps.eu/BookDetail.php?item_id=1470>).

Hall, T., and L. J. O'Toole (2000) 'Structures of Policy Implementation: an Analysis of National Legislation, 1965–6 and 1993–4', *Administration and Society,* 31 (6): 667–86.

Hallstein, W. (1963) 'The European Economic Community', *Political Science Quarterly,* 78 (2): 161–78.

Hallstein, W. (1965) 'The EEC Commission: A New Factor in International Life', *International and Comparative Law Quarterly,* 14 (3): 727–41.

Halsey, A. H., and I. M. Crewe (1968) *Social Survey of the Civil Service* (London, HMSO).

Harmsen, R., and M. Spiering (2004) *Euroscepticism: Party Politics, National Identity and European Integration* (Amsterdam: Rodopi).

Hartlapp, M. (2011) 'Organizing Exits from the Joint-Decision Trap? Cross-Sectoral (Non-) Coordination in the European Union' in G. Falkner (ed.) *The EU's Decision Traps: Comparing Policies* (Oxford: Oxford University Press), 181–98.

Hartlapp, M., J. Metz, and C. Rauh (2010) 'The Agenda Set by the EU Commission: The Result of Balanced or Biased Aggregation of Positions?', LSE *'Europe in Question' Discussion Paper Series,* Paper no. 21, online at <http://dx.doi.org/10.2139/ssrn.1588067>.

Hay, C., G. Ross and W. Streeck (2009) 'Neil Fligstein Euroclash: The EU, European Identity and the Future of Europe', *Socio-Economic Review,* 7 (3): 535–52.

Hayward, J. (ed.) (2008) *Leaderless Europe* (Oxford: Oxford University Press).

Heclo, H. (1978) 'Issue Networks and the Executive Establishment' in H. Heclo (ed) *The New American Political System* (Washington DC: American Enterprise Institute).

Heidbreder, E. G. (2011) *The Impact of Expansion on European Union Institutions: The Eastern Touch on Brussels* (Basingstoke: Palgrave Macmillan).

Heisserer, B. (2008) 'Management Reforms in International Organizations. A Critical Analysis of Influencing Factors on Organizational Change of the European Commission', unpublished manuscript, University of Konstanz.

Helms, L. (2005) *Presidents, Prime Ministers and Chancellors: Executive Leadership in Western Democracies* (Basingstoke: Palgrave Macmillan).

Hennessy, P. (1989) *Whitehall* (New York: The Free Press).

Hennessy, P. (2007) *Cabinets and the Bomb* (Oxford: Oxford University Press).

Héritier, A. (1999) *Policy-Making and Diversity in Europe: Escaping Deadlock* (Cambridge: Cambridge University Press).

Héritier, A., and Farrell, H. (2003) *The Invisible Transformation of Codecision: Problems of Democratic Legitimacy* (Stockholm: Swedish Institute for European Policy Studies).

Heyen, E. V. (ed.) (1992) *Yearbook of European Administrative History*, vol. 4: *Early European Community Administration* (Baden-Baden: Nomos).

Hix, S. (1994) 'The Study of the European Community: The Challenge to Comparative Politics', *West European Politics,* 17 (1): 1–30.

Hix, S. (2002a) *Why the EU Should Have a Single President, and How She Should be Elected*, paper for the Working Group on Democracy in the EU for the UK Cabinet Office, October.

Hix, S. (2002b) 'Constitutional Agenda-Setting through Discretion in Rule Interpretation: Why the European Parliament Won at Amsterdam', *British Journal of Political Science,* 32 (2): 259–80.

Hix, Simon (2005) *The Political System of the European Union*, 2nd edn (Basingstoke: Palgrave Macmillan).

Hix, S. (2008) *What's Wrong with the European Union and How to Fix It* (Cambridge: Polity).

Hix, S., and B. Hoyland (2011) *The Political System of the European Union* (Basingstoke: Palgrave Macmillan).

Hobolt, S. B. (2012) 'Public Opinion and Integration' in E. Jones, A. Menon, and S. Weatherill (eds) *The Oxford Handbook of the European Union* (Oxford: Oxford University Press).

Hood, C. (1991) 'A Public Management for All Seasons?', *Public Administration,* 69 (1): 3–19.

Hood, C. (1995a) 'The "New Public Management" in the 1980s: Variations on a Theme', *Accounting, Organizations and Society,* 20 (2–3): 93–109.

Hood, C. (1995b) 'Contemporary Public Management: a New Global Paradigm?' *Public Policy and Administration,* 10 (2): 104–17.

Hood, C. and B. G. Peters (2004) 'The Middle Aging of New Public Management: Into the Age of Paradox?', *Journal of Public Administration Research and Theory,* 14 (3): 267–82.

Hooghe, L. (1996) 'Building a Europe with the Regions: The Changing Role of the European Commission' in L. Hooghe (ed.) *Cohesion Policy and European Integration: Building Multilevel Governance* (Oxford: Clarendon Press).

Hooghe, L. (1997) 'A House with Differing Views: The European Commission and Cohesion Policy' in N. Nugent (ed.) *At the Heart of the Union: Studies of the European Commission* (Basingstoke: Palgrave Macmillan).

Hooghe, L. (1999) 'Consociationalists or Weberians? Top Commission Officials on Nationality', *Governance,* 12 (4): 397–424.

Hooghe, L. (2001) *The European Commission and the Integration of Europe* (Cambridge: Cambridge University Press).

Hooghe, L. (2005a) 'Several Roads Lead to International Norms, but Few Via International Socialization: A Case Study of the European Commission', *International Organization,* 59 (4): 861–98.

Hooghe, L. (2005b) 'Calculation, Community and Cues: Public Opinion on European Integration', *European Union Politics,* 6 (4): 419–43.

Hooghe, L. (2012) 'Images of Europe: How Commission Officials Conceive their Institution's Role', *Journal of Common Market Studies*, 50 (1): 87–111.

Hooghe, L., and H. Kassim (2012) 'The Commission's Services' in J. Peterson and M. Shackleton (eds) *The Institutions of the European Union*, 3rd edn (Oxford: Oxford University Press).

Hooghe, L., and G. Marks (1999) 'The Making of a Polity: The Struggle over European Integration' in H. Kitschelt, P. Lange, G. Marks and J. D. Stephens (eds) *Continuity and Change in Contemporary Capitalism* (Cambridge: Cambridge University Press).

Hooghe, L., and G. Marks (2001) *Multi-Level Governance and European Integration* (Lanham, MD: Rowman & Littlefield).

Hooghe, L., and G. Marks (2005) 'Calculation, Community and Cues: Public Opinion on European Integration', *European Union Politics*, 6 (4): 419–43.

Hooghe, L., and G. Marks (2009) 'Does Efficiency Shape the Territorial Structure of Government?', *Annual Review of Political Science*, 12: 225–41.

Hooghe, L., and G. Marks (2009) 'A Postfunctionalist Theory of European Integration: From Permissive Consensus to Constraining Dissensus', *British Journal of Political Science*, 39 (1): 1–23.

Hooghe, L., G. Marks, and A. H. Schakel (2010) *The Rise of Regional Authority: A Comparative Study of 42 Democracies (1950-2006)* (London: Routledge).

Hooghe, L., G. Marks, L., T. Lenz, J. Bezuijen, B. Ceka, S. Derderyan, and C. De Vries (forthcoming) *Multilevel Governance Above the State: The Authority of International Organizations (1950–2010)* (Oxford: Oxford University Press).

Hooghe, L., and N. Nugent (2006) 'The Commission's Services' in John Peterson and Michael Shackleton (eds) *The Institutions of the European Union*, 2nd edn (Oxford: Oxford University Press).

Hooghe, L., R. Bakker, A. Brigevich, C. de Vries, E. Edwards, G. Marks, J. Rovny, and M. Steenbergen (2010) 'Measurement Validity and Party Positioning: Chapel Hill Expert Surveys of 2002 and 2006', *European Journal of Political Research*, 42 (4): 684–703.

Höpner, M., and A. Schäfer (2012) 'Embeddedness and European Integration: Waiting for Polanyi in a Hayekian Setting', *International Organization*, 66 (3): 429–55.

Hosli, M. O., M. Mattila, and M. Uriot (2011) 'Voting in the Council of the European Union after the 2004 Enlargement: A Comparison of Old and New Member States', *Journal of Common Market Studies*, 49 (6): 1249–70.

House of Lords (1998) *Staffing of Community Institutions: 11th Report of the Select Committee on the European Communities*, HLP 66, 1987–88 (London: HMSO).

Hughes, J., G. Sasse, and C. Gordon (2004) *Europeanization and Regionalization in the EU's Enlargement to Central and Eastern Europe: The Myth of Conditionality* (Basingstoke: Palgrave Macmillan).

Inglehart, R. (1970) 'The New Europeans: Inward or Outward-Looking?', *International Organization*, 24 (1): 129–39.

Inglehart, R. (1977) *The Silent Revolution: Changing Values and Political Styles among Western Publics* (Princeton, NJ: Princeton University Press).

Janning, J. (2005) 'Leadership Coalitions and Change: The Role of States in the European Union', *International Affairs*, 81: 821–34.

Jenkins, R. (1989) *European Diary: 1977–1981* (London: Collins).

Jenkins, R. (1991) *A Life at the Centre* (London: Macmillan).

Jennings, E. T., and D. Crane (1994) 'Coordination and Welfare Reform: The Quest for the Philosopher's Stone', *Public Administration Review*, 54: 341–8.

Joana, J. and A. Smith (2002) *Les Commissaires Européens: Technocrates, Diplomates ou Politiques?* (Paris: Presses de Sciences Po).

Joana, J., and A. Smith (2004) 'The Politics of Collegiality: the Non-Portfolio Dimension' in A. Smith (ed.) *Politics and the European Commission* (London: Routledge).

Johnson, M., and J. Rollo (2001) *EU Enlargement and Commercial Policy: Enlargement and the Making of Commercial Policy* (Brighton: Sussex European Institute), briefing paper no. 43, <www.sussex.ac.uk/sei/documents/sei-working-paper-no-43. pdf >.

Johnston, A. I. (2001) 'Treating International Institutions as Social Environments', *International Studies Quarterly*, 45 (4): 487–515.

Jordan, A., and A. Schout (2006) *The Coordination of the European Union: Exploring the Capacities of Networked Governance* (Oxford: Oxford University Press).

Jupille, J. (2004) *Procedural Politics Issues, Influence, and Institutional Choice in the European Union* (Cambridge: Cambridge University Press).

Kamarck, E. (2007) *The End of Government . . . As We Know It: Making Public Policy Work* (Boulder, CO: Lynne Rienner Publishers).

Kassim, H. (1994) 'Policy Networks, Networks and European Union Policy Making: A Sceptical View', *West European Politics,* 17 (4): 15–27.

Kassim, H. (2003) 'The European Administration: Between Europeanisation and Domestication' in J. Hayward and A. Menon (eds) *Governing Europe* (Oxford: Oxford University Press).

Kassim, H. (2004a) 'The Secretary General of the European Commision, 1958–2003: The History of a Singular Institution' in A. Smith (ed.) *The Politics of the European Commission* (London: Routledge).

Kassim, H. (2004b) 'The Kinnock Reforms in Perspective: Why Reforming the Commission is an Heroic, But Thankless, Task', *Public Policy and Administration*, 19 (3): 25–41.

Kassim, H. (2004c) 'A Historic Accomplishment? The Prodi Commission and Administrative Reform' in D. G. Dimitrakopoulos (ed.) *The Changing European Commission* (Manchester: Manchester University Press).

Kassim, H. (2006) 'The Secretariat General of the European Commission' in D. Spence with G. Edwards (eds) *The European Commission*, 3rd edn (London: John Harper).

Kassim, H. (2008) ' "Mission Impossible", but Mission Accomplished: The Kinnock Reforms and the European Commission', *Journal of European Public Policy*, 15 (5): 648–68.

Kassim, H. (2010a) 'Leadership and Coordination in the European Commission. A new era?', paper presented at the Council for European Studies conference in Montreal, Canada, 15 April.

Kassim, H. (2010b) 'A Silent Transformation: Leadership and Coordination in the European Commission since 2005', paper presented at ARENA in Oslo, Norway, 24 May.

Kassim, H. (2010c) 'The Presidency and Presidents of the European Commission', unpublished mimeo.

Kassim, H. (2012) 'The Presidents and Presidency of the European Commission' in E. Jones, A. Menon, and S. Weatherill (eds) *The Oxford Handbook of the EU* (Oxford: Oxford University Press).

Kassim, H., and D. G. Dimitrakopoulos (2007) 'The European Commission and the Future of Europe', *Journal of European Public Policy*, 14 (8): 1249–70.

Kassim, H., and A. Menon (2003) 'Les États Membres de l'UE et la Commission Prodi', *Revue Française de Science Politique*, 53 (4): 491–501.

Kassim, H., and A. Menon (2004) 'EU Member States and the Prodi Commission' in D. G. Dimitrakopoulos (ed.) *The Changing European Commission* (Manchester: Manchester University Press).

Kassim, H., and A. Menon (2010) 'Bringing the Member States Back in: The Supranational Orthodoxy, Member State Resurgence and the Decline of the European Commission since the 1990s', paper presented at ECPR Fifth Pan-European Conference in Porto, Portugal, 23–26 June.

Kassim, H., and B. G. Peters (2008) 'Introduction. Coordinating the European Union', unpublished mimeo.

Kassim, H., and K. Wright (2009) 'Bringing Regulatory Processes Back in: Revisiting the Reform of EU Antitrust and Merger Control in Managing Regulatory Conflict', *West European Politics*, 32 (4): 738–55.

Kato, J. (1996) 'Review Article: Institutions and Rationality in Politics—Three Varieties of Neo-Institutionalism', *British Journal of Political Science*, 26: 553–82.

Kellerman, B. (1986) *The Political Presidency: Practice of Leadership* (Oxford: Oxford University Press).

Kellner, P., and L. Crowther-Hunt (1980) *The Civil Servants: An Inquiry into Britain's Ruling Class* (London: MacDonald Futura Publishers).

Keohane, R. (2002) *Power and Governance in a Partially Globalized World* (London: Routledge).

Kern, K., and H. Bulkeley (2009) 'Cities, Europeanization and Multi-level Governance: Governing Climate Change through Transnational Municipal Networks', *Journal of Common Market Studies*, 47 (2): 309–32.

Kessler, M.-C. (1986) *Les Grands Corps de l'État* (Paris: Presses de Sciences Po).

Ketelaar, A., N. Manning, and E. Turkisch (2007) 'Performance-based Arrangements for Senior Civil Servants OECD and other Country Experiences', *OECD Working Papers on Public Governance, 2007/5* (OECD Publishing).

Kettl, D. (2002) *The Transformation of Governance: Public Administration for Twenty-First Century America* (Baltimore: Johns Hopkins University Press).

Kickert, W. (1997) *Managing Complex Networks: Strategies for the Public Sector* (London: Sage).

Kilduff, M,. and W. Tsai (2003) *Social Networks and Organizations* (London: Sage).

Kingsley, D. J. (1944) *Representative Bureaucracy* (Yellow Springs, OH: Antioch Press).

Kisby, B. (2007) 'Analysing Policy Networks', *Policy Studies*, 28 (1): 71–90.

Kitschelt, H. (1992) 'The Formation of Party Systems in East Central Europe', *Politics and Society*, 20: 7–50.

Kitschelt, H. (1994) *The Transformation of European Social Democracy* (Cambridge and New York: Cambridge University Press).

Kitschelt, H., Z. Mansfeldova, R. Markowski, and G. Tóka (1999) *Post-Communist Party Systems: Competition, Representation, and Inter-Party Cooperation* (Cambridge and New York: Cambridge University Press).

Knill, C., and T. Balint (2008) 'Explaining Variation in Organizational Change: The Reform of Human Resource Management in the European Commission and the OECD', *Journal of European Public Policy*, 15 (5): 669–90.

Kohler-Koch, B., and B. Rittberger (eds) (2007) *Debating the Democratic Legitimacy of the European Union* (Lanham, MD: Rowman & Littlefield).

König, T. (1998) 'Modeling Policy Networks', *Journal of Theoretical Politics*, 10 (4): 387–8.

Kriesi, H., S. Adam, and M. Jochum (2006) 'Comparative Analysis of Policy Networks in Western Europe', *Journal of European Public Policy*, 13 (3): 341–61.

Kriesi, H., E. Grande, R. Lachat, M. Dolezal, S. Bornschier, and T. Frey (2008) *West European Politics in the Age of Globalization* (Cambridge: Cambridge University Press).

Kristensen, J. K., W. S. Groszyk, and B. Bühler (2002) *Outcome-Focused Management and Budgeting* (Paris: OECD).

Kupchan, C. A. (2012) *No One's World: the West, the Rising Rest, and the Coming Global Turn* (Oxford: Oxford University Press).

Kurpas, S., C. Grøn, and P. M. Kaczynski (2008) *The European Commission after Enlargement: Does More add up to Less?* (Brussels: Centre for European Policy Studies).

Kusters, H. J. (1998) 'Walter Hallstein and the Negotiations on the Treaties of Rome 1955–57' in W. Loth, W. Wallace, and W. Wessels (eds) *Walter Hallstein: The Forgotten European?* (London: Macmillan).

Laffan, B. (1997) 'From Policy Entrepreneur to Policy Manager: The Challenge Facing the European Commission', *Journal of European Public Policy*, 4 (3): 422–38.

Laffan, B. (2004) 'The European Union and its Institutions as "Identity Builders"' in R.K. Hermann, T. Risse, and M. B. Brewer (eds) *Transnational Identities: Becoming European in the EU* (Lanham, MD: Rowman & Littlefield).

Lamy, P. (2004) 'EU 25—making it work', address to International Advisory Council, Centre for European Policy Studies (Brussels), 19 February, <www.ceps.eu/ceps/download/956>.

Lane, J.-E. (2000) *New Public Management* (London: Routledge).

Laursen, F. (2012) *The EU's Lisbon Treaty: Institutional Choices and Implementation* (Burlington, VT: Ashgate).

Lemaignen, R. (1964) *L'Europe au berceau: Souvenirs d'un technocrate* (Paris, Plon).

Lequesne, C. (1997) 'The European Commission: A balancing act between autonomy and dependence', paper presented at the European Community Studies Association Conference, Seattle, US, 29 May–1 June.

Levi, M. (1997) 'A Model, A Method and a Map: Rational Choice in Comparative and Historical Analysis' in M. I. Lichbach and A. S. Zuckerman (eds.) *Comparative Politics: Rationality, Culture and Structure* (Cambridge: Cambridge University Press).

Levy, R. P. (2003) 'Critical Success Factors in Public Management Reform: The Case of the European Commission', *International Review of Administrative Sciences*, 69 (4): 554–66.

Levy, R. P. (2004) 'Between Rhetoric and Reality: Implementing Management Reform in the European Commission', *International Journal of Public Sector Management*, 17 (2): 166–77.

Levy, R. P. (2006) 'European Commission Overload and the Pathology of Management Reform: Garbage Cans, Rationality and Risk Aversion', *Public Administration*, 84 (2): 423–39.

Levy, R. P., and A. Stevens (eds) (2004) 'The Reform of EU Management: Taking Stock and Looking Forward', *Public Policy and Administration*, 19 (3): 1–6.

Levy, R. P., M. Barzelay, and A.-M. Porras-Gomez (2011) 'The Reform of Financial Management in the European Commission: A Public Management Policy Cycle Case Study', *Public Administration*, 89: 1546–67.

Lijphart, A. (1992) *Parliamentary versus Presidential Government* (Oxford: Oxford University Press).

Lindberg, L. N. (1963) *The Political Dynamics of European Economic Integration* (Stanford, CA: Stanford University Press).

Lindberg, L. N., and S. A. Scheingold (1970) *Regional Integration: Theory and Research* (Cambridge: Harvard University Press).

Linz, J. J. (1990) 'Perils of Presidentialism', *Journal of Democracy*, 1 (1): 51–6.

Loth, W., W. Wallace, and W. Wessels (eds) (1998) *Walter Hallstein: The Forgotten European?* (London: Macmillan).

Loveless, M., and R. Rohrschneider (2011) 'Public Perceptions of the EU as a System of Governance', *Living Reviews in European Governance*, 6 (2), <http://www.livingreviews.org/lreg-2011-2>.

Ludlow, N. P. (2006) 'A Supranational Icarus: Hallstein, the Early Commission and the Search for an Independent Role' in A. Varsori (ed.) *Inside the European Community: Actors and Policies in the European Integration 1957–1972* (Baden-Baden: Nomos).

Luhmann, N. (1964) *Funktionen und Folgen formaler Organisation* (Berlin: Duncker & Humblot).

MacGregor Burns, J. (1978) *Leadership* (New York: Harper and Row).

MacMullen, A. L. (2000) 'European Commissioners: National Routes to a European Elite' in N. Nugent (ed.) *At the Heart of the Union: Studies of the European Commission*, 2nd edn (Basingstoke: Palgrave Macmillan), 28–50.

Madeley, J. (2008) 'The Origins and Nature of Nordic Christian Euroscepticism', paper presented at ECPR Joint Sessions of Workshops in Rennes, France, 11–16 April.

Majone, G. (1996) *Regulating Europe* (London: Routledge).

Majone, G. (2002) 'The European Commission: The Limits of Centralization and the Perils of Parliamentarization', *Governance*, 15 (3): 375–92.

Majone, G. (2005) *Dilemmas of European Integration: the Ambiguities and Pitfalls of Integration by Stealth* (Oxford: Oxford University Press).

Mandelson, P. (2005) 'The idea of Europe: can we make it live again?', speech to the University Association of Contemporary European Studies (UACES), Brussels, 20 July 2005.

Manow, P., A. Schäfer, and H. Zorn (2008) 'Europe's Party-Political Center of Gravity, 1957-2003', *Journal for European Public Policy*, 15 (1): 20–39.

March, J. G., and Olsen, J. P. (1989) *Rediscovering Institutions: The Organizational Basis of Politics* (New York: Simon and Schuster).

Marks, G., L. Hooghe, and K. Blank (1996) 'European Integration from the 1980s: State-Centric v. Multi-level Governance', *Journal of Common Market Studies*, 34 (3): 341–78.

Marks, G., L. Hooghe, N. Nelson, and E. Edwards (2006) 'Party Competition and European Integration in the East and West: Different Structure, Same Causality', *Comparative Political Studies*, 39 (2): 155–75.

Marks, G., and M. Steenbergen (eds) (2004) *European Integration and Political Conflict: Citizens, Parties, Groups* (Cambridge: Cambridge University Press).

Marsden, P. V. (2005) 'Recent Developments in Network Measurement' in P. J. Carrington, J. Scott, and S. Wasserman (eds) *Models and Methods in Social Network Analysis* (Cambridge: Cambridge University Press), 8–30.

Marsh, D. (ed.) (1998) *Comparing Policy Networks* (Buckingham: Open University Press).

Marsh, D., and M. Smith (2001) 'There is More than One Way to Do Political Science: on Different Ways to Study Policy Networks', *Political Studies*, 49 (3): 528–41.

Marsh, D., and R. A. W. Rhodes (1992) *Policy Networks in British Government* (Oxford: Clarendon Press).

Mayntz, R. (1966) *The Study of Organizations: A Trend Report and Bibliography* (Oxford: Basil Blackwell).

Mayntz, R. (1984) 'German Federal Bureaucrats: A Functional Elite between Politics and Administration' in E. N. Suleiman (ed.) *Bureaucrats and Policy Making: A Comparative Overview* (New York: Holmes and Meier).

Mayntz, R., and H.-U. Derlien (1989) 'Party Patronage and Politicization of the West German Administrative Elite 1970–1987—Toward Hybridization?', *Governance*, 2 (4): 384–404.

Mazey, S. and J. Richardson (1993) 'Policy-making styles in the European Community: Consultation of Groups and the Process of European Integration', paper presented to the Third Biennial International Conference of the European Community Studies association, Washington, DC, 27–29 May, <http://aei.pitt.edu/7243/1/002494_1.pdf>, accessed 10 January 2013.

McDonald, M. (1997) 'Identities in the European Commission', in N. Nugent (ed.) *At the Heart of the Union: Studies of the European Commission* (Basingstoke: Palgrave Macmillan), 49–70.

McGarry, J., and B. O'Leary (2005) 'Federation as a method of ethnic conflict regulation' in S. Noel (ed.) *From Power Sharing to Democracy: Post-conflict Institutions in Ethnically Divided Societies*, (Montreal and Kingston: McGill-Queens University Press), 263–96.

McLaughlin, A. M. (1995) 'Automobiles: Dynamic Organiation in Turbulent Times?' in J. Greenwood (ed.) *European Casebook on Business Alliances* (Hemel Hempstead: Prentice Hall) 172–83.

McPherson, M., L. Smith-Lovin, and J. M. Cook (2001) 'Birds of a Feather: Homophily in Social Networks', *Annual Review of Sociology*, 27 (1): 415–44.

McPherson, M., Smith-Lovin, L. and Brashears, M. E. (2009) 'Models and Marginals: Using Survey Research to Study Social Networks', *American Sociological Review*, 74 (4): 670–81

Meier, K. J. (1975) 'Representative Bureaucracy: An Empirical Analysis', *American Political Science Review*, 69: 542.

Metcalfe, L. (1992) 'After 1992: Can the Commission Manage Europe?', *Australian Journal of Public Administration*, 51 (1): 117–30.

Metcalfe, L. (2000) 'Reforming the Commission: Will Organizational Efficiency Produce Effective Governance?', *Journal of Common Market Studies*, 38 (5): 817–41.

Metcalfe, L. (2004) 'European Policy Management: Future Challenges and the Role of the Commission', *Public Policy and Administration*, 19 (3): 77–94.

Meynaud, J. (1968) *Technocracy* (London: Faber).

Michelmann, H. J. (1978) 'Multinational Staffing and Organizational Functioning in the Commission of the European Communities', *International Organization*, 32 (2): 477–96.

Middlemas, K. (1995) *Orchestrating Europe: The Informal Politics of the European Union 1973-1995* (London: Fontana Press).

Minogue, M., C. Polidano, and D. Hulme (eds) (1998) *Beyond the New Public Management: Changing Ideas and Practices in Governance* (Cheltenham: Edward Elgar).

Missiroli, A. (ed.) (2002) *Enlargement and European Defence after 11 September* (Paris: European Institute for Security Studies).

Moe, T. (1997) 'The Positive Theory of Public Bureaucracy' in D. C. Mueller (ed.) *Perspectives on Public Choice: A Handbook* (Cambridge: Cambridge University Press).

Monnet, J. (1978) *Memoirs* (New York: Knopf).

Moravcsik, A. (1998) *The Choice for Europe: Social Purpose and State Power from Messina to Maastricht* (Ithaca, NY: Cornell University Press).

Moravcsik, A. (1999) 'A New Statecraft? Supranational Entrepreneurs and International Cooperation', *International Organization*, 53 (2): 267–306.

Moravcsik, A. (2002) 'In Defence of the "Democratic Deficit": Reassessing Legitimacy in the European Union', *Journal of Common Market Studies*, 40 (4): 603–24.

Morgan, G. (1986) *Images of Organization* (London: Sage).

Mosher, F. C. (1968) *Democracy and the Public Service* (New York: Oxford University Press).

Nelsen, B. F., and J. L. Guth (2000) 'Exploring the Gender Gap: Women, Men and Public Attitudes toward European Integration', *European Union Politics*, 1 (3): 267–91.

Nelsen, B. F., J. L. Guth, and C. R. Fraser (2001) 'Does Religion Matter? Christianity and Public Support for the European Union', *European Union Politics*, 2 (2): 191–217.

Neumayer, L,. and D. Dakowska (2008) 'Élargissement' in C. Belot, P. Magnette, and S. Saurugger (eds) *Science Politique de l'Union Européenne* (Paris: Economica).

Neustadt, R. E. (1960) *Presidential Power* (New York: Macmillan Publishing).

Neustadt, R. (1991) *Presidential Power and the Modern Presidents: the Politics of Leadership from Roosevelt to Reagan* (New York: Free Press).

Niskanen, W. A. (1971) *Bureaucracy and Representative Government* (Chicago, IL: Aldine Atherton).

Niskanen, W. A. (1994) *Bureaucracy and Public Economics* (Aldershot: Edward Elgar).

Nitzan, I., and B. Libai (2011) 'Social Effects on Customer Retention', *Journal of Marketing*, 75 (6): 24-38.

Noël, E. (1992) 'Témoignage: l'Administration de la Communauté Européenne dans la Rétrospection d'un Ancien Haut Fonctionnaire', *Jahrbuch für Europäische*

Verwaltungsgeschichte 4 (Die Anfänge der Verwaltung der Europäischen Gemeinschaft), 145–58.

Noël, E. (1998) 'Walter Hallstein: A Personal Testimony' in W. Loth, W. Wallace, and W. Wessels (eds) *Walter Hallstein. The Forgotten European?* (London: Macmillan).

Nohria, N., and R. G. Eccles (1992) 'Face to Face: Making Network Organizations Work', in N. Nohria and R. G. Eccles (eds.) *Networks and Organizations: Structure, Form, and Action* (Boston, MA: Harvard Business School Press), 288–308.

Nugent, N. (ed.) (1997) *The European Union*, vol. 1: *Perspectives and Theoretical Interpretations* (Aldershot: Dartmouth Publishing).

Nugent, N. (ed.) (1997) *The European Union*, vol. 2: *Policy Processes* (Aldershot: Dartmouth Publishing).

Nugent, N. (2001) *The European Commission* (Basingstoke: Palgrave Macmillan).

Nugent, N. (2004) *European Union Enlargement* (Basingstoke: Palgrave Macmillan).

Nunan, F. (1999) 'Policy Network Transformation: The Implementation of the EC Directive On Packaging And Packaging Waste', *Public Administration*, 77 (3): 621–38.

Nunberg, B. (2000) *Ready for Europe: Public Administration Reform and European Union Access in Central and Eastern Europe* (Washington, DC: World Bank).

OECD (1996) *Performance Auditing and the Modernisation of Government* (Paris: OECD).

OECD (2005a) *Performance-related Pay Policies for Government Employees* (Paris: OECD).

OECD (2005b) *Paying for Performance: Policies for Government Employees* (Paris: OECD).

OECD (2007) *Performance Budgeting in OECD Countries* (Paris: OECD).

OECD (2008a) *Performance Budgeting: A Users' Guide* (Paris: OECD).

OECD (2008b) *The State of the Public Service* (Paris: OECD).

OECD (2009) *Government at a Glance 2009* (Paris: OECD).

OECD (2011) *Value for Money in Government. Public Administration after 'New Public Management'* (OECD: Paris).

Oesch, D. (2006) 'Coming to Grips with a Changing Class Structure: An Analysis of Employment Stratification in Britain, Germany, Sweden and Switzerland', *International Sociology*, 21 (2): 263–88.

Ongaro, E. (2009) *Public Management Reform and Modernization: Trajectories of Administrative Change in Italy, France, Greece, Portugal and Spain* (Cheltenham: Edward Elgar).

Page, E. C. (1992) *Political Authority and Bureaucratic Power: A Comparative Analysis* (New York: Harvester Wheatsheaf).

Page, E. C. (1995) 'Administering Europe' in J. Hayward and E. Page (eds) *Governing the New Europe* (Durham, NC: Duke University Press).

Page, E. C. (1997) *People Who Run Europe* (Oxford: Clarendon Press).

Page, E. C., and V. Wright (eds) (2000) *Bureaucratic Elites in Western European States* (Oxford: Oxford University Press).

Penaud, J. (1989) *La Fonction Publique des Communautés européenes* (Paris: La Documentation Française).

Peters, B. G. (1998a) 'Policy Networks: Myth, Metaphor and Reality' in D. Marsh (ed.) *Comparing Policy Networks* (Buckingham: Open University Press), 21–32.

Peters, B. G. (1998b) 'Managing Horizontal Government: the Politics of Coordination', *Public Administration*, 76 (2): 295–311.

Peters, B. G. (2003) 'Dismantling and Rebuilding the Weberian State' in J. Hayward and A. Menon (eds), *Governing Europe* (Oxford: Oxford University Press).

Peters, B. G. and V. Wright (1996) 'Public Policy and Administration, Old and New' in R. Goodin and H. D. Klingemann (eds) *A New Handbook of Political Science* (Oxford: Oxford University Press).

Peters, B. G., and V. Wright (2001) 'The national coordination of European policy making' in J. J. Richardson (ed.) *European Union: Power and Policy Making*, 2nd edn (London: Routledge).

Peterson, J. (1995) 'Decision-making in the European Union: Towards a Framework for Analysis', *Journal of European Public Policy*, 2 (1): 69–93.

Peterson, J. (1999) 'The Santer Era: The European Commission in Normative, Historical and Theoretical Perspective', *Journal of European Public Policy*, 6 (1): 46–65.

Peterson, J. (2004) 'The Prodi Commission: Fresh Start or Free Fall?' in D. G. Dimitrakopoulos (ed.) *The Changing European Commission* (Manchester: Manchester University Press).

Peterson, J. (2006a) 'Conclusion. Where does the Commission Stand Today?' in D. Spence with G. Edwards (eds) *The European Commission*, 3rd edn (London: John Harper).

Peterson, J. (2006b) 'The College of Commissioners' in J. Peterson and M. Shackleton (eds) *The Institutions of the European Union*, 2nd edn (Oxford: Oxford University Press), 81–103.

Peterson, J. (2008a) 'José Manuel Barroso: Political Scientist, ECPR Member', *European Political Science*, 7 (1): 64–77.

Peterson, J. (2008b) 'Enlargement, Reform and the European Commission: Weathering a Perfect Storm?', *Journal of European Public Policy*, 15 (5): 761–80.

Peterson, J. (2009) 'Policy Networks' in A. Wiener and T. Diez (eds) *European Integration Theory*, 2nd edn (Oxford: Oxford University Press).

Peterson, J. (2012) 'The College of Commissioners' in J. Peterson and M. Shackleton (eds) *The Institutions of the European Union*, 3rd edn (Oxford: Oxford University Press).

Peterson, J., and A. Birdsall (2008) 'The European Commission: Enlargement as Reinvention?' in E. Best, T. Christiansen, and P. Settembri (eds) *The Governance of the Wider Europe: EU Enlargement and Institutional Change* (Cheltenham: Edward Elgar).

Peterson, J., and E. Bomberg (1998) 'Northern Enlargement and EU Decision-Making' in P. H. Laurent and M. Maresceau (eds) *The State of the European Union*, vol. 4: *Deepening and Widening* (London: Lynne Rienner).

Peterson, J., and E. Bomberg (1999) *Decision-Making in the European Union* (Basingstoke: Palgrave Macmillan).

Peterson, J., and E. Jones (1999) 'Decision Making in an Enlarging European Union' in J. Sperling (ed.) *Two Tiers or Two Speeds? The European Security Order and the Enlargement of the European Union and NATO* (Manchester: Manchester University Press).

Peterson, J., A. Byrne, and N. Helwig (2012) 'International Interests: the Common Foreign and Security Policy' in J. Peterson and M. Shackleton (eds) *The Institutions of the European Union*, 3rd edn (Oxford: Oxford University Press).

Peterson, J., and L. J. O'Toole, Jr. (2001) 'Federal Governance in the US and the EU: A Policy Network Perspective' in K. Nicolaidis and R. Howse (eds) *The Federal Vision: Legitimacy and Levels of Governance in the US and the EU* (Oxford: Oxford University Press), 300–34.

Peterson, J., and M. Shackleton (eds) (2012) *The Institutions of the European Union*, 3rd edn (Oxford: Oxford University Press).

Peterson, R. L. (1971) 'Personnel decisions and the independence of the Commission of the European Communities', *Journal of Common Market Studies*, 10 (2): 117–37.

Piris, J.-C. (2010) *The Lisbon Treaty: A Legal and Political Analysis* (Cambridge: Cambridge University Press).

Piris, J.-C. (2012) *The Future of Europe: Towards a Two-Speed EU?* (Cambridge: Cambridge University Press).

Poguntke, T., and P. Webb (2005) *The Presidentialization of Politics: A Comparative Study of Modern Democracies* (Oxford: Oxford University Press).

Pollack, M. A. (1996) 'The New Institutionalism and EU Governance: The Promise and Limits of Institutionalist Analysis', *Governance*, 9 (4): 429–58.

Pollack, M. A. (1997a) 'Delegation, Agency, and Agenda-Setting in the European Community', *International Organization*, 51 (1): 99–134.

Pollack, M. A. (1997b) 'Representing Diffuse Interests in EC Policy-Making', *Journal of European Public Policy*, 4 (4): 572–90.

Pollack, M. A. (2003) *The Engines of European Integration: Delegation, Agency, and Agenda Setting in the EU* (Oxford: Oxford University Press).

Pollitt, C. and G. Bouckaert (2004) *Public Management Reform: A Comparative Analysis*, 2nd edn (Oxford: Oxford University Press).

Pollitt, C. and G. Bouckaert (2011) *Public Management Reform: A Comparative Analysis*, 3rd edn (Oxford: Oxford University Press).

Porter, A. L., Cunningham, S. W., Banks, J., Roper, A. T., Mason, T. W., Rossini, F. A. (2011) *Forecasting and Management of Technology*, 2nd edn (Hoboken, NJ, and Chichester: John Wiley and Sons).

Powell, W. W. (1991) 'Neither Market nor Hierarchy: Network Forms of Organization' in G. Thompson, J. Frances, R. Levacic, and J. Mitchell (eds) *Markets, Hierarchies and Networks: the Organization of Social Life* (London: Sage).

Preston, C. (1995) 'Obstacles to EU Enlargement: The Classical Community Method and the Prospects for a Wider Europe', *Journal of Common Market Studies*, 33 (3): 451–63.

Puchala, D. J. (1971) 'Of Blind Men, Elephants and International Integration', *Journal of Common Market Studies*, 10 (3): 267–84.

Putnam, R. D. (1973) 'The Political Attitudes of Senior Civil Servants in Western Europe: A Preliminary Report', *British Journal of Political Science*, 3 (3): 257–90.

Putnam, R. D. (1976) *The Comparative Study of Political Elites* (Englewood Cliffs, NJ: Prentice-Hall).

Quermonne, J.-L. (1991) *L'Appareil Administratif de l'État* (Paris: Seuil).

Radaelli, C. M. (1999) *Technocracy in the European Union* (London: Longman).

Radaelli, C. M., and A. C. M. Meuwese (2010) 'Hard Questions, Hard Solutions: Proceduralisation through Impact Assessment in the EU', *West European Politics*, 33 (1): 136–53.

Rhodes, R. (1997) *Understanding Governance: Policy Networks, Governance, Reflexivity and Accountability* (Buckingham: Open University Press).

Riley, A. (2003a) 'EC Antitrust Modernisation: The Commission Does Very Nicely— Thank You! Part One: Regulation 1 and the Notification Burden', *European Competition Law Review*, 24 (11): 604–15.

Riley, A. (2003b) 'EC Antitrust Modernisation: The Commission Does Very Nicely— Thank You! Part Two: Between the Idea and the Reality: Decentralisation under Regulation 1', *European Competition Law Review*, 24 (12): 657–72.

Risse, T. (2005) 'Neofunctionalism, European Identity, and the Puzzles of European Integration', *Journal of European Public Policy*, 12 (2): 291–309.

Risse, T. (2010) *A Community of Europeans? Transnational Identities and Public Spheres* (Ithaca, NY: Cornell University Press).

Ritchie, E. (1992) 'The Model of French Ministerial Cabinets in the Early European Commission' in E. V. Heyen (ed.) *Yearbook of European Administrative History*, vol. 4: *Early European Community Administration*. (Baden-Baden: Nomos), 95–106.

Rittberger, B. (2005) *Building Europe's Parliament: Democratic Representation Beyond the Nation State* (Oxford: Oxford University Press).

Rittel, H. W. J., and M. M. Webber (1973) 'Dilemmas in a General Theory of Planning', *Policy Sciences*, 4: 155–69.

Rohrschneider, R. (1994) 'How Iron is the Iron Law of Oligarchy? Robert Michels and National Party Delegates in Eleven West European Democracies', *European Journal of Political Research*, 25: 207–38.

Rohrschneider, R., and S. Whitefield (2009) 'Understanding Cleavages in Party Systems: Issue Position and Issue Salience in 13 Post-Communist Democracies', *Comparative Political Studies*, 42 (2): 289–313.

Rokkan, S., and D. Urwin (1983) *Economy, Territory, Identity: Politics of West European Peripheries* (London: Sage).

Rose, R., and E. N. Suleiman (eds) (1980) *Presidents and Prime Ministers* (Washington, DC: American Enterprise Institute for Public Policy Research).

Ross, G. (1995) *Jacques Delors and European Integration* (Cambridge: Polity Press).

Rost, J. C. (1991) *Leadership for the Twenty-First Century* (New York: Praeger).

Sanchez-Cuenca, I. (2000) 'The Political Basis of Support for European Integration', *European Union Politics*, 1 (2): 147–71.

Sandholtz, W., and A. Stone Sweet (1998) *European Integration and Supranational Governance* (Oxford: Oxford University Press).

Sartori, G. (1994) *Comparative Constitutional Engineering: An Inquiry into Structures, Incentives, and Outcomes* (New York: New York University Press).

Sasse, C., E. Poullet, D. Coombes, and G. Deprez (1977) *Decision Making in the European Community* (New York: Praeger).

Scharpf, F. W. (1999) *Governing in Europe: Effective and Democratic?* (Oxford: Oxford University Press).

Scharpf, F. W. (2009) 'Legitimacy in the Multilevel European Polity', *European Political Science Review*, 1 (2): 173–204.

Scharpf, F. W. (2010) *Community and Autonomy: Institutions, Policies and Legitimacy in Multilevel Europe* (Frankfurt am Main: Campus Verlag).

Scheinman, L. (1966) 'Some Preliminary Notes on Bureaucratic Relationships in the European Economic Community', *International Organization*, 20 (4): 750–73.

Schick, A. (2007) 'Performance Budgeting and Accrual Budgeting: Decision Rules or Analytic Tools?' *OECD Journal on Budgeting*, 7 (2): 109–38.

Schmidt, S. K. (2000) 'Only an Agenda Setter?: The European Commission's Power over the Council of Ministers', *European Union Politics*, 1 (1): 37–61.

Schmidt, S. K. (2011) 'Law-Making in the Shadow of Judicial Politics' in R. Dehousse (ed.) *The 'Community Method'. Obstinate or Obsolete?* (Basingstoke: Palgrave Macmillan).

Schnabel, V. (2002) 'La « mafia de Bruges » : mythes et réalités du networking européen' in D. Georgakakis (ed.) *Les métiers de l'Europe politique: Acteurs et professionnalisations de l'Union européenne*, Collection Sociologie politique européenne (Strasbourg: Presses universitaires de Strasbourg), 243–70.

Schön-Quinlivan, E. (2007) 'Administrative Reform in the European Commission: From Rhetoric to Relegitimization' in M. W. Bauer and C. Knill (eds) *Management Reforms in International Organizations* (Baden-Baden: Nomos).

Schön-Quinlivan, E. (2008) 'Implementing Organizational Change: The Case of the Kinnock Reforms', *Journal of European Public Policy*, 15 (5): 726–42.

Schön-Quinlivan, E. (2011) *Reforming the European Commission* (Basingstoke: Palgrave Macmillan).

Schwanke, K. and F. Ebinger (2006) 'Politisierung und Rollenverständnis der deutschen Administrativen Elite 1970 bis 2005. Wandel trotz Kontinuität' in J. Bogumil, W. Jann, and F. Nullmeier (eds) *Politik und Verwaltung*, Politische Vierteljahresschrift special issue 37 (Wiesbaden: Springer-Verlag), 228–49.

Scruton, R. (2009) *I Drink Therefore I am: A Philosopher's Guide to Wine* (London: Continuum).

Searing, D. (1994) *Westminster's World: Understanding Political Roles* (Cambridge, MA: Harvard University Press).

Searing, D., G. Wright and G. Rabinowitz (1976) 'The Primacy Principle: Attitude Change and Political Socialization', *British Journal of Political Science*, 6: 83–113.

Sears, D. O., and C. Funk (1991) 'The Role of Self-Interest in Social and Political Attitudes', *Advances in Experimental Social Psychology*, 24: 1–91.

Sears, D. O., and C. Funk (1999) 'Evidence of the Long-Term Persistence of Adults' Political Predispositions', *Journal of Politics*, 61 (1): 1–28.

Sears, D. O., and S. Levy (2003) 'Childhood and Adult Political Development' in D. O. Sears, L. Huddy, and R. Jervis (eds) *Oxford Handbook of Political Psychology* (Oxford: Oxford University Press).

Sedelmeier, U. (2000) 'Eastern Enlargement: Risk, Rationality, and Role-Compliance' in M. G. Cowles and M. Smith (eds) *The State of the European Union: Risks, Reform, Resistance and Revival* (Oxford: Oxford University Press).

Sedelmeier, U. (2002) 'Sectoral Dynamics of EU Enlargement: Advocacy, Access and Alliances in a Composite Policy', *Journal of European Public Policy,* 9 (4): 627–49.

Sedelmeier, U. (2005) 'Eastern Enlargement' in H. Wallace, W. Wallace, and M. A. Pollack (eds) *Policy-Making in the European Union* (Oxford: Oxford University Press).

Sedivy, J., P. Dunay and J. Saryusz-Wolski (2002) *Enlargement and European Defence After 11 September,* Chaillot Papers, 53 (Paris: European Union Institute for Security Studies).

Shackleton, M. (2000) 'The Politics of Codecision', *Journal of Common Market Studies,* 38 (2): 325–42.

Sheriff, P. (1976) 'The Sociology of Public Bureaucracies, 1965–75', *Current Sociology,* 24 (2): 1–175.

Shore, C. (2000) *Building Europe: The Cultural Politics of European Integration* (London: Routledge).

Sidjanski, D (1965) 'Some Remarks on Siotis' Article', *Journal of Common Market Studies,* 3 (1): 47–61.

Simon, H. A. (1985) 'Human Nature in Politics: The Dialogue of Psychology with Political Science', *American Political Science Review,* 79: 293–304.

Simon, H. A. (1997) *Administrative Behavior: A Study of Decision-Making Processes in Administrative Organizations* (New York: Free Press).

Siotis, J. (1964) 'Some Problems of European Secretariats', *Journal of Common Market Studies,* 2: 222–50.

Sjursen, H. (2002) 'Why Expand? The Question of Legitimacy and Justification in the EU's Enlargement Policy', *Journal of Common Market Studies,* 40 (3): 491–513.

Slaughter, A.-M. (2004) *A New World Order* (Princeton: Princeton University Press).

Slaughter, A.-M., and D. Zaring (2006) 'Networking Goes International: An Update', *Annual Review of Law and Social Science,* 2: 211–29.

Smith, A. (2003) 'Why European Commissioners Matter', *Journal of Common Market Studies,* 41 (1): 137–55.

Smith, A. (ed.) (2004) *Politics and the European Commission: Actors, Interdependence, Legitimacy* (London: Routledge).

Smith, K. (2011) 'Enlargement, the Neighbourhood and European Order' in C. Hill and M. Smith (eds) *International Relations and the European Union,* 2nd edn (Oxford: Oxford University Press).

Snyder, L. L. (1968) *The New Nationalism* (Ithaca, NY: Cornell University Press).

Spence, D. (1997) 'Staff and Personnel Policy in the Commission' in G. Edwards and D. Spence (eds) *The European Commission,* 2nd edn (London: Cartermill).

Spence, D. (2000) 'Plus ça Change, Plus c'est la Même Chose? Attempting to Reform the European Commission', *Journal of European Public Policy*, 7 (1): 1–25.

Spence, D. (2006) 'The President, the College and the Cabinets' in D. Spence with G. Edwards (eds) *The European Commission*, 3rd edn (London: John Harper).

Spence, D., with G. Edwards (eds) (2006) *The European Commission*, 3rd edn (London: John Harper).

Spence, D. and A. Stevens (2006) 'Staff and Personnel Policy in the Commission' in D. Spence with G. Edwards (eds) *The European Commission*, 3rd edn (London: John Harper).

Spierenburg, D. (1979) 'Proposals for Reform of the Commission of the European Communities and its Services. Report Made at the Request of the Commission by an Independent Review Body under the Chairmanship of Mr Dirk Spierenburg' (commonly called the 'Spierenburg Report') (Brussels: European Commission).

Spinant, D. (2006) 'Barroso: Commission needs "Presidential-style Leadership' *European Voice* (26 October), 2.

Spinelli, A. (1967) *The Eurocrats* (New York: John Hopkins Press).

Stares, J. (2005) 'To Brussels, on the Gravy Train', *The Guardian* (1 March), <http://www.guardian.co.uk/education/2005/mar/01/internationaleducationnews.highereducation>.

Stevens, A. and H. Stevens (2001) *Brussels Bureaucrats? The Administration of the European Union* (Basingstoke: Palgrave Macmillan).

Stevens, H. and A. Stevens (2006) 'The Internal Reform of the Commission' in D. Spence with G. Edwards (eds) *The European Commission*, 3rd edn (London: John Harper).

Stuart, M. (2004) 'Douglas Hurd, 1989–95' in K. Theakston (ed.) *British Foreign Secretaries since 1974* (London: Routledge).

Suleiman, E. N. (1974) *Politics, Power and Bureaucracy in France* (Princeton, NJ: Princeton University Press).

Suleiman, E. N. (1984) *Bureaucrats and Policy Making* (New York: Holmes and Meier).

Suvarierol, S. (2007) *Beyond the Myth of Nationality: A Study of the Networks of European Commission Officials* (Delft: Eburon).

Suvarierol, S. (2009) 'Networking in Brussels: Nationality over a Glass of Wine', *Journal of Common Market Studies*, 47 (2): 411–35.

Suvarierol, S. (2011) 'Everyday Cosmopolitanism in the European Commission', *Journal of European Public Policy*, 18 (2): 181–200.

Szarek, P. and J. Peterson (2007) 'Studying the European Commission: A Review of the Literature', EU-CONSENT working paper, <http://www.eu-consent.net/library/deliverables/D17_Team7_Szarek-Peterson.pdf>.

Szczerbiak, A., and P. A. Taggart (2008a) *Opposing Europe? Volume 1, Case Studies and Country Surveys* (Oxford: Oxford University Press).

Szczerbiak, A., and P. A. Taggart (2008b). *Opposing Europe? Volume 2, Comparative and Theoretical Perspectives* (Oxford: Oxford University Press).

Taber, C. S. (2003) 'Information Processing and Public Opinion' in D. O. Sears, L. Huddy, and R. Jervis (eds) *Oxford Handbook of Political Psychology* (Oxford: Oxford University Press).

Tallberg, J. (2000) 'The Anatomy of Autonomy: An Institutional Account of Variation in Supranational Influence', *Journal of Common Market Studies*, 38 (5): 843–64.

Tallberg, J. (2002) 'Delegation to Supranational Institutions: Why, How, and with What Consequences?' *West European Politics*, 25 (1): 23–46.

Tallberg, J. (2006) *Leadership and Negotiation in the European Union* (Cambridge: Cambridge University Press).

Taylor, S. (2010) 'Reformist of the Centre. Barroso II: A Guide to the New European Commission', *European Voice*.

Thompson, G. (2003) *Between Hierarchies and Markets: The Logic and Limits of Network Forms of Organization* (Oxford: Oxford University Press).

Thompson, G., J. Frances, R. Levacic, and Mitchell J. (1991) *Markets, Hierarchies, and Networks: The Coordination of Social Life* (London: Sage).

Tickell, C. (2004) 'President of the European Commission' in A. Adonis and T. König (eds) *Roy Jenkins: A Retrospective* (Oxford: Oxford University Press).

Tindemans, L. (1975) *European Union: Report by Mr. Leo Tindemans, Prime Minister of Belgium, to the European Council (commonly called the Tindemans Report).* Bulletin of the European Communities, Supplement 1/76.

Topan, A. (2002) 'The Resignation of the Santer-Commission: The Impact of "Trust" and "Reputation"', *European Integration Online Papers* 6 (14), <http://eiop.or.at/eiop/texte/2002-014a.htm>.

Trondal, J. (2007) 'The Public Administration Turn in Integration Research', *Journal of European Public Policy*, 14 (6): 960–72.

Trondal, J. (2007) 'Is the European Commission a "Hothouse" for Supranationalism? Exploring Actor-Level Supranationalism', *Journal of Common Market Studies*, 45: 1111–33.

Trondal, J. (2008) 'The Anatomy of Autonomy: Reassessing the Autonomy of the European Commission', *European Journal of Political Research*, 47 (4): 467–88.

Trondal, J. (2010) *An Emergent European Executive Order* (Oxford: Oxford University Press).

Trondal, J. (2011) 'Bureaucratic Structure and Administrative Behaviour. Lessons from International Bureaucracies', *West European Politics*, 34 (4): 795–818.

Trondal, J., M. Marcussen, T. Larsson, and F. Veggeland (2010) *Unpacking International Organisations: the Dynamics of Compound Bureaucracies* (Manchester: Manchester University Press).

Tsoukalis, L. (2011) 'The Shattering of Illusions—And What Next?', *Journal of Common Market Studies*, 49 Annual Review: 19–44.

Tugendhat, C. (2004) 'The European Achievement' in A. Adonis and T. König (eds) *Roy Jenkins: A Retrospective* (Oxford: Oxford University Press).

Vachudova, M. A. (2005) *Europe Undivided* (Oxford: Oxford University Press).

Vachudova, M. A., and L. Hooghe (2009) 'Postcommunist Politics in a Magnetic Field: How Transition and EU Accession Structure Party Competition on European Integration', *Comparative European Politics*, 7 (2): 179–212.

van Apeldoorn, B., J. Drahokoupil, and Horn, L. (2009) *Contradictions and Limits of Neoliberal European Governance* (Basingstoke: Palgrave Macmillan).

van den Hoven, A. (2004) 'The European Union as an International Economic Actor' in N. Nugent (ed.) *European Union Enlargement* (Basingstoke: Palgrave Macmillan).

Van Riper, P. P. (1958) *History of the United States Civil Service* (New York: Harper and Row).

Vassiliou, G. (ed.) (2007) *The Accession Story: the EU from 15 to 25 Countries* (Oxford: Oxford University Press).

Viñas, A. (2001) 'The Enlargement of the European Union: Opportunities and Concerns for Spain' in R. Gillespie and R. Young (eds) *Spain: The European and International Challenges* (London: Frank Cass).

von der Groeben, H. (1998) 'Walter Hallstein as President of the Commission' in W. Loth, W. Wallace, and W. Wessels (eds) *Walter Hallstein: The Forgotten European?* (London: Macmillan).

Wallace, H. (2000) 'The Institutional Setting: Five Variations on a Theme' in H. Wallace and W. Wallace *Policy-Making in the European Union*, 4th edn (Oxford: Oxford University Press).

Wallace, H. (2010) 'An Institutional Anatomy and Five Policy Modes' in H. Wallace, M. A. Pollack, and A. R. Young (eds) *Policy-Making in the European Union*, 6th edn (Oxford: Oxford University Press).

Ward, S., and R. Williams (1997) 'From Hierarchy to Networks? Sub-Central Government and EU Urban Environment Policy', *Journal of Common Market Studies*, 35 (3): 439–64.

Wasserman, S., and K. Faust (2007) *Social Network Analysis: Methods and Applications* (Cambridge: Cambridge University Press).

Webb, P. (2000) *The Modern British Party System* (London: Sage).

Weber, E. P. and A. M. Khademian (2008) 'Wicked Problems, Knowledge Challenges, and Collaborative Capacity Builders in Network Settings', *Public Administration Review*, 68 (2): 334–49.

Weber, M. (1964) 'Science as a Vocation' in *From Max Weber: Essays in Sociology* (ed. and trans. H. Gerth and C. Wright Mills) (London: Routledge), 129–56.

Weiler, J. H. H. (1991) 'The Transformation of Europe', *Yale Law Journal*, 100 (8): 2403–83.

Wessels, W. (1998) 'Walter Hallstein's Contribution to Integration Theory: Outdated or Underestimated?' in W. Loth, W. Wallace, and W. Wessels (eds) *Walter Hallstein: The Forgotten European?* (London: Macmillan).

Westlake, M. (1998) 'The European Parliament's Emerging Powers of Appointment', *Journal of Common Market Studies*, 36 (3): 431–44.

Westlake, M. (2001) *Kinnock: The Biography* (London: Little, Brown).

Wildavsky, A. (1979) *Speaking Truth to Power: The Art and Craft of Policy Analysis* (Boston, MA: Little, Brown).

Wildavsky, A. (1987) 'Choosing Preferences by Constructing Institutions: A Cultural Theory of Preference Formation', *American Political Science Review*, 81: 3–21.

Wilks, S. (1992) 'Models of European Administration: DG IV and the Administration of Competition Policy', paper presented at the European Group of Public Administration Conference, Pisa, Italy, 2–5 September.

Wilks, S. (1996) 'Regulatory Compliance and Capitalist Diversity in Europe', *Journal of European Public Policy*, 3: 536–59.

Wilks, S. (2005) 'Agency Escape: Decentralization or Dominance of the European Commission in the Modernization of Competition Policy?', *Governance*, 18 (3): 431–52.

Wille, A. (2007) 'Senior Officials in a Reforming European Commission: Transforming the Top?' in M. W. Bauer and C. Knill (eds) *Management Reforms in International Organizations* (Baden-Baden: Nomos).

Wille, A. (2010) 'Political, Bureaucratic Accountability in the EU Commission: Modernising the Executive', *West European Politics*, 33 (5): 1093–116.

Wille, A. (2011) 'Public Sector Leadership in a "Reinvented" EU Commission' in J. W. Bjorkman, R. van Eijbergen, C. Minderman, and H. Bekke (eds) *Public Sector Leadership and Citizen Value* (The Hague: Eleven International Publishing).

Williamson, D. (1998) *Reflection Group on Personnel Policy* (Brussels: European Commission).

Willis, V. (1982) *Britons in Brussels: Officials in the European Commission and Council Secretariat*, Studies in European Policy, vol. 7 (London: Policy Studies Institute).

Wilson, J. (1991) *Bureaucracy: What Government Agencies Do and Why They Do it* (New York: Basic Books).

Wonka, A. (2007) 'Technocratic and Independent? The Appointment of European Commissioners and its Policy Implications', *Journal of European Public Policy*, 14: 169–89.

Wright, V. (1997) 'The paradoxes of administrative reform' in W. Kickert (ed.) *Public Management and Administrative Reform in Western Europe* (Cheltenham: Edward Elgar).

Yee, A. S. (1997) 'Thick Rationality and the Missing "Brute Fact": The Limits of Rationalist Incorporations of Norms and Ideas', *Journal of Politics*, 59: 1001–39.

Yesilkagit, K,. and J. Blom-Hansen (2007) 'Supranational Governance or National Business-As-Usual? The National Administration of EU Structural Funds in the Netherlands and Denmark', *Public Administration*, 85 (2): 503–24.

Yi-Chong, X., and P. Weller (2008) ' "To Be, But Not to Be Seen": Exploring the Impact of International Civil Servants', *Public Administration*, 86 (1): 35–51.

Young, J., C. J. Thomsen, E. Borgida, J. L. Sullivan, and J. H. Aldrich (1991) 'When Self-Interest Makes a Difference: The Role of Construct Accessibility in Political Reasoning', *Journal of Experimental Social Psychology*, 27: 271–96.

Young, O. R. (1991) Leadership and Regime Formation: On the Development of Institutions in International Society,' *International Organization*, 45 (3): 281–308.

Ziller, J. (2000) 'Flexibility in the Geographical Scope of EU law' in G. De Búrca and J. Scott (eds) *Constitutional Change in the EU: From Uniformity to Flexibility?* (Oxford: Hart Publishing).

Zürn, M., and Checkel, J. T. (2005) 'Getting Socialized to Build Bridges: Constructivism and Rationalism, Europe and the Nation-State', *International Organization*, 59 (4): 1045–79.

Index